Jewish Materialism

Jewish Materialism

THE INTELLECTUAL REVOLUTION OF THE 1870S

Eliyahu Stern

Yale UNIVERSITY PRESS

New Haven & London

Published with the assistance of the Frederick W. Hilles Publication Fund of
Yale University and with assistance from the foundation established in memory
of Amasa Stone Mather of the Class of 1907, Yale College.

Yale University Press books may be purchased in quantity for educational,
business, or promotional use. For information, please e-mail sales.
press@yale.edu (U.S. office) or sales@yaleup.co.uk (U.K. office).

Set in Adobe Garamond type by Newgen North America.
Printed in the United States of America.

Library of Congress Control Number: 2017948470
ISBN 978-0-300-22180-0 (hardcover : alk. paper)

A catalogue record for this book is available from the British Library.

This paper meets the requirements of ANSI/NISO Z39.48-1992
(Permanence of Paper).

10 9 8 7 6 5 4 3 2 1

For Sherlley

Contents

Preface, ix

Acknowledgments, xiii

Note on Transliteration, xv

Introduction: Materialisms, 1

1 Tradition, 32

2 Social Materialism, 56

3 Scientific Materialism, 85

4 Practical Materialism, 114

5 The Materialization of Spirit, 147

Conclusion: Jewish Body Politics, 182

Notes, 193

Bibliography, 253

Index, 283

Preface

This book could not have been written had I accessed only the standard collected works of the period under investigation. For in conducting archival research for this project, I discovered that many of the articles and essays that today stand as the authoritative output of Russian Jews in that revolutionary decade had been emended, rewritten, judiciously cut, or simply expurgated by editors and publishers who wished to conceal ideas that clashed with their twentieth-century political worldviews. These acts ranged from simple substitution of words and phrases to the deletion of entire sections within essays to working to suppress the publication of particular writers' archives.

To be sure, I am not the first person to recognize these violent acts of historical suppression. The first authors who wrote on Russian Jewish life in the late nineteenth century—scholars such as Joseph Klausner, Samuel Leib Zitron, Israel Sossis, Morris Winchevsky, Kalman Marmor, and Samuel Agursky—privately noted some of the many malfeasances I found. However, perhaps because of their own political biases, these men did not find it necessary to present the full extent to which primary documents had been doctored. They tacitly—or in some instances willfully—participated in the historical cover-up. Most important, they failed to identify what about the writings of the 1870s later generations found so threatening that they needed to alter them in such profound ways.

One example is revealing. In the 1870s, the future Zionist leader Isaac Kaminer wrote dozens of articles and poems that reflected his general view that "labor is the first principle of human life." Kaminer, whose daughter married the Russian revolutionary leader Pavel Axelrod, was perhaps the first Jew in the Pale of Settlement to own a copy of Karl Marx's materialist bible, *Capital.* But after the pogroms of the 1880s, Jewish intellectuals determined that Jewish cultural unity was more important than Marxist principles. In response, Kaminer's literary executor, Asher Ginsberg, began expunging the materialist themes in his writings, believing they were at odds with the needs of the reigning Zionist movement. From his office desk in Odessa, Ginsberg ensured that Kaminer's works of the 1870s that appeared only in short-run publications with limited distribution would be overshadowed by his later Zionist works. Kaminer's legacy would now be fully controlled by a Zionist narrative. Thus, it is not surprising that when Jacob Krepliak, the editor of the Bundist publication *The Future* (*Tsukunft*), translated Pavel Axelrod's Russian memoir into Yiddish, he deleted Axelrod's claim that he first came across *Capital* in Kaminer's home. Kaminer's Marxist legacy was wiped out by both sides of the political divide.

In some cases, the authors themselves were responsible for obscuring the historical record. In the 1870s, the Russian Jewish leader Moses Leib Lilienblum explicitly wrote that Jews should adopt "a materialistic perspective on life" and championed the ideas espoused by the Russian revolutionary Nikolai Chernyshevsky. In the next decade, however, Lilienblum turned against Chernyshevsky's disciples, whom he considered to be abetting violent anti-Semitism. Fearing that his earlier ideas would be misused, Lilienblum discreetly removed the Russian sources and materialist terminology from his self-published *Collected Writings* (1913) and inserted more neutral, Hebraic phrases and terms. He went so far as to erase citations from Chernyshevsky and the Russian radical Dmitry Pisarev. Further complicating the matter for future scholars, Lilienblum's first biographers were slow to acknowledge that the he had doctored his own works.

My research revealed that the very idea of "Jewish materialism"—a term that I shall define in the introduction of this book—represented the primary point of concern for scholars looking back at the 1870s. The people I discuss in this volume, who became Zionists, Jewish socialists, or Communists, often glossed over or ignored completely positions they espoused in the 1870s. In many instances they destroyed traces of material that might have exposed the political elasticity of their earlier arguments. These acts of historical revision have made it difficult to analyze this period of intellectual history on its own terms and as expressing a distinct intellectual profile. In order to present the historical uniqueness of the 1870s, and its wide-ranging influence on twentieth-century politics and religion, I have taken care to cite from archival data or original publications from the period. All citations to memoirs and reflections written or published at later dates are carefully weighed and assessed against other, more verifiable historical data. Throughout this book, my aim is to present the intellectual revolution of the 1870s, illuminating how it redefined what constituted Judaism and led Jews to join in the vanguard of twentieth-century revolutionary politics.

Acknowledgments

My *mame-loshn* was the key to unlocking a vanished world. Spending the last decade reading Mendele and exploring the eccentricities of Soviet Yiddish with my mother, Batya Rabinowitz Stern, opened new vistas in my life and scholarship. The material of this book was unearthed with the support of academia's unsung heroes, the librarians and archivists who made available academic fields that had been buried beneath mounds of secondary literature. Most notably, I am indebted to the staff at YIVO, the National Library of Israel, the Jewish Public Library of Montreal, the Gnazim Archive, the New York Public Library, the Jewish Theological Seminary Library, W. M. Blumenthal Academy Library in Berlin, Landesarchiv Berlin, and Yale University Library. I wish to thank the efforts of Fruma Moher, Gunnar Berg, Leo Greenbuam, Gil Weisblei, Shannon Hodge, Anne-Marie Belinfante, Stephen Corrison, Ulrike Sonnemann, Nanette Stahl, Julie Cohen, and Sarah Diamond. I greatly appreciate Peter Schäfer's granting me access to the resources of the Berlin Jewish Museum Library during my yearlong stay in Berlin.

David Henkin and Abigail Green were integral in laying this book's foundation. From very different geographic perspectives each repeatedly impressed upon me that I was writing about Jewish materialism. At early stages in the writing process they challenged me to rethink the scope of this project and not fall prey to the traps of nationalist or socialist historiographies or conventional theories of secularism. Alan Brill handed me Joseph Klausner's collected works and told me to read them carefully. Jonatan Meir gifted me with the codes to the major archives of this period and knowledge of Jewish history that circulate only by word of mouth. James Loeffler helped me recognize the political stakes of this work and the long-term impact of its subject matter. I am honored by the time and effort they gave to reading various drafts. Only their friendship outweighs their contributions to this book.

The manuscript was greatly enhanced by the comments and suggestions offered by Brian Porter-Szűcs, Daniel Boyarin, Jonathan Boyarin, Shaul Magid, Eliot Wolfson, Vasudha Dalmia, David Nirenberg, Francesca Bregoli, Allan Megill, David Ruderman, John Efron, Paul Nahme, Marci Shore, Timothy Snyder, Mordechai Zalkin, Noreen Khawaja, David Myers, Paul Bushkovitch, Amos Bitzan, Yishai Schwartz, Marina Zilbergerts, Francesca Trivellato, Martin Jay, Julie Cooper, Elie Jesner, Elias Klienbock, Glenn Dynner, Christine Hayes, David Sorkin, Kathryn Lofton, Joshua Price, Ivan Marcus, Marwa Elshakry, Steven Fraade, Hannan Hever, Michael Silber, and Shaul Stampfer. Shaun Halper, Todd Weir, Samuel Moyn, Eli Lederhendler, and Naomi Seidman provided thoughtful and productive feedback that saved me from a host of unforced errors and helped me to sharpen and better articulate my thesis. My friend and the rising star Vadim Shneyder assisted me in reading many of the Russian archival documents cited herein. Samuel Thrope and Josh Price helped me ensure linguistic consistency throughout the bibliography and notes. I am grateful to Btzalel (Todd) Shandelman for his attention to detail and for providing me with wide-ranging bibliographic knowledge.

As always Noah Strote, Dov Weiss, Daniel Septimus, Meir Katz, Gabriel Posner, Barry Wimpfheimer and Benjamin Skydell have been there to take the 11 p.m. phone calls about matters ranging from the lofty to the lowly. Their critiques and feedback stand behind every sentence of this book. Likewise, I would like to especially thank my team, including George Newmark, Dana and Ilan Rubenstein, Jacob Morris, Shaya Ish Shalom, Jack Rosen, and of course my father, Sholom Stern, for all their support and encouragement.

Finally, over the past seven years I have had the privilege of working with Jennifer Banks at Yale University Press. This is the second time I have thanked her for her deep professionalism and commitment to helping me write the best possible book. I am honored by the attention she and her assistant, Heather Gold, have given to this manuscript. I am greatly appreciative of the remarkably clarifying and exacting editorial work of Susan Laity.

Note on Transliteration

The system of transliteration employed in this book takes into consideration various national, religious, and historical claims over the individuals, towns, and texts addressed herein. Due to the many languages used by the protagonists of this book, it is impossible to re-create a historically precise system of transliteration. Instead, I have chosen the least taxing and cumbersome transliteration rules for a more easily read text. As an aid to future research, proper names follow the spelling of the Library of Congress. In cases in which a name does not appear in the Library of Congress's catalogue, I have adopted the accepted scholarly version as it appears in the *YIVO Encyclopedia* (e.g., Alter Druyanow, not Alter Druyanov). Names appearing here for the first time in English scholarly literature are rendered according to a common Anglicized form. The names of prominent individuals appear in the accepted English spelling (e.g., Peretz Smolenskin, not Perez Smolenskin or Peter Smolenskin; Leon Pinsker, not Yehudah Leib Pinsker). The titles of works in Hebrew follow a simplified system, based on the rules listed in the *Encyclopedia Judaica,* that reflects modern Hebrew pronunciation. Yiddish titles and words follow the YIVO transliteration system. Town and city names match the ones used most often by their Jewish residents in the nineteenth century. However, for stylistic reasons the transliteration of these names conforms to their common Anglicized form (e.g., Vilna, not, Vilne). All titles of works in Russian have been transliterated according to a simplified Library of Congress system, omitting where possible diacritical marks. Russian personal names conform to common usage in English academic studies (e.g., Chernyshevsky, not Chernyshevskii).

Jewish Materialism

Materialisms

A cracked, yellowed wallet haunts the title of this book.[1] At first glance, the wallet resembles any other money holder of its time. Its smooth leather, tight stitching, and hard crease allow it to lie comfortably and inconspicuously in a pocket. However, upon careful examination one notices a peculiar black pigmentation staining the flaps covering its coin pockets. When they are lifted, the culprit is revealed: disturbingly beautiful Hebrew words with delicate small crowns have bled through the wallet's skin.

This wallet was a relic of the carnage left behind by one of the many pogroms that decimated Jewish communities across the Russian Empire. From the end of the nineteenth to the beginning of the twentieth century, mobs, sometimes led by local police officials, engaged in terror sprees against Jews and their businesses that could rage for up to a week. Although Russian government officials sometimes protected a Jewish population, in most cases they ignored or were ill-equipped to prevent the rampant violence. Fueled by longstanding anti-Semitism and fierce economic competition, the Cossacks who perpetrated the pogroms targeted the most valuable possessions of their Jewish victims. Many of the objects that survived were left lying battered on wooden floors, covered in debris and shards of glass, later to be publicly mourned, eulogized by rabbinic leaders, wrapped in prayer shawls, and finally laid to rest. But other objects were snatched by the marauders, hauled out of

A wallet made from the parchment of a Torah scroll desecrated during a pogrom,
circa 1917. (Courtesy of Beinecke Library, Yale University)

synagogues, taken captive, operated on, and circulated in new forms in the
profane world. Such was the fate of the Torah scroll that was sliced up and
reconstructed into the wallet with the unusual coin pockets that now sits on
a library shelf in New Haven, Connecticut.

The inside of the wallet is marked with verses ripped from the story of
Koraḥ's rebellion against Moses and Aaron. In Numbers 16 the rabble rouser
charged the Israelite leaders with placing themselves above the congrega-
tion and appropriating more than their fair share of resources. It is doubtful
whether the Russian militiaman who used an industrial sewing machine to
manufacture the wallet could read these passages, and we can only imagine
the perverse fantasies he might have attached to this piece of merchandise.
The wallet is not only a material manifestation of anti-Semitic physical violence; it also gives testimony to a dark strain of thought running through the
Western intellectual canon.

As the historian David Nirenberg has shown, for fifteen hundred years Gentile thinkers from Marcion to Kant glorified Christendom's spiritual development in opposition to a "materialism" that they further defined as "Jewish."[2] These philosophers demonized what they perceived as Judaism's legalism, particularism, and carnality in order to promote their own theories of spirituality, universal love, and philosophical idealism.[3] Jews did not worship God; they bowed to the idol of Mammon—to the Lord of Shylock. They engaged in mercantile and moneylending activities that reflected a materialistic doctrine inscribed in their sacred scrolls.

Gentiles thus produced the concept of Jewish materialism to justify their own social institutions, economic relations, and political commitments. As Nirenberg explains, they turned Judaism into "a popular arena for contests over the relationship between matter and spirit, man and God, and over the texts and sacraments that mediate between them."[4] This form of anti-Judaism circulated among Western societies in hate-filled sermons and grotesque theater pieces both performed and watched by adults and children alike. Jewish materialism was created by people invested in seeing Judaism's sacred texts as profane artifacts whose sole purpose was to valorize Jews' accumulation of wealth.

The intellectual history of the anti-Judaism that sat at the heart of Western life adds layers of meaning to the violence that led the Russian militiaman to craft his wallet. But it ignores how its victims made sense of these acts of violence and what means were available to them to protect themselves. It fails to address the way oppressed groups understood their own relationship to the material world and the value they attached to the resources being denied to them. In fact, when such atrocities are recorded only from the vantage point of Russian militiamen or other perpetrators of violence, we miss what is actually most remarkable about the fate of this wallet—and for that matter, the fate of various discriminated religious and ethnic minorities in the late nineteenth and early twentieth centuries.

In an irony of biblical proportions, the militiaman would end up selling his wares to a Russian soldier at a local market in Berdichev in 1917. Perhaps he was not aware that his customer was in fact a Jew coming home for the Passover holiday. Perhaps he did know and thought he could demand a higher price. In any case, a small piece of the desecrated Torah scroll was thereby reappropriated by its original people and was soon on its way to Palestine, from whence it was shipped to the United States of America.

Now out in the world, this remnant of Europe's spiritual and political heritage carried a different meaning from the one it had borne when it was sheltered inside a synagogue ark. It was no less sacred, but for most Jews, it could no longer be seen as part of the uninterrupted textual tradition recording two millennia of Jewish law, beliefs, and learning. The dismembered piece of Torah mirrored the Jews' own growing detachment from their religious traditions, as well as their precarious relationship to the material world. Reconstructed through the crucible of European anti-Semitism and industrialized labor, this fragment of scripture came to express not the sacredness of Jewish ideas per se but the material, labor, and resources needed to produce and protect them. Jews would develop their own idea of Jewish materialism that would be positively valued.

The Jewish reappropriation of the wallet and its formerly pejorative association cast new light on the forces that propelled Jews into leadership positions within every twentieth-century ideological movement, be it capitalism, socialism, Zionism, or communism, based on the ownership and distribution of property and resources. Scholars have proffered dozens of theories to account for the pivotal political roles played by Jews, specifically Russian Jews, during the late nineteenth and early twentieth centuries. Most point to the pogroms of 1881 and the subsequent immigration of Jews to the United States, the Russian interior, and Palestine as the impetus for their involvement in these movements. As is common in the story of religious and ethnic minorities worldwide, the persecution narrative tends to divest Jews of agency in their own story; it ignores the social forces, ideas, and beliefs at work within Jewish life.

A more sophisticated theory for Jews' deep investment in these movements was presented by the historian Yuri Slezkine, who pointed to the Jews' sociological position as diasporic nomads. As people who traveled the world and traversed boundaries Jews were uniquely predisposed to embrace the cosmopolitan and universalistic aspects of the modern age.[5] Slezkine's provocative thesis, however, relies mainly on evidence from only a small percentage of European Jews, those who were highly secularized and acculturated into the societies in which they resided.[6]

Some scholars look in the opposite direction, focusing on how Jewish religious predispositions led them to embrace the various modern political and economic movements ranging from capitalism to socialism.[7] The emphasis that spiritual and pietistic movements such as Hasidism placed on divine worship through corporeal means and social fraternity, they argue, predisposed Jews to socialism.[8] Other scholars, such as the American historian Andrew R. Heinze, contend that the tradition of Hasidism that flourished in eastern Europe in the eighteenth and nineteenth centuries prepared Jews to see America as a paradise of luxuries.[9]

In this work I build upon these studies by connecting a set of ideas and cultural predispositions to Jews' involvement in certain political and economic movements. But contrary to these scholars, I argue that the decisive intellectual force that brought Jews to the forefront of these movements was not Hasidism's emphasis on sociability or various forms of cosmopolitanism popularized by a small cohort of Western European Jews. Rather, it was a distinct ideology developed by Russian Jews in the late nineteenth century that defined Judaism and Jewish identity in terms of what its espousers explicitly called—whether in Russian, German, Yiddish, or Hebrew—the "material" (*material'nyi, meteriali, gashmi, ḥomri*) aspects of the universe. They primarily invoked the term "materialism" in three senses: social, scientific, and economic. I take each as a locus of discussion. For many, such as Moses Leib Lilienblum, materialism entailed promoting "a materialistic perspective on life," in which social practices and religious institutions were scrutinized according to universal scientific principles of efficiency and utility.[10] For some, like the Darwinian Joseph Sossnitz, it meant promoting a "materialistic religion," a metaphysical argument about the nature of the universe.[11] For others, like the Marxists Aaron Shemuel Lieberman and Isaac Kaminer, it involved analyzing history based on "labor being the first principle of life."[12] All these social, scientific, and economic definitions of *materialism* circulated throughout Europe in the last quarter of the nineteenth century, often overlapping with monism and certain strands of positivistic thought. What was unique, however, about this book's protagonists was the way they connected these forms of materialism to specific religious and ethnic identities.

Russian Jews wrestled with what it meant to adopt a specifically Jewish conception of materialism. For those discussed in this volume, materialism was a philosophy that brought into focus latent Jewish ideas and beliefs about the physical world. According to Sossnitz and the Marxists Judah Leib Levin, Isaac Kaminer, and Aaron Shemuel Lieberman, Judaism provided philosophical underpinnings for a universal theory of materialism. For them Marxism and the Kabbalah shared the same temporal structures and theories of critique. The Bible was the backstory to Darwin's *On the Origin of Species*.

Materialist ideas had been lying dormant within Jewish literature (Hasidic texts, the Bible, Spinoza's philosophy), they claimed, and only now could be clearly recognized and fully articulated.

In contrast, Moses Leib Lilienblum's Jewish "material perspective on life" reflected the myriad forms of discrimination that operated in society and the limitations of a universal theory of materialism. Jewish particularity was based on specific historical economic differences between Jews and others. What made Jews different—what made people *Jews*—was a certain socio-economic dynamic that distinguished them from their neighbors. For Lilienblum, Jewish materialism was an ideology derived from the reality that Jews living in Russia were not treated as humans. Only by particularizing the universal claims of equality, he believed, could Jews, like those called "German" and "French," ensure their own protection and access to resources.

Though Jewish materialism emerged in the 1870s among a defined group of roughly twenty-five intellectuals born in the northwestern provinces of the Russian Empire who shared a similar intellectual upbringing, it soon could be found among western European Jews residing in England and Germany. Only half-jokingly, the German anarchist Gustav Landauer claimed that what distinguished "the modern 'conscious' Jew from a German was that when the latter writes about . . . the conservation of energy, . . . he writes about the conservation of energy, but when the conscious Jew writes about the conservation of energy, he writes about the conservation of energy and *Judaism*" (emphasis mine).[13] The French intellectual Bernard Lazare would place Karl Marx alongside Aaron Shemuel Lieberman in a tradition of "matérialisme hébraïque." Eventually, there would be those, such as the Englishman Israel Zangwill, who considered themselves adherents to "a religion of pots and pans," and others who identified Judaism as a faith based on "bagels and lox."[14] Over the course of the twentieth century Jews would increasingly come to believe that "there is nothing purely spiritual that stands on its own. . . . Everything spiritual requires a necessary material basis."[15]

Jewish materialism should not, however, be confused with the kind of "Jewish materiality" often associated with, for example, Jewish foodways or purchasing practices. Studying the idea of a Jewish wallet is not the same as studying wallets owned by Jews, wallets made by Jews, or even wallets made out of Jewish objects. Studying these objects is the domain of scholars of material culture, such as Jonathan Boyarin and Barbara Kirshenblatt-Gimblett, whose pioneering work investigates Jewish texts, performances, and actions in terms of their material features.[16] Their studies complement those conducted by Carolyn Walker Bynum on Christian materiality. Historians and anthropologists of materiality explore relics, sacraments, and devotional images and the kinds of meaning that are attached to them. They investigate the way objects "functioned and what they meant religiously."[17]

The people I discuss in this book, however, use *materialism* to describe an intellectual movement. Jewish materialism reveals what modern Jews believed and the values they explicitly associated with the physical world. Building on the work of the theorist Benedict Anderson, in this book I examine the concrete ideological features that hold together a collective or define a social body.[18] I explore the way in which Jews mobilized an imagined concept of land, labor, and body for various national and religious projects. Abstract conceptions of God, dogma, or ritual were not the primary elements that connected modern Jews to one another. Instead, it was a new conception of the physical world. Jewish materialism reflects a set of ideas and forms of praxis in which human beings prepare themselves to act as part of imagined communities of shared material interest.

MATERIALIZATION VERSUS SECULARIZATION

Scholars often discuss modern Judaism within the context of the secularization of the modern state and the transformation of religious groups into confessions. The rise of the modern state, they say, led to both the decline of clerical authority and the weakening of the church's economic grip on Europe: in the name of improving public welfare, the state curtailed independent economic fiefdoms, wresting property from religious institutions.[19] And as the state claimed more of the physical world, Christian theologians further emphasized Christianity's dominion over the worlds of the spirit and of individuals' inner well-being. The state consolidated and centralized its subjects' material resources, and Christianity began to splinter and diversify into various Protestant sects.[20]

To be sure, this process, which is often said to have begun in the sixteenth century with the rise of Protestantism, was never fully realized. Religious leaders often resisted the state's confiscation of church properties. Many Protestants and Catholics pushed back by promoting confessional polities. They began protracted battles with government representatives over the official religion of the state. These heated fights would persist into the seventeenth and eighteenth centuries. However, European states, for the most part, continued to increase their independence from clerical authorities. While it is highly doubtful that economic secularization gave rise to Protestantism (or vice versa), it is clear that in many instances the two were mutually reinforcing processes.[21] Although churches retained some of their economic power, Christians—Protestants and Catholics alike—increasingly understood their religion in nonmaterial terms. Religious leaders detached spiritual concerns from the entanglements of matter: objects, property, and the physical aspects of being.[22]

In the eighteenth and nineteenth centuries western European governments broadened the processes of economic secularization by assimilating Jews into the public welfare.[23] They asked Jews to emulate Catholics and Protestants by relinquishing their status as an independent corporation and integrating their activities into local economies.[24] Jews would financially contribute to the general economic upkeep of society, and in return they would enjoy the protection and securities conferred upon citizens of the state. Economic secularization shadowed the medieval custom of demanding that Jewish converts to Christianity relinquish all their material goods and strip naked before the baptismal font. "Giving up one's belongings physically" embodied, for some in the medieval and modern periods, "the very repudiation of Judaism."[25] The more Jews let go of their material (physical, economic, and demographic) distinctiveness—the less they differed from others in appearance, behavior, speech, and professions—the more they stood to gain from the resources generated by a larger economic entity, the state. By shaving their beards, purchasing new apparel, tossing away headscarves and skullcaps, and ingesting new foods, Jews could be seen by others as human beings. For its part, unlike the medieval church, the state did not demand that Jews deny their ties to Judaism. It simply asked that material forms of Jewish identity remain outside the marketplace and away from public view.

Christian property owners who were now forced to share with Jews what was once under their sole ownership often resisted attempts to integrate Jews into the public welfare. They denounced Jews as Pharisees who traded in the Temple and as Shylocks who hoarded their capital at the expense of the larger public good. These charges would reach a fever pitch in the late nineteenth century in Germany, where a new anti-Semitic movement denounced Judaism as "a religion of material interests."[26] Anti-Semites conflated economic secularization with "Jewish materialism," a view that reflected their own antipathies to sharing property and goods with groups hitherto excluded from the general welfare. It was impossible for Jews to ever become part of a commonwealth, they claimed, because Judaism was a religion based on egoistic forms of Jewish wealth accumulation.

Western European Jews combated the charges of "Jewish materialism" by celebrating the relinquishment of their corporate status for equal access to the state's resources. They consciously formulated theories of Judaism that emphazized the spirit of the biblical prophets. Jews increasingly defined Judaism in confessional terms, distinguishing it from concerns involving economic or physical well-being.[27] New Jewish sects began to emerge, emphasizing immaterial features of their respective traditions, and underlining their beliefs rather than the specifics of their rituals or attachment to Jewish communal institutions. Western European Jews portrayed Judaism in ways similar to those used to describe Protestantism, advertising it as a monotheistic religion.[28] Early-nineteenth-century European Jews pointed to the Bible as epitomizing Judaism's ethical ideals. It was neither a political text nor a blueprint for Jewish sovereignty.

At the same time, Western European Jews politically defined themselves as "secularists" and embraced government institutions as the protectors of their material well-being. German and French Jews formulated a distinct economic theology based on their relationship to the state. "Liberal Judaism in Germany," explains Derek Penslar, "developed a notion of a Jewish mission to serve the state in all arenas, including economic productivity."[29] Jews conceptually embraced the idea of the state—its offices, court systems, and civil service—as the sole entity responsible for the distribution of resources in society and the guarantor of civil rights. Few designations frightened nineteenth- and twentieth-century western European Jews more than "materialistic," and few ideas were more demonized by Reform and Orthodox Judaism than "materialism."

Jewish denominational leaders residing in German lands condemned what they called "Roman materialism."[30] In France, Isidore Cahen and other mid-nineteenth-century Jewish intellectuals repeatedly defined Judaism as opposed to materialism. They were not just refuting the charge that Jews had their own political institutions; they were also rejecting the idea that Judaism endorsed economic, philosophical, or biological materialism. They stressed Judaism's universalist orientation in the context of its support of republican values.[31] Jews' devotion to the state, as noted by Hannah Arendt, among others, would persist until the Holocaust.

However, what Arendt and others overlooked was that the bond between Jews and the state was not present for all European Jews—in fact, not even for the majority of European Jews. For unlike their coreligionists in Paris and Berlin, Jews residing in Russian lands in the second half of the nineteenth century remained landlocked, sidelocked, and locked out of major labor markets and state offices.[32] The state identified Jews as a foreign entity. Jews dressed in different clothes from those of other Russian subjects, they worked in circumscribed labor markets, and, for the most part, they resided in designated lands. They were not alone in their polarization: the Russian Empire also discriminated against Catholics and Muslims at various times. Although Jews disbanded their local corporations in 1844, they were still denied basic access to land and labor markets even much later into the nineteenth century.

True, a number of Russian Jewish elites followed their western European counterparts and strove to reform their practice of Judaism to fit the specific confessional boundaries of the Russian Empire.[33] They emphasized the persuasive aspects of Judaism, downplayed rabbinic coercive power, and supported the civil authority of the tsar and the economic goals of the state. As in France and Germany, Jewish liberals in Russia defined themselves as Russian. They favored the designations "members of a tribe" or "followers of the Mosaic Faith."[34] These reformist efforts, however, did not yield the economic opportunities offered to Jews residing in western Europe.

Whereas in France, Germany, and Britain Jewish reform went more or less hand in hand with property accrual and upward social mobility, religious reform in Russia did not bring about a large-scale change in Jews' socioeconomic situation. In 1897 only 1 percent of the total Jewish population was "bourgeois" by any economic measure.[35]

The ideology of religious reform did not lead to the kind of economic prosperity for Russian Jews that it seemingly had for western European Jews. Jews residing in Russian lands in the 1860s and 1870s lived in poverty. They described their homes as being "sunken into the ground, with floors pounded into the earth, aged broken roofs covered in moss . . . [and] windows stuffed with rags." It was not uncommon for a child to be raised in "one-bedroom quarters that included parents, siblings or in-laws, and some livestock."[36] Many wore the same few tattered clothes their entire adult lives. Roughly one-fifth of the population in the northwestern provinces required charity in order to obtain the basic food needed to celebrate Passover.[37] To be sure, Russia's serfs were still economically worse off than the empire's Jews. However, unlike the serfs, who had been emancipated in 1861, Russia's Jews seemed to live in a state of economic stasis, their physical mobility still limited to a defined geographic terrain. In Russia, the difference between Jews and Gentiles could not simply be described as a cultural, historical, or religious bias; it was empirically witnessed in their physical condition and dress, and defined by the territories in which they resided and the professions available to them.

In marked contrast to Jews in western Europe, Jews in Russia reimagined the central features of Judaism around their material distinctiveness. The daily hardships of Russian Jews led them to identify acquisition of the necessary means of survival and their ability to appropriate the physical world as being essential to what it meant to be Jewish. This was not limited to obtaining kiddush wine and challah for Friday night or matzo for Passover; it also began to encompass owning property, living with a roof over one's head, and securing a loaf of bread to eat on weekdays. Physical well-being became a *Jewish* issue.

The conscious theorization of Judaism in material terms signified a historic change in the way people understood Judaism. This development is captured in its most crude form by one wry Russian Jewish observer who quipped, "Now in the nineteenth century, [the classic rabbinic dictum] 'The world stands on three pillars—the study of Torah, divine worship, and ethics,' has been replaced by three things: money, money, money."[38] Such musings were not simply a description of the actions of certain Jews but rather reflected a new Jewish calculus.

In the 1870s land, labor, and people began dislodging rituals, study, and reason as the new measures by which to define the nature of Jewish identity and of Judaism. In 1872, following a pogrom in Kiev, the poet and future Zionist activist Judah Leib Levin called on his coreligionists to "begin to work on matters that address their bodies. Let Jews heal the crippled back and then they will worry about the spirit [*ru'aḥ*]." With rabbinic and Kabbalistic metaphors he declared: "One first builds a house and only afterward carries in vessels."[39]

The Jewish materialists defined their worldviews in opposition to what they described as an idealist bias in early-nineteenth-century Jewish thought—a bias that ignored the Jews' material well-being. Significantly, the Jewish materialists' call to heal Jews' bodies often was framed in gendered terms, whereby the healing of the Jewish body entailed Jewish men adopting the economic role that often devolved upon Jewish women. Whereas the idealized eastern European Jewish male was understood as spending his day in study, the woman he married was imagined to be an economic agent and producer, working with her hands and gaining economically beneficial knowledge. The Jewish materialists questioned this division of labor and called on Jewish men to embrace the activities and knowledge that had traditionally been left to Jewish women. While few explicitly drew this connection, it is not difficult to see why Jewish women living in Russia embraced the new worldview. Becoming "Jewish women" meant replacing Talmudic study with labor and economically productive activities. The new Jewish man would offer a contrast to both the hunchbacked traditional Jewish Torah scholar incapable of supporting his family and the muscular Gentile male whose energies were directed at conquering and dominating the physical world. Rather, the new Jewish man would be shaped in the image of a healthy traditional Jewish woman who labored to provide for her family's material well-being. Tending to the material aspects of existence would now be seen as the primary feature of Judaism.

HISTORICIZING MATERIALISM

What I refer to as "Jewish materialism" emerged in the context of a global debate that was, as the intellectual historian Frederick Beiser has argued, the most important intellectual dispute of the nineteenth century.[40] The eminent scholar of nationalism Carlton Hayes labeled the entire period of 1871–1900 "a generation of materialism." He hoped, however, "that no one would question [him] too closely about [his] use of the word 'materialism,'" which he defined, in "a common sense way, as denoting a marked interest in, and devotion to material concerns and material things."[41] Hayes thought that materialism was a matter of common sense, but in fact it was something protean and slippery, capacious and complex, provoking heated disputes with important political implications. Aspects of what we might label today monism, positivism, philosophical anthropology, or even idealism were once placed under the rubric of materialism, often by ruling elites who vehemently opposed the political implications of these philosophies.

The scientists, philosophers, and polemicists who used the word *materialism* in the 1860s and 1870s employed it in various, often contradictory ways. Friedrich Albert Lange's monumental second edition of *History of Materialism* (*Geschichte des Materialismus und Kritik seiner Bedeutung in der Gegenwart*) and Georgi Plekhanov's *Essays on the History of Materialism* (*Beiträge zur Geschichte des Materialismus*, 1896) provide examples of the diverse meanings attached to the term.[42] Lange and Plekhanov's differences highlight the disputed legacy of "materialism" and provide historically contextual categories in which to examine how the people I discuss in this book employed the term.

Lange, a German philosopher, noted in the 1860s that, while the philosophical focus on matter had a long history going back to ancient times, the term "materialism" had been coined only in the previous century. Lange endorsed materialism in terms of Democritus's theory of atomism and stressed the importance of scientific research being protected from the encroachments of religion. He was disturbed, however, by the way the concept had recently gained currency among a group of young radical scientists and physiologists. He singled out for criticism the German-speaking scientists Ludwig Büchner and Karl Vogt, who were invoking materialism to dismiss the possibility of all unknowable aspects of consciousness and the subjective nature of sensory knowledge. Büchner and Vogt had popularized the idea that the data obtained through our senses were sufficient to discount the possibility of any nonscientific knowledge. Lange considered them not materialists but rather metaphysicians. For Lange, being a true materialist meant holding back from scientifically asserting ultimate claims about the universe and admitting that there were unknowable aspects of nature. A person could be a materialist, Lange claimed, and still reject the reduction of all ideas and beliefs to social, economic, or biological forces.[43]

Lange's *History of Materialism*—which allowed religion and science to operate in tandem, provided that neither infringed on the domain of the other—would be one of the most influential contemporary philosophical works for Russian Jews.[44] It was translated into Hebrew and even Yiddish two generations before Immanuel Kant's *Critique of Pure Reason* was. Its popularity was, most probably, due to Lange's own argument as well as to its being a compendium of various materialist philosophies. Russian Jewish intellectuals in the 1860s and 1870s expressed the full range of mid-century forms of materialism described by Lange. Social materialists like Moses Leib Lilienblum assumed that people behaved in the same way all other organisms did: according to their best interests. They decried institutions and relationships that blinded people to the material basis of society, the way economic relations determined who married whom and who received communal prestige and privilege. Others, such as Joseph Sossnitz and Tsvi Hirsch Rabinowitz, assumed that nature and science could explain human behavior. Human beings reflected nature because they were its products.[45]

While Russian Jews were attracted to Lange's theory of materialism and the importance of scientific research as the basis for our knowledge of the world, it was Lange's young German Jewish protégé Hermann Cohen who popularized Lange's work in western Europe. In 1887 Cohen penned a foreword to the *History of Materialism* in which he identified Lange as laying the foundations not for a new kind of materialism but rather just the opposite, for a new kind of idealism. Cohen used Lange's insistence on delimiting the boundaries of materialism as an invitation to investigate the possibilities of using the standpoint of the ideal to critically investigate the presuppositions of scientific knowledge.

It is thus not surprising that by the mid-1880s the Russian Marxist Georgi Plekhanov was already condemning Lange's theory of materialism. Cohen and Lange, Plekhanov maintained, were more interested in exploring the implications of what we did not know about consciousness than what we did know by adopting a materialistic worldview. What Lange called materialism, Plekhanov asserted, was in fact idealism. While Lange may have been correct that "we shall never learn how consciousness arises," for Plekhanov this was not the point. The question, Plekhanov maintained, was "whether our ignorance can serve as an objection to *materialism.*" In contrast to Lange and Cohen, Plekhanov was of the opinion that "it could *not.*"[46] To be a materialist required that one disavow the proposition that ideas could transcend material forces. Plekhanov would become the chief proponent of what he termed Karl Marx's "dialectical materialism," in which all aspects of history come into being and perish through a process of negation. Unlike Lange's version of materialism, which left open the possibility of ideas that were not reducible to geographic, economic, and biological factors, Plekhanov demanded that all aspects of history be understood through their relation to the movement of matter in time.

Marx, however, never provided a consistent definition of materialism, allowing for his theories of matter to be understood in multiple ways. "Contrary to common opinion," explain the intellectual historians Allan Megill and Jaeyoon Park, "Marx never claimed that he was a *historical* materialist or that he was an adherent of *the materialist conception of history*—never, ever, at any time, not even once. Nor did he ever declare that he was a dialectical materialist."[47] It was Plekhanov who proposed the term "dialectical materialism," and Friedrich Engels who invoked "historical materialism" to describe Marx's worldview.[48] Those who would have read Marx in the 1870s would more often than not have described him the way he described himself, as a "practical materialist," focusing on the forces blocking human beings from developing their capacities to act freely upon nature and reconstruct matter. For Marx, nature could "not be discussed as if it were severed from human action, for nature as a potential object for human cognition has already been affected by previous human action on contact."[49] The unity of humans with nature is actualized every day in human work, through which humans change nature according to their needs, and in turn are changed by the form of nature that they construct. Instead of a deterministic worldview, Marx's focus was on freeing human beings to act upon the world. Labor relations thus emerged, according to Marx, as the lens through which to evaluate history, as well as the mechanism through which human beings changed the course of history.

Marx identified the accumulation of private property and capitalism as the chief obstacles blocking human beings, as laborers, from developing their full capacities. "Instead of being in the position to sell commodities in which his labour is incorporated," Marx explained, the laborer under capitalism "must be obliged to offer for sale as a commodity that very labour-power, which exists only in his living self."[50] In "Zur Judenfrage" ("The Jewish Question," 1844), he described Judaism as a redacted entity, a stealth carrier of capitalism and social antagonism in Western life. He equated the material features of Jews with both the primary impediments to a universal social revolution: social antagonism and economic inequality.[51]

Even before Marx's death, some Christians and Jews had turned his idea on its head, connecting his theory of a social revolution that rectified social and class imbalances with the messianic program located in the Bible. Moses Hess, the Jewish philosopher from whom Marx borrowed heavily when writing "The Jewish Question," was the first to merge Marx's insights about economic relations with both Judaism and new racial and biological theories. "What Darwin had said regarding the economy of nature," Hess wrote in 1870, "Marx had established for the science of social economy. It is the great merit of these two researchers to have discovered in nature and history the law of progressive development as well as the struggle for existence."[52] Long before Engels's eulogy for Marx in 1883, Hess had equated the German philosopher's insights on history and economics with Darwin's scientific theories. In his final, posthumously published work, *The Dynamic Theory of Matter* (*Dynamische Stofflehre*, 1877), Hess went farther, merging biblical notions of creation and messianism with new biological and economic forms of materialism.[53] While Hess's project represented an important development in the history of Judaism and the relationship between materialism and late-nineteenth-century nationalism, Russian Jewish intellectuals were unaware of his work in the 1870s. When it finally received the attention of a Jewish audience, it was not claimed by Marxists but rather by Cultural Zionists, who were attracted to Hess's reinterpretation of Jews as a national entity.[54]

Among Russian Jews, Aaron Shemuel Lieberman, Judah Leib Levin, and Isaac Kaminer became known as the first and most influential Jewish interpreters of Marx's practical materialism. Like Hess, they were all theists who imparted metaphysical value to the physical world (the Hebrew and Yiddish words for *secularism* had not even been coined). But they also were deeply versed in Kabbalistic and rabbinic literature and were able to identify precisely which strands of medieval and early modern Jewish thought could be woven into a theory of Jewish materialism based on labor.[55] They denounced the liberalism embraced by western European states and described the redistribution of resources in society as a sacred undertaking. They struggled with questions regarding the universal and particular claims associated with materialism. Their Jewish reinterpretation of Marx's theories of capital, human consciousness, and the spreading of propaganda highlights the dynamism of the term *materialism* and the myriad ways it was employed during this period. Most important, it allows us to see the new kinds of metaphysics that emerged around the debates over materialism, nationalism, and ethnicity in the late nineteenth century.

Jewish materialism illuminates a larger phenomenon that appeared in the late nineteenth and early twentieth centuries across Europe, the Middle East, and Asia, especially in the context of struggles for sovereignty and equal access to resources. During this period, we see the conscious reformulation of religious traditions through the lens of "materialism." The history of Catholicism in Polish lands (and more generally in eastern Europe) offers one such parallel case study. According to Brian Porter-Szűcs, defining the development of modern Poland in terms of a "secularization process" obscures the way in which Catholicism had, in one sense, gained more importance for Poles in political terms.[56] What began as a faith adopted by a large contingent of people living in the Polish-Lithuanian Commonwealth later became a universal messianic ideal in the writings of the poet Adam Mickiewicz and eventually a religion that justified the exclusivist and racialist positions e pounded by Poland's Christian Democratic Party.[57] By the twentieth century Poles had come to view Catholicism as a socioethnic marker instead of as a spiritual system based on Roman doctrines. Although the case of Catholicism in Poland tends to highlight the amalgamation of theology and state-based positivism (more than materialism), it remains an important example of how religion was theorized in material terms.[58]

More historically contemporaneous points of comparison to the forms of Jewish materialism advanced in the 1870s can be found in colonial settings. Most notably, it is mirrored in the "Islamic materialism" developed by the Young Turks in the late Ottoman Empire.[59] According to M. Şükrü

Hanioğlu, "a bi-directional process . . . transformed Islam into a materialist philosophy, and at the same time made materialist philosophy Islamic."[60] Science was conceived of as a sacred endeavor; engaging in scientific research was deemed a ritual, and its practitioners were called clerics. Advocates of "Islamic materialism," such as the Young Turk theorist Abdullah Cevdet, were not religious apologists attempting to reconcile Islam and modern science but rather the opposite. They were endowing science and people's physical well-being with new Islamic value.[61] As with Jewish materialism, the form of Islamic materialism developed in the late nineteenth century "was far more than a device for countering accusations of atheism . . . rather it was the creation of a brand new ideology presented as Islam."[62] Its goals were not to defend Islam against a new scientific ideology but to impart metaphysical importance to scientific discoveries.

The rise of Islamic materialism was said to have had an "enormous" effect on Turkish nationalism and upon Mustafa Kemal's worldview, most notably in his attempt to structure Turkey's religious establishment around a progressive notion of faith.[63] Kemal's secularism did not banish religion from all spheres of life; rather, it demanded that Muslim clerics bestow Islamic value on Turkey's scientific and technological advancements.

Hinduism represents the most radical example of an embattled collective consciously reconfiguring (some claim creating) a belief system in line with materialist principles.[64] As with Judaism, this fusion first emerged in the second half of the nineteenth century among what some scholars refer to as "reformist" Hindu thinkers, individuals who asserted that "science seemed to justify and intensify their religiosity."[65] This process can be seen in various competing Hindu national movements.[66]

Most notably, staunch nationalists like the Indian independence advocate V. D. Savarkar gave spiritual value to Darwin, Ernst Haeckel, and Herbert Spencer's theory of "survival of the fittest."[67] Savarkar encouraged the transformation of India from a "fatherland" into a "Holyland" for Hindus. Those included under the rubric of "Hindus," explains the anthropologist Peter van der Veer, were considered to be of a distinct racial ethnic group.[68] Hindus' racial purity was placed on par with that of Jews. This version of Hinduism was devoid of dogmas and clerics, and made few references to Indian gods. Savarkar attempted to distinguish what he termed *Hindutva* (Hindu-ness) from Hinduism. In doing so, he differentiated between a Hindu civilization and the religion of Hinduism. He did not, however, do away with the metaphysical claims associated with Hinduism. Instead he marshaled them to justify particularistic claims over what ostensibly appeared to be universal matter. Explaining what constituted a distinctly Hindu civilization, Savarkar wrote, "If matter is the creation of the Lord, then civilization is the miniature secondary creation of man. At its best it is the perfect triumph of the soul of man over matter and man alike. Wherever and to the extent to which man has succeeded in moulding matter to the delight of his soul, civilization begins."[69] Here too, Savarkar was not engaged in religious apologetics (he considered himself an atheist). He was endowing universal matter with Hindu values—something that he claimed even God could not do. By invoking God as the creator of matter, Savarkar argued that while we may not know the origins of the physical world, what is critical is the way human beings shape it and use it.

Even at the other end of the spectrum, a strong materialist premise undergirded "spiritualist" reinterpretations of Hinduism, such as those advanced by Swami Vivekananda. As noted by the scholar Margaret Chatterjee, Vivekananda's economic theology mirrored that of certain socialist strands of Zionism in promoting "the redemptive role of labor." While Vivekananda is often cited for his denunciation of crass "Western materialism," he was equally adamant in declaring that it was against religious principles and "an insult to a starving man to teach him metaphysics."[70] He emphasized that Hinduism needed to be reformulated with an eye toward addressing social idleness and people's material well-being. Human beings, he argued, could not be reduced to labor, but it was through labor that that they were able to worship God.

Social and political differences aside, these cases illuminate the ways various late-nineteenth- and early-twentieth-century groups consciously infused land, labor, and people with metaphysical value. In all of these cases imperial regimes were blocking collectives from invoking principles of population size and demography to justify their claim over land, labor, and people. When imperial regimes disregarded representational politics or defined them in a manner that ensured the marginalization of certain collectives, Jews, Muslims, Catholics, and Hindus turned to other systems of value to make claims on the physical world. Hindus, Jews, Muslims, and Catholics invoked their respective religions as a way to argue for a more equal and fair universal distribution of resources.

Though mentioned by scholars of respective religious traditions, these various cases have yet to be theorized in terms of the broader history of materialism. The discovery of Muslim, Hindu, Catholic, and Jewish materialisms challenges existing scholarship on the political impact of materialist thought in the second half of the nineteenth century. The intellectual history of materialism is often described as serving the needs of modern universalistic political movements. This connection has been most thoroughly detailed by the historian Todd Weir, who argues that "between the mid-nineteenth and mid-twentieth century . . . [monism] provided an important epistemological foundation to actors in a host of social and political movements. It was an undercurrent in the history of international socialism and had a formative influence on socialist leaders from August Bebel to Mao Zedong."[71] In contrast, my study reveals the ways in which materialist thought contributed to the formation of new national bodies and put into circulation a new theological discourse addressing the organization of people, allocation of resources, and definition of territories. The rise of materialist thought allows us to see more clearly the ideological building blocks of nationalism, the ways in which ideas about the physical world connected people to one another.

However, instead of simply describing these phenomena in terms of religious nationalism or political theology, in this study I investigate the ways human beings create value. I start with the premise that there is no pure human nature in political contexts. [72] For "there is as much making sacred of the profane as there is a secularization of the religious."[73] Instead of debunking the neutrality behind "German lands," "American waters," and "French vineyards," I seek through the idea of Jewish materialism to illuminate what it means to call a science "Islamic," a profession "Catholic," a body "Hindu," or a territory "Jewish." My objective is not to critique various forms of political pseudo-neutrality, but rather to examine the conscious production and manufacturing of *new* and often *conflicting* forms of value toward land, labor, and people. As such, my central concern is not the degree to which something is or is not secular but rather the degree to which various and conflicting forms of value produce and allow for greater or lesser degrees of equality and access to goods and resources.

Identifying an individual, a territory, or a labor force as "Jewish," "Catholic," or "Hindu" was an explicit rejection of a liberal ideal that the physical world could be defined in human terms or through its relative value to a pristine preexisting state. People could not be reduced to citizenship, land was more than something French, German, or Russian, and labor markets were determined by more than productivity and consumption. The bold assertion that there was a Jewish body, either in terms of the physical being of an individual or a defined mass of people; a Catholic profession, an economic role that expressed Catholic assumptions about labor; or a Hindu territory, a landmass that belonged to people called Hindus, generated a different kind of distributional logic and social ordering.

What made materiality so important for these groups was that it also became explicitly invested in something immaterial and unquantifiable.[74] When taken to its extreme, this could become the fetish of sod witnessed in Woody Allen's *Life and Death,* where one estate owner, Dmitri Petrovitch, unearths from his breast pocket a parcel of land that he proudly refuses to sell at any price. Wagging his finger at the useless clod of dirt, he tilts his head back and screams, "This land is not for sale." In other instances, however, it soberly reminded materially oppressed groups that they needed to give greater importance to ensuring the necessary means for their survival. They could no longer afford to see the physical world as a neutral medium. When seen as a historical phenomenon, Jewish, Catholic, Hindu, and Muslim forms of materialism highlight the way we signify and determine how much and in what ways we value the physical world and animate it with new potentialities. Dismissing the Jewish materialists' use of "Jewish" or "religious" language as either philosophically incoherent or a pious facade for a secular worldview prevents us from recognizing how language constructs the objects it references and the way value is produced.

Instead of attempting to uncover philosophical coherency, in this work I pay close attention to the language employed to define an object or a person as well as to the specific political contexts in which value is determined. I assume a philologically conservative definition of what constitutes "Jewish" and "Judaism," including under this rubric only explicit usages of these terms (in their various Hebrew, Yiddish, Russian, and German senses) and only explicit invocations of theological, messianic, or Kabbalistic doctrines. Unless stated otherwise, in the following chapters I reference only writings from the 1860s and 1870s (thus, in many instances, book and article dates appear only in the notes) and focus on the way Jews living in the Pale of Settlement understood the concept of materialism in this period.

MATERIALISM IN MODERN JEWISH HISTORIOGRAPHY

Investigating the formulation of Jewish materialism through a philological and historical prism challenges the way Jewish historians usually associated with competing twentieth-century political points of view portray the intellectual features of the 1870s. Bundist and Zionist historians synchronically limited their discussions of Jewish materialism to its role in inspiring their respective movements. They also diachronically minimized the novelty of Jewish materialism in the 1870s by associating it with ancient biblical—and even rabbinic—ideas. Believing that materialism was already located in the Bible, Jewish historians have failed to see how the very idea was modernized and politicized. Instead of describing the 1870s in terms of the formulation of Jewish materialism, these historians conceptualized it in terms of Zionist and Bundist histories.

The literary scholar Joseph Klausner, for example, insinuated materialism into ancient Jewish sources. Klausner traced Zionism's intellectual origins through a literary narrative that spanned two thousand years and crisscrossed Europe and the Middle East.[75] A child of Lithuania, he made his way to Palestine in the early twentieth century. Although his colleagues at the newly founded Hebrew University looked askance at his undisciplined forays into all corners of history and various political debates, his classes were filled to capacity. His seminal work on the history of Hebrew literature became a primary resource for all students of Jewish history. Klausner was prepared to admit that the Russian materialists such as Dmitry Pisarev and Nikolai Chernyshevsky made a strong impression upon Jewish intellectuals in the 1870s, noting that "it is here that one sees the splitting of ways between on the one side moderate socialism, or at the very least those attempting to solve the Jewish material problem in Russia, and on the other side, the Lovers of Zion (Hovevei Tsiyon) movement, whose strength resides in laying the solid groundwork and material foundation beneath the [Jewish] nation."[76] However, throughout his writings, Klausner criticized those advancing strict materialist theories of Jewish nationalism. He rejected the idea of Zionism being reduced to a precondition for addressing universal class conflicts.

In his article "Historical Materialism and the History of Nationalism" (first published in 1897), Klausner saw the biblical-based socialist ideals espoused by cultural nationalists as the starting point for modern Zionist thought.[77] For Klausner, Zionism mediated the divide between "historical idealism that perceived man to be spirit and nonmaterial and historical materialism that saw only the body and no life-spirit."[78] In 1910, Klausner tagged on an addendum to the article, lambasting thinkers who affiliated with the new Marxist Zionist youth movement Laborers of Zion (Po'alei Tsiyon) and dismissing the materialist Jewish writings of the 1870s as expressing only "the extent to which Jews gave up on their future."[79] This was largely a response to the emergence of specific readings of Marx put into circulation by socialist parties in the 1890s.[80] Klausner still staunchly defended the idea that Zionism was a socialist goal; however, he maintained that the provenance of the Jewish social idea was not located in the materialist theories advanced in the 1870s but rather in the words of the biblical prophets.

A vignette recorded by Klausner in his autobiography reveals how the Jewish materialism of the 1870s has been misidentified by anachronistic theories of the biblical prophets. In 1923, he was invited to an intimate socialist gathering in Haifa. The company included Zionist luminaries such as the socialist theoretician Nachman Syrkin; the future president of Israel Yitzhak Ben Zvi; and Israel's future first prime minister, David Ben-Gurion. The guests were debating, perhaps in Yiddish or Russian, the origins of Jewish socialism. Klausner recalled that "one asserted that it started in Minsk, the other thought that it had emerged in Vilna, finally a third maintained that it originated in Odessa." After listening to their argument, "Mrs. Klausner piped up in Hebrew, 'You are all wrong: the origins of social Zionism were in Jerusalem with the prophets Amos, Isaiah, and Jeremiah and the poets of the Psalms.' The room broke out in applause. 'Right you are, Tziporah,' they proclaimed." According to her husband, "No one thought there was any difference between biblical socialism and class-based socialism."[81] The clapping was more than simply chauvinistic paternalism. As I shall argue, it was the inspiration behind cultural Zionist historiography. What on the surface seemed to be a new form of consciousness born in Minsk, Vilna, and Odessa they now were prepared to assert was as old as scripture.

Bundists applied the same hermeneutics of spiritualization as those found in Zionist writings. They often classified the material elements located in Jewish socialism as reflecting biblical motifs. "Does the rain have a father?" it was asked rhetorically.[82] "The revolutionary fervor that captured the Jewish street had its origin in the Prophets, the Midrashim and messianic expectations," they maintained. Bundists read *Capital* with the same exacting hermeneutic that they employed when reading a folio of the Talmud and referred to Marx and the philosopher Ferdinand Lassalle as both prophets and as modern-day incarnations of Moses.[83]

The German Social Democrat leader Karl Kautsky was so disturbed by this trend among Bundists that he dedicated half his foreword to the first Yiddish edition of *The Communist Manifesto* (*Dos manifest fun di komunistishe partey,* 1899) to admonishing religious readers to stop referring to Marx's

The historian Joseph Klausner (*seated*), the Hebrew poet Shaul Tchernichovsky, and
Fannie Klausner. (Joseph Klausner, *Kitvei prof. Yosef Klausner: otobiyografya*
[Tel Aviv: Massada, 1955], vol. 1)

works as "Torah" or the "Bible." Holding up Marx's *Capital,* he declared,
"This is a book! It is incorrect to associate it with the teachings of Christianity
or Judaism."[84] Yet, even Kautsky, the leading Marxist theorist of his generation, could not keep from making the same mistake. Trying to express the
nature of his own commitment to socialism he explained that "if one were
going to label one of Marx's work's 'Torah' . . . it should not be *Capital,* but
rather the principles advanced in *The Communist Manifesto.*"[85]

The Bundists' and Zionists' attempt to fold materialism into religious or more ancient sources reflects their own desire to give authority to the ideas espoused by their own movements. The Marxist critical theorist Benjamin Feigenbaum laid bare the Zionist and socialist spiritualization and particularization of materialism. The scion of a rabbinic family who became a leader in early-twentieth-century American socialist circles, Feigenbaum imbued his writings with the glee and piercing wit of the young heretic who debunks old rabbis.[86] In his Yiddish article "Materialism in Judaism or Religion and Life" (published in 1896), Feigenbaum heaped scorn upon Jewish socialists and Zionists for employing the Bible as propaganda. Without first proving that Jeremiah knew Marx, Feigenbaum argued, it was disingenuous to claim that class-based Jewish socialism was the product of a prophetic tradition.

Feigenbaum mercilessly satirized "idealist" Zionists, romantics, and members of the Christian Socialist movement who speciously claimed to adopt certain materialist principles. He noted the irony that "for thousands of years religious people have been screaming from rooftops that the world was created in six days, and then all of a sudden . . . Darwin proves that man was the finest son of apes. It was only a matter of time until people began claiming that the 'six days of creation' means six geological periods and 'Adam' means prehistoric man." Feigenbaum chuckled at these exegetes, jeering that such interpretations of biblical literature were as believable as "two plus two equals a noodle pot." Similar hermeneutics were also distorting the historical record of Jewish materialism. "So too," he wrote, "prior to Saint Simon, Charles Fourier, Karl Marx, and Friedrich Engels being dubbed heretics, no one perceived of or discovered a socialist idea in the Bible." Now, all of sudden, everyone says to these thinkers, "Good to see you, my dear friend of religion. What? Who says that socialism is a new idea; its positions can be found right here in the Holy Bible!"[87]

Feigenbaum's biting sarcasm was directed at the anachronistic reading of Jewish history. Because Jews at certain periods expressed anxiety about their material well-being did not mean that they consciously adopted a materialist or socialist understanding of life. That historians and ideologues were suddenly now "discovering" materialist ideas in various time periods and sacred works indicated nothing more than that "the Torah did not determine life but rather life is what determines how people understand Torah."[88]

Feigenbaum's Marxist historiographic model helps peel away the layers of anachronism that now coat the history of materialism. It allows us to see various historical pressures and influences that led to the formation of modern

Benjamin Feigenbaum, "The Most Observant Marxist." The caption reads, "Dedicated to the fanatical heretic B. Feigenbaum who upends all gods except his own, Karl Marx." (*Der Groyser Kundes*, October 25, 1912)

Jewish politics. Still, it is incapable of accounting for the full impact of materialism on modern European history. Feigenbaum was well aware that the categories of "messianic socialism" and "biblical socialism" were also historically new religious phenomena. But in his ideological zeal to criticize what he thought to be the "reactive forces" of religion and expose the hermeneutics of spiritualization, he and others did not articulate how what constituted Judaism and other religions such as Christianity had also been transformed by materialist theories. The rise of materialist consciousness also changed the way Jews understood Judaism. Even contemporary scholarship such as Jonathan Frankel's big-tent political historiography—majestically displayed in his *Prophecy and Politics*—and the otherwise illuminating studies of Jewish social and political life by Ezra Mendelsohn do not address how religious beliefs and ideals were restructured in the nineteenth century.[89] Though both provided a detailed history of Jewish politics, neither scholar addressed the way in which materialism also redefined the nature of Judaism.

Leading Jewish historians such as Israel Bartal, Shmuel Feiner, Eli Lederhendler, Olga Litvak, Michael Stanislawski, and Steven J. Zipperstein have examined the similarities and differences between the philosophy of the Jewish intelligentsia living in Russia in the 1870s and that of the earlier religious reformist movement, the Haskalah (Jewish Enlightenment).[90] Their work, which I reference throughout this study, details the history of Jewish acculturation, secularization, and nationalism. Though their historiographical model was pioneering in its ability to offer a cohesive account of Jews in nineteenth-century eastern Europe, I have not adopted it in this work for a number of reasons. First, virtually all those described here as Jewish materialists distinguished their concerns about Jews' material well-being from a religious reform project (the Haskalah). In addition, a secularization narrative is not capable of explaining why a group of individuals might be committed to imbuing the physical world with metaphysical value. And while many of the thinkers described in this book expressed a strong nationalist orientation, just as many expressed strong Communist or universalistic sentiments.

By examining these individuals according to how they described themselves—as "materialists" (and not as *maskilim,* "enlighteners")—we are able to address a different set of issues, namely, those that revolve around the relationship of metaphysics to materialism and those focused on the way value is generated in society. Though such questions may seem to be of secondary concern to Russian historians or historians focused on Jewish acculturation, secularization, and nationalism, they remain pressing for scholars interested

in the reception of Marx and Darwin in eastern Europe, the formation of
value in modernity, and the outsized role Jews played after 1881 in various
political and economic movements.

THE MATERIALISTS: A PROSOPOGRAPHY

In this book I investigate the relationship of materialism to religion, ethnicity, and nationalism through the lens of roughly twenty-five men and
women in the 1860s and 1870s. Most of these individuals knew one another
and enjoyed relative degrees of social success. Though their worldview, rather
than their biographies, is my subject, it is pertinent to outline some of the
unique social features that define their group identity. The figures I identify
as Jewish materialists include Pavel (Pinchas) Axelrod (1850–1928), Eliezer
Ben-Yehuda (1858–1922), Yitshak Isaac Etkin (1857–1879), Grigory Gurevich
(1852–1929), Henne Helfman, also known as Hessia Meyerovna Helfman
(1855–1882), Mordecai ben-Hillel Hacohen (1856–1936), Isaac Kaminer (1834–
1901), Abraham Uri Kovner (1841–1909), Judah Leib Levin (1844–1925), Aaron
Shemuel Lieberman (1842–1880), Moses Leib Lilienblum (1843–1910), Aaron
Meir Masie (1858–1930), Aaron Porjes (1848–1919), Khasia Shur (1861–1927),
Salomon Shachne Simchowitz (1859–?), Joseph Sossnitz (1837–1910), Morris
Winchevsky (1856–1932), and Eliezer Zuckermann (1852–1884). Others who
borrowed from, and who were in constant conversation with, the materialists
include Shalom Jacob Abramowich (1835–1917), Judah Leib Kantor (1849–
1915), Shlomo Zalman Luria (1857–1908), Ilya Orshanski (1846–1875), Abraham Jacob Paperna (1840–1919), Tsvi Hirsch Rabinowitz (1832–1889), Ḥayyim
Selig Slonimski (1810–1904), and Peretz Smolenskin (1842–1885). While there
were many Jews involved in the debates over the nature of materialism (such
as Jews who took part in the Russian revolutionary movement), these figures
identified as materialists and addressed "Jews'" and "Judaism's" relationship to
what they termed "materialism."

Nearly all the Jewish materialists were born in the 1840s and 1850s into
highly traditional families residing in the northwestern provinces of Russia,
referred to by Jews as Lita (harkening back to the Grand Duchy of Lithuania and today including parts of Belarus, Latvia, Lithuania, Poland, and
Ukraine). Their parents' economic situations varied but they reflected the
limited range of professional opportunities available to Russian Jews: they
worked as teachers, shopkeepers, day laborers, butchers (kosher slaughterers), wheelbarrow makers, and merchants. For the first half of the nineteenth

century, Russian Jews were still legally prohibited from entering universities or purchasing land. While the Russian government did promote Jewish farming settlements in far-flung regions, none of the families of the Jewish materialists took part in these projects. None of them were doctors, lawyers, or professors, and certainly none were civil servants.

Pavel Axelrod, who would later become a founder of the Russian Menshevik Party, grew up in a *bogadel'niia,* a house set aside by Jewish society for impoverished families.[91] The literary critic and apostate Abraham Uri Kovner and his nine siblings lived on the 16 rubles a month (equivalent to roughly $500 today) earned by their father as a schoolteacher. When the father of the future scientist Joseph Sossnitz lost his job as a slaughterer, the family survived on the 75 kopecks a week their mother was paid for doing odd jobs.[92] By contrast, the Mogilev rabble-rousers (and eventual *Narodnaia Volia* revolutionaries) Khasia Shur and Eliezer Zuckermann hailed from the "ghetto aristocracy," elite rabbinic or Jewish mercantile families.[93]

The materialists' relationships to their parents often reflected the way they related to Judaism. If there was antagonism between parent and child, it would be mirrored by the level of hostility the child expressed toward the ancestral religion. At one end of the spectrum were figures such as the future Bundist leader and newspaper editor Morris Winchevsky and Peretz Smolenskin who had positive relationships with their parents and expressed positive feelings toward certain religious features of Judaism.[94] At the other end, the rebellious Eliezer Zuckermann and the precocious revolutionary Henne Helfman expressed more antipathy toward both ritualistic aspects of Judaism and their upbringing.[95] While some, such as the Russian Jewish scientist Tsvi Hirsch Rabinowitz, remained observant Jews throughout their lives, others felt "far more human than Hebrew."[96]

All of these figures' early education was highly conservative. Until their teenage years, most of the men studied in the traditional *kheyder* or were taught by private tutors (only Pavel Axelrod attended a government-sponsored gymnasium).[97] Khasia Shur recalled her father teaching her to write in Hebrew.[98] The poet Judah Leib Levin; Aaron Shemuel Lieberman, the founder of the first Jewish socialist union; and Joseph Sossnitz all also immersed themselves in the Jewish mystical tradition, the Kabbalah.[99] All the Jewish materialists could read and write in German. Few had proficiency in Russian or had Gentile friends before their teenage years.[100] Tsvi Hirsch Rabinowitz founded a Russian newspaper but his Russian was so poor that his business cards read, "author of the natural sciences."[101]

All the Jewish materialists were highly mobile; not one died in the place he or she was born. Some left their childhood homes to avoid arranged marriages.[102] Although some scholars described them as cosmopolitans, this was not a term they used to describe themselves. Many formed a commune in Berlin and developed close ties with the founders of the German Social Democratic Party. The Berlin police watched their every move, taking copious notes on the medical students Masie, Kantor, and Gurevich.[103] Some would spend time in jail for their involvement in revolutionary activities.

Their travels and time spent in Paris, London, and Berlin provided these figures with new sexual freedom;[104] some even engaged in homosexual relations.[105] This autonomy, experienced in tandem with deepening estrangement from family and community, could cause extreme stress, leading in some cases to severe depression and even suicide.[106] While some, such as Kovner, enjoyed the hedonistic lifestyle often associated with certain strands of materialism, most of these thinkers looked askance at such behavior. Echoing the labor-oriented model of materialism exemplified by Rakhemtov, a character in Chernyshevsky's novel *What Is to Be Done?*, Lilienblum castigated Kovner for his decadence and excesses.

Perhaps the most notable shared characteristic of the Jewish materialists was that the majority of them foreswore the two central pillars of early-nineteenth-century liberal Jewish politics. They abandoned their quest to reform the rabbinic tradition and ceased working to win greater political rights for Jews in the Russian Empire. Their interest in the question of Jews' relationship to the material world was a rejection of the aims of Jewish enlightenment.[107] "Even though the writers of the 1860s–1880s . . . have been called maskilim . . . they were different from those who came before them and should be set apart from those Jewish writers who operated in the 1820s–1850s."[108]

Few of the materialists were able to take advantage of the Russian government's decision in 1861 to allow Jews entry into universities: most had not received the education needed to pass the entry exams. Still, a few of the men did receive advanced degrees, and many attended university lectures while living in Riga, Kiev, Saint Petersburg, and Berlin.[109] The women, however, were often forced to literally take back seats in lecture halls.[110] Some managed to gain a working knowledge of the mechanics of the printing press; others took up manual labor.[111] Their knowledge reflected not so much the Russian university-educated *raznochintsy* (members of mixed classes) but rather the eclectic intellectual mixture captured in Todd Weir's description of

Halbgebildete—autodidacts who conflated the scientific and theological fields and the lower and middle classes.[112]

For all their talk about professional diversification, however, the majority of these materialists were writers and teachers. Like their parents, none of them became farmers or guildsmen. Most of the materialists were what Dmitry Pisarev termed "thinking realists," individuals engaged in what they considered the strenuous activity of using their minds. Their source of income was not a corporate communal institution, nor was it the Russian government. It was "a Jewish public," an entity they were both creating and informing. In some instances, they were able to procure as much as 25–35 rubles per month tutoring the children of wealthy businessmen or performing a mixture of literary, tutorial, and administrative functions.[113] Compared to jobs in a tobacco factory or as handcrafters —which demanded on average a fourteen- to eighteen-hour workday at a salary that ranged from half a ruble to 1.5 rubles a week—the self-created profession of "thinking realist" paid relatively well.[114] Most of these materialists, however, depended in one way or another upon finding a public that was prepared to read their writings.

The Jewish materialists contributed to and functioned in a trilingual public sphere that emerged around Yiddish, Hebrew, and Russian newspapers.[115] Each newspaper was directed at a different sector of Jews, with some overlap, residing in Russian lands: the Russian broadsheets appealed to liberals and those who wished to assimilate into Russian society; the Hebrew weeklies spoke to the high-minded rabbinic elite; while the Yiddish papers tended to address the more practical concerns of the masses. Some of the materialists wrote and worked for Russian and Ukrainian revolutionary organs. The medium and format of the papers generated new forms of communication and encouraged writers to address shared social questions and cultural reference points.[116] In the 1870s, these weeklies might have as many as two thousand subscribers, but their readership far exceeded those numbers.

The materialists' role in shaping and participating in an egalitarian trilingual Jewish public sphere starkly differed from the more personal form of letter writing that defined the primary mode of communication for the men of the 1840s. For the latter, the epistle was the primary means through which they shared their ideas. While the men and women of the 1860s and 1870s also carried on robust personal correspondence, their energies and anxieties focused on the interests of the impersonal print-reading public to whom their words were now being addressed.

Following the pogroms of 1881, there would be a split among the Jewish materialists. Many became leaders in emergent Zionist circles, a few assumed prominent positions in the Jewish socialist movement, and others forsook Jewish concerns to focus on Russian revolutionary politics. Many of the characters discussed in this book died prematurely. Etkin, Simchowitz, Orshanski, Zuckermann, Lieberman, and Smolenskin all perished before 1885. By the time the survivors came to write their autobiographies in the early twentieth century, nearly all were interpreting the ideas they had espoused in the 1860s and 1870s either as foreshadowing or in stark opposition to later political and cultural activities.

Tradition

Jewish materialism comprised worldviews and philosophies first formulated in the 1860s and 1870s. But the roots of the problems addressed by this intellectual movement ran back to a religious and economic landscape set in 1795, when the Russian Empire, along with the kingdoms of Prussia and Austria, completed the third and final partition of the early modern Polish-Lithuanian Commonwealth. Russia acquired large swaths of territory spreading east of the Nieman River and down into Volhynian Ukraine. With its territorial expansion it also gained a number of new religious and ethnic groups. Now Russia ruled over not only Orthodox Christians, Muslims, and Catholics but also over roughly one million Jews. The Russian Empire, which had long barred Israelites from residing on its lands, suddenly became the protector of the world's largest Jewish population.

This Jewish community had existed for two hundred years as a corporate entity—a state within a state. Under the Polish-Lithuanian Commonwealth, Jews were allowed to establish their own courts and civic institutions in return for taxes paid by leaders of local Jewish corporations. The corporate leaders negotiated these taxes, as well as the Jews' legal and residential rights, with the Polish aristocracy. The noblemen allowed Jews to reside on their assigned lands and employed them as middlemen between themselves and the peasantry. Jewish residents leased the right to work as small handcrafts producers, tavern keepers, liquor dealers, tailors, and merchants.[1] Jews built their own educational institutions, seminaries, and synagogues. Theirs was a deeply observant society. Communal lay leaders supported rabbis whose authority derived from learning institutions, and Hasidic masters whose power bases were independent large-scale courts. The Polish-Lithuanian Jews did not fit into any preexisting socioeconomic category of the Russian Empire. Their customs, dress, and languages appeared foreign and strange within the largely Christian, agrarian world. Jews were for the most part not agriculturalists. And as Jews they were barred from owning property or joining Christian guilds. The empire struggled to determine how best to rule its new population.

Russia was not the first state to be confronted with a seemingly independent Jewish population. For at least two decades, France and Prussia had been taking decisive steps toward dismantling medieval corporate institutions and assimilating their Jewish populations into new confessional and economic structures. The state removed Jewish leaders from their positions as tax collectors and managers of civic life and forbade rabbis to employ coercive power over their adherents. In France and Prussia, Judaism would be increasingly restricted to family law, rituals practiced in the home, and services conducted in the synagogue.

The policies directed toward Jews mirrored a larger practice: in France and Prussia feudal and guild-based systems were being abolished to make way for economies revolving around manufacturing, private enterprise, and large-scale civil services. Along with the rest of the population, Jews were encouraged to become productive citizens and subjects. No longer required to follow trades based on familial ties or a Christian religious identity, Jews were finding new jobs in new industries. That Prussian and French Jews had never taken part in agricultural labor or Christian guilds was far less a concern for French and Prussian officials than it would be for Russia's leaders, who in 1795 were sixty years away from emancipating the serf population and seizing control of the land from churches and noblemen.

Catherine the Great briefly toyed with the western European model of allowing Jews to join Christian guilds. Ultimately, though, she left local Jewish corporate institutions intact and refused Jews the right to own land. Moreover, she restricted them to a landmass called the Pale of Settlement, which included territories in present-day Lithuania, Ukraine, Belarus, and Poland. In the government's archaic estate system, Jews were classified under at least three different categories (members of an independent estate, national foreigners, and members of various occupational professions), each of which carried its own set of rules and standards. It was thus impossible even to speak of a coherent government policy regarding Jews.

Under the leadership of Alexander I (r. 1801–1825), the government issued dozens of contradictory edicts and laws for Russia's Jewish population. The confusing nature of these policies can be seen in the two most significant proposals. One was to economically integrate the Jews: the government offered Jews resources and territory for their own agricultural settlements.[2] At the same time, to address the religious divide between Jews and the rest of the population, it invited Protestant English missionaries to the empire in the hope of converting the Jews to Christianity.[3] The former created only slightly more farmers than the latter did converts.

By the end of the first quarter of the nineteenth century, the Russian government had failed to weave its Jewish population into the religious and economic tapestry of the empire. Even as the Jewish population ballooned to roughly two million (increasing at twice the rate of the rest of the Russian population), the outward differences between Jews and other Russians remained noticeable. As one traveler from the period remarked, Jewish men wore "a black caftan, tied round the waist by a girdle of the same colour, boots, and breeches. Their head is entirely shaven, with the exception of two locks of hair upon their temples, which fall upon their cheeks, and mingle with the beard." Jewish women appeared equally foreign, "wearing a handkerchief folded like a turban."[4] In the eyes of their detractors they appeared to be "filthy" and garbed in "tattered rags."

For their part, Jewish religious leaders did little to help the situation.[5] They promoted Talmud study over all other forms of labor, "even if it meant [Jews] would have no clothes to wear in the freezing cold and only be able to afford a dry piece of bread dipped in salt water."[6] Some recognized that the Jews' beliefs were adversely affecting their economic well-being,[7] and complained that their co-religionists "hate[d] work, and love[d] the rabbinate."[8] Some even admitted that such sentiments had caused Jews to engage in criminal behavior.[9] While the Jews' economic standing remained relatively stable vis-à-vis the rest of the population, overcrowding, lack of basic civic infrastructure, and minimal retail opportunities were becoming endemic to life in the Pale of Settlement.

Following the ascension of Nicholas I to the Russian throne in 1825, the empire instituted a policy of enlightened absolutism toward Jews, Tatars, and Poles, whereby all religious groups were expected to promote internal reform agendas that supported the ideals and economic aims of the empire.[10] Regarding Jews, this policy was intended to rectify the two most noticeable differences between them and the rest of the empire's subjects: their religious orientation and their refusal to become part of an agricultural workforce.

Nicholas instituted forced conscription of Jews into the Russian military and moved to dissolve the Jews' independent corporate structures to further assimilate them into occupational estates. He enlisted a cohort of intellectuals, known as *maskilim* (the plural of the Hebrew *maskil,* "scholar," "enlightened"), to promote his edicts among the Jewish masses. Largely comprised of autodidacts, this group would become the government's Trojan horse, set among Jews to turn them into productive and loyal subjects. Men such as the rabbi and journalist Samuel Joseph Fuenn (1819–1891) and the scholar Isaac Baer Levinsohn (1788–1860) would provide religious support for Jews serving in the Russian army, attending state-sponsored schools, and adopting agricultural professions. The government would look to Levinsohn and Fuenn to promote its agenda of economic and religious reform among Russia's Jewish population.

Nicholas's ultimate goal for the Jews remains cloudy. Some scholars claim that he secretly wanted to convert the Jews (and all other minority religious groups) to Orthodox Christianity. Others argue that he sought less to convert them than to "Europeanize" them.[11] What is clear is that Nicholas wanted to reproduce within his Russian lands the same economic and religious transformation that he saw taking place among French and Prussian Jews. By the 1840s, most Jewish children residing in Berlin were fluent in German, attended state schools and proudly joined the military. The intense religious observance and practices found among Jews living in the northwestern provinces of the Russian Empire were fast disappearing from western Europe. Most notably, Jewish residents of Berlin and Hamburg had begun adopting the religious norms and mores of their Protestant neighbors. They had instituted mixed-sexed pews and sermons delivered in the vernacular. Their dress, mannerisms, and education were increasingly indistinguishable from those of their Christian neighbors. Nicholas I hoped to encourage the same developments among Russia's Jews.

Russian government officials now called upon Jews to adopt the Protestant ideal of self-identification, expressed as "Russians of the Mosaic Faith."[12] But Nicholas's program deviated from the western European model in ways that proved formative. Western European Jews were becoming integrated into local economic institutions that favored capitalistic enterprises; their new religious ideals were being shaped within increasingly secular economic and Protestant religious contexts. Nicholas wanted Russian Jews to integrate into a feudal economy that had brought only misery upon its peasantry and to adopt a liberal model of religion that contrasted with the traditional character of Russia's major religious groups, Catholicism and Eastern Orthodoxy.

Moreover, Nicholas's plans did not adequately address the important differences between Russia's Jews and their counterparts in western Europe. As one prominent Russian-Jewish enlightener remarked, "The Jewish 'doctors' of Berlin were fluent in the language of their German birthplace and French, and sometimes were even familiar with English." By contrast, a deep commitment to rabbinic knowledge distinguished Russian Jewish intellectuals.[13] The Russian maskilim such as Fuenn and Levinsohn were deeply concerned by the religious and economic inconsistencies and structural problems in Nicholas's program.

Often overlooked by scholars are the theological and economic aspects of the Russian Empire's program. As perceptively alluded to by Yochanan Petrovsky-Shtern, "Nicholas I's enlightened rationalism clashed with his own vision of a Russian Orthodox Empire,"[14] as he tried simultaneously to promote a religious revolution and economic conservatism. The empire hoped to transform Judaism along Protestant lines but demanded that Jews become integrated into a medieval feudal economic system. Russian Jewish enlighteners cautiously noted these inconsistencies. Employing economic and religious arguments that would eventually be fused within the sociologist Max Weber's theory of "traditional authority," they asserted that for Jews to become part of a "traditional" economy based on agriculture and guilds, Judaism needed to promote "traditional" theological models associated with Russia's Catholic and Orthodox populations. To understand the rise of Jewish materialism in 1860s and 1870s, we must first realize the contradictory nature of Nicholas's program and the weakness of the Jewish reform projects during the 1840s and 1850s.

The maskilim argued that the government's idea of making Jews into Russians of the Mosaic Faith was as foreign to Judaism as it was to the Russian Empire. A Mosaic Faith would create deists, heretics, and rabble-rousers; it would be counterproductive for accomplishing what the government really wanted—namely, the adoption by Jews of "traditional" feudal forms of economic enterprise. Russian government officials wanted Jews to become members of professions that were handed down from generation to generation and developed over time: agriculture and the guilds. The maskilim attempted to impose this economic model by promoting a form of a religion that reflected the same values: what they would call "traditional" rabbinic Judaism.[15] The Russian Jewish enlighteners' relationship to the Russian government was mediated through European religious categories but expressed a very different theory of social and economic acculturation from the one advanced by Prussian or French Jews of the 1840s and 1850s as well as from that of the Russian Jewish materialists of the 1860s and 1870s.

THE EMPIRE'S ECONOMIC AND RELIGIOUS REFORM AGENDA

The way Jews living in Russian lands in the 1840s and 1850s described their economic and religious predicament should not be confused with the living conditions of Jews in this period. By the 1840s and 1850s noticeable strains had appeared in the Jews' economic condition. Jews were confined to specific professions and hampered by contradictory laws and regulations. But Jewish enlighteners often exaggerated these complaints and exploited economic problems to make an argument for religious reform and enlightenment.[16] Jews were poor, they maintained, because their religious beliefs and practices were preventing them from acculturating into larger economic bodies. Only by reforming Judaism, they argued, could Jews become part of and benefit from the Russian economy.

The tension between the actual and purported economic situation of Jews living in Russian lands can be observed in archival documents written on the eve of the British philanthropist Moses Montefiore's visit to Russia in 1846. On one hand, the enlighteners admitted that Jews were involved in over forty different occupational professions including farming, chopping wood, carpentry, wheelmaking, and glazing.[17] This variety certainly differs from more monolithic pictures of Russia's Jewish professional profile. On the other hand, Jewish enlighteners often added to their description of these professions caveats such as "the majority of those who engaged in these professions were poor, for they never obtained the necessary knowledge to properly undertake such forms of labor."[18] Some went so far as to claim that "death" and "starvation" engulfed the city of Vilna.[19] Residents who at one time had sufficient means were now said to be beggars; those who were "once considered poor and had previously received bread from generous [merchants] were now strewn across the streets in need of bread, finding none, and waiting for death to come."[20] On the doorsteps of Vilna's hospital, it was said that one could find dozens of sick and impoverished Jews who, because of quotas on Jewish patients, were left to die in the street.[21]

For good reason, the maskilim's description of the Jews' economic situation would make a strong impression on Russian officials. Vilna's chief Jewish accountant in the 1840s, Abraham Simḥa Katsenelenbogen, described in his diary the town's economic situation as making it impossible for the Jews to pay their required taxes:

> Today there are eleven thousand [Jewish] men listed as residing in Vilna [of a city population of thirty thousand Jews]. Eight thousand of them are dirt poor; they lack the means to pay even three rubles a year to the government as the law requires from each and every individual. And of the three thousand men who do possess the means to pay the tax, only fifteen hundred, with great hardship, manage to pay the three rubles. . . . The poverty and lack of funds bring cries every day, and people's ability to obtain capital is slowly deteriorating and vanishing. The taxes on . . . meat continue to rise. Even more burdensome is the fact that the government does not allow Jews to engage in business and live outside three districts. And each day a new generation is born and fathers become responsible for their children, and they are unable to provide for their wives and small children, and especially their older children. And professional opportunities continue to decrease. And the only means one has to provide for oneself is to shortchange one's friends. Sons dishonor fathers and daughters rise up against mothers and daughters-in-law against mothers-in-law; a man's own household has become his enemy.[22]

Though it is not within the scope of this study to assess the accuracy of Katsenelenbogen's claims, we can surmise that they made an impression on Russian officials, who thought highly of Katsenelenbogen. In 1834, when Katsenelenbogen requested imperial permission to publish the first Jewish newspaper in Russian lands—*First Fruits* (*Minḥat bikkurim*)—local Russian officials vouched for his honesty and forthrightness.[23] While the Jews' reported and real economic conditions might not have aligned, the reports played a larger role in determining the policies of the Russian government.

The government accepted the enlighteners' descriptions of Jewish life and insisted that the Jews' miserable condition derived from their religious worldview. "The absence of Jews in any useful labor sector and the harmful occupations they have adopted," asserted a memorandum issued by Russian officials on February 27, 1840, "has forced the government to undertake measures against the Jews to encourage them in agriculture and other useful activities." However, the report continued, "Given the absence of a general plan, these measures have not been successful, and Jews, as before, remain in a peripatetic condition and harmful to the interests of the state." Therefore, Russian officials refocused their energies toward "examining the root of [the Jews'] separation from *grazhdanskiy byt* [civic life]; that is to say, examining the religious teachings that separate them from others."[24]

The memorandum, "The Administration of the Jews in Russia," was issued by the Committee for Defining Measures for the Radical Transformation of the Jews of Russia under the leadership of Count Pavel Dimitrievitch Kiselev.[25] The report concluded that all reforms of the Jews' economic profile would be paired with reforms of their religion. The Jewish question on Russian lands could be solved through a two-prong strategy of religious and economic reform. Specifically, the Talmud, the most authoritative textual corpus of rabbinic Judaism, was cited as the cause of Jewish economic intransigence:

> For the Jews, the Talmud is of divine origin. Its religious truth is claimed to be the essence of truth announced by angels and the word of the living God. . . . The Talmud instructs Jews to hold in contempt all peoples and all other beliefs. These teachings are reinforced by the following rules: the Jews should consider their presence in all places other than Palestine as slavery, and they will be freed from the yoke and brought to their homeland by the arrival of the messiah and therefore should devote their activity to practices which, without acculturating them to foreign lands, provide them with the possibility of leaving these lands with all the fruits of their acquisitions.[26]

The Talmud was said to demean Gentiles and, most important, to encourage Jews to engage in petty trade, pursue unseemly business activities, and rape the lands on which they resided in the hope of one day taking their goods to Palestine.

According to the historian Benjamin Nathans, Kiselev's report not only "set the Committee's agenda for the next decade"; it also determined the way Jews would conceive of their identity as Jews.[27] The report showed a correlation between the Jews' economic makeup and their rabbinic ideals. The government memorandum expressed echoes of the old anti-Semitic charge that Judaism was to blame for Jews' economic unproductivity. Thus it is not surprising that a little more than a year after it was filed, another memorandum was drafted that focused not simply on "the administration of the Jews" but on the reform of the educational and spiritual aspects of Judaism. The latter report was written by the newly appointed Russian minister of enlightenment, Count Sergey Uvarov, and promised that the government would dislodge the traditional *kheyder* school system and institute a Russian school system for the Jewish population.[28] The schools would offer instruction in European languages, geography, mathematics, and practical subjects in the hope of Europeanizing Russian Jews.[29]

Following in Kiselev's footsteps, Uvarov asserted that the Russian Jews' economic predicament derived from their reliance upon the Talmud, which encouraged intolerance, usury, and a lack of respect for the countries in which they resided. The Talmud promoted an egotistic form of Jewish materialism that came at the expense of the economic well-being of the Jews' Gentile neighbors. Uvarov instructed the government-sponsored Jewish school system to "eliminate the Talmud from the subjects of teaching, not only compulsory but also elective subjects."[30] Uvarov believed that the chief reason for the lack of economic and religious development of Jews in the Russian Empire was that "nowhere is the influence of the Talmud so strong as it is here, in the Polish Kingdom . . . where ignorance reigns among the Jews." While other religious minorities living in the Russian Empire held similar religious works dear, Uvarov maintained that "the Talmud acquired an importance that neither the early Muslims nor the early church placed on the commentators of Scripture."[31] By removing the Talmud from the curriculum, the government hoped to change the Jews' economic and religious profile.

German Jewish enlighteners like the rabbi and communal leader David Friedländer inspired the Russian government's proposed religious and economic reforms. In 1791, Friedländer had already given thanks to God that "the Talmud was no longer studied in Berlin."[32] As noted by the historian Derek Penslar, Friedländer made the "direct association between morality and economic utility."[33] Jewish economic unproductivity was a function of the Jews' continued adherence to Talmudic and rabbinic Judaism, he believed. Though Friedländer endorsed having Jews adopt agricultural professions, his main focus was on establishing the moral conditions that would allow them to occupy positions in bureaucratic and commercial industries. Friedländer, who at one point entertained the idea of converting Jews to Protestantism, now encouraged Russian government officials to attack the Talmud and the traditional features of rabbinic Judaism.[34]

Disregarding the differences between Prussian and Russian moral and economic contexts, Nicholas's ministers thought to cultivate their own reformers along the Friedländer model. However, unlike Friedländer, the Jewish enlighteners residing in Russian lands continued to believe in the validity of the Talmud and were primarily concerned about the Jews' ability to acquire greater educational and economic opportunities.[35] Jewish enlighteners would walk a thin line in their theological and economic prescriptions between supporting the government's proposals and trying to win the favor of more observant sectors of the population. The enlighteners' connection to Uvarov and the Russian government carried a serious strategic risk. Identifying with Uvarov made them complicit in a strategy for Jewish economic reform that was based on the Christian idea of eradicating the most revered text in Russian Jewish life. Though worried about the prospect of implicitly supporting an anti-rabbinic project, they knew the government ultimately held the keys to greater economic rights, the possibility of professional diversification, and, most important, their own livelihood.[36]

THE ENLIGHTENERS' THEORY OF "TRADITION"

Jewish enlighteners were in full agreement with the government regarding the need for Jews to diversify economically, but they rejected the government's claim that the Talmud was responsible for their current economic situation. They concurred that the Jews' immiseration was connected to their religious beliefs and specifically to rabbinic Judaism. But the root of the Jews' economic problem, they argued, was not the Talmud per se but rather a specific reading of the Talmud adopted by more conservative sectors of the population, the Hasidim. The enlighteners worked to present a reformed theory of the Talmud and rabbinic Judaism more generally—one that they argued aligned more fully with the government's overall social and economic policies than the Friedländer and western European model being adopted by the government.

Most notably, the Jewish enlightener Isaac Baer Levinsohn, who resided in Kremenets, in present-day Ukraine, maintained that, if understood properly, the Talmud supported the Russian government's social and economic reform agenda.[37] Levinsohn would become known as "the Russian Moses Mendelssohn" for his role in promoting a theory of Jewish acculturation that he justified through the tenets of rabbinic Judaism. Levinsohn was a cankerous individual whose character was more suited to academia than the rough-and-tumble politics of the Jewish city. His ideas, however, ingratiated

Isaac Baer Levinsohn. (Courtesy of the National Library of Israel, Jerusalem)

him with government officials. His first work, *Testimony in Israel* (*Te'uda beyisra'el,* 1828), advanced the idea that rabbinic Judaism encouraged Jews to learn European languages, study secular subjects, and work the land.[38] Levinsohn never condemned the Talmud—only those who interpreted it in a manner that promoted Torah study over labor and secular subjects.

However, by the 1840s Nicholas and his ministers had become convinced that all forms of Jewish unproductivity could be traced to the Talmud itself. Levinsohn was well aware that harsh consequences would follow any public rebuttal of the government's economic and educational programs. Ideology aside, he relied on the government's good graces for financial support. From a young age he had suffered from a nervous disorder and spent much of his adult life bedridden and unable to provide for himself. Instead of a stand-off with his employer, Levinsohn looked for a way to make the case that Talmudic Judaism endorsed Kiselev and Uvarov's economic program.

Throughout Levinsohn's literary career he rhetorically conjured up a threat from outside the Jewish community to justify bold and controversial arguments directed toward Jews. In some instances he concocted "questions" posed to him by governments, while at other times he presented queries raised by Christian religious clerics. Playing the game of "my enemy's enemy," Levinsohn hoped to persuade his Jewish audience to grant him greater license in redefining Judaism to deflect the criticisms issued against it by opponents. Thus, it is not surprising that Levinsohn's defense of the Talmud was built around the strawman of English Protestant missionaries.[39] Instead of confronting the government or the Jewish community, Levinsohn targeted the best-known missionary in Russian lands, Alexander McCaul (1799–1863), who had been based in Warsaw from 1821 to 1830.[40] McCaul would go on to have a distinguished career in the Anglican Church, regarded as an authority on the relationship between Judaism and Christianity. While the English minister's missionizing efforts produced minimal results,[41] he gained the attention of Jews across the Pale, as well as of governments around the world, with the serial publication of his anti-Talmud polemic *The Old Paths; or, the Talmud Tested by Scripture.*[42] Aside from its missionary aspirations, *Old Paths* echoed the position of the Russian government: namely, that as long as Jews held fast to the Talmud they could not be loyal imperial subjects and productive citizens, or, most important, deal honestly in business affairs with their fellow countrymen. McCaul's treatise raised the specter that the Russian state might refuse to grant Jews equal access to labor markets and agricultural resources.

Levinsohn responded with a rejoinder to McCaul titled *Seed of Babylon* (*Zerubavel*), which was written over the course of the 1840s and 1850s, although Russian censors blocked its publication until 1863. In private correspondence from the 1850s Levinsohn intimated that he wrote the book in the hope of winning Christians over to a new understanding of the Talmud. He explained, "I purposely supported my positions by citing the works of various Christian scholars."[43] Levinsohn thought Moses Montefiore might help finance a translation of his reply into Russian.[44] But Montefiore received other requests to carry out the project, most notably from Levinsohn's protégé, Samuel Joseph Fuenn. Almost thirty years Levinsohn's junior, Fuenn represented the next generation of Jewish enlighteners. He would become the editor of the first Jewish enlightenment journal and Hebrew newspaper in Russia. Later he was appointed an instructor in the state-sponsored rabbinical school and became a leader in the early Zionist movement. Unlike the reclusive Levinsohn, who spent his days in libraries far away from the seats of power and influence, Fuenn resided in Vilna, took an active role in communal affairs, and developed close contacts with Russian officials.[45] By 1843, Fuenn had written a 250-page response to McCaul under the title *Paths of God* (*Darkhei Hashem*) that he hoped would win Montefiore's support.[46]

Levinsohn and Fuenn proffered similar defenses against the claim by Mc-Caul and the government that the Talmud encouraged Jews' propensities toward mercantile activities and hoarding goods. They both maintained that Judaism was a tradition based on reason, rearticulated and transmitted anew in each generation. Talmudic statements that seemed to confirm the government's or McCaul's assertions had to be read in the context of a larger theory of "tradition," they explained. In contrast to McCaul and the Russian government, who maintained that Jews regarded the Talmud as sacred scripture, Levinsohn and Fuenn employed the idea of tradition to explain the position of the Talmud in Jewish life. According to Levinsohn, the Talmud was an expression of "the Oral Law":

> This is what the Bible refers to as *lekah*, and I understand this term to mean what is written in the Mishnah [the earliest rabbinic work], as masora and kabbalah, and in another language [German] what is meant by the words *carried, present, teaching, report,* and *telling*. And this is exactly what in Latin is referred to as "Traditio" [Tradition]. The tradition is not to be found in the reading of books, but rather in the knowledge obtained through the intellect and one's explanatory abilities and even through Talmudic argumentation.[47]

Similarly, Fuenn maintained:

> The definition of all forms of Oral Law is a philosophy [*Inbegriff*] of all the laws and rulings and ideas and beliefs not written in a book that comprise the basis of the faith. And this teaching flows necessarily from the Written Law because the writer revealed the foundations of the beliefs, ideas, and laws in his book and left after him many things that he did not find appropriate or necessary to reveal and detail in the written word. The writer's students learned these matters from the writer's life, his practices, and his words and his commandments. This knowledge is referred to also as a *kabbalah* or *ha'takah* [*Tradition*], and this can be found in all faiths, in the Jewish, Christian, and Muslim faiths, and without it a person could not fulfill the written law.[48]

It is no coincidence that Fuenn and Levinsohn espoused similar conceptions of tradition.[49] Other Russian Jewish enlighteners explicitly credited Levinsohn with putting the idea of tradition into circulation among Jews. In 1840 "A Letter from a Learned Russian Israelite from Lithuania" appeared in the German Jewish newspaper *Jewish Yearbook* [*Israelitische Annalen*],[50] which described the distinctive features of Lithuanian Jewry and credited Levinsohn and the Galician Jewish philosopher Nachman Krochmal (1785–1840) with helping the author understand that "tradition only reveals itself as the changing garment of the eternal unchangeable spirit."[51]

The Russian Jewish enlighteners' theory of tradition is best understood through a distinction independently drawn by the scholars Jay Harris and Kathryn Tanner. They distinguish between views of tradition that emphasize *what* is being passed on and those focusing on the process *by which* something is transmitted.[52] For Fuenn and Levinsohn (and other Jewish enlighteners), tradition was not the "stuff" of inheritance but rather the idea and "process" of handing down or over to others. Tradition was the application of eternal doctrines to new situations through the use of reason and debate. Tradition was embodied within a *style* of Talmudic legal disputation that emphasized the use of logic to interpret and apply biblical ideas. The rabbinic debates, as opposed to the content of the rabbinic laws themselves, constituted the Tradition or the Oral Law. Each generation created new laws and customs and discarded those that were no longer practiced. "Just like a doctor who sometimes must amputate a limb in order to save the body," explained Levinsohn, "so too, [Judaism authorized] that laws be rescinded in wake of pressing social concerns."[53] Levinsohn followed other Jewish enlighteners in emphasizing the jurisprudential malleability of Talmudic dicta.[54] Norms and mores could be adopted or eliminated depending on whether they contradicted reason or the needs of the time.

The enlighteners freed the Talmud from the shackles of its own canonicity, internal contradictions, and economically problematic statements. They turned it from a fiat that was eternally binding into a prototype that could be applied in any context and reinterpreted. Jews no longer were forced to engage in mental gymnastics to explain texts that suggested they sought only to accumulate goods and resources. The Talmud was not the word of law or a sacred scripture but a style and a method; it was a means by which a religious person could evaluate or assess the nature of a particular situation. Viewed from this intellectual perspective, Jews were no different from Catholic or Muslim populations in the empire.

CATHOLIC JUDAISM

Fuenn and Levinsohn's understanding of the Talmud and rabbinic Judaism was based on Catholic and Orthodox theories of tradition.[55] To be sure, Fuenn and Levinsohn were far from the first to develop a theory of Jewish transmission; however, they were among the first to appropriate the Catholic and Orthodox category of tradition and develop coherent full models of Judaism based on Catholic theology.[56]

Fuenn and Levinsohn enjoyed warm relations with numerous Orthodox and Catholic priests, many of whom read and commented upon Levinsohn's writings.[57] In particular, Fuenn and Levinsohn's theory of tradition drew from ideas espoused by the seventeenth-century French bishop Jacques-Bénigne Bossuet. Defending the idea of the Jewish Oral Law, Levinsohn claimed,

Samuel Joseph Fuenn. (Courtesy of the National Library of Israel, Jerusalem)

"I saw in the work of the well-known Christian scholar . . . Bossuet that Christians also have an Oral Law, which they call 'tradition.'"[58] Likewise, Fuenn cited Bossuet regarding the idea of a Christian "Oral Law."[59] Both Fuenn and Levinsohn were referring to Bossuet's formulation of the idea of tradition in *Discourse on a Universal History* (*Discours sur l'histoire universelle*, 1681) as "being so adaptable to the light of reason, that it was unimaginable that such a clear and important truth could ever have been dimmed or forgotten among men."[60]

Levinsohn and Fuenn read the work of the Catholic bishop through Johann Andreas Cramer's German translation, *Einleitung in die Geschichte der Welt, und der Religion* (1757), a Protestant critique of Bossuet's notion of tradition.[61] Levinsohn went so far as to fully adopt Bossuet's Catholic template for explaining Judaism's process of transmission and structures of authority. While Bossuet believed that the correct Oral Law was passed on to the church fathers (and not the rabbis), Levinsohn maintained that it was passed on to the Jewish fathers, as found in the rabbinic work *Pirkei Avot,* "Teachings of the [Jewish] Fathers."[62] Levinsohn argued that just as the church fathers put down their doctrine in "books of theology,"[63] so the rabbinic fathers transmitted Jewish doctrine through "the Mishnah, our theology book."[64] The Catholic and Orthodox models of tradition provided Russian Jewish enlighteners with a recognized framework to explain Jewish practice within the Russian Empire. Although the historians Israel Bartal and Shmuel Feiner have noted the influence of radical French enlightenment thinkers such as Voltaire on late-eighteenth- and early-nineteenth-century eastern European Jewish thinkers, Levinsohn and Fuenn's notion of tradition is grounded more in conservative French thought as it appeared in Russian lands in the era of Orthodoxy, Autocracy, and Nationality.[65]

The Catholic and Orthodox concept of tradition contained three important arguments not available to Jewish enlighteners from an existing Jewish corpus. First it supplied a language with which to explain the idea of rabbinic Judaism to Catholic and Orthodox audiences. Second, it armed Levinsohn and Fuenn with a socially and theologically acceptable weapon to fight the government's criticisms of Jewish life and its sacred texts. Finally, it provided them with an argument against more radical reformist religious programs emanating from Protestant lands.

In the same way that Levinsohn defended rabbinic Judaism by comparing it to Catholicism, he attacked reformist sectors of German Jewry by equating them with Protestant reformers. "All other Christians consider you to have left your religion entirely and consider you to be heretics. For you do not hold to the beliefs of your ancestors. So too among us [Jews] are many heretics, who stand in opposition to the Talmud."[66] Levinsohn's defense of tradition, he explained, was written "not for heretics . . . but only for believing Jews and Christians [Orthodox]."[67] By arguing that each religion possessed its own independent tradition Levinsohn hoped to persuade Russian officials that support of the Talmud was in line with the government's general support of "orthodoxy" within each faith.

Fuenn concurred with Levinsohn that "most Christian denominations were, like Judaism, based on an oral transmission and transformed in each generation."[68] He went further than Levinsohn, remarking that "the difference between the religion of Judaism and the religion of Christianity is not that one religion interpreted God's word correctly and the other interpreted God's word falsely." Rather, "the Jewish religion [*hadat hayehudit*] is older and is found in synagogue liturgy, whereas Christianity is a faith [*emuna*] that is learned from the torah of the messiah that is located in the New Testament. Or in other words, Judaism [*hayahadut*] is God's word as understood through the Oral Law and Christianity is God's word as understood through the New Testament."[69]

Levinsohn and Fuenn's use of Catholic ideas was expressed in a Russian theological context that distinguished between Catholic ideas, which were selectively employed, and Catholicism itself, which was denounced. "Catholic circles in Paris," wrote the historian of Orthodox theology Georgy Florovsky, played an important role in the development of Russian thought.[70] "Roman Catholic elements can be found throughout the mystical syncretism" of the first decades of the nineteenth century.[71] Beginning around 1825, Russian Orthodox clerics and scholars began borrowing heavily from Catholic ideas regarding order and hierarchy, "with the unintended effect of rendering the Orthodox church of Old Russia suspiciously like the Catholic church of the 1840's."[72]

A prime example of one who was deeply influenced by Catholic ideas yet critical of Catholicism was the Russian minister of education, Sergey Uvarov.[73] Uvarov cited Bossuet throughout his writings on divine providence, death, and evil.[74] Uvarov specifically invoked Bossuet in his first major work on Russian education, *On Teaching History with Respect to National Education*.[75] In one striking curricular recommendation, Uvarov called for schools to teach about Moses, whom he referred to as "an inspired historian and legislator."[76] Most noteworthy, he cited Bossuet when he identified Moses as "the most ancient of historians, the most sublime philosopher, and the most sagacious of legislators."[77]

The language of tradition provided Jews with a means to make their culture religiously intelligible to Russian officials. Uvarov's invocation of Bossuet's theories of religious education could not have been lost on the Jewish enlighteners, who might have read his work either in Russian or in French. By invoking Bossuet's idea of tradition, Fuenn and Levinsohn would have been confident that they were on safe ground, using a concept from a widely cited and recognized—albeit Catholic—authority in a way that appealed to a wider Russian and Polish audience.

The enlighteners' recasting of the Talmud as part of a tradition set the stage for a new theory of Jewish economics that would remove Jews from marketplaces, fairs, and taverns and establish them in rolling fields and sunny pastures, tilling the land and living off the fruits of their labor. The rabbinic tradition could now be adapted to an imperial feudal context. Instead of a roadblock, the Talmud could become the bedrock of the empire's economic program.

TRADITIONAL ECONOMICS

Fuenn's and Levinsohn's theory of tradition undermined the damaging accusations that the Talmud sanctioned Jews' mistreatment of Gentiles in financial dealings and disregard of state laws. Their rebuttals of McCaul went hand-in-hand with a comprehensive and robust argument for Jews becoming involved in the Russian economy. The Talmud, they claimed, authorized Jews to be part of the Russian political and economic body. In other writings, Fuenn accepted the assumption that mercantile activities led to moral decrepitude and contributed to the perception that Jews were not truly rooted in Russian soil. But he blamed historical forces for this predicament. "The history of Jews in Europe attests that the source of Jews' income was only trade," Fuenn explained. "For as we have seen *shitat ha'arisut* [feudalism] distanced Jews from owning their own land and working the land."[78] There was nothing inherent within the rabbinic tradition that made Jews incline toward trade or that could define Jews as an independent economic entity. "The changes and the challenges brought about by time," Fuenn claimed, "forced Jews to wander from nation to nation, pulling them away from the wellspring of their blessing in agricultural professions to seek redemption only in trade and financial dealings."[79] It was understandable that while Jews operated as a distinct corporate entity (in the same way as they had throughout the medieval period) they gave preference to their co-religionists. However, as many writers before them had also argued, Fuenn and Levinsohn maintained that such practices would cease once Jews were fully integrated into an economic system in which all groups were given equal access to resources and labor markets.[80]

Levinsohn went even further, claiming that it was not Jews who engaged in predatory trading activities but rather slave traders and feudal lords. Levinsohn turned his attention "to present-day practices." "It is well known," he noted, "that most Jews around the world are merchants, and in some instances a few of them are quite wealthy." But the reason for this is that "governments don't provide Jews with the opportunity to invest in fields, towns, and villages." There was no inherent connection between Judaism and any specific kind of materialism. Although Jews were mainly involved in transactional businesses, "all of them refused to engage in the slave trade." Levinsohn's assertion was not entirely accurate. Some western European Jews were in fact involved in the slave trade. But it was a clever rhetorical move, which allowed him to question why the government was singling out Jews when other groups were conducting business that was contrary to the wishes of the empire. After complimenting Alexander I's condemnation of slavery at the Congress of Vienna, Levinsohn targeted Polish noblemen. "Why do Polish noblemen trade slaves with their brothers in other locales?" he queried, implicitly asking how Christianity allowed its adherents to trade in human beings.[81]

Levinsohn's arguments for Jewish economic diversification borrowed what Jonathan Karp refers to as the "stock themes" of western European Jewish economic thinkers and western European government officials who were sympathetic to the cause of Jewish emancipation.[82] Levinsohn cited the Christian jurist Carl August Buchholz's *The Improvement of the Civil Standing of Jews* (*Actenstükke die Verbesserung des bürgerlichen Zustandes der Israeliten*, 1815). Buchholz had represented the Jews of Lübeck, Bremen, and Hamburg at the Congress of Vienna, arguing that their involvement in finance and lending was based not on religious beliefs but on discriminatory policies of European governments.[83] Levinsohn followed Buchholz in asserting that Jewish professions depended more on government policy than on any single Jewish text.[84] Like his western European counterparts, Levinsohn adamantly opposed the notion that Jews were a distinct economic body.

Buchholz, however, had made only passing reference to Jews becoming farmers; instead he focused on permitting them entry into manufacturing and the civil service, such as university teaching.[85] In the 1840s the Russian government was not even considering the possibility of allowing Jews into the civil service. Its primary interest was to induce Jews to join agricultural sectors of the workforce and conform with Russia's feudal economic structures. To this Levinsohn responded that biblical and rabbinic sources privileged agricultural professions and supported the Russian government's proposals for the resettlement of Jews in farming colonies. Agricultural work did not entail a rejection of Talmudic and rabbinic teachings.

Levinsohn's economic theory was further supported by his pragmatic theology. The Talmud and rabbinic Judaism were not made up of a set group of statements and laws that endorsed the discrimination of Gentiles; they represented, rather, a system that could support the economic policies of the empire. To make his point, Levinsohn offered a counternarrative to Kiselev and Uvarov's depiction of Judaism's theology of economics. Instead of an economy that revolved around trade and messianic hopes, Levinsohn and Fuenn argued that Judaism inherently favored agriculture.[86] Jews became merchants solely because of the pragmatic social needs of the countries in which they resided. If anything, Jewish messianic expectations encouraged agricultural pursuits.

According to Levinsohn, the Bible never articulated defined laws for trade. "Even the laws of damages mentioned in the Bible," he maintained, "only pertained to an agrarian economy." Levinsohn suggested that "the original intent of the exalted knowledge stated in Scripture was for the Jewish people to be only a nation of farmers."[87] The holy days and professions mentioned in the Bible, he continued, revolved around agriculture. And Fuenn claimed that "even the rabbis of the Talmud usually employed agricultural metaphors to explain themselves." Fuenn noted that rabbinic descriptions of the messianic era were filled with agricultural metaphors and colored by the assumption that in the end of days Jews would be tilling the land.[88]

Levinsohn not only distanced Judaism from international trade, he claimed that it looked down upon all impersonal modes of exchange. He stressed the local character of biblical economic policies and argued that Jewish scriptures instituted injunctions precisely to prevent large-scale wealth accumulation: "According to what Scripture says about collecting loans in the sabbatical year and its warnings against usury and interest, it is clear that lending and borrowing practices should only be drawn between a person and his fellow man for the needs of his house and field such as wheat to eat or seeds for planting or animals for plowing or money for absolute necessities."[89]

Levinsohn looked askance at economic initiatives involving a high degree of risk and large-scale trade, noting that while these ventures might make some wealthy, most Jews would remain poor. Turning the Russian government's claim on its head, Levinsohn went so far as to interpret King Solomon's sin of acquiring an overabundance of horses from Egypt—the rabbis had asserted that Solomon was deposed from his throne for (among other things) owning too many horses and chariots—as a result of the birth of the maritime trade economy. Levinsohn claimed that the rebellion that brought down Solomon was a response to the king's overseas trade and wealth accumulation. The criticism of Solomon's impersonal forms of economic activity and accrual of capital reflected the Bible's—and more generally Judaism's—distaste for large-scale commercial activities.

Similarly, Fuenn embraced agriculture as a bulwark against the havoc wrought by technological advancements to local industries. Looking ahead, he worried that "even in our lands there will be machines that will do many of the tasks that previously were accomplished by the hands of trained workers. . . . Who will stop machines from performing tasks that would take days for human beings to complete?"[90] Fuenn held fast to the belief that "agricultural work would . . . be a safe and secure profession whose strength would not be diminished even in these turbulent times."[91]

Both men were aware that their interpretation of Judaism conflicted with the reality that the majority of contemporary Jews were involved in mercantile professions and that, if carried forward, it could have an adverse effect on Jewish economic life in the short term. Levinsohn, however, asked Nicholas I to "pay no attention" to more conservative sectors of Jewish life and to curb Jewish mercantile activities. "Heal a sick person against his will," he prodded Nicholas, "and when he is in good health he will be thankful a thousand times over for your making him better."[92]

The point that both of them were trying to make was that the long-standing anti-Semitic association of Judaism with Jewish mercantilism had no textual basis. Levinsohn and Fuenn's support for agrarian ideals, however, was not based on a specifically Jewish view of economics. Both men were merchants. They rejected the idea of what I term "Jewish materialism," a specifically Jewish self-reflective way of looking at or acting in the physical world. Levinsohn returned to his general argument that Judaism was a process-based tradition with no single "Jewish" economic policy: while the Bible reflected and clearly favored agrarian professions, Judaism was not inherently against a trade-based economy. "With the changing times," Fuenn noted, "Jews, and for that matter all people, would need to engage in large-scale domestic and international trade." He cited the early modern rabbi Menashe ben Israel, who emphasized the positive role Jews played as middlemen and traders and the benefits their maritime activities yielded to the states in which they lived.[93] Levinsohn and Fuenn's commitment to agricultural professions was not aimed at undermining French and German Jews' engagement in large-scale trade-based professions. Rather, they emphasized Jews' capacities to conform to their own economic milieus. Unlike the Jewish materialists of the 1860s and 1870s, Fuenn and Levinsohn couched their arguments in terms of Jews' capacities to acculturate wherever they might be. Their argument about Jewish tradition was sufficiently flexible to allow Jews to be merchants in western Europe and farmers in Russia. Their employment of religious texts was meant to enable Jews to follow the laws and economic institutions of other peoples. Judaism did not endorse a specific labor profile but rather the need for Jews to be loyal political subjects.

To highlight the dynamic nature of the rabbinic tradition with regard to material concerns, Levinsohn specifically pointed to the Jews' transformation from a people who embraced agrarian ideals to a people focused on trade. "It's not necessary for the Torah to address every new development," he wrote, "for though when the Torah was given at Sinai Jews were originally only agriculturalists, after a period of time . . . many became merchants."[94] The idea that Judaism was a tradition demonstrated that as easily as Jews became merchants they could become farmers and guildsmen. Though Jews were at the time involved in trade, the Oral Law endorsed an idea of Judaism that embraced local norms and mores. In Russia, Judaism could be reinterpreted to support Jews working the land. Jewish economic peculiarities were not, as the Russian government charged, the result of immutable religious beliefs. Not only did the Talmud express a range of opinions on the subject of economics, but Judaism (even rabbinic Judaism) embraced the same agrarian and traditional economic orientation as Catholics and Orthodox Christians living in Russian lands.

Fuenn and Levinsohn's worldview and economic proposals were directed at making Jews productive subjects of the Russian state and defending the idea of Talmudic Judaism. Their works were not simply apologetics; they raised questions about the coherency of the Russian government's proposals for Jews in light of the religious and traditional terrain of the empire. Jewish enlighteners sought to improve Jews' material conditions by arguing that

Judaism fundamentally encouraged the assimilation of Jews into traditional civic economic frameworks and structures. In other words, there was no such thing as a Jewish economic policy or a Jewish economic body, and certainly not a Jewish materialism. Judaism was a "traditional" religion, like Orthodoxy and Catholicism. Jews' economic well-being was a function of the individuals' ability to be integrated into the economic body constituted by the state or by another sovereign entity.

The Russian maskilim couched their arguments in pragmatic terms, explaining that it was in the government's best interest to recognize the "traditional" character of Judaism and not identify Jews as members of a Mosaic Faith. If being guildsmen or farmers entailed becoming a member of a Mosaic Faith at the expense of their commitments to the legal aspects of the Talmud, Russia's Jews would not only reject religious reforms but also enshrine the idea that teaching and mercantile activities were in fact Jewish professions and farming a non-Jewish enterprise. However, if the government recognized Judaism as a constantly evolving tradition, enlighteners wagered they could persuade Jews to support the state's agricultural economic program. Being a farmer or a guildsman did not contravene rabbinic Judaism.

Both internal (Hasidic and Mitnagdic Jews) and external forces (the Russian government's hostile economic policies) thwarted the Jewish enlighteners' efforts. Instead of embracing Levinsohn and Fuenn's ideas, the Russian government demoted the Talmud and rabbinic Judaism.[95] As much as Fuenn and Levinsohn objected, the government continued to assert that the Jews' economic predilections were a function of their Jewish beliefs. The Russian government's proposals ignored the large stumbling blocks they put in front of Jews, such as residential restrictions, Christian-only guilds, and laws restricting Jewish students from university entry. On a number of occasions the government cut funding for Jewish agricultural colonies or even reclaimed land allotted to Jews; by the 1860s it had begun favoring capitalistic enterprises.

But not only did enlighteners like Fuenn and Levinsohn fail to persuade the Russian government; they also could not convince their co-religionists that Judaism encouraged economic and religious reform. Fuenn's projects were met with deep suspicion in Hasidic and Mitnagdic circles. Fuenn admitted as much when he quipped, "Though I pray the afternoon service five times a day . . . the Vilna townspeople still say that I don't worship."[96] Anonymous public posters derided him for his early attempts at reform.[97] Likewise, Vilna's elders were said to have rebuked the rabbi who endorsed Levinsohn's works.[98] By the mid-nineteenth century, rabbinic authorities had begun giving greater weight to work and labor but still maintained that the main task for pious male Jews was to meditate on the divine or to repeat by heart passages of rabbinic literature while they worked. The well-being of Jews was secondary to the maintenance of their religious institutions and scholarly elite.[99]

Unlike the Jewish materialists of the 1860s and 1870s, the Jewish enlighteners in the 1840s and 1850s actively sought to tie Judaism to the traditional economic and religious character of the Russian Empire. They rejected the idea of Judaism being defined through any theory of *materialism.* Instead they identified themselves as religious traditionalists who sought to defend the claims of rabbinic Judaism and the economic and political proposals promoted by the state. In the 1860s and 1870s Jewish intellectuals who identified as materialists would also selectively employ religious concepts and texts but all of them would reject the binding nature of the Talmud and the policies of the Russian government. For Fuenn and Levinsohn, Jews were first and foremost adherents to a religion, like Catholics and Orthodox Christians, and economic and political subjects of the Russian Empire. The Jewish materialists of the 1860s and 1870s would reject both concepts. Jewish metaphysics contradicted Christian metaphysics, and Jews politically identified themselves in opposition to the state.

Social Materialism

The 1860s mark a watershed in the way Jews conceived of Judaism. During this period Jewish intellectuals began employing empirical methods of analysis to examine life in the Pale of Settlement. By the end of the decade Jewish thinkers were analyzing Jewish life not in terms of its conformity with a rabbinic tradition or the policies and laws of Russian Empire but through the way Jews lived and the economic principles behind their social relationships. These developments arose from new streams of thought as well as in response to the financial strains placed upon all inhabitants of Russia in the 1860s. Increased economic competition in the handcraft industries, periodic famines, and the slow exodus of wealthy Jews to Saint Petersburg affected everyone residing in the Pale of Settlement, but especially its Jewish population. One Prussian Jewish leader who traveled to Kovno in 1869 described visiting an *Armenküche* (public soup kitchen), where he witnessed "five hundred twenty children, naked, afflicted, deteriorated, no longer resembling humans, who with wild ravenousness snatched at plates of soup and morsels of bread in the hope of filling themselves until the following afternoon."[1]

Most Jewish responses to the economic downturn still centered on the "traditional" logic employed by Levinsohn and Fuenn: promoting religious reform and petitioning the government for greater economic rights.[2] In this chapter, however, I focus on a small but influential coterie of intellectuals who strove to ameliorate Jews' economic and social problems using what they called a "materialist" approach.[3] This group was divided between proponents of what I shall call *quantitative* materialism and those who favored *substantive* forms of materialism. Quantitative materialists employed socioeconomic methods to distinguish Jews' productive capabilities and consumption patterns from those of other populations in the Pale. Quantitative materialism carried certain ideological presuppositions—for example, it could show that Jews were a distinct socioeconomic entity. But quantitative materialists continued to endorse the idea that Jews were part of a religion, Judaism. At that time, Jews were a distinct economic subset of the empire's total population, but ultimately there was nothing about them or their religious beliefs that prevented them from being integrated into larger economic groups. Quantitative materialism was only a heuristic for describing the way Jews acted; it made no metaphysical claims and did not contradict the idea that Judaism was a set of ideals, beliefs, and dogmas.

Quantitative materialists did not necessarily deny the claims of heaven or the ideals of the empire. Substantively they should be seen more in line with Levinsohn and Fuenn than with the figures I shall discuss later in this chapter. Even as Jewish intellectuals such as the lawyer Ilya Orshanski and the literary upstart Abraham Uri Kovner charted new methods of analyzing Jews' productive capabilities and consumption patterns, they held fast to the view that Jews were first and foremost adherents to a religion and subjects of the Russian Empire. Their analysis of Jews' distinctive socioeconomic profile was produced in the hope that the differences between Jews and Gentiles in Russia would wane in the same manner as they had been waning in France and Prussia. While quantitative materialists employed mathematical and empirical methods of analysis rather than theological or commentarial (explaining the rabbinic tradition or the Talmud), they continued to substantively believe in political and religious programs similar to those promoted by Fuenn and Levinsohn.

In contrast, Moses Leib Lilienblum put forward a substantive form of Jewish materialism that rejected the claims of the rabbinic tradition and ignored the issue of the Jews' political position within the Russian Empire. Whereas Kovner and Orshanski applied what they saw as universal materialist methods to explain Jewish life in the hope that Jews would become Russians, Lilienblum was the first to argue that Judaism, as a coherent body of knowledge, endorsed the adoption of a *mabat gashmi 'al haḥayyim* (materialist perspective on life).[4] Lilienblum not only provided a full economic profile of the Jews that detailed their productive capacities and consumptive patterns; he also began calling on them to see Judaism as a system of meaning that endorsed a certain set of materialistic principles. While Lilienblum dismissed the binding nature of the rabbinic tradition (in contrast to Fuenn and Levinsohn) and divine revelation, he asserted that certain Jewish ideas promoted the principles of rational egoism and a materialist calculus for making life decisions. Materialism was not external to Judaism but a reflection of a deep intellectual current in its history.

Lilienblum's materialistic perspective on life was inspired by his reading of the Russian social materialists Nikolay Chernyshevsky and Dmitry Pisarev. "Just as there had been a Hebrew [*'ivri*] version of Schiller and Goethe," Lilienblum explained in 1871, "there would also be a Jewish version of Chernyshevsky and Pisarev . . . to answer the all-consuming question of economics."[5] Chernyshevsky's influence on Lilienblum has largely been masked by the latter's own attempt, later in life, to deny what he came to see as "foreign" aspects of his legacy as a founder of Zionism in eastern Europe.

Lilienblum was acutely aware that the kind of social materialism he had embraced in the 1870s under the rubric "a materialist perspective on life" could lead in many political directions, including communism or immigration to the United States. "Yes, I read *What Is to Be Done?* by Chernyshevsky," Lilienblum admitted to his Jewish comrades decades later, "but by no means did it change me into a different person." Eventually, Lilienblum threatened to publicly denounce anyone who dared associate his more mature theories on Zionism with positions used by Russian revolutionaries.[6]

When Lilienblum was interviewed in the early twentieth century about his intellectual debt to the "Russian materialists" of the early 1870s, he told journalists to "refrain from mentioning my name."[7] If we compare Lilienblum's collected writings published in 1913 to the original articles published in the 1870s we can see a concerted effort to remove Chernyshevsky, Pisarev, and other materialist sources from his theories about Jewish economics and the nature of Judaism.[8] While historians have focused on Lilienblum's role in the founding of Zionism, the historical record has yet to fully account for the ways his appropriation of social materialism transformed what constituted Judaism and how people defined the essential features of Jewish life.

The path that leads from Levinsohn and Fuenn's traditional Jewish economics to Orshanski and Kovner's economic analysis of Jews to Lilienblum's

groundbreaking materialistic perspective on life terminates in what I call Jewish materialism and the various forms of late-nineteenth-century Jewish anti-
imperial political ideologies.

LIBERALISM AND QUANTITATIVE MATERIALISM

Lilienblum's call for Jews to adopt "a materialistic perspective on life"
emerged against the background of a fresh set of policies carried out by a new
political and economic regime. Shortly after becoming tsar in 1855, Alexander II enacted his Great Reforms, a series of measures aimed at accelerating
the growth of urbanization and industrialization within the Russian Empire.
Russia had just suffered painful losses in the Crimean War (1853–1856), and
its domestic and international affairs were in a shambles. Alexander took up
the task of revitalizing Russia's depressed economy and harnessing its under-
developed labor potential. In a momentous decision announced in 1861, he
declared that the Russian serfs, a third of the imperial population, would be
emancipated. Alexander's proclamation was at the center of his larger program to provide greater economic opportunities to various groups, including the Jews living within the Pale of Settlement. His hope was to "gradually bring existing regulations on the Jews into agreement with the general
laws for other subjects of the Empire." Thus he granted full residential rights
to wealthy Jewish merchants of the First Guild (1860), allowed Jews entry
into Russian universities (1861), and opened up greater working opportunities for Jewish artisans (1865).[9] These initiatives, one addressing the peasantry,
the other the Jews, led to clashes when the newly emancipated serfs began
moving into urban areas and competing with Russia's 3.5 million Jewish
residents.[10]

Though totaling only 4 percent of the Russian population, Jews made up
12.5 percent of all Russian inhabitants living in the Pale of Settlement.[11] In the
urban areas in which most Jews resided, they often accounted for 25–50 percent of the total population, making up a majority or a plurality of the local
populations. Jews and the newly emancipated serfs flooded the handcrafting,
tailoring, and petty mercantile industries, which resulted in dwindling profits
for Jews and heightened interethnic strife. While the two groups feverishly
competed for customers, their potential clients passed over the shirts and
shoes they were producing and selling in favor of products made at newly
established factories. The Jews living in the northwestern provinces had never
even seen the machines that were now producing people's goods.[12]

"Russian industrialization," explains the economic historian Arcadius Kahan, "put severe constraints upon the growth of employment and income of the majority of the Jewish population."[13] Large-scale changes in Russian society, such as the emancipation of the serfs and the Polish uprising of 1863, severely affected Jewish economic life. Aside from continued residential restrictions, less money was now in consumers' hands, a glut of laborers vied for places in limited industries, and First Guild merchants, the major source of capital and philanthropy, migrated en masse to Saint Petersburg.[14] This "epochal transformation" of the Pale's economic landscape, according to the historian Salo W. Baron, resulted in the pauperization of the Jewish masses.[15]

This common narrative of the Jewish economic crisis of the 1860s, still invoked today, can be traced back to Ilya Orshanski's groundbreaking economic analysis of Jews in Russian lands. Born into a respected Mohilev family, Orshanski was provided with the finest European education a Russian Jew could procure in the 1840s, becoming one of the first Jews to receive an advanced degree in a Russian university.[16] However, given the option of converting to Christianity and assuming an official academic post, Orshanski instead decided to become "the first Russo-Jewish historian to set himself the task of studying the economic position of the Jews on the basis of primary sources and of carefully analyzing the economic aspect of the Jewish question."[17] Orshanski's studies of Jewish manufacturers and tavern owners were pioneering not only in their assessment and conclusions but also because of their innovative methodology. They avoided all mention of Jews' beliefs, central texts, rituals, or theology and instead exclusively focused on the economic factors responsible for Jews' material hardships.

In 1869 he published an article that appeared serially, "Notes on the Economic Situation of the Jews in Russia," in the Russian Jewish weekly he helped edit, *Day* (*Den*). Somewhat disturbed by his own findings, Orshanski asserted, "No matter how strange it appears," the main cause of Jewish economic stress in the Pale of Settlement was "the emancipation of the serfs."[18] He continued, "Although it might not seem to be connected" to their economic state, the serfs' emancipation "exerts a powerful effect on the Jews."[19] Orshanski focused on the crisis in liquor distribution and the handcrafts trade, showing that urbanization, industrialization, residential restrictions, and, most important, greater competition all contributed to the deterioration of Jewish social and economic life.

Influenced by the empirical methods advanced by Friedrich Engels's Russian translator, the radical Nikolai Shelgunov, Orshanski addressed the wid-

Ilya Orshanski. (Courtesy of the National Library of Israel, Jerusalem)

ening gap between wealthy and poor Jews.[20] He calculated the large number of Jewish factory owners spread throughout Russia and in the Pale and noted that most of their "factories" were not much more than small, "pathetic leather-tanning workshops."[21] Of the ninety-eight Jewish-owned factories in Grodno, thirty-five were such tanneries; in Kiev, fourteen of thirty-two. Orshanski's statistics were meant to highlight the small percentage of Jews who operated large businesses in comparison to the increasing numbers of Jews vying with the serfs in far less lucrative markets.

Orshanski was a proponent of liberalism, and he endorsed the Russification of Jews.[22] His interest in "materialism" was only quantitative. He employed social scientific and mathematical methods to analyze Jews, seeing them not only as a religious group but also as a distinct socioeconomic entity. But his goal was to figure out how such economic differences could eventually be overcome and Jews be incorporated into the labor markets of the Russian Empire.

Orshanski's articles were also aimed at combating anti-Semitic claims concerning Jewish wealth. Like liberals residing in western Europe, Orshanski highlighted the productive role that Jews played as merchants and middlemen, and the debilitating poverty of the Jewish masses.[23]

Orshanski laid the groundwork for the widely accepted thesis that the economic crisis of the 1860s was brought about by new forms of economic competition that resulted in a growing Jewish underclass.[24] Orshanski diagnosed the Jews' economic woes by focusing on the external pressures of the state, religious discrimination, and the competition of the peasantry. Jews living in Russia, however, sensed that there were other internal factors impairing their development. While Orshanski focused on their productive capacities, he largely ignored their patterns of consumption. "Those who say we don't have money," one observer remarked, "should look at all the study groups and synagogues each Jew builds for himself."[25] Orshanski's studies largely ignored this insight even though it would become a common refrain among Jews trying to assess their situation. By the end of the 1860s there were eighty-six study houses in Vilna,[26] roughly forty synagogues and study houses in Kovno,[27] and ten Hasidic prayer houses in the town of Mogilev alone.[28] Someone had to pay for all of these institutions. The Jews' economic woes were not simply due to a lack of productive capacity.

Abraham Uri Kovner would be the first to detail the most unusual product of Jewish consumption: religious institutions and functionaries. Two months before the first installment of Orshanski's article appeared, *Day* published Kovner's article "Yeshiva Dormitory" (Yeshibotnaia bursa) as part of a series on Jewish educational institutions in the Pale of Settlement; Kovner documented the number and cost of Jewish higher educational institutions.[29] Kovner's piece ran from June to October 1869, and some of the installments appeared alongside Orshanski's article. Unlike Orshanski, who focused on Jewish production—primarily Jews' involvement in manufacturing, agriculture, small farming, liquor distribution, mercantile activities, and handcrafts—Kovner zeroed in on one of the major Jewish sources of consumption, the disproportionate resources spent on synagogues, study houses, and educating seminary students.

Kovner was Orshanski's antithesis. Whereas the latter's refusal to convert to Christianity cost him a professorship at a Russian university, the former would eventually embrace the cross in the hope of improving his own material condition. Kovner had been raised in Vilna in a home in which every crumb of food was so precious that when a house cat nabbed some chicken fat, Kovner's thin-as-a-rail father threw the feline into a bag and dashed it against the wall.[30] One of ten siblings (he wryly commented that his father drew a sigh of relief when an eleventh died at birth), Kovner attended local Jewish religious elementary schools (kheyders) and yeshivot. By 1875 he would be the subject of a Europe-wide manhunt for identity theft and robbery.[31]

Kovner's article in *Day* addresses the worsening conditions for Jews in terms of the economic costs attached to their religious commitments. Kovner's piece was an exposé of the economic and social hegemony of the yeshiva and the rabbinic intelligentsia of the northwestern provinces of the Russian Empire. Though Kovner is often remembered today for his hotly debated realist critique of Jewish prose, *Analyzing the Issue* (*Ḥeker davar*, 1865), his article in *Day* was far more hostile to the Jewish masses, going to the heart of Jewish spending practices and the price tag on rabbinic culture.[32]

As noted in Chapter 1, from the early modern period on, Torah scholars had been singled out as an excessive expense for Jewish communities. By the 1860s, however, this criticism had reached new heights. Aside from the growing costs of Hasidic and Mitnagdic rabbis, synagogues, schools, butchers, and teachers, Jews were burdened with paying for state schools they did not attend, state seminaries they looked down upon, and state-appointed rabbis whose words they did not heed. All sectors of Jewish society were said to be crying out for the moneys they were being taxed to uphold these institutions.[33] Funds were tight and fights flared up among warring ideological groups. "Each [religious] group," it was claimed, "tried to defeat its opponents based on the amount of money it was able to amass."[34] The costs extracted from the Jews trickled all the way down to their kitchen tables. The Hebrew novelist Sara Foner recalls that in the town of Dvinsk:

> The Mitnagdim brought a judge to the city. . . . They also brought a butcher and established their own slaughter house for meat. . . . In every house, in every study hall and in every store and street, nothing was heard besides, "Mitnaged and Hassid, Hassid and Mitnaged." At first the women made mistakes since they didn't know which butcher shop was Mitnaged and which was Hassidic, and so they mixed up

the products. Then there were great problems such as when a man came home from work and sat down to eat, and while eating asked his wife where she got the meat. She told him Yitzchak Fagin's butcher shop, which was the Hassidic butcher shop. He cried out loudly, "Oy, Oy, You have fed me unclean meat! . . ." A day didn't pass that the kitchen utensils weren't made traif [nonkosher] in many homes on both sides.[35]

Only the restrictions placed on Jews by the government were seen as creating greater hardships than the battles between the eastern European Jewish denominations. Kovner targeted the costs of the yeshiva, the most expensive religious institution in Lithuanian lands and the heart of Mitnagdic culture.

Kovner set out *statistically* and *empirically* to detail the amount spent on Mitnagdic institutions of higher learning. He maintained that yeshivot in Russia had taken on a character distinct from similar Jewish educational institutions in other countries.[36] He described two types of rabbinic institutions: large seminaries (yeshivot) located in the towns of Volozhin and Mir that enrolled two hundred to three hundred students[37] and smaller study halls that were "ubiquitous" in Jewish towns across the Pale.[38] In Vilna alone, he speculated, roughly three hundred to five hundred young people spent their days "studying" at these smaller institutions.[39] Kovner saw the seminaries as sources of indolence and sloth, responsible for perpetuating Jewish poverty.

Kovner's work on the rabbinical seminaries followed the publication of other controversial works. Just a few years earlier he had produced the first Hebrew translation of Ludwig Büchner's "Heat and Life" (Wärme und Leben), a section of the German doctor's *Physiological Portraits* (*Physiologische Bilder*, 1861).[40] There Büchner asserted that "it was chemistry that we needed to thank for revealing to us that which is hidden."[41] Kovner had cultivated a feisty, some would say reckless, persona for his attack on Jewish "idealists," who wasted ink and energies on works that waxed poetic about "droplets of dew, the glow of the moon, woodland shade, love, hope, song, death, the destiny of mankind, time and so on." Kovner asserted that such pleasant scenes camouflaged the harsh conditions he and other Jews experienced in the Pale. "These idealists," Kovner declared, "paint a serene and beautiful picture of the world in which farmers tilled lands on hills of bliss." To his Russian Jewish readers, who were prohibited from owning land, he asked, "Where have you seen the kind of farmer depicted by the idealists?"[42]

In his *Day* series, Kovner described the filth on the floors of study halls, the books piled on tables smothered in wax, young men breathing over one another while engaged in casuistic debates. Instead of the idyllic pictures of passionate budding scholars toiling in spiritual labor, Kovner presented a bunch of rowdy, hot-headed teens packed in dank rooms where they wasted away their prime years. Kovner did not think it important to tell his readers what the boys were studying "because it is almost always the case that the subject matter . . . they were involved in examining . . . has no application in the present."[43]

Kovner drew a correlation between Jewish economic unproductivity and physical maladies. The rabbinical seminaries, he maintained, were responsible for corrupting the Jewish youth and making them unfit for labor. Peering into the students' lodgings, he reviled the boys' physical traits and bedroom practices. "They have rashes on their bodies, boils, sores, and if a healthy boy arrives at the yeshiva, in a very short time, due to contact with the others, he will acquire sores as well. It is clear," at least to Kovner, "that in the students' common room their morality suffers terribly."[44] Insinuating that homosexual practices took place in the lodgings, Kovner remarked that "vices [*poroki*] developed among them in the most extreme form."[45]

Kovner did not specify which yeshiva or seminary he was describing; probably he was repeating common themes among Russian writers of the period who made similar attacks against Christian seminaries.[46] He detailed locker-room shenanigans, bullying, and pranks that took place after a day spent in the study hall.[47] "They don't go to sleep," he admonished. "They gather together; take a piece of paper; roll it up into a narrow tube; stuff it into a student's nose and set it on fire."[48] "Sometimes," he continued, outraged, "they cover someone's head with paper and set it on fire." The prank that Kovner thought "the most original" was placing a sleeping student on the floor, draping a shawl over his body, and encircling him with candles. As the boy lay in slumber, one of the mischief-makers would start eulogizing him, citing biblical texts, crying, and encouraging others to join him in mourning for the "loss" of the "deceased." Gradually the wailing and lamenting would reach a crescendo and the "dead" boy would awake to what he would think was the world to come. His friends would now appear as animals and ghosts, their faces covered in soot. They would crawl around the young man on all fours, "mewing like cats and making the noises of savages."[49] Such mischief was severely discouraged by supervisors, who slapped the students when they engaged in these hijinks; in some instances, the students retaliated by pummeling their supervisors.

Kovner's central criticism of the yeshiva, however, was not the antics of the students it housed, but rather the money being spent on unproductive and degenerate forms of behavior. Kovner was not simply "realistically" describing Jews' lives, he was making an argument about how Jews should manage their resources. "In every house of prayer," he noted, there was a sexton who distributed charity and provided the students with two or, in some instances, three meals a day. In some locales, students ate at townspeople's homes. At the Mir yeshiva students received between 75 kopecks and one ruble a week for breakfast, lunch, dinner, and lodging. Those who did not receive funds slept in the yeshiva on tables or floors; a few kipped down in the open air.[50] The funds allocated to the more elite students were paltry compared to the roughly 8–10 rubles a month Jewish philanthropists allotted to each Jewish student enrolled in Kiev University. However, in toto, the funds given to yeshiva students far outweighed the 2,000 rubles a year allotted to those attending university.[51]

Kovner described the way yeshivot and their students consumed Jews' funds. Aside from their monthly stipend, students "earned extra money by performing all kinds of religious functions." They went to women's homes on the Jewish New Year to sound the shofar; many assisted cantors; some taught children their letters; and others begged for charity. "In many instances," Kovner explained, "these poor students ended up marrying daughters of their teachers. And they themselves became teachers or left their wives and became pariahs." Kovner identified these students as "a 'klass' of people, crippled by their upbringing, perverted by their surroundings, and unsuited for any kind of physical or intellectual work." They consumed but did not produce. Kovner claimed that this permanent Jewish underclass was symptomatic of larger social forces. "Of course it is impossible to blame the yeshiva students themselves," he remarked. "It was the society within which such parasites develop," he maintained, which "encouraged such ways of life."[52]

Kovner's claims are difficult to substantiate. Statistical studies on Jewish occupations in nineteenth-century Russia often overlooked the categories of religious laborers and yeshiva students.[53] "Even statistical analysis that provides an accounting for all people of the land is unable to identify the number of all those engaged in studying the Torah; their numbers fluctuate," one contemporary observer noted.[54] However, those who have attempted to tally the number of people within this amorphous group posit a strikingly high percentage of rabbis, beadles, cantors, undertakers, rabbinical students, semi-narians, and itinerant preachers operating in the Pale of Settlement. Some estimated that over half a million people, one-sixth of the 3 million Jews living in Russian lands, depended at least in part on funds paid to them for performing religious activities.[55] Meanwhile, others maintained that roughly 15 percent of the Jewish population in the Pale belonged to a class of "Torah scholars."[56] The 1897 Russian census suggests that between 7 percent and 9 percent of the population was engaged in what might be considered religious professions.[57] More recently, the historian Glenn Dynner calculated that at least 6.5 percent of Jews living in Russian lands in the 1870s were religious functionaries.[58]

Leaving aside the question of the veracity of their claims, Kovner and Orshanski's studies were methodologically groundbreaking. Taken together their analysis of the economics of Jewish religious institutions and labor rela-tions allows us to see the factors that contributed to the economic crisis of the 1860s. While scholars have sometimes touched on Orshanski's economic anal-ysis of the crisis, they often fail to recognize the innovative quantitative forms of materialism employed in his work on Jewish production. Likewise, while much attention has been given to Kovner's Hebrew realism, his rapacious sexual appetites, his debauchery, and his literary debates, his empirical and economic analysis of educational and religious institutions has been ignored.

Kovner's and Orshanski's analyses, however, were mainly descriptive; their authors adopted a form of quantitative materialism for understanding Jews and Jewish life. Kovner and Orshanski did not promote or develop a mate-rialist conception of Judaism or a theory of Jewish identity based on Jews' physical and economic well-being. Both men remained committed to un-derstanding Judaism as a religion and endorsed the policies of the Russian Empire. Both believed that Jews were members of a liberal religion and that material differences should and would be overcome when they were fully acculturated.

A MATERIALISTIC WORLDVIEW

Moses Lilienblum went beyond Kovner and Orshanski's quantitative materialism to articulate a self-consciously substantive materialist concep-tion of Judaism.[59] The one-time Vilkomir rabbinic scholar turned religious reformer turned self-declared "half-nihilist" would begin describing Judaism as a religion focused on people's material concerns. Unlike Orshanski and

Kovner, Lilienblum broke with the liberal goal of encouraging Jews to acculturate and become economically productive subjects of the empire.

Lilienblum's embrace of materialism followed a period in the late 1860s when he distinguished himself as one of the most militant Jewish reformers in Russian lands. He had burst onto the Hebrew literary scene with his work "The Ways of the Talmud" (Orḥot hatalmud) in 1868 and his follow-up, "Additions" (Nosafot), published in the winter of 1869. His fearless sparring with observant sectors of Russian Jewry won him praise in Jewish enlightenment circles. In his piercing assaults on the rabbinic elite, Lilienblum marshaled liberal precedents from the Talmud to encourage rabbis to address the material hardships of Russian Jews: if rabbis were more lenient regarding kosher laws, he maintained, Jews would have more bread on their table.[60] Lilienblum's economic arguments in the 1860s were still, however, based on proof texts from the Talmud. His method was largely exegetical, and his arguments turned on the true meaning of rabbinic texts. His positions were more radical than those of Levinsohn or Fuenn—he was far more irreverent toward the learned elite—but methodologically he followed their lead, rooting his positions in the rabbinic tradition.

Lilienblum's full break with the movement for rabbinic reform and his embrace of what he would term a materialist perspective on life came in 1871, as he was assuming the editorship of the Yiddish weekly *Voice of the Herald* (*Kol mevaser*).[61] Since its establishment in 1865 the newspaper had called on Jews to petition the empire for greater rights and to establish shared religious institutions that all Jewish groups could agree upon. The newspaper's editor pointed to the deleterious economic and political effects generated by the divide between the religious fanatics on one end of the population (Hasidim) and religious reformers (maskilim) at the other.[62] He encouraged the streamlining of Jewish institutions through ideological compromises among the major religious groups. Its goal was to reform Judaism and make Jews loyal and productive subjects of the empire.[63]

Though Lilienblum had never written an article in Yiddish, his views, as recorded in his previously published essays, made him a suitable editor for the Yiddish weekly. However, in January 1871, Lilienblum recorded in his diary, "I succeeded in reading Chernyshevsky's *What Is to Be Done?* after I had read a month earlier *Fathers and Sons* by Turgenev."[64] Chernyshevsky's work, one of the most politically influential novels ever written, would fundamentally transform the way Lilienblum understood Jews and Judaism. The novel detailed the way a young woman used the principles of rational egoism and biological materialism to win her freedom from her parents, her spouse, and society. Published in 1863, *What Is to Be Done?* (*Chto delat'?*) quickly became the blueprint for young Russian revolutionaries seeking greater social freedom and economic equality.

Lilienblum noted in his diary that he "enjoyed reading Chernyshevsky's work, whose ideas made an impression on me."[65] In fact, Chernyshevsky's work so overwhelmed Lilienblum that he went back and inserted the word *strong* over *impression.*[66] Lilienblum's later protestations aside, there were many reasons why he and others in 1870s paid upwards of twenty-five rubles on the black market (a few rubles less than the monthly salary offered to Lilienblum) to obtain a copy of Chernyshevsky's banned book[67] and came to know it "better than the daily prayer *Ashrei.*"[68] First among these was Chernyshevsky's positive projection of Jewish characters.[69] Chernyshevsky's chief disseminator, Dmitry Pisarev, whose work Lilienblum would not read until later in the summer of 1871, described one of the main revolutionary characters in Chernyshevsky's work, Lopukhov, as possessing Jewish characteristics: "Working a lot [with] little entertainment; [being] enthusiastic over the idea he worships, the idea [with] which the names [Robert] Owen and [Charles] Fourier and a few other true friends of humanity are connected. . . . He feels no necessity of living in unison . . . [Still] he is always ready to help . . . in a moment of trouble or grief."[70]

Lilienblum could also personally and intellectually recognize the logic operating in Chernyshevsky's writings. The socialist Charles Fourier and the German philosopher Ludwig Feuerbach played the same role in Chernyshevsky's deeply religious upbringing that Chernyshevsky would then play in Lilienblum's intellectual development. Feuerbach taught Chernyshevsky, and by extension Lilienblum, that "the dualistic conception between man and God or any other supernatural power or essence [does] not exist. Man [is] matter alone, and he live[s] in a material universe."[71] This principle would become essential to Lilienblum's own development as a critic and Jewish thinker.

Personally, Lilienblum would have been moved by the novel's portrayal of young people struggling for economic, social, and sexual freedom. Since his departure from Vilkomir in 1869, he had been a nervous wreck, anxious about how he, a man with no practical skills, could earn a living, as well as manage his illicit affair with Feyge Novakhovitch (whom he referred to in his correspondence as "N").[72] Novakhovitch was everything that Lilienblum wished for in a partner; she was intelligent and educated in European literature, someone with whom he could share his most intimate feelings.

Lilienblum was struck by Chernyshevsky's call for economic empowerment, demand for gender equality, and embrace of nontraditional sexual unions and divorce.[73]

Vladimir Lenin's claim that *What Is to Be Done?* was the most influential novel in *Russian* history could as easily be applied to *Russian Jewish* history. Starting with Lilienblum, *What Is to Be Done?* became required reading for every Zionist, Bundist, and Jewish Communist, and probably more than a few capitalists. There was no hurdle a young Jewish intellectual would not have overcome to obtain the contraband literature.[74] In the 1870s young Jews tiptoed through narrow back alleys and entered the backdoors of churches to meet with people who would help them catch a glimpse of the outlawed book. As documented by the historian Jeffrey Veidlinger, well into the twentieth century it remained one of the most borrowed items in Russian Jewish libraries. For Jews its message was simple and clear: their well-being depended on their opportunities to pursue what was in their best interests.[75] While historians have noted the enthusiastic Jewish reception to Chernyshevsky's work, they focus more attention on the way "Jews" became (the protagonist) "Vera Pavlovnas," acculturating into the Russian intellectual landscape. Lilienblum's interpretation of the work highlights something else: the way Vera became Jewish. Lilienblum's reading of Chernyshevsky certainly reflected the profound influence of Russian literature and politics on Jews residing in the Pale. It challenges any Zionist narrative that downplays Jews' ties to Russian culture and letters. However, it did not indicate an attempt on the part of Jews to be Russians. Rather, it symbolized and inspired a new understanding of the social and economic forces animating and shaping Jews lives.

Chernyshevsky inspired Lilienblum to see the connection between the Jews' patterns of consumption and their productive capacities. Accommodating Judaism's religious needs and proscriptions not only demanded significant capital, energy, and other resources but also limited Jews' ability to produce or purchase the goods they needed for survival. Jews, Lilienblum realized, had to come to terms with the cost exacted by their rituals, beliefs, and religious educational institutions. On March 11, 1871, Lilienblum published the first of an eleven-part serial, "Jewish Life Questions" (Yidishe Lebnsfragn) in *Voice of the Herald.* In it he employed Chernyshevsky's ideas to analyze the economic cost of Jews' religious culture. In the first installments Lilienblum explained the basic principles of economics and the circulation of capital among Russian Jews. At no point did he mention the Russian state or any law issued by the government. He assumed that he could address Jewish social life on its own terms through the Jews' distinctive economic profile. Contrary to enlighteners such as Isaac Baer Levinsohn, Lilienblum did not ask how Jews could benefit the Russian state. Rather, he addressed their ability to pursue their best interests and retain control over their own capital to ensure their survival.

Lilienblum's series was published under the shadow of events that transpired in Odessa. From March 27 to April 1, 1871, a major pogrom swept through the city. Six people were killed and 21 wounded, and 863 houses and business were damaged or destroyed.[76] As described by the historian Steven Zipperstein, the total costs incurred were twice as high as those of the historically better-known pogrom of 1881. The perpetrators were incited by unsubstantiated rumors that Jews had desecrated the Greek Orthodox church and cemetery.[77] The Jews of Odessa were shocked by the government's lethargic response to the wave of violence. The liberal Russian intelligentsia's weak protestations to the deadly attacks were but one more insult to the injured. Meanwhile, the few media organs that did condemn the violence, such as *The Saint Petersburg Record* (*Sankt-Peterburgskie vedomosti*), put some of the blame on the Jewish manufacturers, merchants, and capitalists for their "exploitation" of the masses.

Five days after the pogrom, Lilienblum wrote to his friend Judah Leib Gordon about the "great tragedy" that had befallen the city.[78] We also know that he penned at least three articles about the devastation, but none of his essays appeared in print.[79] Perhaps his views invited controversy by targeting either Jewish merchants (a common theme in Lilienblum's writings of the 1870s) or (more likely) the government, which he would undoubtedly have criticized for not adequately protecting its Jews.

It might be suggested that Lilienblum's decision in "Jewish Life Questions" to ignore the government indicated a new trend taking shape among Jewish intellectuals, one based on the assumption that the Russian government was incapable of providing Jews with the means to ensure their material well-being. While Lilienblum might have significantly underestimated how dependent Jews were on economic structures beyond their control, his avoidance of both religious and state-based arguments pioneered a new approach to understanding Jewish life and Judaism.

He opens the series with a metaphor: the Jews have become a sick and feeble people in danger of collapsing at any minute. A healthy person, with job security, land ownership, and a means of making a living, can survive even rapid changes to an economic climate. "Those, however, who live in the air [luftmenschen], are hopeless. For them a new railroad, an innovation in commerce, or the introduction of even a minor change in the law, can quickly destroy a whole family."[80] The problem, according to Lilienblum, was not Russian industrialization or the emancipation of the serfs. Rather, "the doctors" of Jewish life continued to misdiagnose "the sick" and prescribe the wrong medicine. "All the Jewish doctors say the problem is the Jewish soul; they claim that Jews are not doing what God wants, they are not following the commandments." The Jewish enlighteners were the very doctors who promoted "*Bildung*, civilization, and enlightenment but were unable to explain how these ideas would benefit people. These enlighteners created a set of institutions that no one would join because it was not clear to people 'what use they had.'"[81]

Lilienblum decried the Jews' emphasis on religious reform as fundamentally ignoring the real issue. "I am not interested in telling Jews to stop keeping the things that are written in the [sacred] books," he explained. "I only want to tell you that it's wrong to say that Jews are sick in their souls." "No!" he declared. "It's their bodies that are sick."[82] The problem was simply that "they don't have bread to eat."[83] Lilienblum was no longer making an anticlerical argument or promoting religious reform, as he had done in the 1860s. "Jews are hungry," he cried, "because they were not trained in their youth to make a living." The cause of their misery is that "no one instructed them how to acquire the means needed to support themselves." Their education was geared toward making them good servants of God, not laborers or producers. It taught them how to spend resources on servicing the divine, not how to produce resources to care for themselves. Jews thought and acted in a manner contrary to the most basic principle: "Every person must eat and drink, have clothing and a place of residence, and some extra capital in case he or she becomes ill and is unable to produce."[84]

Lilienblum's theory focused on the Jews' labor capacities, starting with the idea of the specialization of labor. Merchants, he explained, purchase products from agriculturalists and manufacturers. They "sell these products to craftsmen, and then to the large-scale merchants, who then resell the products to the various manufacturers, who need other materials, which they themselves do not produce. The manufacturers employ hundreds of people who feed families." To these labor profiles, Lilienblum added "other 'classes' of professionals who made their living from their knowledge, *which the world needs,* such as doctors, professors, and diplomats" (emphasis mine). Economic diversification, which the Jews so desperately lacked, was a precondition for group survival.[85]

Jew in tattered clothes and fine prayer shawl, late nineteenth century. (From *Tracing An-sky: Jewish Collections from the State Ethnographic Museum in Saint Petersburg,* ed. Mariella Beukers and Renée Waale [Zwolle: Waanders Uitgevers; Amsterdam: Joods Historisch Museum; Saint Petersburg: State Ethnographic Museum, 1992], 81)

Lilienblum compared a "healthy," "diverse" economic system with that of the Jews. Those living in the Pale, he wrote, were subservient to religious elites who prevented them from acting in their own best interest. "There were more beadles," he claimed, "than those who worked the land."[86] Jews were confined to "the professions of preaching, religious adjudication, teaching, cantoring, matchmaking, writing, Kabbalistics, synagogue work, psalm recitation, prayer recitation, seminary studies, asceticism, those who make their living from dowries, creditors, the fear of heaven and thievery."[87] Jews, Lilienblum only half sarcastically claimed, differed from other people (*folk*) in that they all experienced the same educational upbringing. This simple point was in fact quite radical. In making it, Lilienblum was asserting that Jews were a people and not a class or members of a religion, as their economic profile might suggest.

The Jews' lack of educational and economic diversification had its roots in the religiously conservative sectors of the population, whom Lilienblum labeled *batlanim,* "people of waste."[88] Lilienblum echoed many of Kovner's criticisms, illustrating them with his special brand of exempla and satire, such as the yeshiva students who explained Talmudic commentators while others were "cursing the head of the Yeshiva, yelling at him: 'up your father's . . . [*in taten aryin*]!'"[89] Lilienblum, however, wanted to provoke more than an easy laugh at the expense of the rabbinic establishment. He aimed at showing how the culture of the yeshivot and Hasidic institutions had skewed Jewish economic and social relations. The fundamental difference between Jews and other peoples, Lilienblum maintained, was that they did not economically behave like or recognize themselves as a collective. Their educational system, unified though it was, revolved around the study of otherworldliness, and was geared toward the production of religious functionaries. People were educated exclusively in abstract "ideas" and "heavenly matters . . . that float in the air."[90] Though Lilienblum did not come out and charge rabbinic elites with creating and profiting from these wasteful professions, less than a decade later others would take his theories farther, describing Russian Jewish life in terms of the "capitalism of the commandments" and rabbis as "titans of industry" and "ritual manufacturers."[91]

THE WOMAN QUESTION

Lilienblum used the metaphor of the undervalued woman to explain the economic and collective features of Jewish life.[92] Lilienblum's interest in the liberation of women and Jews came out of a principled valuation of individual freedom above all else, freedom that he defined as economic agency informed by an awareness of an individual's full range of labor options. In "Jewish Life Questions," Lilienblum focused on the way early marriage stunted not only young people's development but more generally the development of Jews' productive capability. Many writers had already described youthful marriages as irrational or hurtful for development and a cause of economic

Moses Leib Lilienblum (*left*) and Moses Kamensky. (Courtesy of the National Library of Israel, Jerusalem)

hardships. Lilienblum was aware of the criticism of early marriage issued by the early-nineteenth-century enlightener Mordecai Aaron Guenzburg.[93] Lilienblum however went far beyond Guenzburg's reflections and passing insights. Lilienblum developed a full theoretical framework to explain how the custom of marrying off children at a young age was rooted in a particular structure of economic power and authority.

According to Lilienblum, marriage was the means through which Jewish society reproduced its own traditional economic hierarchies, keeping young people dependent on their families and religious communities for financial support. At the center of this institution was the "professional matchmaker."[94] This matchmaker was, as a rule, a religious functionary, who had no productive skill set. He or she was like a merchant, but whereas the merchant traded in physical objects, the matchmaker's wares were young people and his profit was the percentage he garnered from brokering a deal between two families. The matchmaker assessed a young person's value through a combination of his or her parents' monetary assets and lineage. He or she also evaluated the sex-specific skills necessary to reproduce the established gender roles of a Jewish marriage: a man's learning potential and a woman's physical beauty. Lilienblum charted the value certain characteristics held in marriage negotiations (see table).

Lilienblum paid most attention to the last category listed on the chart, the European-educated "Mamselle," whose true economic worth and educational

Male	Acquires	Female
Poshutr Bokhur, a simple seminary student, who comes from a poor family		*Maydl,* a young woman, who is average in appearance; an attractive woman who is a *bal mum* (has a disfigurement); or an ugly or a poor woman
Bokhur who comes from a *balie-batishe* (respectable) family		*Maydl* with a fine lineage; an attractive woman with no blemishes; or a woman who comes from a family with some financial assets but is not attractive
Ilui, a Talmudic prodigy, with no secular education, or the son of a rebbe		*Mamzl* (Mamselle), who has a secular education and possesses economic means

attainments were ignored by Jewish elites.[95] Her devaluation in the marriage market underscored, for him, the absurdity of traditional Jewish society and the rabbinic economics. According to Lilienblum, by the middle of the nineteenth century it had become prevalent in Mitnagdic circles for women to be given secular educations, an exaggerated generalization but one that is partially supported by other sources from the period. The historian Shaul Stampfer notes, for example, that "by the mid-nineteenth century there was no lack of families in which boys studied Talmud and their sisters French literature, which looked incongruous to later generations who viewed secular studies as evil or as leading to evil."[96] Among wealthy families it was not uncommon for a sister to be "dressed in the latest fashion, speaking several languages and playing piano," and a brother to be dressed "in a long garment, with longer *payes* [sidelocks], not knowing how to write in even one language, not even ancient Hebrew."[97]

The education given to women from poorer sectors of Jewish society also differed from that given to their male counterparts. A few months before Lilienblum penned his series, a group of prominent Jewish women in Odessa petitioned the government to establish a society that promoted professions and elementary education for poor Jewish girls. "The important role played by women in the economic life of Russian Jews," explains the historian Eliyana Adler, "meant that there were very practical reasons for educating daughters." In other words, a woman's education often revolved around ensuring her family's material well-being. Her education differed from her brother's precisely in terms of its economic utility. "What most strongly differentiated [Jewish] girls' schools from schools of Jewish boys was instruction in the handicrafts." While men spent their days debating Talmudic minutiae, women gained the capacity to work with their hands.[98]

One might suggest that the division of learning that distinguished a Jewish male's from a Jewish female's education reflected the assumptions about what constituted Judaism and Jewish identity. In the early nineteenth century an individual's material well-being was simply not seen in terms of Judaism and as such was not the concern of Jewish men. Women were engaged in worldly matters so that men could focus on matters of the spirit. Judaism was defined by the study of rabbinic literature and the rituals connected with the home and the synagogue. Women could study secular subjects, master languages, and engage in labor precisely because these were not deemed specifically Jewish concerns. Judaism was defined by the knowledge obtained in the study hall and the rituals performed in the synagogue; physical labor and worldly knowledge were deemed non-Jewish and as such were the domain of Jewish women and Gentiles.

Implicit in Lilienblum's critique of Jewish education were certain assumptions about the material world—assumptions that he would eventually articulate as part of a coherent worldview. Rabbinic Judaism was the province of men and deemed superior to the more practical knowledge taught to women. For Lilienblum, this division and its assumptions about the value given to the material world were at the root of Russian Jews' poverty and ignorance. He ironically remarked that the rabbinic elite believed that women should be allowed to study secular knowledge because they did not have the same intellectual capacities as men. Rabbis were under the impression that only a man had the brainpower to become a heretic. Thus women received a proper European education, studying math and science and gaining proficiency in vernacular languages. In other words, knowledge about the physical world was deemed heretical only if it usurped the spiritual domain of rabbinic Judaism.

The partnership of the Talmudic prodigy and the Mamselle revealed the way Jewish wealth was squandered and capacities were stunted. Instead of suiting the Mamselle with an intellectual and economic equal, her fanatical father looked to "betroth her to a Talmudic prodigy or a rebbe's son." "What?" Lilienblum chuckled, "Do you really think he would take as his son-in-law a student from the university, from a gymnasium, from a government-sponsored seminary? Heaven forbid!" Lilienblum then imagined the tragicomedy of the first conversation between the Talmudic prodigy and the Mamselle. "And what are your means of support?" the Mamselle asks her new partner. The Talmudic prodigy has never even heard the word *means* before, and so he sheepishly answers: 'I don't know, I sit on stools and couches.'"[99] Even in the institution of marriage Jews' productive capacities were being smothered by the religious economy. The income Jews produced through industry was squandered on men who sat and studied subjects that had no practical application. Funds were dissipated within the heavenly sphere of yeshivot and deposited in the pockets of sons-in-law who spent their days praying to God and studying the Talmud. For Lilienblum, the reality of Jewish marriages highlighted the way Jews sacrificed their material well-being (the female) to spiritual concerns (the male). The relationship between Jewish men and women was a microcosm of the way Jewish wealth was produced and consumed; it illustrated the diminished status of the material world in the way people had come to understand what constituted Judaism.

Furthermore, Lilienblum argued, such economically unbalanced marriages were at the core of Jews' social strife. Lilienblum went straight to the economic downside of matrimony. Without economic parity between marriage partners, abuse and misunderstanding would inevitably follow, the same misunderstanding he was experiencing at the time with his own wife, whom he had married at young age while he was still considered a Talmudic prodigy destined to be a leading rabbinic figure.[100] Where there was an excess of wealth, Lilienblum argued, following Chernyshevsky, there would be petty arguments over honor and religion; where there was a lack of resources, young people would be indentured servants to preexisting familial sources of authority. The only path to true freedom for both sexes was to follow in Vera Pavlovna's footsteps and become economically self-sufficient!

Lilienblum criticized those who believed that political solutions could alleviate the discrimination against women in society. In other pieces he echoed ideas expressed by Pisarev, who argued that "we have no trust in the kind of emancipation associated with eighteenth-century French thinkers."[101] Lilienblum preferred the goal of economic equality envisioned by Englishmen like John Stuart Mill. For women to be truly free, they needed to become economically independent from spouses who controlled their lives.

Lilienblum's equation of Jews and women is illuminated by the political theorist Wendy Brown in her discussion of the difference in rhetoric surrounding the Jewish question and the woman question in the nineteenth century. Brown notes that whereas the latter was often framed in terms of "equality," the former was based on the weaker category of "religious tolerance." By tying the Jewish question to the woman question Lilienblum was making an argument about the need for Jews to be treated equally.[102] In contrast to enlighteners who continued to promote "tolerance" toward Jews,[103] Lilienblum, the materialist, asserted that Jews were human beings and thus should be treated the same as all other human beings. Lilienblum's demand for "equality" assumed that Jews were not part of a minority religion (not equal) that had to be "tolerated" but were first and foremost in the same category as women, fully human and yet not recognized as such.

There was, however a seminal tension in Lilienblum's own call for Jews to be treated as human beings. Either Jews were a particular group or they were bodies made up of the same substance as all other bodies. It was philosophically incoherent to argue that Jews should adopt a materialist perspective on life but still identify themselves as an independent entity. Lilienblum would have argued that his position had been imposed on him by outside forces that continued to see Jews as different. Still the position itself was philosophically contradictory. The universalist assumptions behind a strictly materialist perspective did not fully cohere with a particularist Jewish identity. The contradictions in Lilienblum's theory are reflected more deeply and personally in his own promotion of the equality of all human beings, including women, even as he mistreated both his wife and his lover. Lilienblum left his wife, Rachel, and their children penniless on more than one occasion. He carried on a very public extramarital dalliance with Feyge Novakhovitch in the 1870s and exposed private details about both women in a tell-all memoir. It is unclear whether he obtained the permission of either to disclose their pillow talk, but it does not seem as though he was much concerned about the pain he might have inflicted upon them. He took pleasure in shocking his wife by violating the Sabbath in their home. When he died he left her without enough money to pay for food or medication in her old age. His son would have to beg other writers for funds to assist his aging mother when she was suffering from typhus.[104] The great promoter of feminism and of the equality of all people treated the women in his life in the most unequal manner. Lilienblum's materialist perspective certainly put forward a new model for making sense of Judaism in the modern age, but it was laced with contradictions and tensions that would reappear in different guises throughout his early writings as well as in his later theories of Jewish nationalism.

Lilienblum's implicit criticism of Jewish society and of the Russian government rankled elites in the Pale and Saint Petersburg.[105] His detractors in the Jewish establishment, including his publisher, had a very different view of how to go about addressing the Jews' economic woes. In opposition to Lilienblum's materialistic perspective they continued to point to the Jews' political and religious profiles as the sources of their problems. By the early 1870s critics such as Eliezer Zweifel, Alexander Zederbaum, and Samuel Joseph Fuenn had endorsed a platform that was variously called "pure-faith Judaism" (*emuna tserufa*), "peace over Israel" (*shalom 'al yisra'el*), and "unity of the Haskalah" (*aḥdut hahaskala*), directed at solving the Jews' economic problems by reforming the rabbinic tradition.[106] This platform supported the centralization and consolidation of religious institutions and functionaries, which it was hoped would win Jews greater rights from the Russian government.[107] Lilienblum jettisoned this entire framework. Not surprisingly, on July 30, only seven months after Lilienblum began his tenure as editor of *Voice of the Herald,* he was dismissed. As we might expect, "differences of opinion" were cited as the cause for the breakup.[108]

JEWISH INTELLECTUAL REALISTS

Lilienblum spent the early 1870s spelling out the philosophical and substantive implications of quantitative materialism. He now privately declared himself to be a half-nihilist[109] and maintained that "Jewish Thought [*ḥokhmat yisra'el*] is not to be understood in terms of medieval philosophy or philology." These approaches "had only been adopted by a small fraction of Jews, failed to leave a strong impression on Jews' spiritual legacy, and were not accepted by the Jewish nation." By the end of the 1870s Lilienblum had dismissed "all the Jewish philosophers who followed Aristotle" and asserted that "until Spinoza Jewish thinkers had failed to advance any new philosophical theories."[110]

Lilienblum opposed the worldview put forward by medieval Jewish thinkers, who saw matter and form, the spiritual and intellectual, as being in an eternal struggle. Moses Maimonides had called matter "'the married harlot,' never free from but always in search of a new form."[111] Maimonides' sexist metaphor highlights the extent to which matter had no purpose other than being "used" by form. For Maimonides, "matter [was] evil and the source of all vices, form [was] good and the source of all virtues."[112] It is not surprising that this metaphor also reflected medieval Jewish philosophers' general denigration of physical bodies, human needs, sexual desires, and women.

Instead, Lilienblum identified the Talmud and Midrash as a reference point for a different kind of Judaism, which stressed the Jews' relationship to the physical world.[113] Lilienblum was not justifying his ideas based on Talmudic principles (as he had done earlier, following the model of Fuenn and Levinsohn); his arguments did not turn on whether they could be proven from the Talmud. Rather, he saw the Talmud, with its emphasis on Jewish life and practice, as a source of inspiration and a text that lent historical authority to his arguments. Lilienblum was prepared to admit that the Talmud had played a formative role in the development of his worldview. His materialism was not simply a function of reading Pisarev and Chernyshevsky or of Russian socioeconomic forces. It was also shaped by the non-theological and this-worldly orientation of Talmudic Judaism. However, his points of reference were Jews and their physical well-being, not a defense or explanation of the Talmud or rabbinic ideals or hermeneutics.

Lilienblum recognized the differences between his worldview and the emancipatory politics adopted by Jewish enlighteners like Fuenn and Levinsohn.[114] He also differentiated his own project from that of Kovner and other

"Europeans" whose materialism amounted to nothing more than the weaknesses of the flesh. Instead of running after the "pleasures of life," Lilienblum explained, he was destined to be a suffering servant. "I don't say that life is meaningless," he wrote to a friend; rather, "I write about matters pertaining to life and its values [*ve'erkam*]."[115] These were difficult years for Lilienblum, who in his diary and articles claims that he and Russian Jews in general were in the throes of a crisis. Unable to afford his nagging cigarette habit and in desperate need of cash, Lilienblum had become acutely aware of the difference between the economic situation of Jews residing in Russian lands and their more well-to-do acculturated co-religionists living in western European countries. "Jews living in Russia," he maintained, "did not find it necessary to work toward the reforming of synagogue practices or rituals. Rather, they needed reforms that would be beneficial to people's lives."[116] This distinction between Russian and western European Jewry signaled the beginning of a discourse that increasingly differentiated the two populations based on their respective social and economic features.

Lilienblum's Jewish materialism did differ from the materialism put forward by Chernyshevsky and Pisarev in one important respect: his was not directed at doing away with religion. "One who honestly believes in the commandments and wants to observe them is fulfilling what he desires," he insisted. He was not bothered by people being religious per se, but rather by their active denial that religious practices could have economic costs, their refusal to acknowledge that if a person wanted to act in his or her best economic interests, he or she would need to reconsider religious practices in light of those concerns. It was not freedom from religion that Lilienblum sought, but rather the freedom of every man and woman to become "a master of a field of knowledge or a trade that has utility."[117] Lilienblum wanted Jews to see themselves first and foremost as laborers and economic actors capable of acquiring resources necessary for their own survival. Religious observance was an economic decision.

Contrary to his writings from the 1860s, in the early 1870s Lilienblum maintained that economic idleness generated nonsensical religious practices and theories, not vice versa. "Illusory ideas and nonsensical actions," which were a focus of criticism by Jewish reformers, were in and of themselves "nowhere near as destructive" as the "idleness and limpness of the hands that surround us, sap our strength, and subject thousands of Jews to painful suffering." The problem was not with the Talmud; it was with the way Jews acted.

Lilienblum asserted that "the issue of labor and income was a more critical issue" than beliefs or ideas.[118]

Lilienblum's materialism, however, was hampered by the same tensions inherent in Pisarev's, and to some degree Chernyshevsky's, materialism. Russian society was so alienated from its own oppressive physical conditions, Pisarev claimed, that to be a materialist, or what he called a realist, in the 1860s required standing in opposition to the social order that made possible such alienation. "The most real [*re'al'nyi*] labor, that which brings the most obvious and indisputable utility presently [i.e., manual labor]," Pisarev wrote in his essay "Realists" ("Re'alisty," 1864), "remains outside the sphere of realism." Manual laborers, the masses, supported regimes of tyranny and stood against their own and others' best interests. The "thinking worker," meanwhile, fought to institute a new worldview based on empirical knowledge and scientific principles.[119] For Pisarev and Lilienblum true realists (or materialists) were people engaged in thinking about the physical world. Materialism was not yet a question of political action; it concerned the way people thought about the world.

Lilienblum repeatedly came back to lack of proper scientific perspective as the root cause of the Jews' idleness. He maintained that Jews "needed to adopt a materialist perspective on life [*mabat gashmi 'al haḥayyim*] . . . for there is no purpose of life, other than life itself, and there is no life without movement, and there is no movement without force, and there is no force without labor, and there is no labor without science and the correct perspective on life." The wrong perspective on life, "the perspective of fantasy, or delusion," he insisted, "leads to idleness and poverty and produces distress and pain."[120] Society was meant to mirror nature. Lilienblum believed that a "materialist perspective" meant seeing objects, movement, and labor in terms of the fixed and objective laws of nature.

Following Pisarev and Chernyshevsky, Lilienblum ultimately based his materialism on a static and objective notion of education and scientific knowledge (studying the laws of nature). He fundamentally differed in his thinking from the traditional (rabbinic) economic thinking of both Samuel Joseph Fuenn and Isaac Baer Levinsohn. But he was not a follower of Marx. In line with Pisarev and Chernyshevsky, Lilienblum believed that the laws of nature were immutable and eternal. Unlike Marx, he did not see "nature" as an entity determined by human economic activity and shaped by the forces of capital. Nature stood outside human subjectivity. Scientific knowledge was objective; it was the means for evaluating human activity and organizing society in a "healthy" and "natural" manner. Thus, for Lilienblum, education was a social imperative because it brought people closer to understanding the laws of nature and, ergo, the most rational mode of existence.

Beneath Lilienblum's social materialism was a particular understanding of scientific knowledge. For Lilienblum it was the responsibility of the intellectual to apply the knowledge produced in scientific laboratories to social life. The world was to be understood through the scientific categories of rational egoism and the principles of utility and productivity. It is thus not surprising that Lilienblum would spend the 1870s trying to pass the university entry exams that would have allowed him to become a "thinking realist," a scientist. While Lilienblum's theory contained the strengths of Chernyshevsky and Pisarev's theories—it allowed Jews to see clearly the material basis of their religious ideals—it also suffered from their weakness, and his failure to gain entry into the university revealed its weakness. Lilienblum's materialism, like Pisarev and Chernyshevsky's, was dependent upon educational institutions and the elites who determined what constituted science and who were admitted into institutions of higher learning.

CHAPTER 3

Scientific Materialism

The social materialists' sensational run-ins with clerics and religious institutions have distracted us from the more radical and intellectually rigorous theories of Jewish scientific materialism formulated in the 1870s. Whereas social materialists dueled with revered rabbinical authorities over the consumption patterns and productive capacities of the Jewish people, Jewish scientific materialists largely remained in cloistered libraries and labs, where they analyzed biological and chemical processes in technical language. Inspired by both the revolutionary politics of the Russian intelligentsia[1] and the German popular science movement,[2] scientific materialists educated Jews about the laws of nature, technological inventions, and, most important, how God and the Jewish people could be understood through biological and chemical processes.[3] Though often overlooked by historians, their views prefigured the major debates in the twentieth century over the scientific and biological basis of Jewish nationalist and cosmopolitan politics.

Most notably, in the 1870s the Darwinist polymath Joseph Sossnitz and the chemist Tsvi Hirsch Rabinowitz dueled over the relationship between Judaism and scientific materialism.[4] Although both men began their careers as strong public opponents of scientific materialism, as they matured they, along with others of their generation, came to embrace many of its assumptions. For the Jewish scientific materialists, the physical world operated according to objective laws of nature. Sossnitz would argue that science did not have to conform to preconceived religious ideals; rather, religion was meant to support scientific advancement and innovation. Scientific knowledge suggested that Jews were a distinct race; their roots could be traced back to nature itself, and the existence of God could be proven from biological processes. Sossnitz would eventually immigrate to the United States, where he became a supporter of the Zionist movement. In contrast, Rabinowitz endorsed "positivist religion." All people, he claimed, had the same origins and were united under the canopy of a religion of civilization. Religion promoted love between peoples and provided a moral system that held together humanity. Although Judaism enshrined these universal ideals, they could also be found in other religious and philosophical systems. Rabinowitz urged Jews to remain in Russia, continue their fight for equal rights, and wait for their neighbors to embrace the principles of peace and tolerance.

The contrast in the philosophical worldviews of Sossnitz the materialist and Rabinowitz the establishment positivist was a reflection not only of the two men's respective scientific and racial theories but of their personalities and politics as well. Rabinowitz's positivism mirrored his acceptance of scientific hierarchies and his endorsement of the political program espoused by the empire. For Rabinowitz, positivism was not simply a philosophy; it was also a way of being: it expressed his deference toward set orders and authorities. In contrast, Sossnitz's materialism reflected his intellectual vitality, his near total disregard for questions involving the Russian Empire, and his challenging of elites. Unlike Rabinowitz, Sossnitz emphasized the dynamism of the physical world: the ways in which nature was constantly transformed and reformed according to various political pressures. Their political differences were based on conflicting conceptions not of God, religious dogmas, revelation, or Jewish law but rather of the status of the physical world and the human race. The conflicts between them foreshadowed the central debate of modern Jewish politics between cosmopolitan liberals committed to Jews' becoming citizens of various preestablished nation-states and Jewish nationalists who challenged the accepted orders of Western politics. More generally, Sossnitz's evolution provides us with a detailed account of the philosophical and political differences between a Hasidic worldview and scientific materialism. Sossnitz's nationalism emerged from a dynamic concept of land, labor, and bodies and not from the secularization of God, beliefs, or commandments.

BÜCHNER'S HERESY

Sossnitz and Rabinowitz came of age during what has been described as a large-scale culture war over the authority of science and organized religion. The debate's epicenter was located in Prussia and involved primarily intellectuals, but its ripples could be felt across Europe and the Russian Empire in government buildings, in classrooms, and in church pews. Following the failed revolutions of 1848 young scientists throughout Europe began registering complaints about being limited to laboratories while religious elites played an outsized role in political and social spheres.[5] In 1855 the physician Ludwig Büchner upended the scientific community with the publication of *Force and Matter* (*Kraft und Stoff*), in which he charged that religious, government, and scientific leaders had conspired to force people to engage in a dual accounting in all life matters. "Bookkeeping by double entry," was how he described the burden placed upon the human mind.[6] Sometimes scientists were merely forced to play a linguistic game: calling themselves God's prophets, identifying the locomotive and steam engine as divine creations. But in other instances, such as the allocation of government funds for education, bookkeeping by double entry was a costly proposition that drained economic and intellectual resources and could not be justified by reasonable and educated modern men and women.

Büchner claimed that the scientists' humility and deference toward religious elites had confused and misled the public. Scientists were at fault for allowing religion to assume such a prominent place in the organization of society. They were too circumscribed in their claims. Scientists needed to be more assertive in social and political matters; they needed to adopt the same posture of certitude witnessed in the writings of the clerics. Science was not simply a presupposition of research or a method of analysis restricted to test tubes. It was a system of values that should be employed in social policy and political decision making. In the same way, matter was not only a way of explaining the laws governing nature; it constituted the sum total of the universe. For Büchner it was clear that if scientific authorities were to replace clerics as the arbiters of social and political value they would have to speak with the same degree of certitude about the claims of science.

Ludwig Büchner and his followers demanded that principles adopted by scientists in their experiments be treated as more than a mechanism to analyze phenomena; they were rather a philosophy.[7] There was no reason to continue to trust in an "unknown dynamical power." Instead of bowing to the gods of the unknown, Büchner proclaimed that science "had a duty . . . to infer the unknown from the known."[8] Science had made sufficient progress to conclude that the world was independent of any outside force. Human beings, like all other entities, were the products of matter; mind and body were indistinguishable, and God did not exist. These "dogmatic materialists," as their detractors dubbed them, called upon science to support their absolute claims over and against religious elites.[9] But the scientific materialists' earlier association with the revolutionary politics of 1848 had made them enemies of government officials and theologians across Europe. Established biologists, chemists, naturalists, and philosophers with ties to state offices lined up in opposition and began attacking them in scientific journals across the continent.

Relatively few Jews living within the Russian Empire in the middle of the nineteenth century, however, had the capacity to access, support, or respond to the scientific theories behind scientific materialism. In the 1850s and early 1860s only a handful of Jews even attempted to do so. Most notably, Ḥayyim Selig Slonimski's *On the Existence of the Soul* (*Metsi'ut hanefesh*, 1851), Ephraim Menkin Zagorski's two-part *Teaching on Immortality:* (*Torat 'al-mavet*, 1860–1863), and Moses Bazilevsky's *Words of Understanding; or, Belief and Scientific Knowledge* (*Divrei bina: o emuna veḥokhmat hateva'*, 1870) all defended the independence of "soul" or "force" from "matter" and rejected the claims of what they called "materialismus." Zagorski's defense of the soul boasted a Who's Who of Jewish endorsement letters, ranging from the titular head of the Volozhin Yeshiva, Rabbi Naftali Tsvi Berlin, to the enlightener Samuel Joseph Fuenn. Slonimski's work was reprinted four times in a decade. The notion of "materialismus" that Slonimski claimed to be refuting, however, was in fact Galileo's sixteenth-century mechanistic philosophy, and Slonimski did not mention a single study written after the 1830s.[10] While Zagorski explicitly attacked the German philosopher Ludwig Feuerbach and Bazilevsky cited contemporary scientific scholarship in chemistry, none of these works directly addressed the scientific materialists Karl Vogt, Büchner, or Jacob Moleschott—probably owing to censorship. Their discussions largely focused on defending medieval theological concepts.

Joseph Sossnitz's Hebrew treatise *Indeed, There Is a God* (*Akhen yesh Hashem*) was the first Jewish monograph that explicitly responded to the scientific materialism of Büchner and his followers. Published in 1875, it combined elements of the Jewish philosophical tradition with research conducted on the conservation of energy, human perception, race, and geology. However, it was not German and Russian atheists whom Sossnitz hoped to convince of

God's existence. Neither Büchner nor the other well-known scientific materialists—with the exception of Moses Hess—could read Hebrew. Rather, Sossnitz targeted the "many Hebrew writers of that generation [who] worshipped materialism and were busy destroying everything holy."[11] Some claim that by the 1870s Büchner's "heretical" ideas had permeated Jewish life, "even reaching the youth in the study house."[12]

Sossnitz's own path toward becoming a critic of scientific materialism reflected the general influence of scientific thought on Jews living in the Pale of Settlement. He had been born into a Hasidic family.[13] In his teens he had gained a reputation for possessing otherworldly powers and was sought out by townspeople for advice and to perform miracles. By his thirties, however, he had been moving away from his youthful dalliances with the occult and was grappling with scientific theories of creation.[14] When he sat down to write his tract he was not known in intellectual circles, and so he asked a better-established Jewish scientist, Tsvi Hirsch Rabinowitz, to vouch for his expertise and the importance of his work.

Sossnitz hoped that Rabinowitz's approval might win him the support of the philanthropic Society for the Promotion of Culture Among the Jews of Russia (OPE), the organization that was chiefly responsible for advancing scientific knowledge and literacy among Russia's Jewish population.[15] The society held Rabinowitz in high regard for his role as a public defender of Russian Jews and an outspoken advocate of the government-backed school system.

Rabinowitz's scientific commitments and support for the acculturation of Russian Jews was fostered through his educational upbringing.[16] Raised in a family of Mitnagdim, Rabinowitz was a child of a Lithuanian Jewish culture that prized intellectual achievement. His mother taught him Hebrew; a copy of Luther's translation of the Bible borrowed from a local Gentile became a manual for gaining proficiency in German.[17] Although early in his career he faced rabbinic opposition to his efforts to spread scientific knowledge in the Pale,[18] by the mid-1870s he had settled in Saint Petersburg, where he became a darling of the Jewish capitalist elite. His close contacts with the wealthy and mighty earned him a lab fully stocked with equipment, test tubes, and machinery for conducting experiments. He enjoyed the support of the Russian minister of education Ivan Delianov and the company of various Saint Petersburg academics.[19]

Sossnitz and Rabinowitz had very different temperaments. Whereas the former was known for his "sarcastic tendency" and wide-ranging intellectual interests,[20] "logic and order accompanied Rabinowitz in all his pursuits."[21]

Rabinowitz was stingy with his contacts, refusing to open his Rolodex for Sossnitz. Still, he obliged when Sossnitz requested an endorsement letter. In keeping with Rabinowitz's general character, the letter was measured in tone, and contained a subtext. Rabinowitz complimented the work but confessed to his discomfort with Sossnitz's depiction of scientific materialists as heretics. The problem with Büchner's disciples was not that they were too "scientific" or "heretical," Rabinowitz maintained, but rather that they had become "BELIEVERS in materialism."[22] Rabinowitz was a serious man who was deeply suspicious of charismatic authority. A cold and analytic thinker, he recoiled at the thought of scientific knowledge being exploited to serve the needs of an ideology. Implicitly, Rabinowitz had dismissed Sossnitz's work as beneficial only for those who lacked the capacity to understand the scientific theories behind Büchner's writings.

Rabinowitz's critique was more than a clever turn of phrase; it situated Sossnitz at the center of political and religious debates swirling around Büchner. As described by the historians Andreas W. Daum and Todd Weir, religious dissidents in the early 1870s touted Büchner's ideas to argue that they should be granted the same economic and political rights as people associated with state-recognized confessions. Adherents of what was called the Free Religious Movement, they began "evangelizing nature."[23] They combined the insights of scientific materialism with a religious worldview reflecting "a shift from Christian dualism to an immanent monism."[24] Arguing that their scientific system of belief was no less worthy of being granted the benefits offered to religious groups, those associated with the Free Religious Movement provided the lower classes with a "systematic understanding of the world replete with moral, aesthetic, historical and religious dimensions."[25] They offered the less educated the requisite knowledge to challenge the elite monopoly over what constituted *Bildung* (education), though their conservative opponents intellectually considered them to be *Halbgebildet* (semi-educated). This was a reference not simply to the group's low socio-intellectual standing but also to its members' incomplete and unorthodox knowledge of science and theology. The amalgamation of these two spheres of knowledge represented both a false idol and an illogical worldview. Rabinowitz believed that science should not be vulgarized or confused with theology. His endorsement subtly distinguished him from Sossnitz, whom he saw as a theologian and scientific popularizer.

Rabinowitz denounced the vulgarization of science and the cultivation of unquestioning acolytes. He equated the newfound respect being given to scientists and scientific knowledge with the religious idea of the worshipping of clerics (*emunat ḥakhamim*). In their zeal to destroy the claims advanced by the rabbi and the priest, scientific materialists had fallen prey to the entrapments of the church's ideological fervor. For Rabinowitz, science was not a matter of certitude; rather, it promoted the evolution of knowledge, with each generation of scholars replacing outdated theories with new propositions.[26] Rabinowitz saw scientists as individuals tasked with challenging religious doctrines. Enthusiasts were the products of a religious worldview, not a scientific one. Rabinowitz believed that science was distinguished from religion by its refusal to speak in absolute terms.[27]

Rabinowitz's status as a Jewish scientist reflected that of a new class of Jewish intellectuals who had emerged following the Russian government's educational reform projects. Whereas in 1840 only 48 Jewish students had attended Russian gymnasiums, by 1872 that number had jumped to 2,362.[28] In that period, Alexander II granted Jews entry into universities, allowing them to become doctors and scientists. Between 1831 and 1881 well over a hundred private schools for Jewish women had opened.[29] By the mid-1870s, 14 percent of the 480 medical students at the University of Saint Vladimir in Kiev were Jews.[30] By 1886 one in three students at the women's medical courses in Saint Petersburg and 14 percent of the total number of students in Russian universities were Jewish.[31] Rabinowitz was in close contact with many of those who had attended medical schools, and he saw Sossnitz as a man of the Pale, a man who addressed popular Jewish concerns and religious anxieties but was not a real scientist.

Rabinowitz's insinuation that Sossnitz was writing for the Halbgebildete was not altogether wrong. Sossnitz's target audience was not the small number of Jewish university students. Rather, he was addressing the tens of thousands of Jews steeped in rabbinical lore but increasingly interested in new scientific discoveries. Though operating outside of institutions of higher learning, Jewish men and women were progressively seeking employment in new industries and professions built on new technological insights. Sossnitz's tract targeted such individuals and presented them with a model for how to negotiate the seeming conflict between religious and scientific worldviews.

The differences between Rabinowitz and Sossnitz quickly moved from the intellectual to the personal. "You opened up your evil mouth . . . without properly reading my work," Sossnitz privately told the Saint Petersburg scientist. "You claimed . . . that it was only of value for the barbarians who did not understand Büchner." [32] Sossnitz was hurt by Rabinowitz's hesitancy to assist him with obtaining funds and was not appreciative of the tepid recommendation letter.

Sossnitz and Rabinowitz, however, shared more than either man was prepared to admit. Their public stances against scientific materialism belied their own appreciation for the very works they were criticizing. It would not be long before these concealed aspects of their work came to the fore.

FOUNDATIONAL ETHER AND LEAPS OF FAITH

Many elements of Rabinowitz's theories can be traced back to ideas associated with the scientific materialists. But we would be hard pressed to see these connections based on his response to Sossnitz. His most developed position on the subject of materialism can be found in his multivolume work *Collection of Knowledge and Wisdom: Fundamentals of the Natural Sciences* (*Otsar haḥokhma vehamadda': yesodei ḥokhmat hateva'*, 1876). In it he claimed to offer "a new theory for the laws behind the creation of the world from one matter and the law of the existence of the world through the action of one force."[33] Rabinowitz spent years working on his treatise, and by the time it was published he could boast of having more than a thousand presubscriptions, as well as the endorsement of the science faculty of Saint Petersburg University.[34] He dedicated the work to the Jewish French statesman and Freemason Adolphe Crémieux.

The contents of the work testify to the author's erudition, originality, and access to the most recent research on magnetism, electrodynamics, and theories of perception. Rabinowitz argued that "foundational ether" had preceded the creation of the universe and was the basis for all inorganic and organic matter. He insisted that this foundational ether was not a metaphysical entity but rather something that could be detected in the cosmos. Rabinowitz used "ether" and "atoms" to explain in scientific terms the way matter functioned. Like others of his generation, such as the German scientists Aaron Bernstein and Philip Spiller, Rabinowitz believed that "foundational ether could be witnessed from the slowing rotation of Comet Enke around the sun."[35] Scientists noticed that with each rotation Enke lost speed. Since there was no object blocking its way, some scientists posited that an unseen drag of "ether" accounted for this phenomenon. Rabinowitz argued that ether was the medium through which force traveled between elements. Foundational ether was the unseen rigid vessel that transmitted light, which in turn created heat and eventually gave rise to life. Rabinowitz described foundational ether as being made up of matter. He explained: "Within each point of ether there is the foundational matter [*haḥomer hayesodi*], and a movement that is the foundational force [*hakoaḥ hayesodi*]. And when the composites of ether created the various universes [*'olamot*] they did so according to their matter and force, because form and matter cannot ever be detached from one another."[36] Rabinowitz distinguished his own theory of etherism from Democritus's and Epicurus's philosophical materialism (atomism). There was also a difference, he maintained, between the kinds of atoms referred to by medieval philosophers and those employed by nineteenth-century chemists.[37] Whereas the former understood atoms as an abstract metaphysical concept that explained the process behind creation, the latter invoked the term *atom* to account for microscopic entities.

However, Rabinowitz refused to concede how close his views were to those adavanced by medieval metaphysicians.[38] Rabinowitz claimed that ether preceded not only the creation of the earth but also of all worlds. Ether was not an empirically observable substance; it was a placeholder that accounted for missing information. Rabinowitz would have rejected the insinuation that he was proffering a metaphysical argument. Yet the foundational ether he postulated could not be seen, touched, sensed, or detected by a microscope. Rabinowitz was treading on the threshold of metaphysics. His foundational ether hypothesis bordered on a theory of first causes.

At least in one sense, Rabinowitz's theory of creation reflected the shortcomings of his theory of ether; no one had ever seen it. Rabinowitz claimed to have composed an unpublished treatise addressing "the creation of the universe [*'olamot*] based on [Immanuel] Kant and Pierre-Simon Laplace's [nebular theory] as well as [the creation of] the earth according to the position of geologists and Darwin."[39] As Sossnitz later noted, although Rabinowitz "promised to write books on a new theory of Creation, they never appeared in any known scientific publication."[40] Rabinowitz repeatedly mentioned this tract while shying away from explaining the process and role played by God in the creation of the universe.[41]

Rabinowitz tiptoed around the question of creation and metaphysical truths. He rebuked those he called "enlightened priests" for "working as hard as possible to find ways to address all the contradictions between knowledge and religion and faith and empiricism."[42] In their desire to harmonize these two fields of knowledge, these "enlightened priests" had misinterpreted both. He defended his silence on metaphysical issues by citing the "biblical prophets who investigated and sought to understand the phenomenon of nature and what it allowed them to know but did not ask about what was beyond them . . . metaphysics."[43]

In the rare instance in which Rabinowitz broached matters pertaining to the intersection of science and metaphysics, he offered only cursory and vague speculations. He cited the narrative of the biblical story of Creation but refused to define the terms *world, God,* and *Creation.* Citing the discomfort of Talmudic rabbis with such matters, he recused himself, claiming, "It is better to remain brief when discussing these topics and not to speak about Creation in public lest untutored students be led astray," trailing off with "the vessel of the mind is weak . . ."[44] Addressing the question of who or what created "motion," he shrugged his shoulders: "All the forces of nature are only different appearances of motion and the first source that causes, the source that gives birth to, all of these movements will always be hidden from us. Our knowledge reaches only to the point at which we see how things are created from other movements."[45] Rabinowitz's prose is highly deceptive. Although he seems to place a wall between science and God, his silence on metaphysical concerns was also an admission of how much of the universe he had placed within the domain of science. Readers of Rabinowitz's work are often given the impression that he sometimes equated nature with God. Even Sossnitz noted privately that at first glance Rabinowitz's work "seems to indicate that the author believes that knowledge of the Creator was equivalent to nature creating itself." Sossnitz felt obliged to add that "such an interpretation of Rabinowitz's writing contradicted his homilies and instructions to students in which he expressed his belief in God, as all kosher Jews are required to do."[46]

Nonetheless, Rabinowitz was accused of promoting materialism. Such was the opinion of Ḥayyim Selig Slonimski, the man who Stalin claimed invented the telegraph and a close friend of the geographer and naturalist Alexander von Humboldt.[47] It was ironic, Slonimski remarked, that proponents of "etherism" were often the first to attack materialists. Slonimksi insinuated that the Saint Petersburg scientist's work was comparable to another recent study on foundational ether composed by Philip Spiller, *The Primordial Force of the Universe* (*Die Urkraft des Weltalls,* 1876). Like Rabinowitz, Spiller railed against materialism while ascribing to ether the properties that were once ascribed to matter. "Though Spiller's stated goal was to fight against all those who deny God and the materialists," Slonimski claimed, "anyone who read his book would know that he in fact raised the materialist thesis to a higher rung and called it by a new name, Etherism."[48] Clearly inferable from

Slonimski's comments was that Rabinowitz's notion of foundational ether was also a theory of foundational matter. Rabinowitz was a closet materialist!

Joseph Sossnitz defended Rabinowitz against Slonimski's charges. He asserted that Rabinowitz's work differed from that of philosophers "who postulated a theory of matter that was attached to the 'chaos' prior to Creation."[49] Sossnitz insisted that Rabinowitz was a chemist (not a metaphysician) and focused on matters that were posterior to the creation of the universe. He shielded Rabinowitz against the explosive charge of blurring the lines between science and metaphysics. Sossnitz's defense, however, failed to address the fact that Rabinowitz clearly believed that ether existed prior to the solar system and all universes.[50]

Sossnitz's defense of Rabinowitz's piety appeared in the context of a larger argument about the compatibility of Charles Darwin's scientific theories with Judaism. *On the Origin of Species* appeared in Russian in 1864 and was hotly debated in scientific and intellectual circles across the empire.[51] Sossnitz challenged Büchner's claim in *Darwin's Theory of the Origin and Development of the Living World* (*Die Darwin'sche Theorie von der Entstehung und Umwandlung der Lebewelt*, 1868) that Darwin's theories confirmed the nonexistence of God. Sossnitz hoped to insinuate the British scientist's theories into Jewish letters by pitting him against the bogeyman of materialism, Büchner.[52] Sossnitz cited the German scientific writer Julius Dub, who distinguished "Darwin as a scientist of nature—for even after all of the studies conducted on nature known today, he does not argue that the forms were created through nature"—from Büchner, "who was a philosopher of nature—for after researching a few phenomena he claims that the source for all can be understood through no other means than through nature. Since we are incapable of imagining anything through a different means, we are forced to conclude that this is the totality of truth."[53] Sossnitz highlighted Darwin's own silence on the question of first causes and accepted the position Darwin articulated in the conclusion of the sixth edition of *Origin of Species* (1872). "It accords better with what we know of the laws impressed on matter by the Creator," Darwin wrote, "that the production and extinction of the past and present inhabitants of the world should have been due to secondary causes, like those determining the birth and death of the individual." Dub and Sossnitz's distinction allowed them to entertain, or at the least not be forced to deny, the possibility of an outside force governing nature.

For Sossnitz, the theory of natural selection proved that nature contained within itself something logical, suggesting that a master plan or planner existed that made matter function according to set, defined rules. Sossnitz religiously sanitized Darwin's theory, deifying it as the "Natural Selector." Instead of God being an agent that put a process into motion, Sossnitz saw God in the development and process of nature. Sossnitz suggested that there was a divine spirit located within the evolutionary process.[54] God (the Natural Selector) was the logic (natural selection) that explained how nature evolved.

Sossnitz came daringly close to promoting a pantheistic theory of the world. He argued that human beings were distinguished from other animals by their ability to comprehend nature. Embracing certain unitary and organic aspects of *Naturphilosophie,* Sossnitz assumed that because man is on the highest rung of the chain of being, the fullest expression of the unity of nature, he is capable of penetrating and grasping the life processes of other animals.[55] Human beings could recognize the features of nature that united various phenomena. Comprehension allowed humans to identify laws and processes within the natural world. God, that which unified and explained all, could be witnessed through nature.

In the early 1870s Sossnitz's worldview oscillated between a form of pantheism in which nature was associated with God but its forms of diversity—or at least certain forms of individuality—were upheld and taken to be real, and acosmism, in which all differences between extension and thought or between particular things was seen as illusory. The line between acosmic and pantheistic theories concerning God's relationship to nature has often been reduced to semantics. But the theories contain some basic differences. The former leads from nature into mysticism, theology, and idealism, while the latter points in the direction of immanence and materialism. Acosmists are often depicted as God-intoxicated, focused on metaphysical questions, while pantheists are deemed closet atheists whose sole concern is the physical world.[56] Whereas for the former all difference in nature collapses into one unity that exists beyond human comprehension, for the latter the whole of nature is one, but its parts—that is, all bodies—vary in infinite ways.

Sossnitz's worldview—operating in the space between the idealist-materialist divide—reflects not only his eclectic scientific and philosophical commitments but also a transformation of certain paradoxical strands of Hasidic theology. As a child Sossnitz studied the works of the various masters of the Ḥabad (Lubavitch) branch of Hasidism, and from 1855 until 1862 he traveled annually to the town of Lubavitch to visit its leading rabbinical figure (rebbe).[57] In *Indeed, There Is a God,* Sossnitz repeatedly cites the third Ḥabad rebbe, Menachem Mendel Schneersohn (including unpublished manuscripts to which he seems to have been given access). Sossnitz's student Mordecai Kaplan described his teacher in the early twentieth century as "not only a mathematician and physicist but also a Hasid in the fullest sense of the term."[58] Ḥabad's paradoxical philosophy of matter would act as both a bridge and a barrier to Sossnitz's path toward a materialistic conception of Judaism.

For more than a few modern Jewish thinkers, Ḥabad would become a path toward philosophical materialism. According to the philosopher Elliot R. Wolfson, Ḥabad places spirituality and materiality on par with each other.[59] In Ḥabad, empirical knowledge and reason are ultimately overwhelmed by the divine reality that fills the entire cosmos. All existence is perceived as an image, which is meaningless compared to its source in God. Human beings strive to understand the way God permeates the universe but in so doing eventually come to recognize the equality of all things and the ultimately illusory nature of the differences that exist in the physical world. However,

Boris Schatz, Portrait of Joseph Sossnitz with his head covered and dressed in pious garb. (Courtesy of Forsythes Auctions, LLC, Russellville, Ohio)

Joseph Sossnitz, bareheaded,
in modern attire.

Ḥabad also maintains that the physical world is the only porthole through which humans can encounter the infinite God. The stones and dirt are where God resides.[60] Understanding how God placed himself into the stones and dirt (creation) is how human beings understand the divine.

For Ḥabad, the paradoxical nature of the universe began with Creation. Understanding Creation requires the individual to embrace the idea of *dillug* (leap).[61] Within Ḥabad's theology the terms *walking* and *leaping* are used to distinguish between mechanistic actions (walking) and supernatural activities (leaping).[62] The leap both represented the limits of a materialistic worldview and bypassed the need to explain how an outside force accounts for the creation and maintenance of the physical world.

Sossnitz understood Ḥabad's concept of the leap in terms of what F. W. J. Schelling identified as *Sprung.* For Schelling, the Sprung was the only means of fathoming the discontinuity between the phenomenal world and its origins in the Absolute (God). In 1878, while working as an editor at the Hebrew-language scientifically oriented newspaper *The Morning* (*Hatsefira*), Sossnitz published an article by the Galician Jewish philosopher Fabius Mieses (1824–1898) in which Mieses noted the parallels between Ḥabad and Schelling. "The creation of differentiation [according to Schelling] can only be rendered intelligible according to a theory of the 'dillug' (Sprung) or a onetime sudden supernatural occurrence," Mieses explained. "And all those who are experts in the books of the recent Kabbalists who subscribe to the theory of Ḥabad [Wisdom, Understanding and Knowledge] will be surprised to notice how this concept of [the Sprung] in its nature, origins, and implications coincides with the words of Schelling and his students."[63]

Sossnitz was not prepared to accept unconditionally either Schelling's or Ḥabad's theory of Creation as involving an outside force. While Schelling's work had enjoyed popularity in Russia, by the 1870s the wider scientific community had cooled to his ideas. "Characteristic of the new German scientific community on the philosophical front was a replacement of the older *Naturphilosophie* with no philosophy at all."[64] Schelling's philosophy was severely discredited by scientists who rejected all knowledge beyond that which could be identified through strict empirical methods based on observation and experimentation. While Sossnitz conceded that many found the idea of nature "leaping" inconceivable, he was not prepared to accept a strictly causal theory of evolution.[65] Sossnitz was still committed to identifying a force that set into motion the process that would create the world.[66]

Sossnitz relied upon the German physiologist Emil du Bois-Reymond's much-discussed Leipzig lecture "Limits of Our Knowledge of Nature" to justify a force existing outside of matter. According to du Bois-Reymond:

> Though there is no fundamental difference between the forces operating in the crystal and in the organized being, still the two are incommensurable, just as a simple building is incommensurable with a factory into which coal, water, and raw material pass, on this side, while at the other side carbonic acid, water, vapor, smoke, ashes, and the products of the machinery are sent out. The building we may regard as so made up of parts, each resembling the total result, that, like the crystal, it is separable into like parts; the factory, like the organic being (if we abstract from the cellular constitution of the latter, and the divisibility of sundry organisms), is an Individual.[67]

As to the cause that transformed inorganic into organic matter, du Bois-Reymond declared, *Ignorabimus!* (We will not know!). Even if nature could not act in a noncausal manner, Sossnitz asserted, scientists still could not *discount* the possibility of an outside force—what Sossnitz called God—to explain the origins of organic matter. Ultimately, Sossnitz's work rejected a pantheistic theory of the world.

Sossnitz's invocation of du Bois-Reymond's theory of consciousness to highlight the limits of Büchner's position echoed arguments most cogently expressed by F. A. Lange in his groundbreaking *History of Materialism.* For Lange, the totality of life could be divided into the categories of the real-existence and ideal-value. The latter term emerged at the border of the former and pointed to something that could not be fully accounted for through a scientific and empirical lens. Ideas could not be proven to be true or false from a scientific point of view; rather, ideas were based on values generated by the subjectivities of human beings. So long as consciousness remained unquantifiable, materialism had no right to assert itself beyond the realm of phenomena. The subjectivities of sensory experiences pointed to the limits of materialism and the possibility of nonempirical and nonscientific forms of knowledge.

Sossnitz followed Lange in marshaling du Bois-Reymond's claim of ignorance to discredit Büchner. Religion and morality could not be rejected simply because they could not be proven to be real. For Lange, religion was something beyond a strict material calculus; it inspired the masses to correct social imbalances and political abuses. Religion disrupted reality and stood outside the realm of scientific knowledge. Lange, however, did not address in the *History of Materialism* how these two spheres, the real and the religious, truth and value, cohered or could be reconciled. He simply noted that consciousness could not be fully accounted for and that therefore one could not reduce all ideas to their relation to material forces alone.

Sossnitz's theories reflected many of the ideas put forward by Lange, but he refused to categorize religion as relative or subjective. Rather, Sossnitz invoked God as an *x* that could explain the unknowns of science; at other times he went farther, justifying God's intervention in history and revelation at Sinai. Sossnitz employed Ḥabad's theory of the leap to explain the way binary compounds of inorganic matter became organic substances. Sossnitz acknowledged that his argument for "natural leaps of nature" was a weak defense of Judaism against the challenge of scientific materialism. It was neither an original idea nor an especially convincing one. More than anything else it reflected some overlap between a certain strand of materialist thought and a Hasidic worldview that privileged the idea of divine worship through the physical world (*avodah bagashmiyut*). However, in general it highlighted the incompatibilities between Ḥabad's acosmism and the new forms of scientific materialism advanced in the mid-nineteenth century.

BUT NATURE DOES NOT LEAP

Sossnitz must have known that he was philosophically trapped between Ḥabad acosmism and scientific pantheism. What once seemed to be a paradox would eventually turn into a contradiction. Increasingly, he described himself as torn between either granting the material world ultimate value or dismissing it as a chimera. As soon as *Indeed, There Is a God* left the printing press, Sossnitz began to reconsider his commitment to Ḥabad and to Schelling's supernatural concept of the leap. Sossnitz's studies were causing him to doubt the ideas espoused by Ḥabad, and he drifted away from Hasidism.[68]

Sossnitz's intellectual struggles coincided with financial difficulties. Ḥayyim Selig Slonimski had offered Sossnitz a position as co-editor at his Berlin-based newspaper *The Morning*.[69] Sossnitz moved to Berlin, where he became part of Slonimski's circle, which included Aaron Bernstein and other scientific luminaries.[70] Before Sossnitz could establish himself in the Prussian capital, however, Slonimski had turned on his young protégé for refusing to defend him in an academic debate over mathematics, sending him back to Russia "empty-handed."[71] Back in Riga, Sossnitz supported himself by teaching at the government-sponsored Jewish school and working on barges to obtain extra funds.[72] He rekindled his friendship with Gothard Schweder (1831–1915), an instructor at the Riga gymnasium and the director of the Nature Society of Riga, who provided his student and friend Joseph with borrowing privileges at the gymnasium library.[73]

Sossnitz's material hardships and spiritual wrestling had shaken his constitution. His friends urged him, "Greater is the strength of faith and hope in God, as you know from having been raised by Hasidim. Rise up from the dust of the philosophy . . . for not a shred of grass grows from it."[74] But Sossnitz could find little solace in Ḥabad. He searched in vain for answers to the issues he had raised in his book. He traveled widely, visiting with respected rabbis such as Eliyahu Ḥayyim Meisel and Yitsḥak Elḥanan Spektor of Kovno. He recalled, "I confronted them with various questions about religion . . . but they were unable to provide me with scientific answers, and I told them that I have to follow my own judgment."[75] Sossnitz was undergoing an intellectual crisis; he had grown tired of leaping over nature. The claims of scientific materialism were becoming too great to ignore. He was now being forced to accept the very positions he had just denounced.

Sossnitz's growing doubts must have been compounded by his friends and colleagues' endorsement of positions he had deemed heretical. The newspapers that were publishing his articles were also running pieces supporting Ernst Haeckel's materialistic monism. In 1879 one socialist-leaning Hebrew broadsheet ran a review of *Indeed, There Is a God* that subtly criticized Sossnitz along with Büchner. The reviewer argued that the "the concept of God is not within the boundaries of form and is beyond all form or matter."[76] Sossnitz critics asserted that God existed entirely outside human comprehension. God's essence was a lack of essence, an incomprehensible formlessness. God could never be imagined, let alone understood, through the natural world. Sossnitz was rattled by this criticism and began a full-length rebuttal. For unknown reasons, however, he never published the piece.[77]

Meanwhile Sossnitz's former employer, Slonimski, had patched up his rift with Rabinowitz and now endorsed scientific materialism. Soon after his harsh review of Rabinowitz appeared, Slonimski repudiated it. In a remarkable about-face Slonimski privately admitted that he too was a proponent of Rabinowitz's theory of etherism (which he had earlier dubbed a form of materialism). His "critical remarks" had reflected his "frustration with not being given proper recognition." Admitting to a bruised ego, Slominski conceded that his gripes against Rabinowitz could be reduced to the question, "What, you were not able to cite old man Slonimski?"[78] The aging Jewish scientist now praised the young Saint Petersburg intellectual for taking up his own mantle and promised to defend him against a growing chorus of Hasidim who were denouncing his work.[79]

Eventually Rabinowitz and Slonimski would join forces in editing *Theory of Life and Its Forms* (*Torat haḥayyim veḥezyonoteihem*, 1880), a posthumous work by Yitsḥak Isaac Etkin.[80] Before his untimely death at the age of twenty-two, Etkin had been a rising star in Jewish scientific circles; he had also been one of Sossnitz's public critics. Etkin's posthumously published work praised Ernst Haeckel's "excellent response to the old man of the sciences du Bois-Reymond's lecture in Leipzig on 'The Limits of Nature.'" He pointed to "Haeckel's (and many others who supported him) new scientific data that suggested there was no boundary to consciousness [*ru'aḥ ha'adam*] and that

Tsvi Hirsch Rabinowitz.
(Courtesy of the National Library
of Israel, Jerusalem)

human beings were capable of [fully] understanding" the nature of matter and force.[81] There was no hidden reality behind what the eye encountered, and certainly no need to cry *Ignorabimus!* The unknowns behind human perception did not justify jumping to outside forces to explain Creation. In his introductory letter to Etkin's work, Slonimski turned 180 degrees from where he had stood in the 1850s. What Slonimski had once deemed heretical, maintaining that it propounded a materialist conception of the universe, he now supported. He asserted that a scientist could be a religious materialist: "While simpletons will find the new discoveries of the well-known physiologists lacking in faith in the existence and eternality of a soul, we no longer should cover from the eyes of the masses of our people these well-known positions. And even if at first they will retreat from hearing such things, in the end they will embrace these ideas and will know how to refine their faith in a manner that

Ḥayyim Selig Slonimski. (Courtesy of the National Library of Israel, Jerusalem)

will conform to their intellect."[82] Slonimski's blessing of Haeckel's theories indicates a much larger transformation in the way Judaism was being conceived around modern biological and chemical categories.

Sossnitz recognized the increasing acceptance of scientific materialism among his peers and their dismissal of the position he had espoused in *Indeed, There Is a God*. His discomfort with his own ideas can be seen in his handwritten emendations to a printed copy of *Indeed, There Is a God*.[83] In the original publication Sossnitz wrote, "Even following Darwin there still are those who believe in the possibility of a sudden spiritual event [that can alter nature]. For even if nature will not leap [*yedalleg*], still God passed over all the ways of nature when punishing the Egyptians, and God leapt over the mountains when he revealed himself to the people of Israel [at Sinai]."[84] At some point following the publication, Sossnitz crossed out both the mention of God "leaping" and the statement that God performed the "miracles" of Passover and Sinai. Now it read, more cryptically and ambiguously: "Even if nature will not leap [*yedalleg*], still God passed over all of the ways of nature and covered the universe in its entirety."[85] While in the emended version it is not clear whether Sossnitz was equating God with nature, he certainly was no longer endorsing the idea that God would act against the laws of nature.[86] This subtle but profound difference between his original position that God involved himself in specific historical events and his later position of an impersonal God passing over all of nature reflects a shift from an acosmic worldview in which the world lacked absolute rules or logic to a form of pantheism in which God and the logic of nature were one and the same.[87]

Sossnitz's rejection of acosmism also appeared in a critique of Schelling's Naturphilosophie. In archival drafts to a work he later edited and published under the title *The Luminary* (*Hama'or*, 1889) Sossnitz argued:

> As the philosopher (in name only for he studied philosophy at a university and was recognized with a doctorate), Schelling said all scientific knowledge is a false palace (for it teaches only the external aspects of knowledge, so that one does not refer to it as the unknown) built on the foundations of experimentation. This kind of philosopher is no more than a believer. [He] lacks the kind of understanding seen among those who reject the knowledge of material existence in favor of activities and dreams in the upper spheres in which they reside without proof, without ever having any consciousness of these matters. In contrast stand the sages of the Talmud and the philosophers of God, who cherish and respect the sciences.[88]

Sossnitz charged Schelling with fundamentally misunderstanding Kabbalah and diminishing the religious value of a scientific worldview. Schelling looked on the Kabbalah as a system of thought that pointed beyond the realm of scientific knowledge. Sossnitz agreed with Schelling that certain aspects of the Kabbalah expressed nonempirical and nonscientific wisdom; however, he asserted that Kabbalistic texts and authorities had endorsed the importance of scientific and empirical knowledge. In other words, the Kabbalah encouraged people to study nature and science in order to understand not the absence of God but his presence in this world. Sossnitz selectively cited Jewish authorities ranging from the sixteenth-century Judah Loew ben Bezalel of Prague, to the seventeenth-century anti-Sabbatean Moses Ḥagiz, to the *Zohar*, all of which, he claimed, endorsed the knowledge obtained through the empirical study of the natural world, the sciences, and medicine.[89] Instead of attempting to reinterpret canonized religious texts to conform to new scientific theories, Sossnitz was now prepared to admit that canonized religious texts contained outdated, irrational, and illogical ideas.

Sossnitz argued that science did not justify the specific theories advanced by the Kabbalah; Kabbalah endorsed new scientific developments. The positions Kabbalists assumed about the natural world and human development were not scientifically valid and should be rejected. But, Sossnitz maintained, Kabbalistic texts supported the study of scientific knowledge. No longer would science kneel before the altar of theology. It would now be theology that would strengthen and authorize science's claims. This was an important shift in Sossnitz's thinking, one that pinpoints a profound intellectual shift in modern Judaism. Sossnitz and others like him had moved away from defending biblical, rabbinic, and Kabbalistic ideas about the nature of God and the universe to marshaling biblical and Kabbalistic metaphysical authority to support new scientific theories.[90]

MATERIALIST AND POSITIVIST RACIAL POLITICS

Sossnitz's embrace of scientific materialism dovetailed with a new theory of Jewish bio-politics first articulated in an article he published in 1879. There he departed from the line of reasoning central to his earlier work and criticized the "philosophical religion" of the prophet Ezra that first infected Judaism in the fifth century BCE. "Philosophical religion," Sossnitz claimed, emphasized "spiritual matters such as blessings and prayers."[91] It was based on visions and dreams and ignored human needs and the claims made by science. In a remarkable turnabout from earlier writings in which he generously cited Kabbalistic and philosophical texts, Sossnitz now dismissed even Kabbalah as speculative knowledge. After all, while Kabbalah may have described the Godhead in material terms, its point of departure was not the natural or physical world but the nature of the divine as understood through a circumscribed set of concepts. Even though the lines between these two positions could be blurry, Sossnitz's position had clearly evolved. His notion of religion did not begin with abstract conceptions of the divine. It now was rooted in matter.

In contrast to "philosophical Judaism," Sossnitz held up two other forms of religion, one ancient and the other modern. He asserted that Moses introduced the Israelites to a *dat ḥomrit,* a materialistic religion. And lest there be any confusion regarding the meaning of this loaded phrase, Sossnitz printed alongside it in Hebrew characters: "materialische religion."[92]

Sossnitz's "materialist" religion was based on a number of sources. He somewhat disingenuously claimed that the medieval philosopher Maimonides supported his theory of the ancient Israelite kingdom embodying the ideals of a materialistic religion.[93] A far stronger case, however, can be made that Sossnitz's new worldview was based on the ideas espoused by the Amsterdam heretic Baruch Spinoza. While Maimonides privileged knowledge of the physical world as the source for prophecy, it was Spinoza who asserted that Moses's *political* authority stemmed from his ability to demonstrate his control over the natural world. Sossnitz's earlier work was directed at "the Enlightened Spinozist," whom he mentioned in an introductory poem coupled with the "Hasid" and the "Talmudist." Sossnitz's students from the late 1870s also cited and praised Spinoza in their writings,[94] and in speeches Sossnitz delivered in the United States he placed Spinoza alongside Sabbatai Zevi as a founder of the enlightenment.[95] While many thinkers noted the similarities between Spinoza's pantheism and Kabbalistic ideas, Sossnitz's most illustrious student, the American rabbi Mordecai Kaplan, would claim that "Spinoza is as Jewish as Maimonides."[96] Sossnitz was one of the first Jewish writers to describe the Israelite religion as materialistic and Moses as a political leader.

For Sossnitz, the authority exerted by Moses over the Israelites reflected his insight that the various forces of nature could be consolidated under a single unifying principle, God. Cryptically Sossnitz wrote that those "who understand will know the true meaning of the rabbinic interpretation 'Moses was a godly man [Deut. 33:1]. This means that from his midsection down he was man [but] from his midsection up he was God'" (Deuteronomy Rabbah, 11).[97] Sossnitz believed that nineteenth-century Jews should follow in Moses's footsteps by formulating a theory of God that reflected new biological and chemical knowledge.[98] Judaism needed to be reconceived according to the materialistic principles of nineteenth-century science.

Sossnitz's presentation of Moses as the father of a "materialistic religion" may have been a response to a similar but ultimately opposed depiction of Moses put forward by Rabinowitz in the introduction to the government-sponsored Jewish catechism, *Fundamentals of the Law of Moses* (*Osnovy Moiseeva zakona*,1874).[99] The book was reprinted in 1881 and incorporated into the curriculum of the Jewish girls school in Saint Petersburg.[100] The Russian government placed it on the list of recommended books for Jewish educators. There, Rabinowitz argued that Moses was the founder of a *pozitivnaia religiia* (positivist religion), whose aim was to "encourage life in the broadest physiological and psychological sense of the term."[101] Rabinowitz cited

Moses's declaration in Deuteronomy 30:15: "Behold I have set before thee this day life and good, and death and evil." The Mosaic teaching, according to Rabinowitz's reading, was directed at cultivating human potential and "the unity of all human beings."[102]

Rabinowitz contrasted Moses's universal ethical teachings with those of scholars who had historically employed "religion to establish impermeable barriers between people of different faiths and inflame animosity between them." "Universal human history," he asserted, "provides abundant facts that indicate that people who deceive others . . . have committed terrible misdeeds, finding some false testament to justify themselves."[103] Acts of violence perpetrated in the name of religion ran counter to the biblical cosmopolitan ideal.

Rabinowitz's identification of Moses as advancing the cause of positivism did not so much contradict his insistence that the spheres of religion and science be separated as it illustrated the importance he granted to a scientific worldview. Rabinowitz attacked philosophers who conflated Moses's law with otherworldly ideals. He heaped scorn on "the blasphemous Kabbalistic ideas that had crept into numerous theological works." Echoing a commonly invoked rhetorical trope, Rabinowitz asserted that Moses "was concerned not only with life that is *vechnaia-zagrobnaia* [eternal and beyond the grave] but also with the *nastoiashchaia-zemnaia* [present earthly]."[104]

There were important political differences between Rabinowitz's "positivist" and Sossnitz's "materialist" religion. Rabinowitz asserted that all humanity shared a single ancestor. He seems to have endorsed Darwin's monogenetic theory of human evolution, which assumed that all human beings came from the same forefather.[105] Races and nations, Rabinowitz held, were historical, not natural entities. Rabinowitz was a cosmopolitan who believed in the idea of progress and in the universal ideals of civilization. Moses might have been a lawgiver for the Jews, but his message, Rabinowitz insisted, was ultimately one that applied to all peoples irrespective of time and place.

Rabinowitz's immediate goal was to provide a model of biblical Judaism that encouraged Jews to draw socially and economically closer to other Russians. His long-term hope was to bring about "a unity among all people, who would consider themselves as children of the same ancestor living in peace and agreement."[106] Throughout his life, his friends recalled, Rabinowitz remained optimistic about the Jews' place in Russian society. Even after the pogroms of 1881, he believed that eventually Russians would come to see Jews as their fellow countrymen.[107] "Religious positivism" was a code name for Jewish acculturation, international politics, and scientific advancement.

Rejecting the notion that Israel's lawgiver was a cosmopolitan, Sossnitz was, by contrast, deeply skeptical about the ability of Russian Jews to acculturate, and was more concerned about Jewish poverty in the Pale than about supporting the capitalistic industries of Jews residing in Saint Petersburg. The Sossnitz family's papers even contain a document claiming that he had been associated with certain revolutionary cells in Russia. In contrast to Rabinowitz, Sossnitz maintained that Moses taught people to pay political heed to scientific principles and the laws of nature, principles and laws that did not demand they join a universal faith or a religion of humanity. Whereas Rabinowitz portrayed Moses as the presumed founder of a positivist religion, Moses as the father of a *materialische religion* believed that "Nature governs over bodies, and over the course of time bodies will dissolve back into their origin. These origins will combine with other bodies or will generate new bodies. Even if multiple bodies are united," Sossnitz continued, "they will ultimately dissolve, and the elements will go back to being independent of one another. [Just like atoms] parts of the body will break away and will return to their origin."[108] In contrast to positivist religion's prescription for various collectives merging into a single united religion of humanity, Sossnitz argued that scientific knowledge and the forces of nature suggested the opposite. Collectives would eventually splinter off and return to their independent states of being. Like the atoms, the Jewish people could merge with other peoples but ultimately they were a distinct body. Sossnitz used the idea of fundamental "origins"—atoms as indivisible particles—to draw a significant analogy to the indivisible, *sui generis* nature of social groups, races, and nations.

Sossnitz's theory of national bodies was rooted in the racial theories of the scientific materialist Karl Vogt. Sossnitz had in his earlier work already endorsed Vogt's views on the genesis of man: "The well-known and highly praised zoologist Karl Vogt, in the second section of his book *Lectures on Man* [subtitled *His Place in Creation and in the History of the Earth (Vorlesungen über den Menschen, seine Stellung in der Schöpfung und in der Geschichte der Erde,* 1863)] . . . states that there is no means by which animal and plant life could have come from the same source. For one reason, their cell makeup is fundamentally different."[109] Sossnitz endorsed Vogt's insistence on distinctions between humans and other animals and seems to have also adopted Vogt's criticism of Darwin's theory of evolution.[110] Human beings did not come from a shared ancestor.[111] Sossnitz was among a minority of scientists in Russian lands who privileged Vogt's polygenetic explanation of human development over Darwin's monogenetic theory.[112]

For Vogt, human beings originated from different ape-men scattered around the world. Sossnitz admitted that in following Vogt he was rejecting the literal reading of the Bible. "It is permissible to entertain the possibility," he wrote, "that there was more than one person who was the forefather of the species in general."[113] To be sure, Sossnitz, unlike Vogt, was not a racialist. In unpublished commentaries on Genesis he clearly asserted that "all human beings possess a divine spark and there is no difference between nations."[114] Later in life he seems to have believed that differences, whether between individual humans or between collectives, were primarily the result of historical circumstances (perhaps once again shifting his position and embracing a more cosmopolitan position).[115] If he continued to believe in polygenetic creation, he must have also believed that differences could be overcome through the eventual unification of nations. For Sossnitz, cosmopolitanism and messianism meant overcoming racial differences. It was the task of humanity to unify the various aspects of nature. He accepted the philosophical justification for cosmopolitanism. But he argued that in the present day Jews should reject such ideals on temporal (political) grounds. Groups were splintering off from one another, and people were at war with each other over resources. The time was not ripe for Jews to acculturate or attempt to bind themselves to other peoples.

Writing in the 1870s under dire economic conditions and with nationalist fervor, Sossnitz was not inclined to believe that his was a messianic age. Warning against the political dangers of cosmopolitanism he told Jews: "For just as it is currently impossible for the wolf to lie in peace with the lamb, so too it is currently impossible for there to be one idea that unites mankind . . . just as the Asiatic will not be the decider, the Eskimo will not be a philosopher. . . . Not all lands are similar in their nature and not all nations who sit on them are similar in their makeup [*tekhunatam*]."[116] Sossnitz's scientific assumptions about racial differences fundamentally differed from positions advanced by Russian Jewish liberals and western European Jews. As noted by Lisa Moses Leff, in the French context Jewish racial differences were "used primarily as a way of describing diverse groups coexisting harmoniously, a 'holy alliance of peoples,' each contributing something particular to the world." In contrast to Sossnitz's theories, French Jewish identity was based on history and biology, but its goal was "a very practical kind of world reconciliation, with France, guided by Mosaic principles, explicitly at the helm."[117] Sossnitz also believed that it was imperative for humanity to strive toward the goal of unification. But he asserted that it was both futile and foolhardy to act as though history were on the precipice of redemption. Those who promoted Jewish acculturation—such as Rabinowitz and various liberal Jewish intellectuals—had failed to properly understand the laws of nature and the Jews' contemporary political situation in Russia. Sossnitz's "materialische religion," which posited an independent Jewish body, directly challenged the fundamental political program of European Jewish liberals and cosmopolitans.

The nationalist and revolutionary kernels in Sossnitz's theories would not be lost on Jews residing in the Pale of Settlement, especially his detractors. On December 19, 1879, the religiously conservative Jewish newspaper *The Lebanon* (*Halevanon*) published a front-page, three-part article bemoaning the popularity of scientific materialism among Jews and identifying it as the basis for a new kind of Jewish national identity. Though published in Palestine, *The Lebanon* in the 1870s vehemently opposed the embryonic Jewish nationalist movement in the Russian Pale of Settlement. The writer blamed Jewish scientists and nationalists. "Who would have believed that so many of our own youth residing in Russian and Polish lands would join this front?"[118] This was not the first time the paper had warned about the spreading of Büchner's ideas among Jews, but its prime target was now the individual who a few years earlier had made his name as the leading Jewish opponent of scientific materialism: Joseph Sossnitz.

Halevanon condemned Sossnitz for turning biblical Judaism into a *materialische* religion, despiritualizing it, and making it a vessel of nationalism. (He was compared to the leading Jewish nationalists of the 1870s.) Unlike the well-respected Rabinowitz, Sossnitz was identified with the most revolutionary, anti-establishment Jewish groups. He was labeled a heretic, a destroyer of religion, and an enemy of God. Sossnitz was now lumped together with Moleschott, Büchner, Vogt, and even Haeckel! His earlier attacks against those he had deemed heretics were completely ignored, and the figures that he had once pointed to as his archenemies were said to be his teachers.

Sossnitz was deeply wounded. Located in his archive are two responses to the attack issued by *Halevanon.* In one note, he lashed out at his critics, telling them "to purchase a dictionary with more words . . . so that you would no longer have to keep using the term *heresy.*"[119] In another, he described the article's author (whom he refers to as "Mr. Kahane") as "a man for whom every whiff of knowledge smells like heresy."[120] In both notes he refused to respond to the charges, arguing instead that the author was a dilettante whose philosophical knowledge was cribbed from secondhand sources familiar to any yeshiva student. Sossnitz fumed at the newspaper's editors for running the articles while refusing to publish his own work.

Eventually, even *Indeed, There Is a God* would be "burned" by the Orthodox and described as a work that clandestinely endorsed scientific materialism.[121] By the end of the nineteenth century the rabbinical judge and scholar Yehuda Halevi Lifshutz (the brother of the Kovno-based Orthodox polemicist Ya'akov Halevi Lifshutz) was charging Sossnitz with dissimulation. Sossnitz and his cohorts, Lifshutz cried, reduced Judaism to empirical forms of knowledge. Describing Sossnitz's approach he declared that "in our generation heretics veil their heresy."[122] Sossnitz's citations of Maimonides and other traditional figures were just a cover, Lifshutz inveighed, for his real sources: scientific materialists.[123] Lifshutz called on Sossnitz "to rise and testify" that he honestly thought that "spiritual forces could be understood through the concepts of electricity and magnetism."[124] The man who began his career as Judaism's primary defender against scientific materialism and its "heretics" had now come to be seen as the chief espouser of Jewish materialism.

JEWISH NATIONALISM VERSUS RUSSIAN COSMOPOLITANISM

Sossnitz's and Rabinowitz's theories highlight the ways in which the reconstitution of Judaism around scientific materialism gave rise to new political identities. Over the course of the late nineteenth and early twentieth centuries the differences between Sossnitz and Rabinowitz would become more apparent and begin to reflect two distinct political struggles. Rabinowitz continued to ingratiate himself with the wealthy liberal-capitalist Poliakov and Gintsburg families as well as the Russian government, which granted him honorary citizenship and supported his scientific research. In 1879 he began publishing a newspaper, *Russian Jews* (*Russkie Evrei*), whose editorial stance supported the acculturation of Jews into Russian society. Carefully navigating around both Jewish nationalists and highly observant Jewish factions, Rabinowitz won the admiration of his coreligionists with his broad knowledge and deep piety.[125] A staunch positivist until his dying day, Rabinowitz defended the tsar and scientific authorities and encouraged Jews to continue to wait for their condition to improve. When he died in 1889 he was eulogized by philanthropic elites as one of the leading Russian Jewish intellectuals of his generation.[126]

Rabinowitz's intellectual contributions would be most notably championed by the first president of the State of Israel, the world-renowned chemist Chaim Weizmann, who in recalling his own intellectual development identified Rabinowitz's scientific work as the well from which "I drew my first taste of chemistry."[127] However, Rabinowitz's legacy would be primarily confined to the history of Jewish liberalism in the Pale of Settlement. Like Jewish liberals in France and Germany, Rabinowitz championed Judaism's moral and ethical qualities. After the outbreak of the pogroms of 1881, the newspaper he edited considered endorsing immigration to Palestine and the United States but ultimately sided with those who urged Jews to stay where they were and continue their struggle for greater rights. Rabinowitz used the newspaper to promote his brand of cosmopolitanism, integrating Jews into the Russian Empire and encouraging the Russian government to adopt more liberal ideals and values.[128]

Sossnitz's mixture of race science and Jewish politics, meanwhile, can be seen as the start of "the story of integral Jewish nationalism that expressed itself in biomedical language."[129] In contrast to the positivist Rabinowitz, Sossnitz, the originator of a Jewish "materialische religion," aligned himself with Zionist groups and others who advocated immigration. While in Riga, he taught two of the most important future Jewish scientific writers: Nehemiah Dov Hoffman, who helped establish the Jewish community in South Africa, and the physician and Russian American Jewish communal leader Simon Brainin.[130] Sossnitz also developed close ties to Boris Schatz, the originator of the Jewish art movement.

Eventually, Sossnitz made his way to the United States, where he became one of the founding members of the Hebrew Educational Alliance. Most notably, he was the teacher of arguably the most influential American rabbi, Mordecai Kaplan, who named Sossnitz as the person who inspired him "to synthesize the spirit of religion with that of science and to become aware of ethics as the indispensable prerequisite for worship."[131] Kaplan credited Sossnitz with "freeing [him] into an expanded space after being entrapped by the thistles and brush of *pardes* [the garden of knowledge]."[132] Kaplan became an outspoken advocate of Darwin as well as of Jewish nationalism. Like Sossnitz, he was also at the forefront in developing a theory of Jewish difference that did not conflict with scientific knowledge. The tensions between the universal claims of Darwin and Jewish political difference would become one of the central themes in Kaplan's work. What Sossnitz addressed in theory, Kaplan would politically harness and develop into a full-blown argument for minority rights in the United States and Europe and for the Jewish Zionist cause in Palestine.

CHAPTER 4

Practical Materialism

In the preceding chapters, I considered how certain Jewish thinkers in the 1870s redefined Judaism in terms of land, labor, and bodies. What they did not do, however, was lay out a comprehensive program of action that might help us account for the outsized role Jews played in various late-nineteenth-century political and economic movements. Sossnitz's and Lilienblum's respective social and scientific materialisms offered diagnoses of the Jews' maladies, but their prescriptions could not be fulfilled. They made Jews aware of their collective material identity, but neither developed a theory of group action.

Both assumed that opportunities would arise in Russia, either through government legislation or new markets, for Jews to gain greater access to resources and diversify their labor profile. Although they recognized tensions among various groups within the Pale of Settlement and the precarious status of its Jewish inhabitants, they had seen reason to trust that the opening up of Russia's educational institutions would lead to greater economic prospects. Jews might not yet have the same opportunities as their Gentile neighbors, but the situation was slowly improving. By the late 1870s Jews made up 19 percent of the gymnasium population in the Pale of Settlement. Jews were flooding Russian universities and increasing numbers were entering the legal and medical professions.[1] Lilienblum himself spent most of the

1870s preparing for university entry exams. While he still was skeptical about the government's ability to alleviate Jewish poverty, he held fast to the idea of education as a panacea for all social and economic maladies. However, Lilienblum, like the overwhelming majority of Jewish men and women of his generation, never matriculated at a Russian university. Denied access to educational institutions and professional mobility, Jews, however attuned to their circumstances they might be, were incapable of improving them.[2]

The discovery of Karl Marx's writings by Russian Jews in the mid-1870s changed the way they viewed their situation and provided a framework for them to become political actors. Marx emphasized something that Chernyshevsky and Büchner, and for that matter Lilienblum and Sossnitz, did not: the capacity of human beings to transform their social and economic environment, an idea that gripped Russian intellectuals who were disillusioned with the unfulfilled promises of the country's new liberal program. Through Marx, Russian intellectuals began to see how not only the empire but its educational systems and social hierarchies had kept its various subjects from obtaining equal access to resources. Jews could now envision building a society independent of the Russian Empire or religious institutions. Marx provided a blueprint for every individual invested in alleviating economic imbalances and social discrimination.

For Jews, Marx's most enduring legacy was neither his secularism nor his critique of Judaism as an insidious form of capitalism. It was the emphasis he placed in his work *Capital* (*Das Kapital*) on the social and political structures that blocked human beings from acting and the ways in which the distribution of resources in society limited people's freedom and mobility.

My discussion of Jews' reception of Marx in the 1870s offers a different narrative from the one presented by the historian Yuri Slezkine in *Jewish Century*. According to Slezkine, "Whatever the relationship between Judaism and Marxism, large numbers of Jews seemed to agree with Marx before they ever read anything he wrote. Emancipation from haggling and from money, i.e. practical, real Judaism, would be the same as the self-emancipation of our age."[3] Slezkine maintains that Jews saw Marx as a modern-day Christ, whose mission was to overcome the original sin of history: humanity's turn to nationalism. "The Jews, as a group, were the only true Marxists because they were the only ones who truly believed that their nationality was 'chimerical'; the only ones who . . . had no motherland."[4] Jews knew that national identities were ephemeral, created and destroyed by various economic and political forces. For Slezkine, the Jews' reception of Marx centered on their detachment from familial ties and rejection of Judaism. Marx brought Jews to reject the concept of nationality and religion.

Slezkine's theory helps explain the disproportionate number of Jews who held leadership positions in the Communist Party. He focuses on a group of secular Jews who in the late nineteenth and early twentieth centuries forsook their Jewish identities and adopted Russian revolutionary politics. Slezkine's narrative is rooted in strong historical precedents. Starting in the late 1860s a cohort of secular Jews such as the Chaikovsky circle leader Mark Natanson, the future People's Will (Narodnaia Volia) Party gunrunner Aaron Zundelevich, and their comrades Lev Deutsch and the future Siberian anthropologist Benjamin Jochelsohn renounced their Jewish upbringings and emerged as leading figures in revolutionary organizations and terrorist groups.[5] These men dismissed Judaism as "irrational" and asserted that Jews "lacked a common national interest."[6] Some of them would attend Russian universities, where they found their way into revolutionary cells.[7] They dismissed the Russian Jewish enlightenment and claimed that the problems facing their families could best be solved through larger political struggles that addressed the inequalities of the lower classes throughout society. Eventually, they migrated "from one chosen people to another."[8] Their disdain for Judaism and denial of its nationalist characteristics provide the background for Slezkine's narrative about these and other Jews' affinity toward Marxism.

Whereas Slezkine's view corresponds to a cosmopolitan and secular narrative of modern Judaism, I look at Marx's first Jewish readers in terms of the way they incorporated his deeper insight about the nature of history: the capacity of human beings to act freely and appropriate the physical world. Although Slezkine's narrative explains the role Marx played in influencing large numbers of Jews to join Russian revolutionary circles, it does not address Marx's reception among the majority of Jews who encountered his writings.[9] By the early twentieth century, Marx would be claimed not only by Jewish Communists but also by leaders in the minority rights movement, by Bundists, by Jewish socialists, and by Zionists, as well as, in a modified form, by the founders of arguably the two most influential twentieth-century Jewish religious movements: Rabbi Mordecai Kaplan,[10] who introduced the concept of Jewish peoplehood, and Abraham Isaac Kook, the first chief rabbi of Palestine and the spiritual forefather of the settler movement.[11] Both Kook and Kaplan identified certain strands of historical materialism as reflecting Jewish ideals.

Slezkine argues that the Jews' nomadic and mercantile identities stimulated their interest in Marxism, but a careful reading of Jewish philosophical texts and propaganda literature from the late 1870s suggests that their understanding of Judaism and Jewish collectivity was in fact what drew Jews to Marx. The Jewish materialists viewed Marx in conjunction with, not in opposition to, the Hebrew Bible and the Kabbalah. Their primary target was the Russian state, not their Jewish parents. While this intellectual development does not account for the appeal of Russian revolutionary parties to Jews, it does challenge the idea that their attraction to Marx was because of his criticism of Judaism. Whereas Slezkine's nomadic Jews drew attention to the secularizing and cosmopolitan goals of Marxism, the Jewish materialists teased out the messianic universal aspirations and nationalist assumptions that they saw behind Marx's theories of revolution.

Those who viewed Marx within a Jewish framework did so not to spiritually authorize a secular program but rather to propose rigorous and sustained arguments about the overlapping nature of Judaism and Marxism. Slezkine's narrative places a great deal of historical weight on the self-critical aspects of Marx's "On the Jewish Question" (Zur Judenfrage). Yet it is not clear whether any major Russian Jewish Marxist even read "On the Jewish Question" before the late 1880s.[12] None of Marx's Jewish followers in the 1870s directly referenced the work, and their near-total silence regarding "On the Jewish Question" is deafening.[13] This was in large part due to the Prussian government's confiscation of the journal in which Marx's essay appeared. Prussian authorities seized roughly one-third of the thousand copies of the *German-French Annual* (*Deutsch-Französische Jahrbücher*), an action that transformed it into a rare and dangerous piece of literature to own.[14] Like many Jewish Communists and socialists who came after them, the Jewish materialists ignored "On the Jewish Question" and employed other Marxian insights to reinterpret Judaism as a universal program to alleviate poverty and establish a materialistic argument for Jewish collectivity.[15]

Instead, Marxists such as the Kiev poet Judah Leib Levin and the Vilna intellectual Aaron Shemuel Lieberman studied *Capital*[16] and *The Communist Manifesto* (*Manifest der Kommunistischen Partei,* 1848)[17] with the same reverence and exacting hermeneutic that they employed when reading Jewish sacred texts.[18] Though overlooked by Slezkine, this circle had an influence on the history of Jews and the spreading of Marxism among oppressed groups in eastern Europe that cannot be ignored. Aside from their own projects, such as establishing the first Jewish labor organizations and newspapers, the hundreds of works written about Lieberman and his followers by Communists, Zionists, socialists, and Bundists testify that this group's reading of Marx was more than a matter of intellectual curiosity.[19] It reflected a radical transformation in the way Jews envisioned themselves and Judaism, and for many it was the birth of modern Jewish politics.[20]

MARXISM AND JUDAISM

The story of the Jews' reception of Marx in the Pale of Settlement begins in the 1870s with the formation of two revolutionary cells, one in Mogilev and the other in Vilna. Each consisted roughly of fifteen to twenty core members. Most of the men in these groups attended either the Vilna or Zhitomir state-sponsored rabbinical schools but had become intellectually disenchanted with liberal state-based politics and reformist religious ideals. The men and women in these revolutionary groups were often running away from arranged marriages. They were inspired by contraband socialist literature secretly passed to them by revolutionaries in Saint Petersburg associated with the Chaikovsky circle, one of the leading Russian socialist propaganda organizations. The Chaikovsky circle opposed the use of terrorist tactics and promoted self-education among young people living in the countryside.[21]

With the assistance of Aaron Zundelevich (1853–1923) and the revolutionaries Anna Epstein (d. 1895) and Rosalya Idelsohn (b. 1851), works of various socialist writers were smuggled into Vilna, where they were quickly consumed by cell members such as Aaron Shmuel Lieberman.[22] The future founder of the Mensheviks, Pavel Axelrod, did the same in Mogilev, where he was tutoring Jewish students.[23] In these cells, budding revolutionaries listened to one another analyze the latest political and scientific developments in Europe and America "through the perspective advanced by Pisarev . . . and the materialist method."[24] These groups were still, however, mainly concerned with Jewish affairs. Axelrod was penning articles in local Russian newspapers denouncing Jewish "liberals" for being beholden to "capitalists" and documenting in Jewish communities the way "capital combined with fanaticism . . . enslaved the poor and ignorant masses."[25] While Axelrod would be given access to Marx's *Capital* through the circle surrounding his employer and father-in-law, Isaac Kaminer, Marx's works had yet to circulate in Vilna.

Many of the cell members were social provocateurs, flaunting their disdain for accepted norms and mores. The future Russian revolutionaries Khasia Shur and Eliezer Zuckermann reveled in parading the streets of Mogilev hand in hand on the Sabbath. The rocks thrown by their co-religionists only further emboldened them to flout their parents.[26] Both were determined to break free from their comfortable but stifling lives in the upper echelons of Jewish society. "It was criminal to live off of our parents' capital," Shur would later explain.[27] Many cell members from Mogilev escaped their families and ran away to Kiev, where they soon came under investigation by Russian authorities, subsequently fleeing to Berlin.

In March 1875 the Russian police discovered contraband literature in the possession of the Vilna reading group and began interrogating its members.[28]

Pavel and Nadezhda Axelrod and their son. (Courtesy of the Boris I. Nicolaevsky Collection, Hoover Institution Archive, Stanford University)

Aaron Zundelevich. (Courtesy of YIVO Institute for Jewish Research)

Thirty-eight individuals were accused of smuggling banned socialist propaganda into the empire and fomenting revolution. Arrests began on July 12, 1875. Before the Vilna police could apprehend him, Aaron Shemuel Lieberman fled to Berlin along with a few friends.[29] Their escape from Vilna marked the beginning of their journey into revolutionary politics as well as their struggle to read Judaism and Jews into Marxist literature and Marxist literature into Jewish life and Judaism.

In Berlin, the Vilna and Mogilev émigrés sharpened and refined their political and philosophical positions.[30] This was first time many of the members had been in a major European city; they were awed by the width of the streets, the museums, and the art galleries. They finally understood, explained Axelrod, the nature of bourgeoisie society. Berlin police records reveal that Jewish students congregated in apartments across the city, on Zionskirschplatz, Bergstrasse, Elsasserstrasse, and Grenadierstrasse. At the apartment building on Zionskirschplatz a Jewish commune was formed. The Mogilev revolutionary Grigory Gurevich and Axelrod established "a Jewish Section of the Revolutionary International League" that attempted "as much as possible to interact with other local revolutionary groups."[31] The émigrés spent their days at hard labor and their nights arguing about the state of the world and enjoying new sexual freedom.[32] Writing to one of his childhood friends on October 13, 1875, the Mogilev rebel Eliezer Zuckermann described in metaphorical terms the transformation he was undergoing: "Do you remember the young Rabbi Eliezer who studied under the tutelage of Rabbi Yudel? Do you recall how we both used to look up into the women's section of the study house . . . ?" The boundaries separating men and women that defined so much of his upbringing no longer existed.[33] As Zuckermann explained in another context, "The days of my youth and darkness have passed. . . . There is no more Rabbi Yudel and no more *beit midrash* [study hall]."[34]

Gender differences played an important role in the lives of the young revolutionaries. Khasia Shur complained about rampant discrimination; she even had to dress herself as a man in order to attend certain meetings.[35] The women of the group fashioned themselves after Vera Pavlovna, the unbridled heroine of Chernyshevsky's novel. "Communism in every sense of the word" was the way one of its members described the group's sexual relationships. "The women of the commune practiced free forms of love, not allowing any man to make an eternal claim upon them."[36] This new sexual freedom could lead to bouts of emotional anguish, severe depression, a sense of traditional identities disappearing, even suicide.[37] For some it led to marriage outside the faith; for others it meant the ability to have sex with whomever they pleased; for a few, especially women, it demanded the rejection of emotional attachments as a way to remain autonomous, unhampered by the restrictions of traditional gender roles.

As first detailed by the historian Bernard D. Weinryb, Berlin police shadowed the commune's members, whom they labeled "nihilists" and "socialist agitators," suspicious of their close contact with Eduard Bernstein and other leaders of what would become the German Social Democratic Party. Notes taken by police agents document the daily activities, reading habits, and correspondence of nearly forty Russian Jews who moved to Berlin between 1875 and 1878. Suspects interviewed by the police referred to the Jewish revolutionaries, and specifically Lieberman, as *socialitsischen Utopien.*[38] Berlin police were in contact with governments across Europe, sending letters to officials in London and Warsaw to help them ascertain and gain information about the students' backgrounds and whereabouts. The police reported that during their time in Berlin the émigrés seemed "far less involved in their studies and

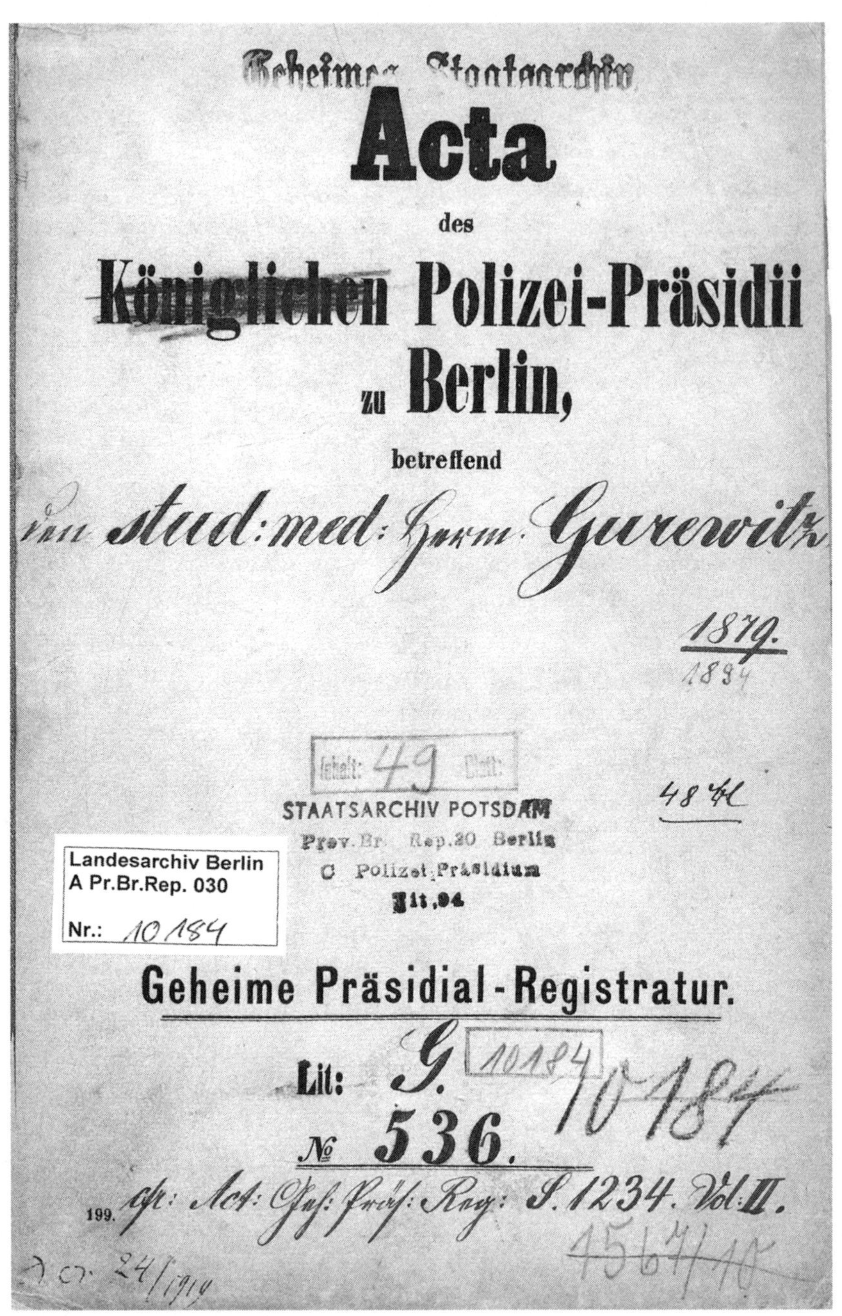

Berlin secret police records of the graduate medical student Grigory Gurevich.
(Landesarchiv Berlin, Akte A Pr. Br. Rep.030 nr. 10184. Courtesy of Landesarchiv Berlin.)

more focused on promoting socialist and nihilistic propaganda and in meeting with members of local Social-Democratic circles."[39] Agents were assigned to investigate and follow dozens of Jewish students.[40]

The Berlin group soon splintered into a number of ideological factions. Some, like Moses Aronsohn, who married the sister of Eduard Bernstein, leaned toward socialist politics; others, like Zundelevich, wanted the group to join larger Marxist revolutionary circles; some, like Lieberman, hoped to establish a Jewish Section within the International (the Revolutionary International League). It is unclear how this group operated or what connections they had to other groups within the Communist orbit. While the commune would eventually split apart, the members agreed to give financial support to Lieberman's proposal to develop a theory of Jewish socialism and spread its principles among Jewish workers.[41]

Lieberman, arguably the most brilliant, learned, and committed of the young revolutionaries, set his sights on the emerging sector of Jewish manufacturing workers residing in the East End of London. The son of a prominent Jewish reformer and the grandson of a Kabbalistically orientated rabbi, Lieberman remained torn between the world of Lithuanian learning and the revolutionary goals of Russian Marxists. He wanted to be part of both of these groups and was determined to resolve the contradictions between them. Having left his wife and children in Vilna when he fled to Berlin, he moved on to London, where he began carrying on affairs with partners of both sexes.[42] There was, however, nothing frivolous about the man. He was driven and ambitious, a perfectionist whose economy of language reflected the focus he brought to the task at hand and the careful attention he demanded from his readers. Even for revolutionaries, who lived on adrenaline and with the prospects that the next day might be their last, the abandonment with which Lieberman worked was extraordinary.

Lieberman arrived in London in 1875, finding employment as a typesetter at the print shop of Peter Lavrov's Russian revolutionary journal *Forward!* (*Vpered!*). This kept him housed and fed while he pursued his other vocation, the London Jewish Socialist Union, of which he was a founder.[43] The Union comprised roughly thirty-five individuals, whose goal was to establish a tailors union. But since many of the group's members came from Russian lands and were seen by the local Jewish population as rabble-rousers, its historical significance lies less in its tangible results, which were few, than in its introducing Jews to a new way of organizing around their economic and material needs.

Jewish socialists in Berlin, ca. 1876. (Smirnov Archive 37/69. Courtesy of the International Institute of Social History, Amsterdam.)

During his time in London, Lieberman became immersed in studying Marx's works and began composing a translation of the *Communist Manifesto*.[44] By 1876, he was telling his Jewish comrades that it was required reading. In a letter written to his friend Eliezer Zuckermann, Lieberman referred to Marx's magnum opus as "*Ha-Keren,*" indicating the ways in which "capital" functioned not only as a form of monetary value but also as both a "fund" and the "foundation" of society.[45] Both Marx and Lavrov deeply affected Lieberman. Whereas in the late 1860s, Lieberman was writing Hebrew letters to Jewish newspapers endorsing the liberal policies of Alexander II, by 1876 he was at the forefront of the intellectuals challenging the Russian government and writing articles in Russian that called for a social revolution.

Lieberman remained in close contact with budding revolutionaries in the Pale of Settlement, with whom he discussed the relationship of Marxism and Judaism. Most notably, he corresponded with the Kiev poet Judah Leib Levin, who was working on his own translation of *Capital* into Hebrew.[46] Like Lieberman, Levin had been raised in an observant home: "In my youth I studied the *Zohar* until I knew it by heart and had mastered Ḥabad Hasidic writings, until I became a Kabbalist of sorts."[47] Upon reading *Capital* in 1875, Levin began assimilating Marx's theory of the commodity form into his diagnosis of the Jews' economic situation. Jewish students attending the university in Kiev soon urged him to "compose a Hebrew translation of Marx."[48] It seems that Jewish university students in Kiev found it "very difficult to understand the first chapter of Marx's *Capital* in which he described the metamorphosis *shel seḥora* [of commodity]."[49] Even the Menshevik leader Pavel Axelrod later in life admitted that when he had first come across *Capital* in Kiev he had trouble understanding the first chapters of the book.[50] Levin's Hebrew translation of the first chapter of *Capital* in 1875 was only the third recorded translation of Marx's work, coming on the heels of the Russian (1872) and French (1872–1875) editions and preceding the English edition (1886) by eleven years.[51] "It was the Hebrew translation," Levin maintained, "that allowed [Jewish] students in Kiev to fundamentally understand Marx's ideas."[52]

However, Lieberman would go further than simply translating Marx into Hebrew and making his works accessible to new audiences. He proposed a new theory of history that merged Marx's insights with Jewish ideas. In his essay "The Development of Medieval Society," Lieberman argued that Judaism had become deformed through its encounter with European scholasticism and feudalism. The scholastics had envisioned life as dualistic, comprising the holy and profane, good and evil, the elite and the masses. Addressing both medieval Christianity and Judaism, Lieberman remarked, "The love and equality [the scholastics] promoted were only a chimera. It was a love of faith and an equality before the laws of the Lord." For Christian and Jewish scholastics, nature reflected the will of heaven; it was something fixed that expressed objective truths. The purpose of life was to conform to the laws established by the deity. "Humans, it was said, could not change Nature. Thus [for medieval Jewish thinkers], social relations were something connected to Nature itself." Lieberman explained that the laws of nature and those established by kings were based either on fate or on powers beyond people's control.[53]

Lieberman detailed the ways feudalism and scholasticism were connected through not only a shared politics but also a shared ontology and theodicy. He noted the preponderance of medieval *musar* (ethical) literature within

Jewish society and attacked Thomas Aquinas and Moses Maimonides for valorizing asceticism. In medieval society form was elevated to divine spirit; matter was base and human. Citing the Talmud and medieval Jewish sources, Lieberman argued that man was said to have created evil by acting on his will in a manner that went against God's edicts. Medieval scholastics assumed that will and desire had to be suppressed because they reflected an attempt to defy God's edicts. Humanity's desire for material things signaled a lack of belief in the divinely ordained order of the world. Lieberman asserted that feudalism politically embodied the philosophical principles informing scholasticism.[54]

According to Lieberman, human beings were assigned specific professional niches from birth. Their material condition was beyond their control. A person's station in life was based on fate, and any attempt to alter or contest social and economic structures constituted an act of sedition and a form of rebellion against the sovereign. Just as desire produced sin, individual will produced rebellion. Human assertiveness had to be suppressed. Feudalism and scholasticism had thus conspired to make human beings believe that the material situation to which they were born was not something that should concern them.

Lieberman fully grasped Marx's theory that capitalism was built on the ruins of medieval feudal regimes. According to Marx, the collapse of the feudal economy was a function of new forms of industrialization and communication. The establishment of manufacturing industries and technological advances in communication gave rise to new kinds of economic classes and labor relations. "The prelude of the revolution that laid the foundation of the capitalist mode of production," Marx wrote, "was played in the last third of the 15th, and the first decade of the 16th century." It was then that "a mass of free proletarians was hurled on the labour market by the breaking-up of the bands of feudal retainers."[55]

Specifically, Lieberman translated into Hebrew the part of chapter 27 of the French translation of *Capital* that detailed the clearing of Scottish estates and the actions taken by the duchess of Sutherland to promote capitalistic eneterprises.[56] From 1814 to 1820, the duchess removed fifteen thousand inhabitants from her land and replaced them with tenant farmers who could operate sheep farms. The clan that had at one time lived on the 794,000 acres was now relegated to 6,000 acres on the shore. "This land that had until this time lain waste, and brought in no income to their owners" was now rented "at an average rent of 2s. 6d. per acre to the clansmen, who for centuries had shed their blood for her family. The whole of the stolen clanland she divided into 29 great sheep farms, each inhabited by a single family, for the most part imported English farm-servants."[57] Lieberman's goal was not to explain the clearing of the estates per se but rather to document the demise of scholasticism's value form along with its feudal economic base structure.

Lieberman explained how just as capitalism arose from the ruins of feudalism, Protestantism and the modern Jewish reform movement were produced out of the remnants of medieval scholasticism. Scholasticism's ascetic qualities could also be found in Protestantism, which gave a religious imprimatur to ruling political elites. Lieberman identified the Jewish reform movement, or what he called "Protestants of the Mosaic Faith," as reflecting the foreign influence of capitalism and Christianity. Protestantism and the Jewish reform movement were not, however, progressive forces. Rather, like capitalism, they only confused the masses and strengthened the claims of ruling elites. Lieberman explained:

> In truth, the religious reforms have damaged the intellectual development of human beings far more than the old and weak institution of Catholicism, as we see witnessed today among the nations of the world and our Jewish brethren. . . . Among the reformers no one sought more than Calvin to bring back the crown of scholasticism. He sought to hang all human affairs on faith and he subsumed all human affairs under an entirely novel principle that was unknown to the Roman priests. God designed from the beginning the development of every person. God willed that the world would be a place of suffering and pain, and man should not complain about his fate. . . . Those who rule are the servants of God. He gave to them his honor and they take his place in the world. . . . And in the same way that Christian Protestants follow in this path so too our [Jewish] Protestants. And all those who try to reform religion according to these principles are only hurting the success and development of the nation. So too we beseech those who are enlightened in our nation: do not listen to these reformers.[58]

Long before Max Weber's studies on the religious origins of capitalism were published, Lieberman explicitly tied capitalism to Protestantism through the work of John Calvin. He argued that Protestantism affirmed the nation-state, promoted political quietism, and supported capitalistic enterprise. Lieberman's critique of "Jewish Protestants" was mirrored in his critique of Jewish capitalists. "The Jewish aristocracy is responsible for Jews being pursued up to today, especially in eastern Europe," he explained.[59]

Lieberman held up the Kabbalah as a counterepistemology to the dualistic regimes of capitalism (feudalism) and Protestantism (scholasticism). Specifically, he pointed to the Kabbalistic ideas put into circulation by the sixteenth-century Safed scholar Isaac Luria and further developed by the eighteenth-century Italian messianist Moses Hayyim Luzzatto. "As the wise one Rabbi Moses Hayyim Luzzatto explained," Lieberman wrote, "'beauty and pleasure emerge from worldly power (*malkhut*) only when worldly power is fully connected to the divine (*yesod*). But when they are misaligned the opposite is the case; privation and misery emerge.'"[60] Luzzatto adopted Luria's basic temporal scheme, which identified privation and misery as a function of historical time. Central to their system was the idea that evil and injustice were built into the very nature of the Godhead and were further revealed in the creation of the universe. Evil was not something produced by human beings or something that indirectly emanated from God but was part of God and thus ontologically conjoined with good.[61] Creation was a "cathartic" process in which God attempted to rid the world of evil and invited human beings to join in this process. Thus, instead of an elite trying to distance itself from an evil material world in order to draw closer to a pure heavenly intellectual sphere (scholasticism), all of nature, for Luria, was connected to and comprised both good and evil elements. The task of human beings was to engage and act upon the physical world and continue the process begun at Creation by fully purging the universe of evil.[62]

The political implications of Luria's Kabbalistic theory were further developed through Lieberman's rereading of Luzzatto's work, *138 Gates of Wisdom*. As I have detailed elsewhere, Lieberman's citations of Luzzatto's work were not merely a matter of scholarly integrity. Lieberman built on Luzzatto and Luria's theory of the divine by pointing to human labor as a precondition for cleansing the world of evil.[63] Lieberman adopted, with modifications, Luria and Luzzatto's theory that evil was inherent in God's nature and the creation of the universe. He used it to redefine the relationship between elites and the masses. Lieberman rejected Gnosticism and claimed that "good and evil"

> are connected together in the upper spheres and emanate from the source of Infinity and the will of that which stands above. . . . However, the evil side is not distinguished from the Godhead as it is with the Persian God Ahriman. . . . The secret of the evil side in [the Kabbalah] is that it allows people to have freedom to choose good or bad and be rewarded for every deed (mitzvah). [Because good and evil are

part of the upper spheres and nature itself] that which is good is not kept hidden for holy men [*tsadikim*] alone.[64]

By locating evil within the Godhead and the physical world, Lieberman empowered human beings with the capacity to critique social institutions and reject asceticism. If form and matter were presented as one, good and evil were part of the Godhead, and desire and will were part of nature, then asceticism was no longer a virtue or a marker of elite status. Lieberman claimed that humans, at each moment, were being given the opportunity to confront, reject, or attempt to resist institutions and laws that promoted social hierarchies, economic inequalities, and social antagonisms. These forms of evil were part of history and were established in order to give human beings the opportunity to question them and to create a new world order that promoted freedom. Humans did not need to distance themselves from social and political institutions (asceticism), but rather to change them. Labor was virtuous and held out the possibility for a full rectification of social and economic imbalances and inequities. For Lieberman, it was only a matter of time until "a prophet" would reveal himself as God's messenger responsible for punishing the wicked, fixing the *sephirot* (the elements that make up the Godhead), and transforming the social order of the world.[65] State law would be eliminated. A new society based on the principle of *hakol lakol,* "everything for the whole," would replace private property and the principle of *sheli sheli veshelkha shelakh,* "what is mine is mine and what is yours is yours."[66]

Lieberman fundamentally differed from Marx in two critical respects. First, Lieberman cryptically and somewhat homiletically broadened Marx's theory of consciousness by defining the agent connecting and motivating human beings toward action. Whereas Marx argued that consciousness began with labor, Lieberman went a step farther and asked about the agency involved in praxis. For Lieberman, human beings' impetus to move forward and attempt to attain "wholeness" was based on their hearing "the voice of God that travels within the sphere of the universe [*bekerev teiveil*] and calls out to our minds: speak to humanity and move forward!" Citing from a biblical passage (Exodus 14:15), Lieberman removed the term "the Jewish people" (*bnei yisra'el*) and instead inserted the word "humanity" (*bnei adam*). This reflected Lieberman's own attempt to see Marx's universal goals as flowing from biblical principles. Lieberman reinterpreted these biblical verses to argue that God was the force that connected human beings to nature and enabled action. God was not consciousness but rather the condition that made consciousness possible and allowed humans to change nature and develop new capacities. "We have the capacity to appropriate nature and make it work for us," Lieberman explained.[67] God provided human beings with the mechanism to conceive and alter the seemingly natural order of things.

Second, in contrast to Marx, who identified Jews as a strictly religious group, Lieberman assumed that Jews were also a historical national collective and as such would follow the internal program of all nations described in *The Communist Manifesto.* Seeing Jews as a national entity allowed Lieberman to promote the cultivation of a specifically Jewish cadre of propagandists. Jews would first develop revolutionary cells within a Jewish social sphere and then later join a larger federated Communist International that would overcome social and political distinctions. This reading of Marx's theory of propaganda would have radical political implications that would be further developed by Zionists, Bundists, and Jewish socialists at the turn of the century.

MARXISM AND JEWS

Lieberman's project was one of the first attempts to broaden Marx's theory to include the diverse nationalities and ethnicities in the Russian Empire. Up until the 1870s Marx's writing had largely been restricted to addressing the formation of capitalism in western Europe and the United States. The rise of Russian revolutionaries in the 1870s brought Marx to reconsider many of his presuppositions about oppressed minority groups who were subjects of larger empires. Lieberman's attempt to reconceive Jewish collectivity through a Marxist prism was an especially surprising development, however, considering Marx's own views on nationality and the Jews. In *The Communist Manifesto,* Marx argued that before moving on to communism people would politically organize around national entities. Each national entity would develop its own class consciousness, thus creating the conditions that would enable workers belonging to different national entities to identify with one another. Some intellectuals understood Marx as indifferent to or standing in opposition to all forms of nationalism. Others, however, maintained that he approved of the development of nationalism among oppressed minority groups, such as the Poles, seeing it as a precondition for a universal class revolution.[68] With regard to Marx's own position on the Jews, "it was clear that Jews belonged to the same class as the Czechs," as an entity that was destined to disappear.[69] Jews would slowly become entangled within larger national class struggles and lose their separate identity.

Much in the way that Marx's theories were ill-suited for understanding the development of Russian society, his theories about Jews failed to explain their material situation in the Pale of Settlement. In the 1860s and 1870s only a handful of highly acculturated Russian Jews considered themselves fully Russian.[70] Most Jews living in Russian lands still defined themselves in religious and ethnic terms. Although they might have invoked the Russian words *narod* (people) and *plemia* (tribe), or the Latin word *natio* (nation),[71] most Jews did not attribute political connotations to these terms. These terms were nearly identical to what liberal western European Jews called *Stamm,* an ethnic designation based on a shared historical religious identity.[72] The discourse of Stamm circulated among Jewish liberals across Europe. For some it involved biological definitions of Jews; for others it meant a shared identity based on culture and descent. These liberal thinkers' use of biology and history as defining elements of identity was predicated on the assumption that different races represented different moral orientations. The moral orientation of Jews, however, was one of harmony and coexistence, and Russian Jewish liberals, following their counterparts in France and Germany, embraced the concept of a Jewish *Stamm.* Tsvi Hirsch Rabinowitz, Alexander Zederbaum, Judah Leib Gordon, Eliezer Zweifel, and their cohort all invoked the concept of Jews as a people that promoted unity and tolerance within the empire and for all humanity.

Jewish materialists, most notably Lieberman and Levin (and even Lilienblum), however, roundly rejected the idea of Jews being a Stamm or of Judaism being a beacon of liberal and republican ideals. Just as proponents of Jewish Stamm defined Judaism in opposition to a materialist worldview, so the Jewish revolutionaries defined Jewish identity in opposition to the concept of a Jewish Stamm. The Jewish revolutionaries maintained that a materialist interpretation of society justified seeing Jews as a distinct socioeconomic group within the empire. Jews living in Russian lands had their own languages, professional profile, political hierarchies, and educational institutions. Lieberman put forward a theory of Jewish identity based on his own materialist reinterpretation of Jewishness. Instead of promoting cultural harmony, Lieberman asserted that Judaism was a tradition of revolution. Instead of acculturated university students, he pointed to the yeshiva students as potential leaders of a social revolution.

At the prodding of his comrades in Jewish and Russian revolutionary circles Lieberman drafted a socialist clarion call, "Shelumei baḥurei yisra'el" (To the Finest of Israel's Youth), in the hope of winning rabbinical students to the cause. Published on May 20, 1876, the pamphlet encouraged yeshiva students to stand up to government authorities, "to sacrifice themselves on the altar of the government that rules the land—to heal the nation and lead it toward progress!" According to the historian Boris Sapir, Lieberman "referred to the debt of the Jewish intelligentsia . . . and envisaged the building up of socialist cadres in the same manner as *Vpered!* [Forward!] and its editor Peter Lavrov."[73] Lieberman's pamphlet pitted yeshiva students against liberal, university-educated Russian Jews. These "so-called enlighteners," Lieberman claimed, "worshipped money and the state." At the same time, yeshiva students represented an ideal type of revolutionary, those who were willing to freely give of themselves without material longings or concerns. Lieberman beseeched yeshiva students to "draw closer to all those who work the land. For the proletariat will come together and remove kings from their seats of power." The reconciliation of these different groups through a shared class identity "would lead to a social revolution and the lifting of the red flag."[74]

Lieberman's propaganda strategy, which focused on the yeshiva students, was based on the Russian revolutionary leader Peter Lavrov's theories of the intelligentsia as well as on ideas culled from Kabbalistic literature.[75] In an article titled "The Work of Satan" ("Ma'aseh Satan," 1877), Lieberman drew on Kabbalistic metaphors to map out the path toward revolution. Lieberman cautioned that "if revolutionary activities are undertaken by those who lack the requisite knowledge [*sodot hamitsvot*] to effect radical change, they are not only doomed to failure; even worse, they could actually strengthen the current regime."[76] It was therefore necessary for the intelligentsia to educate the Jewish "proletariat" about how to conduct a socialist revolution. Lieberman justified his faith in the yeshiva students, whom he referred to as "our *Softas*" (lovers of learning), by proclaiming that they "were the only sector of the youth population that still believed in the Jewish people."[77] The respect they garnered within Jewry, Lieberman assumed, would provide them with the authority to persuade the masses to join in a social revolution.

Lieberman encouraged the yeshiva students to stand up against "the Jewish aristocracy." The latter, he maintained, were responsible for the continued oppression of Jews, "especially in eastern Europe."[78] Repeating his attacks in the pages of *Forward!* Lieberman denounced Jewish capitalist philanthropic families such as the "Gintsburgs, Poliakovs, and Warshavskys, whose interests were in opposition to those of the Jewish people."[79] He described the exploitation and unfair treatment of factory workers and the strikes springing up at tobacco factories across Lithuania.[80]

אֶל שְׁלוּמֵי בַּחוּרֵי יִשְׂרָאֵל.

Aaron Shemuel Lieberman, "To the Finest of Israel's Youth," 1876.
(Courtesy of YIVO Institute for Jewish Research)

Lieberman dismissed the philanthropists' and industrialists' efforts to reform Jewish schools and lambasted the Jewish intellectuals who supported their initiatives. Social change "could never come about through enlighteners who had attended the government schools, benefited from the philanthropy of the rich, and at every opportunity tried to distance themselves from their own people."[81] The Jewish enlighteners were not only deluded in their attempts to reform Judaism into a "liberal" religion but were stooges of the industrialists and pawns of the Russian government.[82] Jewish enlighteners shared in the blame for the abject state of Russian Jewry. As Lieberman's comrade Eliezer Zuckermann concisely explained, the enlighteners' sole interest was "to increase [their own] private property."[83]

It was the job of the yeshiva students to teach the masses the secret of capitalism: that acts of "mercy," such as philanthropy, might appear to be godly but in fact ensured the continuance of class differences, leaving the wealthy in positions of power over the poor. Lieberman offered a detailed strategy for cultivating revolutionary yeshiva students and sending them out to agitate among the masses. In a letter to Valerian Smirnov (the co-editor of *Forward!*), published on April 16, 1877, Lieberman explained, "The socialist revolution among Jews depends on . . . sending propagandists to circulate among our seminarians." These individuals should "outwardly continue to appear as full seminarians, with long coats and sidelocks"; "they must remain [so accoutered] and stay in that environment [in the yeshiva]" so that they could propagandize better. Lieberman explained to Smirnov that the covert Jewish propagandists would "agitate, upset and prepare [their] fellow seminarians to weaken and unmoor them from their Jewish foundations."[84]

Lieberman presented a violent and arresting image for the transformation of the Jewish intellectual class into revolutionaries: the yeshiva student who has become so intellectually riled up by the injustice of his condition that he liberates himself from the sacrosanct ground on which he is standing. The yeshiva student pulls himself out of his own environment and in turn creates an upheaval that revolutionizes the Jewish masses.

Lieberman readily admitted that the path from seminary to revolution was a long and arduous one. "Currently, the children of the yeshiva," he admitted, "are deeply conservative (they observe that which has been established and hate that which is new)."[85] But he saw yeshiva students as having the appropriate personality for fomenting the socialist revolution. The personal sacrifice they made to attend seminary, and the shared group bonds within it, made them ideal agents and propagandists. Thus, Lieberman was prepared "to wait for the yeshiva students. In waiting, we will better know how to instill within their hearts life concepts that will bring the nation to its fullness." Eventually, he believed, "They will transform the old ideal into a new ideal."[86] With time he hoped the yeshiva students' religious orientation would broaden to include a social worldview—instead of thinking about abstract ideals they would focus their intellectual attention to the Jews' physical conditions—and the beit midrash would become the womb of revolution.

Lieberman dreamed that the yeshiva students would ultimately bring their new philosophy to the Jewish masses and identify with the intelligentsia of the larger revolutionary movement. As his childhood friend Aaron Zundelevich explained, Lieberman believed that "the Jewish youths who had given themselves over to the study of the Talmud were a *national intelligentsia*."[87] The very group Lieberman was targeting, however, condemned his proposal. The students at the Volozhin yeshiva who read his pamphlet were terribly confused. "What is 'the red flag,' they asked; is it the little red flag that the kids play with when we celebrate Simchat Torah?"[88]

The laughter of yeshiva students offered a lighthearted counterpoint to the serious theological response by Jewish communal leaders. Most notably, Lieberman's arch-enemy, the Vilna preacher and businessman Isaac Elijah Landau (1806–1876), delivered a blistering rebuke of the Jewish revolutionaries.[89] Landau was a staunch supporter of the tsarist regime, playing an active role in government-sponsored rabbinical conferences.[90] Before moving to Vilna in 1866, he himself was a government rabbi in Kiev. He was also extremely wealthy, involved in business dealings throughout the Pale of Settlement. In 1844 his properties in the Jewish quarter of Vilna were valued at 500 rubles, a small fortune.[91]

Landau took it upon himself to publicly attack the Jewish revolutionaries.[92] Speaking at Vilna's main synagogue on April 4, 1876, Landau praised the tsar and denounced the "stupid and rebellious" youth. "Not long ago" he began, "there emerged a group of ignorant and brainless people . . . who through their pernicious books . . . sought to inspire traitorous behavior among the masses."[93] Landau depicted the Jewish revolutionaries as enemies of both God and the empire.

Tsar Alexander I, Landau proclaimed, was a messenger of God himself. "According to our Torah, one whom God appointed to lead has been graced with part of His greatness. . . . This person is holy. God placed this man on the earth to be his messenger. Those who do harm to God's appointed one, it is as though they were hurting God himself."[94] Judaism stood in opposition to free speech and any form of critique of the government. "Just as you are not permitted to think about God without an elevated state of mind, so too you should think about the tsar with an elevated state of mind," he maintained.[95]

Landau warned rabbinical students "not to associate with any people who made a schism between the fear of God and the fear of the king."[96] Citing the Bible and the Talmud he proclaimed that "the respect of the king was equivalent to the respect one shows to God." Moreover, "God made Jews swear that they would not rebel against kings." This vow would become the basis for later polemics against Zionism, but Landau employed it to support political quietism and subservience to all political leaders. He even positively cited the prophet Jeremiah's reference to Nebuchadnezzar as a servant of God (Jeremiah 27:6) without adding the Talmudic caveat that he was a messenger for evil. Irrespective of whether a king was wicked or virtuous, Landau maintained that Jews must always support the ruling power, going so far as to assert that any Jewish expression of political criticism was tantamount to a denial of God himself. As proof that Jews had always stood in opposition to revolutionary groups he recalled the rabbinic opposition to the Polish rebellion in 1831: "The Torah holds the idea of the king in such high regard that our pious ones never associated with rebels. Tsar Nicholas, may he rest in peace, after the events of 1831 issued a decree that stated that no Jew was to be involved in any organization, and he issued this statement for eternity. As the Talmud teaches us, those who take care of the king are to be treated in the same way as the king. Those who sin not only sin for themselves but also bring other people down."[97] An abridged Hebrew version of Landau's comments (originally delivered in Yiddish) was published a few weeks later in Vilna's Jewish newspaper *The Garden Land* (*Hakarmel*). There he concluded by warning parents to "watch over your sons and daughters lest they follow the advice of the wicked ones who rebel against the government."[98] The rabbi's words were clear: the yeshiva and the rabbinic intelligentsia would do everything in their power to support the state and protect the tsar as if he were God himself.

Lieberman's toughest critics, however, came from within his own revolutionary camp. The leading Yiddish writer of the 1870s, Shalom Jacob Abramowich (aka Mendele Moykher-Sforim), criticized what he saw as the elitist strategy behind Lieberman's program. The same sentiments were expressed in bold relief by Yehoshua Mordecai Lifshitz, the pioneer of Yiddish lexicography, who chastised Lieberman for being an "egoist" seeking the approval of the Jewish intelligentsia at the expense of the masses. Both attacked Lieberman for his decision to spread propaganda in Hebrew, the language of the intelligentsia, instead of Yiddish, spoken by the broader public. Writing in German but using Hebrew characters Lifshitz reminded Lieberman that "the dismissal of the living Jewish language [Yiddish] . . . is also a dismissal of the very people who speak the language. "I wager one thousand to one," Lifshitz continued, "your sharpest critics were precisely the Jewish intelligentsia that you are targeting." Instead of looking to the learned elite, Lifshitz advised Lieberman to develop a strategy for reaching the masses directly.[99]

Judah Leib Levin issued the harshest indictment of Lieberman's program. On the pages of the short-lived Yiddish newspaper *The Old Jew* (*Der alter Yisrolik*), Levin asked, "Must one write in Hebrew?"[100] Although in his Hebrew autobiography Levin dismissed critics who thought that his article signaled a shift in linguistic preferences, the two-part article viciously attacked those who continued to write in Hebrew and offered a full endorsement of Yiddish. He denounced the economic forces behind the fetishization of Hebrew as the Jews' primary language. The "old hunchback" elite profited through the sales of journals and books written in Hebrew. Those privileging Hebrew as the "holy of holies" or the "pride" of the Jewish people were like communal tax collectors, who gathered moneys to support teachers, ritual slaughterers, and rabbis.[101]

Hebrew's proponents, Levin charged, were taking resources away from the Jewish narod. "While I myself enjoy writing in Hebrew," Levin admitted, I would be an "egoist if I thought that what was in my best interest was in the best of interest of all of Israel." Levin doubted that learning Hebrew would help the masses and the poor. Although Hebrew was sweet, "like the land of Israel—a language flowing with milk and honey, Jews didn't need confections"; they needed bread and meat. Levin realized that his words would be considered scandalous by his friends, but he was prepared for their ire. "I am not a blabbermouth, who blabbers for the sake of blabbering," he asserted; "I write in order to communicate with the poor and speak to their interests."[102]

Lieberman's opponents also objected to his broader elite socialist strategy. Writing from Kiev in 1876, Levin begged Lieberman to publish more accessible articles for the Jewish masses. Living in London, Lieberman seemed tone-deaf to Russian Jews, who were only beginning to come in contact with economic forms of analysis. Using the coded language of the slaughtering business to denote the spreading of socialist propaganda, Levin asked, "If a rabbi wants to appoint slaughterers in a town whose residents do not know the first thing about slaughtering or kosher food, and he fails to explain to people what a slaughterer is and why he is needed, people will wonder, Why is this person spilling blood!" Levin beseeched Lieberman to "communicate ideas simply; just as the truth is simple and life is simple, so too the ideas must be simple. . . . You have amazing ideas, but you are not cut out to write in a popular fashion."[103]

A debate even broke out in Jewish revolutionary circles over Lieberman's strategy of targeting the Jewish intelligentsia over the masses. Levin, Zuckermann, and the Bundist leader and newspaper editor Morris Winchevsky maintained that the seeds of a socialist revolution were lying dormant within the more populist spiritual Hasidic movement.[104] Zuckermann and Winchevsky wanted to appeal to the masses, identifying the Hasidim as a Jewish underclass who retained strong communal and social consciousness. "I was the son and grandson of fervent opponents of Hasidism," explained Winchevsky. However, by 1875, he claimed, he had realized that "Hasidism expressed a kind of democratic movement within the religion." Unlike the Talmudists and yeshiva students, who looked down upon the masses and even despised them, Hasidim recognized the needs of the people. In Hasidism, Winchevsky saw "shared communal bonds and a deep contempt for the Jewish Talmudic

Morris Winchevsky. (Courtesy of the National Library of Israel, Jerusalem)

aristocracy."[105] Winchevsky would eventually immigrate to the United States and become known as the grandfather of the Jewish labor movement.

The debate between proponents of Winchevsky's populist-Hasidic tactics and those of Lieberman's Mitnagdic yeshiva-students strategy mirrored the one raging among followers of the two leading Russian revolutionaries of the 1870s, the anarchist Mikhail Bakunin (1814–1876) and the intellectual Peter Lavrov (1823–1900).[106] Originally a professor of mathematics, Lavrov was banished by the Russian government to the remote Ural Mountains for inciting revolutionary activities. In 1870 he was spirited out of Russia by his students and eventually moved to London, where he and other Russian émigrés, such as Lieberman, established *Forward!*, in which Lavrov promoted the causes of "equal rights for individuals, the struggle of the worker against the classes of his exploiters, and the struggle for free association against government compulsion."[107] Specifically, he praised the role students—as members of the intelligentsia—could play in educating the peasants to ensure the revolution would be enacted on socialist principles. The university students, were those most capable of reaching the working classes and preparing them for revolution. "Anyone looking to come close to the people with revolutionary propaganda," Lavrov maintained, "should first develop his intelligence with scientific criticism. He should enrich his thought with foundational knowledge." Lavrov was adamant on the point: "Knowledge, I repeat, is a necessary preparation for revolutionary activity."[108] Lavrov encouraged the masses to study the "laws of the composition of capital, of the formation of rents, and of the fluctuations of prices, divisions of labor, statistics, the life of the worker and his exploiter abroad, and the history of Russia."[109]

Bakunin, who had spent most of his adult life in Geneva, mocked Lavrov's heady ideals and called on his comrades to start the revolution immediately. There was no need to wait for the masses to be intellectually prepared. The peasants would figure out how best to conduct their affairs after they revolted against their oppressors. Anyone who argued that the peasantry first needed to be educated was denying the masses their freedom. What was important was the revolution itself.

The Mogilev revolutionary Grigory Gurevich pithily described the difference between the two leaders: "a long list of books" was a prerequisite for Lavrov's form of agitation; "In Lavrov's eyes, for one to be a true revolutionary socialist one would have to spend years studying in school." Bakunin, however, "laughed at Lavrov's program and said that to be a good revolutionary . . . one only needed to be capable of reading pamphlets."[110] Whereas Lavrov placed his emphasis on the use of critical reason and education, Bakunin was first and foremost focused on disturbing established political orders.

Jewish revolutionaries in the 1870s were split between Lavrov's and Bakunin's camps.[111] "We mocked Lavrov," Lev Deutsch recalled, "dismissing him as a cultural figure and not a revolutionary."[112] Deutsch's fellow Menshevik leader Pavel Axelrod had more positive recollections about the Russian professor but also noted that "Bakunin made a stronger impression as a revolutionary thinker and fighter."[113] Unlike Lavrov, whose following stemmed from the power of his intellect and his intricate theory of social and economic development, Bakunin enjoyed a popularity based less on the technical aspects of his philosophy than on the magnetism of his personality and on "the simplicity, clarity and constancy of his point of view."[114] While the Vilna group tended to be more sympathetic toward Lavrov, those from Kiev and Mogilev favored Bakunin.[115]

Lieberman applied Lavrov's theory of the intelligentsia to the yeshiva students, while Levin and Winchevsky promoted the Hasidim as the people likely to support Bakunin's call for a proletarian revolutionary movement. Both strategies, however, incorporated something that neither Lavrov, Bakunin, nor Marx was prepared to embrace: the idea that religious denominations could be interpreted not only in terms of class but also in terms of various parts of a Jewish nation.

THE LIMITS OF THEORY

As the Jewish revolutionaries debated whether to direct their energies at the masses of Hasidim or the elite intelligentsia of the yeshivot, their comrades in Russian revolutionary circles rejected the assumptions behind a materialist interpretation of Jews' life in the Pale of Settlement, both philosophically and historically denying the existence of a specifically Jewish body. Russian revolutionaries were confused and annoyed by the theoretical transformation of yeshiva students into intelligentsia and Hasidim into a proletariat. Lieberman appeared to be engaged in either a terribly disingenuous reinterpretation of Marx or an ill-fated, eccentric enterprise that was destined for failure. Even those who appreciated Lieberman's zeal and dedication to the revolutionary cause were confused. Did such strategies suggest a materialist interpretation of society or a covert form of nationalism? How did Marx become a theorist for a Jewish nation? These questions seem to have been posed to Lieberman as early as 1876 by Valerian Smirnov (1849–1900).

Smirnov believed that Lieberman and his followers were using Marxism to invent a Jewish national entity. Married to the Vilna-born revolutionary Rosalya (Rozalija) Idelsohn, Smirnov was acutely aware of the liminal situation of Jews living in the Pale of Settlement. Upon hearing of Lieberman's plans to publish a Hebrew socialist newspaper in Vienna, Smirnov queried, "Why is a Jewish idea different from any other idea?" Lieberman responded to Smirnov by accusing him of not understanding the materialist assumptions behind the spreading of propaganda and ignoring the Jews' living conditions. In a letter dated November 23, 1876, a sarcastic Lieberman apologized, "I have sinned terribly, for I was unable to find any hint of nationalism in German, French, or English socialist publications."[116] Smirnov, argued Lieberman, was applying a double standard to Jews. The French could write in French and conduct a class-based critique of the religious elements of French society, but Jews were prohibited from writing in Hebrew and examining their social makeup in terms of labor relations and class.

The ideological division between Lieberman and Smirnov went to the heart of how to define class among oppressed and discriminated peoples. "Why do you consider me to be engaged in promoting nationalism" Lieberman asked Smirnov, "when all I want to do is produce a socialist newspaper in a language read by nearly 4 million Russian inhabitants?" Lieberman argued that addressing his readers in Hebrew did not indicate a nationalist orientation. For all intents and purposes, Lieberman was prepared to declare, "I hate Judaism in the same way I hate all 'isms.'" He conceded that if in fact he was promoting "the idea of the synagogue ruling over the church or the restoration of Palestine as a Jewish homeland" (an idea that had already begun to percolate in the Anglo-Jewish press), Smirnov's accusation would have had validity. But such was patently not the case. Asserting a Jewish collective, Lieberman claimed, was part of a program to end discrimination against all oppressed peoples.[117]

For Lieberman, the printing of a Hebrew newspaper did not indicate a love of all Jews, or a love for all humanity, but rather, "only those people who were oppressed or who identified with the socialist cause." Furthermore, he averred that he had never spoken of Judaism as "being exceptional in terms of its religious and historical aspects and also never in terms of any racial superiority." His focus on Jews was based on a Marxist materialist critique of society that "recognized only peoples and classes."[118] Lieberman's identification of a Marxist program with all oppressed groups and not only the classes that followed a certain western European historical pattern reflects one of the first attempts to revise Marxist thought in light of the specific material conditions of groups in the Russian Empire.

Lieberman observed that Jews were a distinct entity within Russia who had their own languages, social hierarchies, economic structures, and communal institutions. What Smirnov saw as simply religious institutions and denominations Lieberman translated into socioeconomic categories. Jews were not *inherently* different from other people—just as someone who was born in Russia was not *inherently* different from someone born in Germany. But *practically*, Russian Jews' material situation was unique and needed to be addressed accordingly. Thus, he informed Smirnov, "I don't subscribe to a particular nationality, but only to the moral position of those who reside in a territory, according to the place I have been born. For this is the land I know best and whose interests I can best explain." In effect, Lieberman was arguing that national identity was not something that could be abstractly conferred upon a group but had to be based on local and regional factors. Insulted by the charges brought against him, Lieberman asked Smirnov point-blank, "Have you forgotten what I wrote about in the press [*Forward!*]?"[119]

Lieberman's vision of Jewish life in the Pale highlighted the limits of Marx's western European–centric theory of communism. In this regard Lieberman, along with his mentor Peter Lavrov, was among the first to reconceive Marx's theory of revolution through the various populations residing in the Russian Empire. Both men emphasized that to spread propaganda, the propagandists needed to choose a language and identify distinct populations that did not always neatly map onto the historical-national boundaries as originally conceived of by Marx. Lieberman's answer to this problem reflected Lavrov's more general positions and his ongoing conversations with Marx in the 1870s over the status of oppressed groups in the Russian Empire. Lavrov insisted that nations did not contain essential characteristics; at any given moment a group could adopt an idea it had once discredited or that had subsequently been associated with another nation. The two possible exceptions to this rule, Lavrov acknowledged, were the racial homogeneity of the Germans and the shared historical tradition of the Jews. He dismissed the former because "even among the Germans it was easy to find racial diversity," while regarding the Jews he wondered, "Can one really for a moment suppose that the prophets of the time of the first fall of Jerusalem, the medieval Kabbalists, Talmudists, and translators of Averroës, and the contemporaries of Heine, Rothschild, and Meyerbeer, have all represented the same idea in history?"[120] Lavrov considered nations to be no more than composites of individuals;

"national" ideas were simply the beliefs of people living in a specific moment in time under certain economic conditions.

Lieberman and Lavrov believed that nations would also ultimately dissolve in the face of a socialist revolution. However, unlike religion, which Lavrov outright rejected, he conceded that in the short term, "nationalism was a perfectly legitimate principle."[121] In Lavrov's mission statement for *Forward!* he argued that "nationalities represent existing and real foundations for every social process." Thus, for those promoting socialism, "It is necessary to act in a given location, in a society speaking in a given language, developing within a given culture." Lavrov believed that socialism should be promoted in "various locations, and among various nationalities. Depending on the locale," the tactics used "might be different; thus, each nation should perform its own task." Lavrov warned that if national differences were not taken into account in the promotion of socialist propaganda, "then the goal of social activity will have only abstract significance and will not be realized."[122] In other words, a strict materialist conception of life required recognizing the differences among various populations.

The materialist argument for a Jewish national identity was first put forward in January 1876 in a charter drafted by Lieberman for a newly established Vilna socialist reading cell. It proclaimed, "National and cultural conditions . . . are of course temporary and currently produce some differences in means of action depending upon the locality and nationality. It is this that inspires us to adopt the name of the Jewish section of the Russian social revolutionary party."[123] The charter addressed only people who "were residents of this region: Lithuania, Poland, Ukraine, Bessarabia, and the Caucasus."[124] Residents outside the region should not consider themselves part of a Jewish nationality but rather join the ranks of the Russian socialist movement. Thus the charter demanded that

Anyone who is transferred to a locality where socialists speak a different language or belong to a different nationality—any socialist who finds himself in that situation—will be obligated to follow the socialist section there, without singling himself out as a Jew. Especially for Russia, those who find themselves outside of the western region will devote their strength to acting among the Russians and along with them working toward the social revolution in Russia. Only while we are in the place of the necessity of propaganda and agitation among the Jews in their particular dialect, given their particular cultural foundations, do we intend to begin organizing forces specifically directed to the activity in this particular environment.[125]

Their "nation" was not based on an ontological notion of "the Jewish people," a transhistorical "Jewish Geist," or an ethnic concept of a "Jüdische Stamm" but rather predicated on the material differences of Jews who lived in the Pale.

Other groups living in Russian lands were also at the forefront of using Marx's materialist theories to formulate their own theories of nationality. The Ukrainian socialist leaders Mykhailo Dragomanov, Antin Liakhotsky (Kuzma), and Mykhailo Pavlyk supported the materialist argument for a Jewish collective in the context of their own struggle for national recognition. Marx no more considered the Ukrainians a historic people than he did the Jews. Originally, Marx maintained that Ukrainians should be represented in the International League under a Polish banner. Just as the Jews were to be subsumed under other national headings, the Ukrainians would be assimilated into other entities. In the case of Jews, however, the matter was even more complicated. They were geographically dispersed, with communities spread across Europe, North Africa, the Middle East, and America. Jews living in one region often disagreed with those living elsewhere regarding what constituted Jewish identity. In addition, although in some places, such as Germany, it would be possible to say that the Jews saw themselves primarily as part of a religion, it was still unclear whether Jews living in the Pale considered themselves a religion, a nation, or an ethnicity.[126]

In 1875 Dragomanov was already declaring that based on their unique material situation, Ukrainians and Jews should be treated as distinct collectives. Dragomanov and other Ukrainian socialists were in contact with Jewish revolutionaries.[127] Dragomanov appointed Khasia Shur to correspond in Hebrew with Jews residing in Lvov.[128] On July 15, 1880, Dragomanov, Liakhotsky, and Pavlyk signed a document written by Eliezer Zuckermann (who worked as typesetter for Lieberman's *The Truth* (*Ha'emet*) and Dragomanov's journal *Community* (*Hromada*), asserting that Jews were a nation that needed to be specifically approached as such by revolutionary propagandists.[129] The document recognized the profound material differences between Jews living in western and eastern Europe, and the way in which those differences had led to a different political dynamic. "In Russia and in the regions of Austria and Romania," the signers noted, "Jews numerically, culturally, linguistically were different from Jews who live in other regions."[130] They then offered a material argument for why Jews in Russia constituted a distinct national entity. "France has no more than 56,000 Jewish people; England has no more than

50,000, and in Italy there are barely 45,000." In those places, "Jews are nearly completely assimilated with the local populations." However, "due to peculiar historical reasons in eastern Europe, Jews constitute a single isolated and closely bonded mass, numerically greater than 4 million differentiated from the local nations by their worldview and peculiarities of their daily life."[131] Following Lieberman, Zuckermann and Dragomanov maintained that the socioeconomic conditions of the Pale had produced an autonomous Jewish nation.

In the 1880 document, Dragomanov and Zuckermann asserted, however, that socialist propagandists needed to address Jews in the language they spoke: Yiddish. "As socialists," the authors declared, "we are not concerned if a language is ugly-sounding or rough; it would be impractical to ignore a population of 4 million just because its language is not graced by classical virtues." The use of Yiddish would allow revolutionaries to target two sectors of the population: "the intelligentsia" and "the Jewish trade worker."[132] Finally, citing the deliberations at the Geneva Congress of the International League in 1866, the document declared that "it was time to attract the mass of the working Jews to the task of social revolution."[133] Suffice it to say, the Ukrainian-Jewish proposals met with stiff resistance. Not only did other Ukrainian and Russian socialists reject its goals and assumptions but Jewish assimilationists such as Lev Deutsch scoffed at both Jews and the Ukrainians for using the guise of a materialist analysis of society to promote nationalism.[134]

Jews' reception of Marx in the 1870s ran in two distinct directions, both of which led to a variety of political and intellectual movements in the early twentieth century. On one hand, Judaism was understood as a messianic tradition that would inaugurate a new social and economic order. The Jewish revolutionaries' assumption that biblical and Kabbalistic traditions illuminated Marx's theories reveal how the Bible and the Kabbalah were reconceived in modernity to reflect a universal revolutionary political program and an economic theory of equality. On the other hand, Marx's theory of revolution also led to a new particular national Jewish identity as well as to other national identities of oppressed groups in Russian lands. Jews could now be described in terms of their labor profile and economic hierarchies. Levin and Lieberman's propaganda strategy would eventually come to define the heady and intellectual character of the Jewish labor movement and various Marxist Zionist groups. Jews who early in their lives called themselves Hasidim or Mitnagdim would come to define themselves in labor terms and as members of a distinct and particular national-economic entity. Just as Judaism had

פּובֿליק-מיטינג
פיר אידישע ארבייטער.

עס איז בעקאַננט, אז דיא ארבייטער בעפינדען זיך אומעטום
אין איין טרויריגע לאַגע און זייער שׁוֵוער קומט זיי אָן צוא פֿערדיענען
זייער שטיקֿל ברויט. אָבער וויא שׁוֵוער עס איז אויך דער לעבען פון
אַללֵע ארבייטער, ווערט דער אידישע ארבייטער ווייט מעהר פֿארשׁוֵוארצט
אלס אללע איבריגע, און בפֿרט נאַך היער אין לאנדאַן. דער איד מוז
מעהר שׁטונדען ארבייטען אין בעקומט וועניגער בעצאַהלט אלס דער קריסט.

אין וואַרום איזט עס זא ? וֵוייל דיא אידישע ארבייטער זיינען
ניט אזוי פֿעראיינינט אונטער זיך וויא אללע אנדערע, דיא קריסטליכע
ארבייטער זיינען פֿעראיינינט צוא געזעללשאפֿטען. היער אין ענגלאנד איז
דא דיא טראַדעס יוניאַנס, איין פֿעראיין פון טויזענדע ארבייטער
געזעללשאפֿטען פון פֿערשׁיעדענע פֿאַרפֿעססיאַנען, וואס זייא האַלטען זיך
אללע פֿעסט צוזאַממען און לאָזין זיך ניט אונטערדריקקען פון זייערע
פאַבריקאַנטען און מייסטער ; אָבער ביי א אונזערע אידישע ארבייטער איז
ניטא קיין אחדות, דעריבער קענינען דיא מייסטער אונז דריקקען וויא זייא
ווֵוללען.   פֿון אונזער אונאיינינקייט ליידען מיר אלליין און לאָדען נאָך אויך
זיך דעם האַסם פון דיא ענגלישע ארבייטער וואס בעשׁולדיגען אונז, אז
דורך דעם וואס מיר ארבייטען מעהר צייט און פֿאַר וועניגער לאָהן בֿנהוען
מיר זייא אויך אין שׁאַדען.

דארום רופֿען מיר צוזאַממען אינע אפֿפֿענטליכע פֿערזאַממלונג און
לאָדען האפֿפֿליכסט דאַצו אין יעדען אידישען האַנדווערקס-
געזעלל, אום צוזאַממען ראַמה צוא האַלטען וויא צוא פֿערבעסטערן דיא
לאַגע פון אונזערע אידישע ארבייטער און צוא בילדען אין געזעללשאפֿט
פֿון אללערליי האַנדווערקער. מיר האַפֿֿען, אז יעדער ארבייטער, וואס זיין
איינענעס אינטערעססע איז איהם טהייער, וועט נעהמען אנטהייל אן דעם
מיטינג. — איינינע מיטגליעדער פֿון אונזער פֿעראיין וועלן האַלטען רעדען
איבער דיא ארבייטער-אינטערעסטען און יעדעם ארבייטער וועט שׁטיין פֿריי
אויסצושׁפרעכען זיין מיינונג אפֿפֿענטליך אין דער פֿערזאַממלונג.

דער מיטינג וועט זיין אור ליים ז' אלול ה' תרל״ו —
(26) אויגוסט (1876) שבת צוא־נאַכט אום אכט אֿחר אין
זֵעטלאַנד האַלל, 51 מאַנסעלל סטריט, גודמאַן'ס פֿיעלדס, E. (ביי
אלי׳ ווילנער).
                אגדת הסאָציאַליסטהים העברים.

A PUBLIC MEETING
OF JEWISH WORKING MEN,
WILL BE HELD AT
ZETLAND HALL, 51, MANSELL ST., GOODMAN'S FIELDS, E.,
On Saturday August 26, 1876, at 8 o'clock in the Evening.

Yiddish poster for a meeting of the London Socialist Union, August 26, 1876. (Smirnov Archive 156. Courtesy of the International Institute of Social History, Amsterdam.)

been reformulated in Marxian terms of equality and revolution, Jews would see themselves as part of a collective with its own class structures. Perhaps alluding to the possibility of Jewish nationalism being a side effect of Marxism, Salo W. Baron noted the irony of the Russian revolutionaries who "in order to bring communist literature to their most backward subjects . . . laid the foundations for many a new national movement."[135]

CHAPTER 5

The Materialization of Spirit

A most unusual conduit brought practical materialism to Russian Jews in the 1870s. Without the forefather of Cultural Zionism, Peretz Smolenskin, it is unclear what role—if any—Lieberman and Zuckermann would have played in the course of Jewish history. Raised in Lithuanian territory, the charismatic Smolenskin spent his youth dueling with rabbis in yeshivot, mocking Hasidic leaders, and unmasking charlatans who preyed on the poor. He understood the struggles of students who toiled in study houses as well as the laughter of those who enjoyed the finer things in life. After wandering about the colorful religious terrain of the Pale of Settlement, this Jewish David Copperfield made his way to Prague and Berlin, developing contacts among central and western European Jewish leaders. Finally, in 1868 he crossed the border into Austria and arrived in Vienna hungry for employment, still looking for a spouse and a cause toward which to direct his energies.

The handsome, mustached bachelor soon ingratiated himself with a handful of Jewish elites, who supported his initiative to launch a Hebrew broadsheet. Published in a city that lay on the boundary between eastern and western Europe, Smolenskin's *The Dawn* (*Hashaḥar*) would become the leading Jewish nationalist newspaper. Although the paper's editorial stance did not favor Jewish statehood, territorial ambitions, or specific political policies, it did view Jews as a historic people and a defined collective. By the late

1870s Smolenskin's newspaper had become the mouthpiece for the various conflicting currents in European Jewish life: its nationalist editorial line did not fit neatly into any of the denominational, confessional, or establishment ideological boxes. It crossed geographic and religious boundaries, demonizing anything that threatened the unity of the Jewish people. Smolenskin and his paper would be celebrated in Zionist historiography as the means by which a Jewish national ethos was first propounded and disseminated.

Smolenskin's newspaper exemplifies the kind of national project described by Benedict Anderson in his *Imagined Communities*. According to Anderson, the materialistic concept of the nation was formulated and consolidated around the circulation of printed words in eighteenth- and nineteenth-century Europe. Nations were made up less of established collective entities than of new reading coalitions and the construction of ethnic identities that consolidated history into a coherent narrative. "The lexicographic revolution in Europe," Anderson explained, "created, and gradually spread, the conviction that languages (in Europe at least) were, so to speak, the personal property of quite specific groups—their daily speakers and readers—and moreover that these groups, imagined as communities, were entitled to their autonomous place in a fraternity of equals."[1]

For Smolenskin a shared lexicography was essential to developing the idea of a Jewish public, people with similar interests and concerns who lived apart but acted in concert. This Jewish public could be seen as a genuine body even if it existed only in theory. As anonymous as the bodies that lie in the tombs of the Unknown Soldier, this Jewish body would become the basis for constructing a national entity. The newspaper devoted its resources and cultural capital to conjure an idea of Israel for which Jews would be willing to sacrifice their lives. Most of Smolenskin's readers across eastern and western Europe had never met; they had not voted for the same elected officials; and they might have even fought on opposite sides in European wars and various political battles. But Smolenskin's broadsheet unified these individuals through the idea that Jews as a people had a shared set of needs and concerns and that Hebrew was their national language.

As paradoxical as it might seem today, Smolenskin's closest allies in the 1870s were members of Aaron Shemuel Lieberman's Marxist camp. While most histories of Jewish nationalism stress the ideological differences between Cultural Zionists and Jewish Marxists, I shall argue that the founding principles of Cultural Zionism advanced by Smolenskin were shaped and molded by the practical materialism advanced by Lieberman and his Marxist circle. In

1875 Smolenskin invited Lieberman to join his printing operation in Vienna and publish the first Jewish socialist newspaper, *The Truth* (*Ha'emet*). Smolenskin's connection to Lieberman embodies the complex architectonics that went into the building of cultural nationalism. Though appealing to ancient ideas, cultural forms of nationalism often piggybacked on modern movements inspired by calls for economic equality, spiritually appropriating and culturally particularizing the resources practical materialists were attempting to wrest away from discriminatory and oppressive political regimes.

Smolenskin opened his broadsheet to Jewish materialists of all kinds and his printing press to Jewish Marxists. He welcomed Lieberman under a national Jewish banner. But not too long afterward the two men began competing with each other, and Smolenskin grew concerned about the political and social repercussions of Lieberman's ties to the Russian revolutionary parties. The more Jewish materialists insisted that Jewish questions ought to be addressed by focusing on the Jews' economic standing and scientific theories about nature, the more Smolenskin asserted that Judaism was based on a philosophical notion of *Geist*. Tensions between these parties would come to a head in 1880 with a debate over the relationship of Jewish nationalism to the Jews' physical well-being. The dispute involved Smolenskin, the future founder of the first Zionist umbrella group, Moses Lilienblum, and Eliezer Ben-Yehuda, the father of modern Hebrew.

THE POLITICS OF A VIENNESE PRINT SHOP

Many scholars have wondered why, as one Yiddish writer observed long ago, the first Jewish socialists "would find no other platform from which to promote their agenda than Smolenskin's journal *The Dawn*, the flaming torch of not only an abstract but a real form of Jewish nationalism."[2] Smolenskin is best known for promoting what he called *ru'ah le'umi*, "national spirit," or in the German that Smolenskin and his colleagues all read, national Geist. He staunchly opposed materialist brands of socialism and was said never to have set eyes on a word written by Marx or Proudhon.[3] At the same time, his closest professional associates in the 1870s identified themselves as socialists, Marxists, or materialists. These biographical contradictions reflect the mixed composition of late-nineteenth-century cultural nationalism.

Smolenskin's partnership with the materialists would come to play a formative role in the shaping of his worldview. It began, however, as a sensible business decision. Smolenskin was a poor immigrant from the Pale whose

Portrait of Peretz
Smolenskin by his son
Albert Smolenskin.
(*Ost und West* [1901])

knowledge of German was never strong enough to allow him to take part in
Austrian intellectual or political life. His greatest strength was his capacity to
understand the tastes, concerns, fears, and hopes of Jews. He was especially
attentive to the changing views of his Jewish readers, who were increasingly
drawn to media addressing their economic concerns, new technological advancements, and developments in medical science. Despite the controversy
surrounding such issues in the 1860s, by the late 1870s an empirical and scientific worldview was seeping into Russian Jewish life through popular Hebrew
novels, Yiddish newspapers, and translations of German and French scientific
works.

By the end of the 1870s many fully developed theories of Judaism as a
materialistic religion had emerged. Most notably, Smolenskin had published
the young Slutsk physician Salomon Shachne Simchowitz's widely circulated
and hotly debated *Der Positivismus in Mosaismus: erläutert und entwickelt auf
Grund der alten und mittelalterlichen philosophischen Literatur der Hebräer*
(Positivism in Mosaism: Discussed and Developed on the Basis of Hebraic

Aaron Shemuel Lieberman, ca. 1876 (Smirnov Archive 37/28. Courtesy of the International Institute of Social History, Amsterdam.)

Ancient and Medieval Literature), in which he refuted "the common mis-conception" that Judaism should be considered an "idealistic," a "transcen-dental," or a "supernatural" religion.[4] As the scholar Joakim Philipson notes, the "positivism that Simchowitz claims to be the essence of Mosaic Judaism is little more than a common materialist empiricism, clothed partly in religious disguise."[5] Simchowitz, who died shortly after the publication of his work, argued that Judaism incorporated a belief in the eternality of matter that co-hered with Ludwig Büchner's scientific materialism.[6] "Soul and life could not be understood in any other state than through body and matter."[7] God was an entity developed through humanity's knowledge of nature. For the Jewish intelligentsia, the line between Judaism and materialism was growing thinner, with God and the natural world progressively moving closer to one another.

Even banned Russian nihilist literature was making its way into local Jewish libraries, as one-time opponents of nihilism now embraced many of its positions as their own. Perhaps the earliest and most well respected detractor of the nihilists of the 1860s, the novelist Shalom Jacob Abramowich, was now promoting the positions of his one-time adversary Abraham Uri Kovner.[8] Whereas in 1866 Abramowich had heaped scorn upon Jewish writers who lifted "stupid stories from [Chernyshevsky's journal] *The Contemporary* [*Sovremennik*]," by the end of 1870s he was asserting that literature had to be written for the sake of the people and not for abstract notions of beauty. Following Turgenev, he renamed one of his books *Fathers and Sons* and wrote articles with the same title as that of the novel he at one time denounced for its frivolity, *What Is to Be Done?*[9]

The onetime editor of *Voice of the Herald* (*Kol mevaser*), Moses Lilienblum, had moved even farther toward the positions advanced by Lieberman's circle. "Every aspect of a national identity is only based on chance or convention," he now claimed. "It is against my will that I will be a Jew until the day I die. That the laws of our country [Russia] prevent the impoverished of Israel from studying the natural sciences deprives Jews of the hope of obtaining bread."[10] Lilienblum materially distinguished Russian Jews from those who lived in western Europe. "Regarding Jews who live in Germany and other enlightened lands, questions pertaining to life are not Jewish questions. Rather, they are general questions that pertain to the entire country in which they [Jews] participate alongside numerous other scholars trying to understand such matters. However, in such dark lands in which Jews have not received the same benefits of enlightenment, questions pertaining to life regarding the Jews are particular questions and have nothing to do with the general question pertaining to those who live in those lands."[11] In other words, Jews in Russian territory were not to be considered human beings, as they were politically considered in western European countries. For Lilienblum, Jews represented a defined political body. By 1879, Lilienblum was arguing in Russian newspapers that it was necessary "to transform the Russian Jewish proletariat into craftsmen and farmers and to raise the general level of intellectual and moral development." Appropriating Peter Lavrov's theory of the debt that intellectuals owed the folk, Lilienblum told Russia's Jewish youth, "All of this constitutes your direct obligation and debt [*dolg*]."[12] The debt Lilienblum was speaking about was not toward the Russian people but rather to a Jewish collective.

By the end of the 1870s the impact of *Voice of the Herald* on Jewish youth, especially women who could read Yiddish (but not necessarily Hebrew), was becoming manifest.[13] The revolutionary Henne Helfman explained that the newspaper generated heated debates within her hometown of Berdichev, setting family members against one another.[14] In 1881 Helfman became a cause célèbre for her role in the assassination of Alexander II, for which she was sentenced to death in the Trial of the Fifty. In the 1870s, however, Helfman was writing articles for Yiddish newspapers in which she described Jewish parents chastising their sons and daughters for "fearing neither God nor the devil."[15] Recalling the upbringing her children and their generation received, the perceptive memoirist from the period Pauline Wengeroff noted that they were raised on an entirely new set of household words. These included *nihilism, materialism, assimilation, anti-Semitism,* and *decadence*.[16] By 1879 there would be new Jewish revolutionary groups in Saint Petersburg, and only two years later the first Yiddish labor newspaper appeared in the capital city.[17]

The growing acceptance of social and scientific materialist positions, and even Marxist theories, for understanding the nature of Judaism and evaluating the status of Jews was not lost on Smolenskin. Since 1868 he had been editing his floundering Hebrew newspaper *The Dawn* from Georg Brög's print shop in Vienna. In the early 1870s it was still struggling financially—in 1872 it had only one subscriber in the entire town of Mogilev (home to a deeply religious older population as well as a large number of young radicals).[18] But in 1873, Smolenskin began printing articles espousing positions found in the work of Marx, Darwin, and Chernyshevsky, and the paper's fortunes soon turned.[19] The increased revenues could not have come at a better time. Peretz's romantic dalliances were costing him a pretty penny.[20]

In the early 1870s Smolenskin published materialistic poems and articles by Judah Leib Kantor and Mordecai ben-Hillel Hacohen. In 1874 Smolenskin ran Kantor's "We Are Believers" (Ma'aminim anaḥnu), a forceful poem contesting the popular claim that Jewish materialists were atheists. "This is a lie," Kantor declared; "we are believers." We believe that "human beings will no longer work in a disgraceful manner, that the forces of nature will become a means of procurement, and that people will know their own worth."[21] And he published Hacohen's essays in which it was asserted that "there was no happening on this earth that was the result of Geist [*ru'aḥ*]. . . . In the case of the Jews, the reforming of religion would never change their material condition. . . . For life itself gathers forces that produce changes in the laws governing human beings."[22] Inspired by Smolenskin, Hacohen would eventually immigrate to Palestine, where he was one of the founders of the city of Tel Aviv and played a leading role in various Zionist organizations.

More important, Smolenskin published the first Hebrew exposition of both Darwin's theory of natural selection and Marx's theory of capitalism. Smolenskin provided a platform for the leading expositor of Marxism among Jews living in the Pale of Settlement in the late 1870s, Judah Leib Levin. Smolenskin first began publishing Levin's work while the latter was under the influence of the classical economists David Ricardo and Adam Smith. In his essay-poem "Slave of Slaves" ('Eved 'Avadim) Levin applied Ricardo's theory that value was a reflection of labor costs to address social imbalances. For a Jewish audience, he translated the Talmudic phrase *kol de'alim gvar* (the strongest prevails) with reference to Smith's notion that self-interest is an instrument for stimulating collective economic growth. However, even in "Slave of Slaves," Levin expressed skepticism about the explanatory capacity of reigning political economic theories. Addressing Smith's and Ricardo's proposals, he remarked: "When I look around and see the thousands of lost and downtrodden workers starving and thirsty . . . it is funny to hear that [Smith and Ricardo] think they will be strengthened. Only a minority of individuals will be empowered."[23] Levin would find an answer to his critique of Smith and Ricardo in the writings of Karl Marx.

In 1875 Smolenskin published Levin's four-part, sixty-page *poema* (narrative poem) that applied Marx's historical materialism to the situation of Russian Jewish society. In the poema, "Capacity of Praxis" (Kishron hama'aseh), Levin posited that behind the "poor man, without food or clothes," stood a system of capitalism "as wide and deep as the ocean—to which all waves flow and [it] is still never satiated." Levin's metaphor of the ocean echoed Marx's *Kapitalistenheißhunger,* which expressed the view that capitalism (rather than the philanthropist capitalist or well-meaning industrialist) was the source of the social imbalances. Implicit in Levin's argument was that only a radical transformation of reigning social-economic orders could improve the material condition of Jews in the Pale of Settlement. Simply targeting Jewish merchants or industrialists, or promoting Jewish economic diversification or education, could not solve the Jews' economic woes. Levin noted the way governments and bankers priced commodities according to their exchange value and "reduced them to paper alone." But he did not direct his ire at the

Judah Leib Levin,
ca. 1910. (Courtesy of
the National Library of
Israel, Jerusalem)

bankers or industrialists themselves, perhaps because he worked for one, but more probably because he agreed with Marx's own indictment of the system. Levin's poema was the first sustained Jewish treatment of Marx's works published in Hebrew. It captured the deep critical orientation of Marx's dialectic and refrained from offering any form of messianic or utopian solution.[24]

Years later, Levin accounted for the differences between "Slaves of Slaves" and "Capacity of Praxis" by noting the influence exerted by Marx's theory of value and the commodity form on his own worldview. In contrast to the embryonic critique issued against Ricardo and Smith in "Slave of Slaves," in the "Capacity of Praxis," he wrote, "I was explaining how the banker's capital is only in bills and contracts. . . . In all his acquired wealth one will not find even a loaf of bread. The point is clear: even though the laborer produces bread, it is not he who determines its price in the marketplace. The exchange value [*lehotsi'am lashuk betor sekhora*]," Levin translated into Hebrew, "is determined by the promissory notes of the millionaire."[25] Levin made the case that Marx's theory of the abstraction of commodity explained the discrepancy between exchange value and labor wages that he and so many other young Jews in the Russian Empire were beginning to see as unjust.

Smolenskin was buoyed by the growing interest in the articles written by the Jewish materialists. In 1874 he boasted to Aaron Shemuel Lieberman that *The Dawn* had eight hundred subscribers in the Russian Empire alone, drawing its readership from diverse sectors of society.[26] Never one for understatement, Smolenskin used his exaggerations and embellishment as a form of self-promotion and good salesmanship. While Smolenskin's correspondence with his distributors suggests a more modest number of subscribers—according to one count there were only thirty-six subscribers in Vilna and fifteen in Grodno[27]—they too were of the opinion that "*The Dawn* was on the rise."[28]

Smolenskin's chief distributor urged his employees to "pay close attention to the articles that were being published in *The Dawn,* and read the piece 'Vision of Everything' by my friend Aaron Shemuel Lieberman. Make sure to read it two or three times. Trust me, you will enjoy it very much."[29] He also encouraged them to befriend Levin, whom he considered "wise beyond praise."[30]

Smolenskin's editorial decision to publish the materialists brought criticism from some intellectual quarters. Still, he defended Levin against detractors. "Your critics," he privately wrote to Levin, "don't have the intellectual capacity to understand the value of your writing. . . . Don't be concerned, continue to pen articles and reveal the truth."[31] Smolenskin even requested that Levin move beyond poetry, which Levin claimed warmed Smolenskin's heart, and send him "prose articles on economic theory [*torat ekonomya*]."[32] Smolenskin objected to the Kiev poet's "lack of attention to specifically Jewish matters," but he still told Levin that he considered the path he had adopted "as also glorious for Israel."[33]

In the early 1870s it is unclear where Smolenskin personally stood on the issue of materialism and how it related to Jews. In 1867, the same year that *Capital* first appeared in German, he published a small tract on "why money is now the cause for all action," in which he detailed the ways human history was driven by the accumulation of wealth and capital.[34] His early writings about Jews and Judaism, however, place greater weight on ideas as the prime mover of history. Furthermore, he seems not to have fully grasped the point of Levin's translation of Marx's historical materialism. He incorrectly translated Levin's "Capacity of Praxis" into the German "Arbeit und Lohn" (Work and Wages), which suggests that he might not have fully understood what he was publishing. That said, it was clear that his newspaper's readership was growing and there was a demand for writers who were penning articles on the issue of Jewish economics and science.

Over the course of the 1870s Smolenskin was increasingly forced to confront the material imbalances facing Jews in various lands. In 1874 he was invited by the Jewish French international charity organization Alliance Israélite Universelle to lead a fact-finding mission to Jewish communities in Romania that had been ravaged by pogroms. Smolenskin spent three months visiting Jewish leaders in Bucharest and Iasi and obtaining information on the living conditions of Romania's Jewish populations. In his reports he focused on the need to build new Jewish schools but also indicated that the chief problems facing Romanian Jews could not be remedied by the French philanthropists. He explicitly addressed the staggering unemployment numbers and material problems facing Romania's Jews and asserted that no charity was capable of alleviating them. Furthermore, it was the business of the state and not Jewish leaders to tackle the issue of Jewish unemployment. Smolenskin recognized that their material difficulties were the most pressing problem for Romania's Jewish population, but currently he could address only their spiritual and intellectual welfare.[35] Smolenskin called for the state to take a more active role in addressing the economic conditions of the Jews.

It is thus not surprising that Smolenskin invited Lieberman to Vienna to publish a new newspaper, *The Truth,* that had an economic-materialist orientation. The lack of government oversight or censorship in Vienna allowed Smolenskin to print the works of the Jewish materialists without fear of political retribution.[36] He sent copies of the newspaper into Russia in the guise of a book (sending one per year), a procedure that enabled him to avoid the highly conservative Russian newspaper censors (but makes it difficult for later historians to know exactly when an article was written). With the support of Jewish revolutionaries in Berlin, most notably Grigory Gurevich, Lieberman was able to procure 100 rubles for printing costs.[37] While Gurevich, who at the time was a member of the Russian Section of the International League in Berlin, noted his "dissatisfaction" with certain aspects of Lieberman's work as well as with Smolenskin's editorial policies, he was prepared to support his friend's publication.

The year 1876 seemed like an auspicious time to begin propagandizing among Russia's Jewish population. Russia had just mobilized a third of its military, 225,000 men, down to the Danube in support of the Balkan countries' struggle for independence from the Ottoman Empire. "We heard the calls of war," Lieberman cryptically noted about his decision to found the paper in 1876. Russia was now focused on reclaiming Crimea and supporting Slavs on its southern border. It no longer could afford to waste its energies combating what it considered an internal annoyance. While "the great Satan" (Russia) was occupied, Lieberman and his comrades hoped to spread their revolutionary message without being detected by authorities.[38]

Smolenskin's formal support of Lieberman's goals was encouraged by the company he kept, including numerous individuals with strong Marxist leanings. Smolenskin's confidants included Gurevich and Moshe Kamensky, who had also moved to the Austrian capital from Berlin.[39] Moreover, Smolenskin's typesetters included Mordechai Adelman and the future Russian revolutionary Eliezer Zuckermann, both staunch supporters of Lieberman. The editor instructed both his employees to assist in the publication of *The Truth*. These men all self-identified as materialists. More personally, Smolenskin's friend Isaac Salkinson, a Protestant minister who had converted from Judaism and Shakespeare's first Hebrew translator, quickly took a strong liking to Lieberman, with whom he shared a similar upbringing. Before long it was rumored that they were sleeping together, or that, as one observer from the period recalled, Salkinson "strongly desired" Lieberman and the latter, "who was not all that scrupulous with such matters, succumbed to his entreaties." The affair between the two men soon fizzled out, as Lieberman grew increasingly disgusted with the lecherous minister.[40] Smolenskin, who had recently married the lovely and refined Lenora Temkin (1848–1925), seems to have paid less attention to Lieberman's sexual forays and more to the possible dangers posed by his Marxist newspaper.

When the first edition of *The Truth* appeared in 1877, Smolenskin made sure not to send it through regular distribution channels in order to avoid arousing suspicion. Smolenskin had always warned Lieberman not to jeopardize *The Dawn*'s status with Russian officials; one requirement for *The Truth* was that Lieberman not write about Christianity.[41] He also reminded Levin "to be careful about the Russian government [monitoring] your actions and writings as well as the language used in your articles."[42] Smolenskin's precautions were not enough. The Russian authorities confiscated the newspaper and severely curtailed its circulation.

Smolenskin's association with the materialists provided his conservative and liberal critics with ample fodder for dismissing him as a "heretic" who not only posed a threat to the traditional character of Jewish life but was also guilty of "sedition" for supporting anti-government forces. Liberal Jewish enlighteners who sought to curry favor with the Russian government denounced him for associating with revolutionaries. Smolenskin was described as "trying to destroy the foundations of authority . . . the first of the ten commandments of the nihilists."[43]

Traditionalists discredited Smolenskin by citing his ties to "nihilists" who had rejected Judaism. Starting from "the evil one [Abraham Uri] Kovner's 'life question' and on through Kaminer and Smolenskin," the Orthodox polemicist Ya'akov Lifshutz complained, "each person followed his own God and not the God of Israel." *The Dawn* was described as a mortal enemy of Judaism, the newspaper that "sought the destruction of religion."[44]

Smolenskin's liberal and traditionalist enemies tried to poison the distribution wells that carried *The Dawn* by associating it with Lieberman's materialism. Writing to one distributor in Kovno, Lifshutz and his brother Yehuda claimed, "Today the *Shakharistin* [connoting the *The Dawn's* connections to materialists and people whom Jews referred to as *nihilistim*] have students. Those who follow in their footsteps hate the nation and the seed of Israel more than the Egyptians. The *Shakharistin* assist [those who hate Israel] in hurting both our spiritual and our material well being."[45] Others turned to the front pages of rival newspapers to publicly charge Smolenskin with being a materialist. They compared Smolenskin's cultural nationalism to Joseph Sossnitz's "materialische religion," claiming that the two men had created a new version of Judaism. "To everything uttered by Büchner and Karl Vogt," one critic griped, "Smolenskin responds with an Amen."[46]

There was more than some truth in traditionalists equating Smolenskin with Lieberman. Even the radical twentieth-century Hebrew writer Yosef Haim Brenner maintained that "in his force, in his worldview, in his disdain toward those who upheld the law, in his compassion toward suffering, and in his prophetic spirit, Smolenskin was very close to the circle of the writers of *The Truth*."[47] While Brenner's statements were made long after the events of the 1870s, Levin himself described the difference between *The Dawn* and *The Truth* in terms of the former being the "exterior appearance" and the latter being the "inner secret" of the same project.[48]

The two papers had a great deal in common and were vying for the same readership. Writers were confused because the two publications shared a print shop. "It was not clear where my poetry was being directed," Levin later wrote. "At the same time that I sent my poem 'Why' to *The Truth* I was also sending other poems to *The Dawn.*"[49] Isaac Kaminer approached Eliezer Zuckermann—Lieberman and Smolenskin's typesetter—for help in retrieving his writings from Smolenskin. "I am enclosing a sealed letter," Kaminer wrote to Zuckermann, "to be delivered to Smolenskin. It instructs the editor of *The Dawn* to hand over all of my writings to you, and you shall entrust them to Lieberman, and he should do with them as he sees fit."[50] Lieberman was poaching Smolenskin's writers, making it even more difficult to distinguish between the two broadsheets.[51]

The same forces that were propelling Smolenskin's newspaper were undercutting it. Smolenskin recognized the increasing popularity of materialistic writers but he was not interested in having his own paper banned within the Russian Empire or in picking a battle with the Russian government. Smolenskin was not a petty man, but he had a healthy ego and was not accustomed to being upstaged. In addition, Lieberman's operation was becoming a serious threat to his own income. Smolenskin had received 6,000 rubles as part of his wife's dowry, but it was soon spent, and by 1877 he was in need of funds. He could ill afford to lose his writers, his subscribers, or his income as a result of Lieberman's principles and politics.

Smolenskin always kept a distance between his own ideas and those associated with materialism. He used the 1876 publication of the fourth section of his popular serial novel *The Wanderer in the Paths of Life* (*Hato'eh bedarkhei hahayyim*) to denounce the universalistic program of the Jewish materialists. On the pages of *The Dawn,* he carped at the notion, put forth by one of his writers, that economic conditions were the only reason for discrimination against Jews,[52] and in 1877 he explicitly attacked Lieberman's broadsheet, even as it was being published under his own auspices.[53]

Compared to the scathing criticism that Smolenskin levied against his other ideological foes, his admonishment of Lieberman was relatively mild.[54] Rather than dismissing Lieberman's practical materialism as foolish or nonsensical or liable to lead to the destruction of Judaism (all typical Smolenskinian rhetorical gestures), Smolenskin seemed genuinely puzzled by his friend's lack of interest in Jewish history, his reluctance to criticize religious fanatics, and, most important, his indifference to promoting a love for the Jewish nation. "It is not so simple to judge the effect the paper [*The Truth*] will have on people," Smolenskin humbly confessed. He was terribly confused about who constituted Lieberman's target audience. Lieberman's practical materialism, Smolenskin believed, would have no appeal among Jews who saw their future through a religious or national lens.[55]

Smolenskin's more exacting philosophical and political critique of the materialist position can be found in his rebuttal to Lieberman's and Levin's respective essays titled "The Jewish Question" (She'eilat hayehudim). Lieberman's piece, published in the first edition of *The Truth,* asserted that certain anti-Semites were invested in perpetuating the idea that Jews were a distinct cultural and economic entity. Jews, Lieberman explained, had been restricted to undesirable professional niches and were thus constrained to play specific economic roles. This in turn made them vulnerable to discrimination. However, both the professions that Jews were forced to adopt and the discrimination and social antagonism they endured were a function of capitalism. Lieberman believed that that the problems facing Jews were not due to their lack of education or any inherent fault. Larger economic forces put Jews in precarious professional positions and encouraged discrimination.

Lieberman maintained that *Religionhass, Rassenhass,* and *Nationalhass,* could be eliminated only if capitalism were first eliminated. Lieberman asserted that the most productive way to analyze the Jews' economic situation was to locate it within a specific historical and political context. Jews were first and foremost human beings who were being discriminated against and forced into limited and undesirable economic roles. Lieberman concluded his remarks by asserting that true economic equality would be guaranteed only when people ceased focusing on particularistic (religious, racial, or national) issues.[56]

Many of Smolenskin's supporters agreed with Lieberman's economic approach to the Jewish question. Most notably, Judah Leib Levin echoed him in his assertion that the Jewish question could be answered only by seeing it in the context of the problems faced by all oppressed peoples and classes, such as African Americans in the United States.[57] Writing in 1879, Levin explicitly tied "the black question" in the United States to "the Jewish question" in the Russian Empire, arguing that in order to properly understand a particular instance of oppression, people needed to see it in its specific economic context. Jews and blacks both played critical economic roles for ruling elites—but roles that put them in precarious positions. Privately, he explained that "if people understood how and why they were oppressed, they would come to unite with other oppressed peoples to stand up and seek justice from the hands of their oppressors."[58]

Smolenskin responded to Lieberman and Levin with his own two-part article on the topic, "The Jewish Question—The Question of Life" (She'eilat hayehudim—she'eilat haḥayyim), written over the course of two years

(1879–1881). The double title explicitly distinguished his ideas from the views of Jewish materialists, who saw the two questions as one and the same. Smolenskin insisted, however, that "the Jewish question is not to be equated with the material question."[59] According to Smolenskin, material concerns were a universal issue applicable to all peoples at all times, and they were especially pertinent in an age marked by the rise of large-scale business. The life question, he continued, "was a material question [*she'eilah ḥomrit*] and thus not a Jewish question."[60] Implicit in his argument was the contention that there was no such thing as a Jewish view of science, economics, or the distribution of resources. Judaism was not relatable to individual Jews' material conditions; such issues were the problem of states or political entities. Smolenskin's distinction between the spiritual and the material directly contradicted the articles he had been publishing in his own newspaper. "For human beings," wrote Lieberman on the pages of Smolenskin's broadsheet, "are part of nature and a small part in both quantity and quality, and in the same way in which a human being is limited in terms of his material side so too there is a limitation on his spiritual capacities—those that are called forces of the soul or spirit—these features are in fact material features from which [the spiritual capacities] were created and nothing more."[61]

For Smolenskin, the Jewish question involved addressing issues specific to the Jewish people, such as matters concerning God, the Torah, and Redemption (the coming of the Messiah and return of Jews to their homeland). Smolenskin was concerned about the risk of assimilation among Jewish youth, but even here his concern was with Judaism. Smolenskin maintained that the demise of Judaism and not the poverty of Jews should be considered the Jewish question. The economic issues raised by Lieberman were anything but a "Jewish" question.

Intellectuals with ties to both men recognized that they were talking past each other. "Smolenskin's answer to the Jewish Question," his disciple Mordecai ben-Hillel Hacohen wrote years later, "differed from the one provided by those associated with *The Truth*'s camp."[62] Smolenskin's position reflected his concern about Jews assimilating into the social fabric of the countries in which they resided. Living in Vienna, Smolenskin knew firsthand that it was possible for Jews to integrate into local economies and find opportunities to provide for themselves. For Smolenskin, the long-term problem for Jews was not their material situation, for this would eventually be resolved by the lifting of anti-Semitic legislation.

Rather, Smolenskin saw Jews as suffering from a more fundamental deficiency, which he referred to as a *mahsor ruhani,* a term that is best understood as "deficiency of Geist." Smolenskin's notion of Jewish Geist, as we shall see, had novel elements, but was presented by him as something that had animated Jewish history for thousands of years. Following the pattern of other nineteenth-century nationalists, described most notably by Eric Hobsbawm and Benedict Anderson, Smolenskin crafted a new tradition of Judaism, whose sole purpose was to forge national bonds and ensure the future of a people he identified as Jewish. Smolenskin hoped to establish a religion for Israel that could support and give spiritual value to a national collective.[63]

Fundamentally, Smolenskin and Lieberman differed over the temporality of the Jewish nation. Lieberman's materialism recognized that in the present there was a Jewish national collective residing in the Pale of Settlement; however, not only was there no guarantee that this collective would continue to exist, but Lieberman sought its eventual dissolution in a larger social revolution. For Smolenskin, Lieberman's materialism was but another example of a goal identified as Jewish that endorsed the eventual dissolution of Jews into class-based categories. Smolenskin's invocation of a Jewish "Geist" was his temporal antidote to the historical and economic definition of Judaism offered by the materialists. Smolenskin supported his contention that the life question was not the same as the *Jewish* question by introducing a notion of Judaism that posited a transhistorical *essence*—something that defied social and political circumstances. For the next fifty years Smolenskin's conception of Jewish Geist would become a lightning rod in all debates about the nature of Zionism and Jewish cultural nationalism.

SARA, ELIJAH, AND THE JEWISH GEIST

Smolenskin presented his theory of Jewish Geist with the drama of a second revelation of Moses, claiming that it was an ancient concept rooted in ideas presented in the Bible and reappearing in different guises over the ages. Although the Jewish Geist had always existed, for hundreds of years it had been obscured by countless Jewish rituals and beliefs, submerged even further with each passing generation. Smolenskin never claimed to have invented Jewish Geist; but he did claim to have resurrected its message.

According to Smolenskin, Jewish Geist comprised three essential qualities: "monotheism, the study of the Torah, and the belief in the Messiah."[64]

These qualities were all notably immaterial, transcending time and historical context. The Torah was revealed to the Jews when they were exiled from their homeland—it was not a text but an idea; monotheism transcended history and had no form; and the coming of the Messiah, the Redeemer, lay in the future.[65] Jews were "a nation without government, a people who held dear to the teachings and faith without priests. They possess no shared spoken language. . . . They are a nation based on Geist and not action."[66] Smolenskin was deeply committed to seeing Jews as a nation (rather than a religion), but a nation without a land, language, or political apparatus.

These three qualities—God, Torah, and Messiah—were not only touchstones that Jews could use to determine the nature of Judaism; they also distinguished Jews from all other national entities. Whereas "all other peoples . . . calculate their ideals in terms of their economic best interests and power,"[67] Jews were a nation based purely on an abstract notion of spirit.

Smolenskin's theory of Jewish Geist grew out of his own life experiences in eastern Europe as well as the criticisms he issued against Jewish groups.[68] Jewish Geist challenged those who adhered to rabbinic Judaism. For Smolenskin "only those [religious] laws that serve to fortify and unify our nation" were important.[69] Smolenskin was not observant in a conventional or rabbinic sense of the term. In his youth he was rumored to have mockingly put phylacteries on a cat (a claim strenuously objected to by his more conservative biographers).[70] The purpose of laws, rituals, and holy days such as observing the Sabbath, circumcision, and the Day of Atonement, he proposed, should be to generate shared national bonds.[71] This was a novel theory—and it broke with both strict Orthodoxy, which stressed the immutability of Jewish law, and Reform, which jettisoned the law entirely or made it subservient to ethics.[72]

Jewish life was radically altered by Smolenskin's notion of Geist. The synagogue, he hoped, would be replaced by the study house, and instead of denominations defining the nature of Jewish identity, Jews would be unified around their commitment to study. While Smolenskin was very clear about what did not constitute the Geist of Torah—mysticism and scientific knowledge—he never specified what did, a vagueness that enabled him to freely embrace certain aspects of rabbinic Judaism and disregard others.

The closest Smolenskin came to defining the nature of the Geist of Torah was in his presentation of institutions and individuals whom he believed embodied its ideals. Most notably, he identified Sara Copia Sullam, a seventeenth-century Italian Jewish poet, who was renowned for her knowledge of the Bible as well as European languages and literatures. Sara Copia

Sullam carried on a love affair with the Christian writer Ansaldo Cebà but rejected his requests for her to convert to Christianity.[73] Sullam was not simply a woman who had been educated in "secular" knowledge; she was a scholar immersed in *Jewish* literature and was prepared to risk her life and well-being for her commitment to Judaism.

For Smolenskin, Sullam expressed the importance of women's Torah study in the cultivation of Jewish Geist. We might conjecture that Smolenskin's own dynamic and brilliant wife, Lenora, influenced his strong endorsement of women's Torah study. Lenora, who adored her husband, became one of the founders of the Viennese women's Zionist organization Hadassah (the forerunner of the American-based movement) and a leading voice for various Zionist causes. Lenora and Peretz frequently conversed about literary and political matters. As her brother-in-law recalled, she was not the kind of woman written about in the Bible whose sole purpose was to serve her husband. She was a force in her own right, known as an "enlightened" woman who was fluent in French and well-read in contemporary literature. Peretz's biographers describe Lenora as an idealist.[74]

Unlike Lilienblum and Lieberman who gave lip service to sexual equality but treated their own wives shabbily—leaving them betrayed and destitute—Smolenskin deeply admired Lenora's intellectual prowess, and from the day he met her in 1874 until the day he died he sought to provide for her and his family. He made it a point to criticize writers for not being mindful that many of their readers were women. He warned them not to use "foul language," fearing that women like Lenora might find it distasteful.[75]

According to one of his nineteenth-century admirers, Shayndle Borsky, "[Peretz] Smolenskin was the first to wage the battle of the *daughters* over the *shortsighted fathers* who cited passages in the Talmud to prevent their [female] offspring from [receiving a full Jewish education], and he instead taught them anything they wanted to know about worldly knowledge."[76] To bring the Jewish Geist to full fruition, Smolenskin maintained that women needed not only to receive a secular education; they also had to be given the same Jewish education as their brothers.

Smolenskin envisioned a new Jewish entity that blurred the traditional divide between Jewish men and women. In contrast to Lilienblum's materialist perspective that Jewish men should be studying economically productive subjects that had been associated with traditional women's education, Smolenskin's Geist orientation saw Jewish women taking on the intellectual roles that had been often associated with traditional Jewish men. Jewish men were

Lenora Smolenskin with her children. (Courtesy of YIVO Institute for Jewish Research)

not to become traditional Jewish women; Jewish women would adopt the ideals of Jewish men. For Smolenskin the egalitarian nature of Jewish cultural nationalism was the heretical idea that women have the opportunity to become Torah scholars.

Smolenskin also held up the model of the cloistered eighteenth-century Genius [Ga'on] of Vilna, Elijah ben Solomon as the embodiment of the Geist of the Torah. Elijah was one of the most revered figures in Jewish history, a man whose memory continued to loom large over nineteenth-century Jews.

Both the adherents of the yeshiva movement, who saw him as inspiring their Talmudic-centered lifestyle, and the enlighteners, who valued his endorsement of the sciences and love of Hebrew, claimed Elijah as a forefather. Smolenskin was most impressed by the eighteenth-century rabbi's refusal to accept political or communal appointments because of his commitment to intellectual study over practical action.[77] Jewish Geist was not to be found in the petty political machinations of Jewish communal life or the mundane practice of Jewish law.

For Smolenskin, Elijah of Vilna expressed the same deep commitment to Jewish literature and its ideals that he found in Sullam, who had lived on the margins of Jewish and Christian communities. Modern Judaism, he argued, did not begin with the acculturated Moses Mendelssohn and the intermarried women of the Jewish salons but rather with the cloistered Elijah and the brave Sullam. In a radical act of historical revision Smolenskin claimed that Elijah even preceded the German Jewish philosopher Moses Mendelssohn in promoting the dissemination of secular sciences among Jews and even indirectly influenced Mendelssohn's own knowledge. This act of historical revision reflected Smolenskin's attempt to particularize the universal elements of Western liberal culture.

Smolenskin believed that the core of Elijah and Sullam's worldview lay deep in the recesses of the yeshiva. To be sure, Smolenskin had little respect for the pseudo-piety, parochialism, and sexism of the Lithuanian study halls. He remained an unrelenting critic of rabbinic leaders who reduced Judaism to a set of laws or religious rituals. But behind the dross that besmirched the institution, Smolenskin maintained, remained a glimmer of the Jewish people's essential Geist. While he defamed the rabbis who led these institutions, he held out hope that their students would rebel against them and become champions of Jewish Geist.[78] Smolenskin believed that the yeshiva was the foul receptacle that protected the metaphysical spirit of Judaism.

Smolenskin's theory of the Jewish Geist as epitomizing the idealist nature of Judaism was certainly influenced by the five years he spent as a yeshiva student in the city of Shklov.[79] In sections 2 and 3 of his novel *The Wanderer*, Smolenskin describes the idealist aspects of the yeshiva that deeply impressed him: the respect for knowledge and the ethos of study. Pavel Axelrod, with whom Smolenskin reportedly studied for a year in Shklov,[80] also claims that the ethos in these study halls fostered in him a philosophy of idealism: "I think these impressions did not pass by without leaving a mark on my subsequent life. The understanding of the infinity of the spiritual over the material, the external, and the everyday, the understanding that these spiritual foundations were opposed to one another, left a trace in my psyche," he explained.[81] For Jewish Communists who came of age in the 1870s, Torah study was often philosophically translated into a system of idealism that stood in opposition to materialistic worldviews. Whereas for Axelrod, Marxist materialism would ultimately win him away from his earlier allegiance to the idealism of the yeshiva, for Smolenskin the idealism of the yeshiva became the basis for his romantic notion of Jewish Geist and the essence of Jewish nationalism.

Smolenskin presented his theory of Geist as pouring out of ancient and deep biblical and rabbinic wells.[82] However, for many it had been drawn from a more foreign and recent source. "The term 'national Geist' is new to us," one of Lieberman's apparatchiks noted with regard to Smolenskin's theories. "There is no mention of it in any of our ancient writings. Rather, it was born out of the new political literature around the national question."[83] Smolenskin's attempt to buttress his ideas with a pastiche of biblical and even some rabbinic sources was immediately uncovered by his critics. Like so many other romantic theories of nationalism it was carried into Jewish life through new historical currents.

Jewish Geist mirrored the notions of collectivity advanced by other European nationalist thinkers in the first half of the nineteenth century. Following the first Polish uprising in 1833, writes the historian Brian Porter, Polish writers began to elevate "the nation into the realm of 'the spirit' and transformed the goal of statehood into a more grandiose ethical vision." Like the Polish nation, Smolenskin understood Jewish Geist as beyond the empirical or physical; it was "an ideal, a principle that gave meaning to history."[84] Smolenskin's was also influenced by the concept of Geist put forward by the nineteenth-century German philologist Friedrich August Wolf as well as the founder of the Wissenschaft des Judentums movement, Leopold Zunz, and the Galician enlightener Nachman Krochmal.[85] As noted by the historian Amos Bitzan, for Zunz, Geist was an abstract quality comprised of various cultural expressions that differentiated a people from all other groups.[86] While on one hand, Smolenskin attacked the religious worldview of the Jewish enlightenment, on the other, his theory of Jewish Geist was in part indebted to two of the best-known figures associated with the reformist Jewish movement, Krochmal and Zunz.

Smolenskin's definition of Geist contained both universal and culturally particular elements. The core principles of his definition of Jewish Geist —monotheism, the Torah, and Redemption—were concepts that had first emerged in history through the literature of the Jews but had been co-opted by many other collectives in Western civilization. Targeting German anti-Semites and Jewish Marxists, both of whom identified Judaism as anything but a Geist, Smolenskin brashly declared that Judaism's "life source" was different from those of other nations in that "it is not located in materiality but rather in the realm of spirit."[87]

IDEALISM AND THE POSSIBILITY OF ZION

Smolenskin never articulated the precise relation between Torah study and his other two touchstones of Jewish Geist, monotheism and Redemption. In 1872, Smolenskin was already stressing that belief in Redemption was an essential component of Jewish Geist. "And even if it seems impossible for Jews to return [to their homeland]," he asserted, "it is still incumbent upon them to continue to hold on to this hope."[88] For Smolenskin, Redemption was a form of hope and the belief in the Jews' eventual return to their homeland to occupy a more dignified position on the world stage.

In contradistinction to the idealist features associated with the Geist of Torah that transcended all concrete national expressions, Smolenskin seemed to suggest that Redemption was a process of materialization. Redemption was the moment in which the abstract values would redefine the nature of the material world. Describing the nature of Redemption he exclaimed, "The first pillar upon which Jews stand is that the spiritual and the material are one, and the second pillar also combines both the material and the spiritual and that is the belief in Redemption."[89] Smolenskin remained vague about what he meant by *spiritual* and *material;* however, it was clear that in contrast to the Geist of Torah that stood outside the contingencies of the physical world, the Geist of Redemption was to be enacted upon the physical world. The two Geists were not of the same quality; they expressed a different set of values.

In other words, according to Smolenskin, Jewish Geist had two focuses, Torah and Redemption (with each sharing the idea of God). Torah was the idea that carried Jews through diaspora life; Redemption was a commitment to the application of Jewish ideals in the physical world. For Smolenskin, Redemption was a future state in which Judaism would be able to emerge in an embodied form, materially represented. Still, Smolenskin never made this distinction in his writings; he therefore left readers confused about what he meant by a Jewish nation.

The tension in Smolenskin's theory of Geist between an idealist conception of the Torah and a material conception of Redemption provoked a large-scale debate in Jewish intellectual circles. Many were disturbed by Smolenskin's essay "The Jewish Question—The Life Question" (She'eilat hayehudim—She'eilat haḥayyim), in which he repeatedly emphasized the abstract qualities of Judaism and its commitment to Torah study and emphatically dismissed the idea that Jews had a unique material identity. Reading the essay alongside others in the coffee shops of the Latin Quarter in Paris, the Lithuanian expatriate Eliezer Perlman (Ben-Yehuda) was exasperated by the precociousness of Smolenskin's theory of nationalism. Ben-Yehuda idolized Smolenskin, but in "The Jewish Question—The Life Question" he thought that his hero had not only gone against his own principles but had squandered a priceless political opportunity. Russia was at war with the Ottoman Empire, providing assistance to the Russians' "younger siblings," the Bulgarians and Serbians. If the Bulgarians could gain Russia's support for their own national struggle, might not the Jews persuade Russia to aid their return to Palestine? How could the Bulgarians claim to have the status of a nation with a homeland but not the Jews?[90]

Smolenskin seemed oblivious to the possibility that Russia might assist Jews to return to Palestine and was moving in the opposite direction by denying the Jews' claims to a unique language, homeland, and polity. Aside from his commitment to Hebrew as a spoken language, Ben-Yehuda had come to identify himself as a staunch follower of Peter Lavrov, an avid reader of Russian materialist literature and a supporter of Russian revolutionary parties.[91] He was dismayed by Smolenskin's position. Smolenskin had not only disavowed Judaism's ties to physical world; he had even seemingly denied the viability of his own goal to present Judaism through cultural media. Instead of taking the opening provided by the current political climate, Smolenskin had become anti-materialist and anti-political, in effect denying the Jews' claims to nationhood.

A few months before the 1881 pogroms began in southern Ukraine, Ben-Yehuda sent Smolenskin a letter outlining his critique of "The Jewish Question–The Life Question." In it the young university student attacked Smolenskin's positions, calling on Jews to begin immigrating to Palestine and speaking Hebrew. Though he stopped short of demanding an independent Jewish state or sovereign political entity, he made it clear that he was preparing for his own immigration to Palestine and wanted others to follow suit.

"In your article 'The Jewish Question—The Life Question,'" Ben-Yehuda wrote to Smolenskin, "you tore down everything you had been trying to build for ten years." How could the so-called flag bearer of Jewish nationalism equate a national project with the Geist of the Torah, he asked. How could Smolenskin, who wrote in Hebrew, deny that Jews had their own language? Smolenskin's insistence on the unique idealist essence of Jewish nationalism had compromised the viability of the entire notion of a Jewish collective entity. Smolenskin's theories left the Jewish nation as "something abstract, lacking foundation." Ben-Yehuda had exposed the fundamental contradiction within Smolenskin's theory of Geist: How could one be a nationalist without praxis, political will, or at the least a concrete collective culture?[92]

Ben-Yehuda's letter came in the wake of personal and political developments that occurred while he was studying at the Sorbonne in the late 1870s. During that time he met Moritz (Mordecai) Adelman (1847–1922), who had emigrated from Vienna, where he had been an editor of *The Dawn* and then assisted Lieberman on *The Truth*.[93] Adelman would eventually immigrate to Palestine and help Ben-Yehuda establish the the Hebrew newspaper *The Gazelle* (*Hatsvi*). In the late 1870s he had already begun conversing with Ben-Yehuda in Hebrew.[94] Their conversations are often described in Zionist lore as the first recorded instances of Hebrew being spoken casually. In Paris, Ben-Yehuda also became acquainted with French philanthropists who were working to establish Mikveh Yisrael (The Hope of Israel), the first agricultural school in Palestine. He recalled his conversations at Café de la Source in the Latin Quarter, where students discussed Russia's support of the Bulgarians in their struggle for self-determination.[95] Ben-Yehuda, who had recently read George Eliot's proto-Zionist novel *Daniel Deronda,* wondered why no one was actively working toward bringing Jews back to Palestine. He might also have been aware of Judah Leib Gordon's anonymously published essay arguing that the imminent breakup of the Ottoman Empire provided an opportunity for Jews to begin considering the establishment of a Jewish homeland in Palestine.[96]

Ben-Yehuda was confused about where Smolenskin, the so-called leader of Jewish nationalism, stood on the issue of the Jews' return to Palestine. Smolenskin had explicitly rejected the reduction of Jewish nationalism to a struggle for independent statehood. States are "only the creations of mankind," Smolenskin declared.[97] Smolenskin assumed that "any intelligent person recognized that [in biblical times] Jews were given a state only as a means and not as an end goal, in order to speak truth at the gate, to fight against war, and to prevent the powerful from stealing justice from the poor."[98] These positions were anything but a ringing endorsement of a specifically Jewish political entity.

Ben-Yehuda attacked Smolenskin for idealizing something that ought not to be idealized—the Jewish nation was not located in the mind but rather in people's guts and was an outgrowth of their lives *as Jews.* Being a nation, Ben-Yehuda asserted, required *acting* as a nation. Borrowing from Herbert Spencer, Ben-Yehuda asserted that nationalism was born out of "feeling." Jews were a race; their language was tied to nature itself. Human beings were all connected to various racial groups and through instinct were tied to these natural bonds. "Stop asking 'Questions,'" he scolded Smolenskin; "people are not convinced by arguments. Feeling determines human action. . . . Speak to their hearts and tell them: Here before us is the land of our forefathers; let us return and become masters of the land and become like all nations."[99] Ben-Yehuda was determined to convince Smolenskin that he had the wrong line of argument and had misunderstood the material dimension of nationalist thought. Thinking in national terms meant thinking about land, labor, and bodies and not about abstractions like God, Torah, and the Messiah.

Ben-Yehuda's call to action and willingness to overlook the practical problems of immigration would prefigure his own version of Zionism, which led him to support Theodore Herzl's proposal that Jews accept a territory in Uganda. Ben-Yehuda cared less about where or how to establish a state than about the Hebrew culture it would generate. Jews needed a territory so they could create the demographic situation that would allow them to speak their own language—Hebrew—and develop their own cultural identity.

If there ever were a time in Smolenskin's life when material concerns assumed an importance that transcended theoretical debate, it was when he received Ben-Yehuda's letter. In 1880 Smolenskin was being criticized from all sides, and his paper was floundering. Reform as well as Orthodox Jews were attacking him for his nationalist position; his readership was dwindling, and his profits were diminishing. Moreover, he and Lenora had become parents, and Peretz was finding it difficult to support his growing family. He was facing his own personal crisis of the fork and knife.

Smolenskin treated Ben-Yehuda's criticism as an opportunity to clarify his positions on Jewish nationalism and the life question. While greeting the young man's words with applause, he scolded him for his naïveté and accused him of mischaracterizing his, Smolenskin's, positions. Smolenskin conceded that there was an apparent contradiction in calling for the rebirth of a Jewish nation while stripping it of a material basis. But had Ben-Yehuda looked carefully at his earlier writing, Smolenskin charged, he would have realized the productive ambiguities in Smolenskin's concept of Redemption. While in one respect it appeared abstract, an idea that stood outside the vicissitudes of history, viewed from another perspective it ensured that the Jewish nation always held on to the possibility of actualizing its Geist and having it assume a political shape.

Understood through this lens, the messianic age would inaugurate the materialization of the Jewish Geist, the moment when Jewish ideas (the Geist) would be applied to and transformed by the material world. Smolenskin claimed that he had obscured the dual nature of his theory of Jewish Geist in order to avoid setting off alarm bells for government censors. Smolenskin insinuated that he always harbored a hope that Jews would eventually take concrete steps to establish themselves as a political collective in Palestine.

Smolenskin cautiously endorsed Ben-Yehuda's call for immigration to Palestine and the rebirth of Hebrew as a spoken language. However, he refused to compromise philosophically on his identification of Jewish nationalism as located in Geist. Presaging the mission of Ahad Ha'am's (Asher Ginsberg's) Cultural Zionism,[100] Smolenskin corrected Ben-Yehuda, who had assumed that Smolenskin's definition of a Jewish nation was the same as his definition of any other national entity: "Though I am in full agreement with you that Redemption is something that should be sought," he told Ben-Yehuda, "I never said that Jews are like every other nation." Pointing to the prophet Jeremiah's scolding of Jews for defiling the land with their idolatrous behavior, Smolenskin asserted:

> All those who love their nation will follow [in Jeremiah's footsteps] and assert that the Torah and the Geist of Israel are more precious than land (which should not be understood to mean that land is not precious to us). We lived in the land only eight hundred years. Not all of that time was peaceful, and most of the time we were running after false gods and defiled it. But for thousands of years our Torah and Geist have remained with us. . . . Let me tell you, Ben-Yehuda, a traitor is he who accepts the offering of land at the cost of his belief in our Faith and Torah.[101]

For Smolenskin, Jewish Geist could not be reduced to material manifestation of Jewish nationality. Geist was the means by which Jews could evaluate their relationship to the physical world, resources, economics, and land. Geist was the idea of Judaism as a value. It was the idea of Judaism that could be redeployed to evaluate people, land, and labor. Ben-Yehuda's call for immigration had failed to account for the fact that Jews had once governed a land, and it caused Jews to compromise their beliefs and ideals.

Smolenskin was concerned about the ethical costs of a materialized form of nationalism. Writing in the last quarter of the nineteenth century, Smolenskin recoiled at the possibility of a Jewish political entity in Palestine being under the control of men who sat and studied in the beit midrash and depended upon charity for survival. Revealing the radicalness of his theory of Jewish Geist, Smolenskin asserted that Jews who resided in Palestine and spent their days studying the Torah would bring about the ruin of a Jewish state. The very Torah that Smolenskin claimed inspired diaspora Jewish life would ultimately threaten the viability of a Jewish political entity. Torah scholarship in a messianic age no longer reflected Jewish Geist. Smolenskin declared that a state run by present-day Torah scholars would bring about "rampant stealing, killing, and bloodshed on the streets of Jerusalem." The very people Smolenskin praised as the backbone of the Jewish people—the yeshiva students—would, he feared, defile a Jewish state. He went so far as to argue that it would be better to have no state at all than to have a state ruled by those who pledged their allegiance to the rabbis of the study hall. The idea of a state run by rabbis was as foreign to Smolenskin's conception of Judaism as the abominations that, in Jeremiah's words, brought about the destruction of the First Temple.[102] While Smolenskin was convinced that Jews' well-being could never be guaranteed by liberal enlighteners, he was equally disturbed by the prospects of the rabbis turning a Jewish state into a bastion of religious and political fanaticism.

Smolenskin conditionally endorsed Ben-Yehuda's desire to take concrete steps to ensure the return of the Jewish nation to the Land of Israel, supporting slow and cautious immigration to Palestine, all the while warning about the dangers of reducing the "Jewish nation" to its people's physical needs. The land should not be privileged over the ideals of the Jews' Geist, he asserted. Smolenskin encouraged Ben-Yehuda to "focus on building colonies that could alleviate poverty and provide a resting place for workers and the oppressed." Smolenskin concluded with the hope that one day Jews would "rebuild the ruins of Zion and return to live in their land not simply as a poor and weak people dependent upon religious charity [ḥalukka]."[103]

Both Smolenskin's and Ben-Yehuda's arguments contain serious flaws, most of them involving the feasibility of a massive population transfer to a land that lacked basic social infrastructure. There was no point in a people fleeing one land because it failed to provide them with the necessary means of survival only to go to another where they would have even less access to basic amenities and work opportunities. Yet neither man seemed interested in addressing this obvious criticism of their plans.

The weaknesses in Smolenskin's and Ben-Yehuda's articles would be underlined by Moses Lilienblum, who at the time was beginning to develop his own theory of Jewish nationalism. By the late 1870s Lilienblum had grown despondent about his own predicament and was resigned to living in a state of destitution. His response to Ben-Yehuda and Smolenskin would mark a turning point in his life and in the history of Jews in Russia. This was the first time Lilienblum would articulate the logic that made him the founder of political Zionism.

Lilienblum's nationalist orientation was fueled by his early materialism. He dismissed both Ben-Yehuda and Smolenskin as idealists. Unlike the former, who believed that "feeling" and "nature" were the basis of the nation, and the latter, who pushed the idea of "Geist," Lilienblum economically deconstructed the very notion of a nation. In an essay titled "On Israel and Its Land," published in Smolenskin's paper, Lilienblum described the numerous conflicting means that nations in the nineteenth century employed to constitute themselves as such. Both Smolenskin's Geist and Ben-Yehuda's instinct were passé notions of nationalism. Their beliefs that the nation was a metaphysical or organic concept based on a shared idea or language were, for Lilienblum, indications that both men had terribly misunderstood the purpose of a national movement.[104]

In contrast to Ben-Yehuda and Smolenskin, Lilienblum stressed that nations were established in order to facilitate the construction of an entity that could ensure freedom and the sovereignty of individuals—namely, the state. The whole point of "nations" was the centralization of resources in one body. Instead of relying on abstract hope or obsoletely "believing in Redemption," Lilienblum preferred to talk about "obtaining Redemption"—the actions that needed to be undertaken, the labor necessary to become free and sovereign. Redemption existed only to the extent that Jews were prepared to act in ways that would tangibly improve their material well-being. The idea of Redemption, or, for that matter, of the Land of Israel, was meaningless unless it allowed people to survive and flourish. Nations were constructs, and states were a vehicle to protect people and provide them with goods. National rhetoric and bombast might move a person's soul or fire the imagination but it could not feed, clothe, protect, or ensure the freedom of a people.[105]

Instead of focusing on abstract ideals or emotional instincts, Lilienblum considered the means available for Jews to improve their basic living conditions. "With the exception of those who were idealists," Lilienblum asserted, "Ben-Yehuda's words would fall on deaf ears." Lilienblum argued that Jews had two options: immigrate to the United States or to Palestine. Each option had material benefits and drawbacks. In remarks that Lilienblum later edited out of his *Collective Writings,* he qualified this argument, declaring, "I am no idealist," and chuckled at what he saw as Ben-Yehuda's cockeyed logic of promoting immigration to Palestine in order to facilitate the development of the Hebrew language. The purpose of going to Palestine was not to develop a language; it was to ensure the well-being of an oppressed group. A Jewish state was about bread, not Hebrew metaphors and coffeehouse papoter.[106]

Lilienblum's treatment of Smolenskin was even more dismissive. He rejected Smolenskin's position that "Jews are a nation of Geist and the Kingdom of the Jews is a Kingdom of Geist." While Lilienblum and Smolenskin are often linked as former enlighteners who became founders of Zionism, the two men promoted radically divergent philosophies. "Never in my life," Lilienblum privately told Smolenskin's supporters, "was I ever in agreement with Peretz Smolenskin." Lilienblum considered Smolenskin "a nationalist without any foundation; his ideas floated in the air." If it were up to Smolenskin, Lilienblum grumbled, "the Jewish nation would entirely flow from Jewish education located in the wells of Europe." For Lilienblum, Smolenskin's theory of Geist contained nothing inherently Jewish. It did not reflect some metaphysical Jewish ideal; it was a product of European Romantic nationalism.[107]

For Lilienblum, Smolenskin's ideas made for good speeches and could stir people's emotions but lacked the practical content needed to deal with the Jews' most immediate and pressing concerns. Encouraging Jews to immigrate to Palestine or the United States had to be first and foremost conceived of in terms of improving people's living conditions and ensuring their survival. If Palestine or the United States could not guarantee the Jews' well-being, there was no point in uprooting them. There was nothing to be gained from going to a land that could not provide basic security for its inhabitants.

Smolenskin was determined to get the last word, and he used his editorial privilege to address Lilienblum's charges. Smolenskin knew that Lilienblum "despised" him, but he still greatly respected his prickly interlocutor. Placing a marker next to Lilienblum's claim that he and Ben-Yehuda were promoting "idealism," Smolenskin unabashedly asserted,

Not only is there nothing wrong with being an idealist, but rather, just the opposite. One who is not an idealist is no better than an animal. Only Pisarev and his followers expressed this kind of nonsense. While in its time [Pisarev's position] was considered a form of wisdom, today all knowledgeable people know that this is sheer nonsense. Furthermore, those who cry out against idealism—they too are idealists. For why do they fight against idealism, if not because of an idea in their spirit that awakens within them? . . . And one who denies the Geist of the Jewish nation as being idealism is in effect saying, I don't believe in what you are saying because your words are not held together by a rod of wire, for look at bridges—they are held together by large pieces of wire.

In effect Smolenskin charged Lilienblum with being a vulgar materialist, someone who failed to recognize the ways in which language and consciousness transforms the material world. Smolenskin claimed that his critics had misunderstood him. "If only I had used the German phrase, 'Die Macht des Geist[es]'" ('The Power of Spirit'), he claimed, "everyone would have understood what I meant." For without "Geist, there is nothing that connects Jews."[108]

Smolenskin pushed back against Lilienblum, but if we examine his argument closely we see how much he had conceded to the materialists and the extent to which his cultural nationalism relied on the positions put forward by Lilienblum and even Lieberman. Over the course of the debates with Lilienblum and Ben-Yehuda, Smolenskin's theory of cultural nationalism had subtly shifted away from a fully abstract idea to one in which Geist became the determinative factor in the organization of society. Instead of ignoring or disregarding the need for land, labor opportunities, and healthy bodies, Smolenskin now was arguing that these were the primary sites for what constituted the sacred.[109] What he had earlier claimed was devoid of metaphysical content—land, labor, and people—he now claimed should be understood through the prism of materialism. Land, labor, and people would be conceptualized as Jewish.

It is unclear whether Smolenskin's position had changed as a result of the pressure exerted by Lieberman's materialism or whether it emerged more organically out of a theory of Redemption. There were certainly biblical precedents for Smolenskin's theory of Redemption, which demanded that material concerns defer to metaphysical principles, but it was far from a traditional theory of Jewish eschatology. As the historian Eli Lederhendler has shown with regard to Smolenskin and other early Jewish nationalists' messianic rhetoric, "It was evidence not of the *continuity* of messianism with Judaism, but of *discontinuity*." The language of Redemption was a metaphor, he argues, a political code for a nontraditional Jewish nationalism. Lederhendler correctly admonishes historians who "indulged in a form of anachronistic analysis," simplistically coloring Zionism as a political restoration of the biblical monarchy and notes that the messianic rhetoric of early Zionists was empty of eschatological meaning.[110]

Smolenskin's notion of Redemption differed from the one presented in rabbinic literature. His break with the rabbinic tradition paralleled moves by other European cultural nationalists who sought to wrest control of their respective traditions from ruling religious elites. Following Moses Hess (whose work exerted a considerable influence on him), the Italian Giuseppe Mazzini, and the Polish Adam Mickiewicz, Smolenskin's theories challenged traditional religious doctrines and structures of authority.[111]

Still it is wrong to identify Smolenskin's project as a form of secularization. Smolenskin's Jewish nation was not simply a means for providing resources and economic opportunities for Jews, it was the vehicle to actualize the idea of Jewish Geist. Whereas Lilienblum saw Jews primarily as a historically oppressed group of people with certain social and economic differences, Smolenskin saw Jews as constituted by an eternal idea of exceptionality. Jews were a chosen people not because various groups had mistreated them but because of the unique aspects of their Geist. Any attempt to establish a Jewish state would have to conform to that ideal. Discrimination and oppression were not reason enough to justify Jews having a political entity. Only if the Jewish Geist could be materialized could a state be considered Jewish.

Overlooked in Smolenskin's cultural nationalism is the way it ultimately subjected the struggle for resources and territory to a novel set of ideas that broke with rabbinic doctrines. His focus was no longer on proving the abstract and nonmaterial nature of Jewish identity, but rather on the material shape of Jewish ideals. Smolenskin's theory of Redemption took the "merely" material, which he earlier had insisted was not a specifically Jewish concern, and forced it to conform to sacred Jewish ideals and beliefs. Jews could not participate in politics, could not struggle to obtain goods and resources, and could not own land as Jews if doing so meant they acted in the same way all other peoples did. Their survival was not enough reason to return to the Land of Israel; if Jews wanted to return as Jews to the Promised Land, that land would have to be governed by principles based on Jewish Geist. Though he would claim that he had always believed in the importance of Redemption as an ideal, Smolenskin had begun to develop his theory of Redemption in material terms.

Debates over various secular and religious forms of nationalism—debates that are established staples of Jewish historiography—overlook the more fundamental role materialism played in the development of modern political and religious history. The fact that Smolenskin's theory of Redemption significantly differs from rabbinic eschatology might for some "legitimate" Zionism's break with medieval rabbinic Judaism, but it does not mean that Smolenskin and his followers' theory of Jewish Geist operated without its own metaphysical assumptions—assumptions that privileged certain peoples and marginalized others. Smolenskin's cultural nationalism redefined the spiritual conditions for the acquisition of resources, goods, and property and the appropriation of land in Palestine. Far from a secularization of rabbinic ideals, Smolenskin's theory of Redemption achieved something else entirely: the possibility of matter being made Jewish.

ZION

The political ramifications of placing the physical world at the center of a spiritual project was highlighted in Smolenskin's final novel, *Revenge of the Covenant* (*Nekam berit*, 1883).[112] Written while he lay on his deathbed, the novel concerns Jews' response to the pogroms of 1881, in which Russian Cossacks destroyed 215 Jewish communities, leaving 20,000 homeless and 100,000 without means of support. The Russian government was slow to react, failing to protect the Jewish population from the violence. Revolutionary parties were even less sympathetic, refusing to condemn the attacks, which they saw as an unfortunate but understandable expression of the Russian people's will. Devastated Jews living in the Pale were paralyzed, uncertain how to respond. Should they continue lobbying the government for greater rights, attempt to ingratiate themselves with their Russian neighbors, prepare to fight against those who threatened them, or board ships to America, Palestine, or some other destination? Individually and collectively, they considered all of these possibilities.[113]

In *Revenge of the Covenant,* Smolenskin addressed the various struggles and doubts through the story of an acculturated Jewish medical student living in "the capital city." Though proud of his Jewish ancestry, the young man supports the government program of liberalism. So fervent is his belief in becoming acculturated into Russian society that he is prepared to forgive daily anti-Semitic slights he receives. The condescension of his Gentile friends and taunts of superiors can all be dismissed with the shrug of a shoulder or, if the moment calls for it, a meaningless slap back in his accuser's face.

The young man's dreams of melding with his Russian neighbors are soon dashed, however, when he learns about the havoc wrought by pogroms in his hometown. He returns to his ransacked childhood home, where he spends painful days with of his family, until his conciliatory mother encourages him to visit the nobleman's daughter, with whom he had been on intimate terms prior to leaving for the university. He travels to the young lady's estate, where they immediately rekindle their romance. The two spend the next few days enjoying conversation, riding horses, and dining together. The medical student begins to consider marriage with the young woman. Marriage, joining bodies and sharing resources, is Smolenskin's metaphor for the longing for integration and assimilation. Like the young medical student, many Jews wanted to move beyond the atrocities committed against them.

But just as the medical student starts thinking seriously about marriage, his eyes fall upon a medallion dangling on the young woman's bosom. It is the ornament that was ripped from his sister's chest during the pogrom. Dangling before his eyes is a symbol of the violence perpetrated against his family and the barriers that stand between him and his Russian neighbors. The medallion is not simply *someone else's* property; it is *Jewish* property, taken from his sister simply because she *is* Jewish. The nobleman's daughter has no intention of giving it back to its original owner because in her mind it has not been stolen; possessions held by Jews are not really theirs. The young man can no longer ignore the meaning residing in the dangling medallion.

The answer Smolenskin offers to the violence symbolized by the stolen medallion is Zion. After a hurried and rough exchange with the woman's father and brothers about the medallion's origins, the medical student finds himself thrown outside the gates of the estate, severely beaten, with a gun in his hands, while the brothers jeer at him: "Jew! Do you like the price of jewelry?"[114] Burning with rage he contemplates killing them. But he recognizes the futility of such an act. Instead he calls upon his fellow Jews to "revive that which they [Gentiles] kill and reestablish that which they [Gentiles] destroy." In the prophetic tradition he declares: "Behold the flag of vengeance on which we shall glorify the name of Jerusalem! Not by might and not by power; not with the fist of the wicked and not with blood and murder; but rather by spirit!"[115] In Russia, only through the sword, only through blood, only through power can Jews thrive. At the novel's end, the medical student is preparing to immigrate to Palestine, where he and fellow Jews can build their lives in peace.

In retrospect, Smolenskin's nonviolent vision of Palestine as the physical home for a Jewish national body seems not only naive but contradictory, revealing the limitations of his theory of Jewish nationalism. For Jews to appropriate a land without violence ignores the fundamental question of who would be excluded in making Palestine a Jewish territory. Smolenskin's answer to the Jewish question begs a new question, which was most starkly posed a few years later by the Austrian sociologist Ludwig Gumplowicz to Theodore Herzl: "You want to found a state without bloodshed? Where did you ever see that?"[116]

Jewish Body Politics

In the history of Western civilization only the Jews' killing of Christ features more prominently in justifications of anti-Semitism than their "materialism." Jews were persecuted for hoarding their wealth and controlling financial markets. From Russian pogroms to German gas chambers Jews living in European nation-states paid dearly for their "nefarious" adherence to "matter." The anti-Semitic depiction of Jewish materialism relied on conspiracy theories that posited the existence of a small but powerful cabal—Rothschild and his banking cohorts pawing the globe—that manipulated world markets. In reality Jewish materialism was an ideology developed in the second half of the nineteenth century by Jews who were socially oppressed and lived in dire poverty. Far from hoarding goods and resources, Jews developed a theory of materialism to argue for a more equitable and just distribution of resources with their Gentile neighbors. Jewish materialism decisively broke with the rabbinic Judaism of the much-maligned Pharisees. It provides a framework within which we can understand not only Zionism but Jews' involvement in the early-twentieth-century minority rights movement and certain strands of communism. More fundamentally, it allows us to identify the most commonly articulated metaphysical sensibilities of twentieth-century Jews.

Since the eighteenth century no group has been more anxious about being labeled materialist than liberal Jews residing in Russia, Europe, and the

United States. To counter anti-Semitic accusations, liberal Jews couched their claim to be given full civil rights and access to labor markets by defining Judaism in anti-materialist terms, as a faith. As Judah Leib Gordon explained, a Jew should be "a man in the street and a Jew in the home." Gordon recognized that this division between Jews as political subjects and Jews as religious adherents was first and foremost predicated on Jews' "turn[ing] over their wealth to the state."[1] Jewishness was something invisible and private. As individuals or as humans Jews would reap the material benefits of being part of a larger collective. For most liberals, the very idea of a Jewish body or Jewish materialism contradicted the political and philosophical tenets of liberalism.

Jews who identified as liberals often considered their Jewish identities either a historical fact that could be ignored when it came to the distribution of resources or something to be confined to the realm of ideas. Judaism was based on revelation or reason. It was practiced in homes, synagogues, and private educational institutions but not in marketplaces, battlefields, or scientific laboratories. While a Jew could be a liberal, they maintained, it was oxymoronic to describe someone as a Jewish liberal. It was inconceivable that a state-administered institution would acknowledge the existence of a materially distinct Jewish body. Jews who imagined themselves as part of such a Jewish body threatened the ability of all Jews to become part of the societies and cultures in which they resided. The idea of a political Jewish body posed a serious problem for liberals who were Jews.

Most nineteenth-century western and central European Jews considered themselves a "religious minority," not a "political minority." They may have engaged in Jewish politics, but they did not see their Jewishness as a category that should be taken into account when addressing the distribution of resources in society. "At international diplomatic conferences of the Great Powers held in Vienna in 1815, Paris in 1856, and Berlin in 1878," the historian James Loeffler explains, "European diplomats had treated Jews as a vulnerable religious community like the Armenian Christians in the Ottoman Empire."[2] As the French historian Philip Nord writes, "To be a Jew" in France in the nineteenth century "meant to be a citizen and a patriot."[3] Likewise, the European historian Abigail Green explains that nineteenth-century liberal Jews believed that "their Jewishness was—or should be—irrelevant to their politics."[4] In the nineteenth century, when Jews who were liberals referred to themselves as part of a "minority," they were referencing their status vis-à-vis adherents of other religious groups.

Western European Jews that identified as liberals were the first to reject the Russian physician Leon Pinsker's materialist theory of Jewish nationalism expressed in his work, *Auto-Emancipation* (1882). This short essay, which has now been canonized within Zionist historiography, rejected the possibility that courts and government institutions could uproot ingrained anti-Semitism. Pinsker argued that anti-Semitism was an eternal "disease" that had infected Europe. But Jews were also a "a sick patient." "The world," Pinsker claimed, saw the Jews as "a ghostlike apparition of a people without unity or organization, without land or other bond of union, no longer alive, and yet moving about among the living. . . . Fear of the Jewish ghost . . . opened the way for Judeophobia . . . a psychic disorder. As a psychic order it is hereditary, and as a disease transmitted for two thousand years it is incurable."[5] The more laws states passed demanding that citizens ignore any identifiable material features of Jews, the more Jewishness became something mysterious and a subject ripe for conspiratorial theories. The more Jews were defined by an abstract concept of faith, the fewer empirical and physical traits Jews were said to possess, the more their Jewish identities assumed a ghostlike quality in people's minds. Jews were more than ever before present in public life—they now occupied positions in government offices and academic and financial institutions—but it was increasingly difficult to empirically identify them as such.

Pinsker's prescription was for Jews to see themselves as possessing "Jewish" bodies. His reformulation of Judaism and Jews in material terms (he even stripped the heavenly idea of the Jewish soul down to the imaginative false idea of a ghost) represented a radically new Jewish political and spiritual profile, one that was based on the philosophical assumptions of the Jewish materialists of the 1870s.[6] Pinsker did not focus on the legal status of Jews in European nation-states (something he had repeatedly stressed in the early 1860s as the editor of the Russian Jewish weekly *Sion*). He conceived of Jews in medical and biological terms. For Pinsker, a state was necessary not in itself but only because it enabled others to clearly recognize a Jewish body, which could then move freely as such throughout the world. Only an embodied version of Judaism would ultimately ensure the protection of Jews. When people started seeing Jews as economic actors they would stop conjuring theories of hidden cabals and secret groups plotting to overtake the world. They would judge, critique, and praise Jews the way they would all other groups. Only a Jewish body could once and for all put an end to the false stereotypes that followed the identity of the Jewish ghost.

Liberals across Europe cried out that Pinsker was destroying one hundred years of arguments about the religious and faith-based nature of Judaism. Leading mainstream German Jewish newspapers printed editorials that diagnosed the Jewish doctor as "suffering from the Russian nihilistic outlook." He had reduced all issues to "the struggle for existence."[7] For Jewish liberals, Pinsker's materialism undermined their attempts to convince Gentiles that Judaism was restricted to matters of the soul. Pinsker and his ilk, they feared, gave ammunition to longstanding anti-Semitic tropes and traps and thus severely compromised European Jewish acculturation. The liberal charge against Pinsker was not simply that he was promoting Jewish nationalism but, more fundamentally, that he was politically and biologically committed to the idea of a Jewish body.

Perhaps surprisingly, Jewish materialists in the Zionist camp conceded the point to liberals. They were guilty as charged. Following the pogroms of 1881 they justified immigration to Palestine on the principle that "man is a *gashmi* [material] being, and will always act in his best *gashmi* interests."[8] They explicitly differentiated Judaism from Christianity by arguing that "in contrast to Christianity, which works to lift man up to the heavens, the purpose of the Jewish religion is to bring God down to earth."[9] What the materialists addressed in this study would not concede, however, was that their notions of Jewish materialism were chauvinistic or exclusionary in their economic orientation. They also rejected the liberal claim that their ideas necessarily led to atheism or the denial of their Jewish religious ties. While there would be many who would see in Zionism the end of Jewish metaphysics, most Jews saw it as a worldview that redefined Judaism around people's ability to appropriate a place within the physical world and a new set of values that justified the redistribution of economic resources.

Liberal Jewish elites' critique of those headed for Jaffa would also be leveled against those streaming into Ellis Island. Russian Jews who immigrated to the United States at the turn of the twentieth century were often reproached for their godlessness and the materialistic aspects of their Jewishness. A poll conducted by the *New York Times* in 1919 claimed that upwards of 90 percent of American Jews were unchurched, suggesting that Jews posed a threat to America's religious and cultural fabric.[10] Jewish liberals grew increasingly anxious about the involvement of eastern European Jews in labor politics and their sympathy with certain strands of communism. While many of the so-called unchurched retained deep spiritual ties to Judaism through a sense of peoplehood, labor, and social organizations, such forms of religiosity were unintelligible in a Protestant landscape in which religion was equated with church attendance and inner faith. Of the 1.5 million Jews who arrived to the United States from eastern Europe between 1881 and 1911, most practiced *Yiddishkeit*, a set of undefined religious beliefs, practices, and rituals that transcended synagogue attendance, dogma, or defined rabbinic laws.[11] These religious expressions, however, were largely ignored or looked down upon by Jews invested in establishing denominational identities as well as by the secular leadership of Jewish workers organizations. Eager to acculturate into a new American religious landscape, liberal Jewish leaders locked arms with American Christian ministers to battle against the increasingly materialistic identity of America's Jews and to bring Russian Jewish immigrants back to their religious roots.

Most historians place a physical and ideological ocean between Palestine/Zionism and America/Yiddishkeit. I suggest that the two shared far more than Zionist, Bundist, or American Jewish denominational historiography would suggest. Both assumed that the organizing structure of Jewish identity was a Jewish body. Most Jews did not perceive immigration to the United States or Palestine as a choice between the "idealism" of Eretz Yisrael and the "economics" of the United States, as depicted by the idealist Zionist Asher Ginsberg.[12] Rather, they saw them as two sides of the same coin. There were profound differences between the material imaginary of Palestine and that of the United States, but both were idealized in terms of what they materially promised Jews.

Jewish Immigrants to Palestine at the turn of the century saw in Zion the actualization of materialism as first imagined in the 1870s. The students of the Marxist Ber Borochov, such as Yitzhak Ben Zvi and David Ben-Gurion, identified Palestine as a response to the crisis of the fork and the knife originally theorized by Aaron Shemuel Lieberman. They envisioned a new kind of Jew, the *ḥaluts* (pioneer), who was attached to the physical world. As described by Avraham Shlonsky, the twentieth-century Ḥabad Hasid turned Zionist poet, the *ḥaluts* would be the embodiment of the idea that "a human being is meat, and he toils here in the sacred / and the land / bread."[13]

In opposition to the Zionist narrative, the legacy of the Jewish materialists of the 1870s also inspired the core features of American Jewish Yiddishkeit. Most notably, Mordecai Kaplan developed a theory of Jewish peoplehood and Judaism as a civilization for the so-called American Jewish "unchurched."

Kaplan, a student of Joseph Sossnitz and a child of Lithuania, never fit well into the landscape of American Jewish denominations first established by German Jewish émigrés in the nineteenth century. In contrast to his liberal rabbinic colleagues, Kaplan strongly endorsed materialistic interpretations of Judaism in the 1920s and 1930s. Only the fear that his wealthy modern Orthodox congregants would desert him prevented him from publicly expressing sympathy for historical materialism and arguing for its compatibility with Judaism.[14] Kaplan's theory of Judaism as a civilization gave ultimate value to embodied and empirical aspects of Judaism. It was developed through a sustained engagement with both scientific and economic materialism. "If the Jewish religion is to play a part in the life of Jews in the future," Kaplan asserted, then it would have to "say yea" to an interpretation of this and the next world based on materialistic principles.[15] While Kaplan himself carefully distinguished his position from mechanistic and strictly economic theories of materialism, he was equally uncomfortable with Cultural Zionists and liberal Jews who claimed that Jewish identity was based on their ethical or intellectual superiority.[16] It is not surprising that in 1921 denominational leaders threw down the gauntlet. They delegitimized Kaplan in the same way their German colleagues had delegitimized Pinsker. Leading New York Orthodox rabbis railed against him not only as a heretic but also as a proponent of a "materialistic concept of the universe."[17]

In the first half of the twentieth century Kaplan would politically join forces with a cluster of Jews who helped to found the minority rights movement. For Kaplan the idea of a "Jewish body," a term he used repeatedly in his writings, became the lynchpin for a theory about the need to protect all minority groups. Proponents of minority rights were committed to the state as an organizing framework for society but also believed in specifically protecting vulnerable collectives around the world. As described by Loeffler, "These wards of humanity did not wish to be protected as political invalids or naked individuals. They asked to be treated like an independent nation with legal rights and an equal share in the Law of Nations, even if they did not (yet) possess an army or a country of their own."[18] Advocates for minority rights assumed that there was, at least in political terms, a Jewish body that needed protection. They might not have philosophically believed that a Jewish body was different from other bodies, but they asserted that individual bodies that were socially signified as Jewish were under attack, and it was politically impossible to ignore the violence being perpetrated against them. For Jews to

ניט פיהרען, נור שלעפּען

דער „אַמעריקאַן דזשואיש קאָמיטע'ס" „אידעאל" פֿון פֿיהרערשאַפֿט . . .

"Not Leading but Dragging." The caption reads, "The American Jewish
Committee's 'Ideal' of Leadership." (*Der Groyser Kundes,* August 20, 1915)

be protected they would have to become a political (not merely a religious)
minority. The assertion that Jews were a "political minority" and not simply a
"ghost people" was predicated on the thesis I have been arguing in this book.

Only at the end of the nineteenth century did Jews begin asking to be recognized as a political minority, and as such to be entitled to certain rights not
as human beings but as Jews. Not surprisingly, many of the founders of the
early-twentieth-century minority rights movement were also Zionists. They

originated from the northwestern provinces of Russia and, like Kaplan, were weaned on the writings of those discussed in this book.

For the most part, however, American Jewish communal leaders in the first half of the twentieth century vigilantly sought to uproot or deny the materialistic Judaism of eastern European Jewish immigrants. "Throughout the ages," Reform rabbis declared in the Columbus Platform of 1937, "it has been Israel's mission to witness to the Divine in the face of every form of paganism and materialism." They opposed or offered tepid endorsements of the minority rights movement. Their political activities for Jews abroad were couched in philanthropic and religious terms.

Concern about the label "Jewish materialism" continues to occupy Jews. Similar forms of discomfort expressed toward Kaplan's and Pinsker's worldviews can be heard in the critiques issued today against the religious proclivities of American Jewry's fastest-growing sectors, the new Jewish unchurched. They are replacing the onetime hallmarks of the American Jewish denominational system with a new set of identity markers, including combating anti-Semitism, visiting Jewish museums, erecting Holocaust memorials, building hospitals, promoting economic equality, and defending or speaking out against the State of Israel. Social scientists refer to this group as "nones" for their insistence on being considered "nonreligious" Jews.

The nones do not see their Judaism as per se a private affair or something preventing them from being fully American. A whopping 94 percent of American Jews agree that they are "proud to be Jewish." This is an astonishing number for any student of modern Jewish history and complicates any simplistic understanding of acculturation and group identity. Even the authors of the 2013 Pew report on Jewish life note that the "nones" "defy easy categorization." Still, when these findings were revealed, liberal Jewish leaders bemoaned this group's slide into atheism, secularism, and, of course, intermarriage. They glossed over a point stressed by the authors of the Pew report, namely, that the fact that "many Jews say religion is relatively unimportant in their lives does not mean that *being Jewish* is unimportant to them." For example, close to 50 percent of Jews who self-identify as "nonreligious" still say they believe in God. More important, more than four of five American Jews say being Jewish is more than a matter of "religion" alone. In other words, just because they do not relate to the category of "religion" does not mean that they do not identify with a body of Jews or embrace certain Jewish metaphysical positions regarding the nature of the physical world.[19] It would be derelict to overlook the different levels of investment in Jewish communal life between the nones visiting museums, memorializing the Holocaust, and fighting for social justice and early-twentieth-century American Jews marching at rallies against anti-Semitism and establishing Jewish labor unions and defense organizations. Still, both groups share the assumption that Judaism is primarily rooted in people's material well-being and the distribution of resources in society.

Echoing the German American Jewish establishment's response to Pinsker and Kaplan, Jewish liberal intellectuals lampoon contemporary Jewish practices and spiritual proclivities. "It would be a shame if Jews lost the bagel but a tragedy if they lost Maimonides," the literary critic Leon Wieseltier has on more than one occasion quipped about American Jewry's hankering for bread and distaste for medieval philosophy (in far more eloquent terms than my memory or pen can do justice to). These critiques are now also directed at scholars of Judaic studies, whom Wieseltier also chides for having fallen "under the spell of matter."[20] They are criticized for focusing on the material and overlooking Maimonides' scholasticism. True enough. But Lieberman and Lilienblum would not think twice about trading Maimonides the philosopher for Maimonides the hospital. Those who shed tears over the spiritual losses incurred while American and Israeli Jews ensured their physical survival and well-being miss one of the biggest stories of late-nineteenth- and early-twentieth-century global politics: the ways in which the discourse of materialism allowed people to reconceive their relationship to land, labor, and bodies, and the way in which oppressed peoples came to reevaluate and appropriate the physical world. While this story is illuminated through the case study of the Jewish materialists of the 1870s, it was by no means just a Jewish story.

In 1967 Michael Meyer concluded his groundbreaking study *The Origins of the Modern Jew* by expressing apprehension that in the face of Protestant pressure, "Jewish consciousness would gradually dissipate and dissolve into the free American milieu." Meyer offered the arresting image first drawn by the German Jewish Protestant convert Eduard Gans that Judaism might become little more than the "current [that] lives on in the ocean."[21] Meyer's fears may have been realized in certain intellectual quarters where Judaism and Jews all too often appear as little more than a small subplot in the wider story of Protestantism.[22] However, among those who call themselves Jews Meyer's fears have not been realized. At least from the publication date of Meyer's work, the issue confronting Jews has not been Protestantism but the challenges of Jewish materialism—namely, ensuring that the claims of equality that have been instrumental for the well-being of Jews in the United States and Israel are not denied to other peoples.

The same idea that inspired Europe's most oppressed to lift themselves out of poverty and fueled their drive to appropriate the physical world has been seized by a vocal minority of American Jews and an increasing number of Israelis for very different purposes. Today, biblical texts are cited to promote the consolidation of wealth and corporate greed. Genetic studies are marshaled to prevent Jews from intermarrying or non-Jews from converting to Judaism. Some now justify Jewish bio-territorial politics by claiming that Jewish blood and the soil of the Land of Israel are composed of the same molecules. The dynamism of Jewish materialism—originally intended as an argument for equality but often invoked as a justification for exclusivity—remains the central political and philosophical challenge of those who proudly identify themselves as Jews in the modern world.

Notes

Unless otherwise indicated, translations are my own.

ARCHIVAL COLLECTIONS

BINC   The Boris I. Nicolaevsky Collection
Documents cited from the BINC Archive are full copies of documents origi-
nating from the Geheimen Staatsarchivs Preußischer Kulturbesitz GStA PK,
I. HA Rep. 84 a Justizministerium, Nr. 49650.

CAHJP   Central Archives for the History of the Jewish People
Tsvi Hirsch Katzenlenbogen, HM2/9776.7

CZA   Central Zionist Archives
Alter Druyanow Collection A9/59/

GN   The Gnazim Archives of Hebrew Writers
Asher Braudes Archive

IISH   International Institute of Social History, Netherlands

JNUL   The Jewish National and University Library, Manuscripts and Archives
Division
Yalkut Reshumot, F 69276
Saul M. Ginzburg, ARC 4* 1281A
Samuel Joseph Fuenn, ARC 4* 1527
Mordecai ben Hillel Ha-Cohen, ARC 4* 1068 01
A. S. Katsenelenbogen, MS. A236
Joseph Sossnitz, B 710 38°5774
Abrahm Schwadron

JPLM   Jewish Public Library of Montreal
        Reuven Brainin Collection
JTS   Jewish Theological Seminary Archives
        Ephraim Deinard Papers, ARC 29
NYPL   New York Public Library, Archives and Manuscript Division
        ***P Joseph Sossnitz
LAB   Landesarchiv Berlin
        A.Pr.Br.Rep.030
PL   The Pinchas Lavon Institute for Labor Movement Research
        Judah Leib Levin, IV A104 71
        Kalman Marmor, IV-104
YIVO   YIVO Institute for Jewish Research
        Kalman Marmor Collection, RG 205
        Rabbinical School and Teachers' Institute, Vilna, 1847–1915, RG 24
        Nokhem Shtif Archive, RG 57
YU   Yale University Library, Archives and Manuscripts
        Jacob Berman Papers, MS 2014
        Uncatalogued, "Tsava'a: hana'asa 'a.y. R. Ya'akov Avraham b.m. Yehuda Leyb
           hanikra R. Avraham Shklefer mi-Novohardak"

INTRODUCTION

1. The wallet is located in YU, Jacob Berman Papers, MS 2014, box 2. It was given to the
   religious Zionist leader Rabbi Jacob Berman in 1917 and deposited in his archive with
   a note describing its history and how he acquired it.

2. David Nirenberg, *Anti-Judaism: The Western Tradition* (New York: Norton, 2013), 87–
   100. See also Jonathan Karp, *The Politics of Jewish Commerce: Economic Thought and
   Emancipation in Europe, 1638–1848* (Cambridge: Cambridge University Press, 2008), 2.

3. David Nirenberg, "Judaism as a Political Concept: Toward a Critique of Political Theology," *Representations* 128, no. 1 (Fall 2014): 1–29.

4. Nirenberg, *Anti-Judaism*, 214.

5. See Yuri Slezkine, *The Jewish Century* (Princeton: Princeton University Press, 2004).

6. Eugene Avrutin, "Visibility and Invisibility in Modern Jewish History: A Comment
   on *The Jewish Century*," *Ab Imperio* 1 (2005): 151–156.

7. For an overview of Jewish religious and cultural predispositions to capitalism see Jerry
   Z. Muller, *Capitalism and the Jews* (Princeton: Princeton University Press, 2010), 83–
   94. For a comprehensive philological study of eastern European Jews' relationship to
   money see Isaac Rivkind, *Yidishe gelt in lebnshteyger kultur-geshikhte un folklor: leksikologishe shtudye* (New York: American Academy for Jewish Research, 1959).

8. The first attempt to identify Hasidism with modern movements can be witnessed in
   the late 1850s in the writings of the Zhitomir scholar Eliezer Zweifel, *Minim ve'ugav*
   (Vilna, 1858), 46, and *Shalom 'al yisra'el,* 3 vols. (Jerusalem: Mosad Bialik, 1972), 1:68.
   On the claim that Hasidism shared affinities with certain elements of a materialistic worldview see the response of E. Trubich to G. Gelbak published in the Russian

newspaper *Razsvet* in 1860, cited in Joakim Philipson, "The Purpose of Evolution: The Struggle for Existence in the Russian-Jewish Press, 1860–1900" (Ph.D. diss., Stockholm University, 2008), 211. It was not until the 1890s that Hasidism was romanticized as the "origin" of Jewish socialism and communism. See Israel Bartal, "The Secularization of Jewish Spirituality: Hasidism Reinvented," American Association for Polish-Jewish Studies, http://www.aapjstudies.org/index.php?id=42 (accessed January 14, 2016). On the reconceptualization of Hasidism and its relationship to materiality and materialism see Chapters 3 and 4 of this volume.

9. On the adaptation of Jews to a characteristically American attitude toward material abundance see Andrew R. Heinze, *Adapting to Abundance: Jewish Immigrants, Mass Consumption and the Search for American Identity* (New York: Columbia University Press, 1992), 32, 40; and Rebecca Kobrin, ed., *Chosen Capital: The Jewish Encounter with American Capitalism* (New Brunswick, N.J.: Rutgers University Press).

10. Moses Leib Lilienblum, "'Olam hatohu," *Hashaḥar,* 1873.

11. Joseph Leib Sossnitz, "Hadat vehahaskala," *Hatsefira,* October 21, 1879.

12. See the conclusion to Isaac Kaminer's article "'Al derekh avodat ha'adama" in *Hakol,* May 7, 1879.

13. Gustav Landauer, "Sind das Ketzergedanken" in *Gustav Landauer, Der Werdende Mensch: Aufsätze über Leben und Schrifttum,* ed. Martin Buber (Potsdam: Kiepenheuer, 1921), 122. Hermann Helmholtz's *Über die Wechselwirkung der Naturkräft* (Köningsberg, 1854) was one of the first nineteenth-century scientific works to be translated into Hebrew. See Reuven Kalisher, *Ma'amar 'al hakoḥot hapo'alim babri'a* (Warsaw, 1862). On the reformulation of Judaism based on Helmholtz's theories of the conservation of energy see the work of Joseph Sossnitz addressed in Chapter 3, below.

14. Bernard Lazare, *L'antisémitisme: son histoire et ses causes* (Paris, 1894), 344–347; "pots and pans": Meri-Jane Rochelson, "'A Religion of Pots and Pans': Jewish Materialism and Spiritual Materiality in Israel Zangwill's *Children of the Ghetto,*" in *Victorian Vulgarity: Taste in Verbal and Visual Culture,* ed. Susan David Bernstein and Elsie B. Michie (Burlington, Vt.: Ashgate, 2009), 127; "bagels and lox": Jenna Weissman Joselit, *The Wonders of America: Reinventing Jewish Culture, 1880–1950* (New York: Holt, 1994), 171. On the rise of Jewish racial theories and Jewish materiality in the 1880s and 1890s in western Europe, see John Efron, *Defenders of the Race: Jewish Doctors and Race Science in Fin-de-Siècle Europe* (New Haven: Yale University Press, 1994), 64. On the attempt to render Judaism intelligible in scientific and medicinal categories see Mitchell B. Hart, *The Healthy Jew: Symbioses of Judaism and Modern Medicine* (New York: Cambridge University Press, 2007), 13–27. On American Jewish material identity see Ken Koltun-Fromm, *Material Culture and Jewish Thought in America* (Bloomington: Indiana University Press, 2010), 2.

15. Mikhah Yosef Berditsevski, "Lezekher Moshe Leib Lilienblum," *Davar,* February 15, 1935. See also Jonathan Frankel, *Prophecy and Politics: Socialism, Nationalism and the Russian Jews, 1862–1917* (Cambridge: Cambridge University Press, 1981), 85.

16. See Jonathan Boyarin and Daniel Boyarin, eds., *Jews and Other Differences: The New Jewish Cultural Studies* (Minneapolis: University of Minnesota Press, 1997); and Barbara Kirshenblatt-Gimblett, "The Corporeal Turn," *Jewish Quarterly Review* 95, no. 3

(Summer 2005): 447–461. See also Kirshenblatt-Gimblett, "Objects of Ethnography," in *Exhibiting Cultures: The Poetics and Politics of Museum Display*, ed. Ivan Karp and Steven D. Lavine (Washington, D.C.: Smithsonian, 1991), 386–443.

17. Carolyn Walker Bynum, *Christian Materiality: An Essay on Religion in Late Medieval Europe* (New York: Zone, 2011), 25.

18. See Benedict Anderson, *Imagined Communities: Reflections on the Origin and Spread of Nationalism* (New York: Verso, 1991), 6.

19. On the relationship of secularization to the state's seizure of church property and material see C. John Sommerville, *Secularization of Early Modern England: From Religious Culture to Religious Faith* (Oxford: Oxford University Press, 1992), 5.

20. For an overview of the Reformation see the classic work of Steven Ozment, *Reformation Europe: A Guide to Research* (Saint Louis: Center for Reformation Study, 1982). For recent historical studies on the Reformation and the establishment of Reformed churches see Anne Jacobson Schutte, Susan C. Karant-Nunn, and Heinz Schilling, eds., *Reformationsforschung in Europa und Nordamerika: Eine historiographische Bilanz anlässlich des 100. Bandes des Archivs für Reformationsgeschichte* (Gütersloh: Gütersloher Verlagshaus, 2009).

21. See Philip Benedict, *Christ's Churches Purely Reformed: A Social History of Calvinism* (New Haven: Yale University Press, 2002), 328, 533–542.

22. On religion and matter in the nineteenth century, see Peter Pels, "The Modern Fear of Matter: Reflections on the Protestantism of Victorian Science," in Brigit Meyer and Dick Houtman, eds., *Things: Religion and the Question of Materiality* (New York: Fordham University Press, 2012), 32–33. See also Webb Keane, "Materialism, Missionaries and Modern Subjects on Colonial Indonesia," in *Conversion to Modernities: The Globalization of Christianity*, ed. Peter van der Veer (New York: Rutledge, 1996), 137–170. On the longstanding discursive description of "religion" as opposed to materiality, see Webb Keane, "Sincerity, 'Modernity' and the Protestants," *Cultural Anthropology* 17, no. 1 (2002): 67–74; Brigit Meyer and Dick Houtman, "Introduction," to Meyer and Houtman, eds., *Things*, 6, 9–11; and Brigit Meyer, "Aesthetics of Persuasion: Global Christianity and Pentecostalism's Sensational Forms," *South Atlantic Quarterly* 9 (2010): 744–750.

23. On the economic opportunities granted to European Jews in the early modern period, see Jonathan I. Israel, *European Jewry in the Age of Mercantilism* (Oxford: Oxford University Press, 1985), 170–183. On early modern Jewish economic theorists, see Karp, *The Politics of Jewish Commerce;* Karp, "Can Economic History Date the Inception of Jewish Modernity?" in *The Economy in Jewish History: New Perspectives on the Interrelationship Between Ethnicity and Economic Life*, ed. Gideon Reuveni and Sarah Wobick-Segev (New York: Berghahn, 2011), 23–42; and Benjamin Ravid, *Economics and Toleration in Seventeenth-Century Venice: The Background and Context of the "Discorso" of Simone Luzzatto* (Jerusalem: American Academy of Jewish Research, 1978). On the corporate structure of European Jewish life in the early modern period, see Jacob Katz, *Tradition and Crisis: Jewish Society at the End of the Middle Ages*, trans. Bernard Dov Cooperman, rev. ed. (Syracuse: Syracuse University Press, 2000), 63–103.

24. On Jewish integration into the European state I have benefited greatly from the articles published in Michael Brenner, Vicki Caron, and Uri R. Kaufmann, eds., *Jewish Emancipation Reconsidered: The French and German Models* (Tübingen: Mohr Siebeck, 2003); Rainer Liedtke and Stephan Wendehorst, eds., *The Emancipation of Catholics, Jews and Protestants: Minorities and the Nation State in Nineteenth-Century Europe* (Manchester, U.K.: Manchester University Press, 1999); and Pierre Birnbaum and Ira Katznelson, eds., *Paths of Emancipation: Jews, States and Citizenship* (Princeton: Princeton University Press, 1995). For the Russian context see Michael Stanislawski, "Russian Jewry, the Russian State, and the Dynamics of Jewish Emancipation," in Birnbaum and Katznelson, eds., *Paths of Emancipation*, 3–36. On the emancipation of Jews in Germany and France see Jacob Katz, *Out of the Ghetto: The Social Background of Jewish Emancipation, 1770–1870* (Cambridge: Schocken, 1973), 9–41; Pierre Birnbaum, "A Jacobin Regenerator: Abbé Grégoire," in *Jewish Destinies: Citizenship, State and Community in Modern France,* ed. Pierre Birnbaum (New York: Hill and Wang, 2000), 11–30; Bart Wallet, "Napoleon's Legacy—National Government and Jewish Community in Western Europe," *Simon Dubnow Institute Yearbook* 6 (2007): 291–309; and Christopher Clark, "The 'Christian State' and the 'Jewish Citizen' in Nineteenth-Century Prussia," in *Protestants, Catholics and Jews in Germany, 1800–1914,* ed. Helmut Walser Smith (London: Bloomsbury, 2001): 67–93.

25. Paula Tartakoff, *Between Christian and Jew: Conversion and Inquisition in the Crown of Aragon, 1250–1391* (Philadelphia: University of Pennsylvania Press, 2012), 77. I would like to thank Phyllis Granoff for making me aware of this source.

26. Todd H. Weir, *Secularism and Religion in Nineteenth-Century Germany: The Rise of the Fourth Confession* (Cambridge: Cambridge University Press, 2015), 58–63, 214 (quotation). On economic anti-Semitism, see the overview of Derek Penslar, *Shylock's Children: Economics and Jewish Identity in Modern Europe* (Berkeley: University of California Press, 2001), 13–23.

27. On the formation of Jews' confessional identity in Western Europe, see Jens Neumann-Schliski, *Konfession oder Stamm? Konzepte jüdischer Identität bei Redakteuren jüdischer Zeitschriften 1840 bis 1881 im internationalen Vergleich* (Bremen: Lumiere, 2011), 212–273.

28. On the influence of Protestantism on modern Judaism, see Michael Meyer, *The Origins of the Modern Jew: Jewish Identity and European Culture, 1749–1824* (Detroit: Wayne State University Press, 1967), 115–143; Susannah Heschel, *Abraham Geiger and the Jewish Jesus* (Chicago: University of Chicago Press, 1998), 188–192; and Jonathan M. Hess's rich discussion of David Friedländer in *Germans, Jews and the Claims of Modernity* (New Haven: Yale University Press, 2002), 179–193. On Jewish anti-Catholicism in France and Germany, see Ari Joskowicz, *The Modernity of Others: Jewish Anti-Catholicism in Germany and France* (Stanford: Stanford University Press, 2014), 16–19.

29. Penslar, *Shylock's Children,* 89. On the parallel movement of modern European intellectuals "idealizing certain strands of Judaism" to support Jews being granted greater rights see Adam Sutcliffe, *Judaism and Enlightenment* (Cambridge: Cambridge University Press, 2003), 18, 210–212.

30. Samson Raphael Hirsch, *Judaism Eternal,* trans. Isidor Grunfeld, 2 vols. (London: Soncino, 1959), 2:208. See also Isaac Wise, *The Cosmic God* (Cincinnati, 1876), 24, 77–85. As early as 1856 Hirsch's journal *Jeschurun* began running indictments against the new forms of scientific materialism. See for example the anonymous article "Der Materialismus in der Naturwissenschaft," *Jeschurun* 2, no. 5 (1856): 271–279.

31. See Isidore Cahen's defense against the charge of materialism brought against members of the Consistoire and Camille Sée in "Chronique israélite de la Quinzain," *Archives israélites de France* 29 (1868): 388–389, and his more in-depth philosophical critique of materialism in "Sur une polémique récente a propos du Darwinisme," *Archives israélites de France* 36 (1875): 175–178.

32. For an overview of the economic situation of Jewish residents of the Pale of Settlement in the 1870s see Ezra Mendelsohn, *Class Struggle in the Pale: The Formative Years of the Workers' Movement* (Cambridge: Cambridge University Press, 1970), 1–26. On the differences between Russia's Jewish population and other groups living in the Russian Empire see Eugene Avrutin, "The Politics of Jewish Legibility: Documentation Practices and Reform During the Reign of Nicholas I," *Jewish Social Studies* 11, no. 2 (2005): 151–153.

33. On Jews' attempts to conform to the confessional boundaries of the Russian Empire see Eliyahu Stern, "Catholic Judaism: The Political Theology of the Nineteenth-Century Russian Jewish Enlightenment," *Harvard Theological Review* 109, no. 4 (2016): 483–511. On Jewish liberals in Russia see Benjamin Nathans, *Beyond the Pale: The Jewish Encounter with Late Imperial Russia* (Berkeley: University of California Press, 2002).

34. On Jewish republicanism and the idea that Jews constitute a tribe (*Stamm*), see Heidi Knörzer, "Ludwig Philippson et Isidore Cahen: Deux journalists, deux pays, un discours politique commun," *Archives Juives* 43 (2010): 128, Till van Rahden, "Germans of the Jewish *Stamm:* Visions of Community Between Nationalism and Particularism, 1850–1933," in *German History from the Margins,* ed. Neil Gregor, Nils Roemer, and Mark Roseman (Bloomington: Indiana University Press, 2006), 27–48; and Lisa Moses Leff, "Self Definition and Self Defense: Jewish Racial Identity in Nineteenth-Century France," *Jewish History* 19 (2005): 7–28. More generally, see Philip Nord, *The Republican Moment: Struggles for Democracy in Nineteenth-Century France* (Cambridge: Harvard University Press, 1995), 64–90.

35. See Eli Lederhendler, *Jewish Immigrants and American Capitalism, 1880–1920: From Caste to Class* (New York: Cambridge University Press, 2009), 7n23.

36. Moses Aaron Shatzkes, *Der yudisher far-peysekh* (1881; Warsaw, 1896), 14.

37. On Russian Jews' culture of poverty, see Arcadius Kahan, "The First Wave of Jewish Immigration from Eastern Europe to the United States," in Kahan, *Essays in Jewish Social and Economic History,* ed. Roger Weiss (Chicago: University of Chicago Press, 1986), 123–124.

38. Abraham Tsukerman, letter to Ephraim Deinard, dated 10th of Tevet, 5635, in JTS, Ephraim Deinard Papers, ARC 29, box 5, no. 39.

39. Letter from Judah Leib Levin to Judah Leib Gordon in "Mikhtav me-Yehalel le-Yalag," *He'avar* 1 (1918): 195–196.

40. See Fredrick C. Beiser, *The Genesis of Neo-Kantianism, 1796–1880* (Oxford: Oxford University Press, 2014), 182–183.

41. Carlton Hayes, *A Generation of Materialism, 1871–1900* (New York: Harper and Row, 1941), xii.

42. Lange's work was first published in 1865 and then significantly developed and republished in two volumes (between 1873 and 1875). A few years later Nikolia Strakhov translated the work into Russian as *Istoriia Materializma* (Saint Petersburg, 1881–1883). On the influence of Lange's work in Russian intellectual circles, see Alexander Vucinich, *Science in Russian Culture, 1861–1917* (Stanford: Stanford University Press, 1970), 260–262. Jewish materialists were already reading Lange's works by the 1870s. In the archives of the Prussian police there is a document that contains a list of books that the police confiscated from the Russian Jewish émigré Moses Aronsohn (one of the defendants in the 1879 trial of the Russian Jewish nihilists). Among the works listed in Aronsohn's possession was F. A. Lange, *Die Arbeiterfrage: Ihre Bedeutung für Gegenwart und Zukunft* (1865). See BINC, series 79, box 132, Geheime Präsidial-Registratur Lit: S. nr. 1234, vol. II, 200.

43. Frederick Albert Lange, *The History of Materialism and Criticism of Its Present Importance,* trans. Ernst Chester Thomas, 3 vols. (Boston: Houghton, Mifflin, 1881), 1:41–42, 236.

44. Lange's work had a profound influence on Russian and Polish Jewish thinkers. Shraga Feivel Frankel translated Lange's work into Hebrew under the title *Toldot hamaterialismus uvikoret 'erko bizmaneinu* (Warsaw, 1922). It was translated it into Yiddish by Z. M. Blat as *Geshikhte fun materyalizm un kritik fun zayn badaytung in der kegnvart* (Warsaw, 1929). On Lange's influence among eastern European Jews see Eliezer Y. Sheinbaum, *Hatsiyonut vehamateryaliyut* (Vilna, 1906), 17; and Kalman Shem Tov Geffen, *Torat hanevu'ah hatehora* (Cairo, 1923), iv.

45. On the general distinction between scientific materialism and scientists who adopted materialistic methods see Frederick Gregory, "Scientific Versus Dialectical Materialism: A Clash of Ideologies in Nineteenth-Century German Radicalism," *History of Science Society* 68, no. 2 (June 1977): 208. See also James Scanlan, "Nicholas Chernyshevsky and Philosophical Materialism in Russia," *Journal of the History of Philosophy* 8, no. 1 (1970): 74.

46. Georgi Plekhanov, "Cant Against Kant: or Herr Bernstein's Will and Testament," in Plekhanov, *Selected Philosophical Works,* trans. Julius Katzer, 5 vols. (Moscow, 1976), 2:352–378.

47. On the multiple ways Marx employs the term *materialism,* see Allan Megill and Jaeyoon Park, "Misrepresenting Marx: A Lesson in Historical Method" (manuscript, courtesy of the authors, July 2016). See also Victoria S. Frede, "Materialism and the Radical Intelligentsia: 1860s," in *A History of Russian Philosophy, 1830–1930: Faith, Reason and the Defense of Human Dignity,* ed. G. M. Hamburg and Randall A. Poole (Cambridge: Cambridge University Press, 2013), 68–89.

48. See Zbigniew A. Jordan, *The Evolution of Dialectical Materialism: A Philosophical and Sociological Analysis* (New York: St. Martin's, 1967), 404n67.

49. Shlomo Avineri, *The Social and Political Thought of Karl Marx* (Cambridge: Cambridge University Press, 1968), 70.

50. See Karl Marx, *Capital: A Critique of Political Economy,* trans. Samuel Moore and Edward Aveling (Chicago: Charles H. Kerr, 1909), 2:6:4, p. 187.

51. Karl Marx, "On the Jewish Question," in *The Marx-Engels Reader*, 2nd ed., ed. and trans. Robert Tucker (New York: Norton, 1978), 48; see also Julius Carlebach, *Karl Marx and the Radical Critique of Judaism* (London: Routledge, 1978); Yoav Peled, "From Theology to Sociology: Bruno Bauer and Karl Marx on the Question of Jewish Emancipation," *History of Political Thought* 13, no. 3 (1992): 464–485; Wendy Brown, "Rights and Identity in Late Modernity," in *Identities, Politics, and Rights*, ed. Austin Sarat and Thomas R. Kearns (Ann Arbor: University of Michigan Press, 1995), 85–131.

52. Moses Hess, "Die Soziale Revolution," *Volksstaat*, February 1870, cited in Theodor Zlocisti, *Moses Hess: Der Vorkämpfer des Sozialismus und Zionismus, 1812–1875* (Berlin: Welt Verlag, 1921), 408.

53. On Moses Hess's *Dynamische Stofflehre* (Paris, 1877) see Theodor Zlocisti, *Moses Hess, Jüdische Schriften* (Berlin: von Lious Lamm 1905), clxii–clxvi; and Karl Erich Grözinger, *Jüdisches Denken. Theologie-Philosophie-Mystik*, vol. 4: *Zionismus und Schoah* (Frankfort: Campus Verlag, 2015), 85–91.

54. As perceptively noted by Jonathan Frankel in *Prophecy and Politics*, 83, there was a "paradox" in how Hess was received among Russian Jews. It was not the self-declared materialist Lieberman or "half-nihilist" Lilienblum but the founder of Cultural Zionism, Peretz Smolenskin, who was said to have first appropriated Hess's theories and promoted them among Russian Jews. I discuss this in Chapter 5, below.

55. On the scholarly debate over the "ascetic" versus "materialistic" features of medieval Judaism, see the dueling positions of Yitzchak (Fritz) Baer, *Yisra'el ba'amim* (Jerusalem, 1955), 20–57, and Ephraim E. Urbach, *The Sages: Their Concepts and Beliefs* (Jerusalem: Magnes, 1975), 443–448. For an overview of this debate see Steven Fraade, "Ascetical Aspects of Ancient Judaism" in *Jewish Spirituality: From the Bible Through the Medieval Ages*, ed. Arthur Green (New York: Crossroad, 1986), 253–277. See also Daniel Boyarin, *Carnal Israel: Reading Sex in Talmudic Judaism* (Berkeley: University of California Press, 1993), 33–36. For an overview of rabbinic and medieval Jewish philosophical materialism, see Sarah Pessin, "Matter, Form and the Corporeal World," in *The Cambridge History of Jewish Philosophy: From Antiquity Through the Seventeenth Century*, ed. Steven Nadler and Tamar Rudavsky (Cambridge: Cambridge University Press, 2009): 269–302. On early modern Jewish atomist thought, see Tsvi Langerman, "Yosef Shlomo Delmedigo's Engagement with Atomism," in *Jewish Culture in Early Modern Europe: Essays in Honor of David B. Ruderman*, ed. Richard I. Cohen et al. (Cincinnati: Hebrew Union College, University of Pittsburgh Press, 2014), 124–133.

56. Brian Porter-Szűcs, *Faith and Fatherland: Catholicism and Modernity* (Oxford: Oxford University Press, 2011), 15.

57. See Piotr H. Kosicki, "Masters in Their Own Home or Defenders of the Human Person? Wojciech Korfanty, Anti-Semitism, and Polish Christian Democracy's Illiberal Rights Talk," *Modern Intellectual History*, published online January 23, 2015 (http://dx.doi.org/10.1017/S1479244314000857).

58. Nineteenth-century Polish intellectuals preferred positivist thinkers (Buckle and Spencer) who supported their historical claims to the lands in which they resided over more materialist thinkers who focused on the issue of labor and class relations. See Brian Porter, "The Social Nation and Its Futures: English Liberalism and Polish Nationalism

in Late Nineteenth-Century Warsaw," *American Historical Review* 101, no. 5 (December 1996): 1476n17; and Porter, *When Nationalism Began to Hate: Imagining Modern Politics in Nineteenth-Century Poland* (Oxford: Oxford University Press, 2000), 70. The difference between the ideas espoused by Jewish positivists living in Polish lands and the positions advanced by Russian Jewish materialists has been perceptively recognized by Ela Bauer, *Between Poles and Jews: The Development of Nahum Sokolow's Political Thought* (Jerusalem: Hebrew University Magnes Press, 2005), 41–43, 49. There were numerous differences between materialists such as Levin, Lieberman, Lilienblum, Zuckermann, and Kaminer and positivists such as Sokolow. The Russian materialists in the 1860s were not focused on currying favor with state-based institutions, usually did not see history as progressing, and were far more critical of traditional religious beliefs. On Polish positivism and the Jews, see Stanislaus A. Blejwas, "Polish Positivism and the Jews," *Jewish Social Studies* 46, no. 1 (1984): 21–36. On positivism in Russia more generally see Andrzej Walicki, "Variants of Positivism" in his *A History of Russian Thought from the Enlightenment to Marxism* (Stanford: Stanford University Press, 1979), 349–370.

59. Turks, like Jews, were especially taken by the way pre-Marxian forms of materialism had been mobilized by the early *narodnik* revolutionaries in Russian lands. See M. Şükrü Hanioğlu, *The Young Turks in Opposition* (Oxford: Oxford University Press, 1995), 21–23.

60. M. Şükrü Hanioğlu, "Blueprints for a Future Society: Late Ottoman Materialists on Science, Religion and Art," in *Late Ottoman Society: The Intellectual Legacy,* ed. Elisabeth Özdalga (New York: Routledge Curzon, 2005), 58. See also Marwa Elshakry, *Reading Darwin in Arabic, 1860–1950* (Chicago: University of Chicago Press, 2013), 99–131.

61. See Hanioğlu, "Blueprints for a Future Society," 29.

62. Hanioğlu, *The Young Turks in Opposition,* 202.

63. Ibid. 82–89.

64. On the reconstruction of Hinduism in the nineteenth century, see the overview of Vasudha Dalmia and Heinrich von Stietencron in their introduction to *Representing Hinduism: The Construction of Religious Traditions and National Identity* (London: Sage, 1995), 17–26. See also Vasudha Dalmia, *Nationalization of Hindu Traditions: Bharatendu Harischandra and Nineteenth-Century Banaras* (Delhi: Oxford University Press, 1997), 6–10, 340–341.

65. David Kopf, *The Brahmo Samaj and the Shaping of the Modern Indian Mind* (Princeton: Princeton University Press, 1979), 51–85 (quotation, 66). See also Kenneth W. Jones, *Arya Dharm: Hindu Consciousness in Nineteenth-Century Punjab* (Berkeley: University of California Press, 1976), 45.

66. See Brij Gopal Tiwari, *Secularism and Materialism in Modern India* (Jabalpur: Motilal Banarsidass, 1964), 106–112

67. Savarkar specifically mentions these writers as among those whose works that he read during his time in jail. V. D. Savarkar, *The Story of My Transportation for Life,* trans. Majhi Janmathep (Bombay, 1984), 269, 429.

68. Peter van der Veer, "Hindus: A Superior Race," *Nations and Nationalism,* 5, no. 3 (1999): 419–430.

69. See V. D. Savarkar, *Hindutva* (Bombay: Veer Savarkar Prakashan, 1969), 92.

70. Margaret Chatterjee, *Studies in Modern Jewish and Hindu Thought* (New York: St. Martin's, 1997), 23–48. More generally on the relationship between Hinduism and Judaism see Alan Brill, *Judaism and World Religions: Encountering Christianity, Islam and Eastern Traditions* (New York: Palgrave Macmillan, 2012), 203–235.

71. Todd Weir, "The Riddles of Monism: An Introductory Essay," in *Monism: Science, Philosophy, Religion, and the History of a Worldview,* ed. Todd Weir (New York: Palgrave Macmillan, 2012), 2.

72. Aside from the studies associated with the groups discussed previously, in recent years scholars have overturned the old model of seeing nationalism in terms of the decline of religion. See George L. Mosse, *The Nationalization of the Masses: Political Symbolism and Mass Movements in Germany from the Napoleonic Wars Through the Third Reich* (Ithaca: Cornell University Press, 1975). More generally, see Brubaker, "Religion and Nationalism." See also Hartmut Lehmann, "Über die Varianten einer komplementären Relation. Die Säkularisierung der Religion und die Sakralisierung der Nation im 20. Jahrhundert," in *Religion im Nationalstaat zwischen den Weltkriegen,* ed. Christian Maner and Martin Schulze Wessel (Stuttgart: Fritz Steiner Verlag, 2002), 13–27; and the essays in Martin Schulze Wessel, ed., *Nationalisierung der Religion und Sakralisierung der Nation im östlichen Europa* (Stuttgart: Franz Steiner Verlag, 2006). For a view beyond Europe, see the essays in Peter van der Veer and Hartmut Lehmann, eds., *Nation and Religion: Perspectives on Europe and Asia,* eds. (Princeton: Princeton University Press, 1999); and Annika Hvithamar and Margit Warburg, "Introducing Civil Religion, Nationalism and Globalisation," in *Holy Nations and Global Identities: Civil Religion, Nationalism and Global Identities,* ed. Annika Hvithamar, Margit Warburg, and Brian Arly Jacobson (Leiden: Brill, 2009), 1–10. In a Jewish context, see, most recently, Naomi Seidman, "Secularization and Sexuality: Theorizing the Erotic Transformation of Ashkenaz," paper available at http://www.ajsnet.org/seidman.pdf (accessed November 11, 2015). There she writes, "If Protestantism bore within it the seeds of the secular, the Jewish secular embrace of the Jews as a people already carried within itself the seeds of its embrace of the Jewish religion" (48–49).

73. Michael Löwy, *Redemption and Utopia: Jewish Libertarian Thought in Central Europe: A Study in Elective Affinity,* trans. Hope Heaney (Stanford: Stanford University Press, 1992), 22.

74. See Daniel Miller's introduction to his edited volume *Materiality* (Durham, N.C.: Duke University Press, 2005), 28n9. On value, see Viviana A. Zelizer, *Pricing the Priceless Child: The Changing Social Value of Children* (New York: Basic, 1981), 21.

75. On Klausner's nationalist historiography and his role as a public intellectual see David N. Myers, *Re-inventing the Jewish Past: European Jewish Intellectuals and the Zionist Return to History* (New York: Oxford University Press, 1995), 94–98, 137–138; and Myers, "Between Diaspora and Zion: History, Memory, and the Jerusalem Scholars," in *The Jewish Past Revisited: Reflections on Modern Jewish Historians,* ed. David N. Myers and David B. Ruderman (New Haven: Yale University Press, 1998), 96–97.

76. Joseph Klausner, *Historya shel hasifrut ha'ivrit hahadasha,* 6 vols. (Jerusalem: Hebrew University, 1953–1960), 4:271. Klausner's statements were expressed in the context of his analysis of Moses Lilienblum. Klausner noted that "again and again one sees Lilienblum adopting a materialist perspective" (4:271; see also 3:105–115).

77. Klausner specifically singled out for praise the works of Peretz Smolenskin and Asher Ginsberg. See Joseph Klausner, "Hamaterialismus hahistori vehatnu'a hale'umit," in *Kitvei prof. Yosef Klausner: yahadut ve'enoshiyut,* 2 vols. (Tel Aviv: Massada, 1955), 1:105. On Klausner's more general attempt to locate precursors of Zionism in Jewish history, see Daniel B. Schwartz, *The First Modern Jew: Spinoza and the History of an Image* (Princeton: Princeton University Press, 2012), 113–140.

78. Joseph Klausner, "Hamaterialismus hahistori vehatnu'a hale'umit," 1:85.

79. Ibid., 1:104–106.

80. For an overview of the way Marx's ideas were formulated into a theory of history see Allan Megill, "Marxism," in *New Dictionary of the History of Ideas,* ed. Maryanne Horowitz, 6 vols. (New York: Scribner's, 2005), 4:1357–1364; and Jordan, *The Evolution of Dialectical Materialism.*

81. Joseph Klausner, *Kitvei prof. Yosef Klausner: otobiyografya,* 2 vols. (Tel Aviv: Massada, 1955), 1:27.

82. See Abraham Liessin, "Epizodn," in Elias Tcherikower, ed. *Historishe shriftn,* 3 vols. (Vilna: YIVO, 1939), 3:174–175.

83. Abraham Liessin, *Zikhronot vahavayot* (Tel Aviv: Am Oved, 1943), 128.

84. Karl Kautsky, "Forvert," in Karl Marx and Friedrich Engels, *Dos manifest fun di komunistishe partey* (Geneva, 1899), 15.

85. Ibid., 16.

86. On Feigenbaum's political activity, see Joshua D. Zimmerman, *Poles and Jews: The Politics of Nationality* (Madison: University of Wisconsin Press, 2004), 127–146.

87. Benjamin Feigenbaum, "Materyalizmus in yidishkayt oder religyon un lebn—ver firt vemen?" *Di tsukunft* 5, no. 10 (October 1896): 13 [466].

88. Ibid., 19 [472].

89. See Mendelsohn, *Class Struggle in the Pale;* and Steven J. Zipperstein, *The Jews of Odessa: A Cultural History, 1794–1881* (Stanford: Stanford University Press, 1986).

90. Shmuel Feiner and Israel Bartal have explained how some of those identified in this work as Jewish materialists bridge Jewish political movements that emerged at the end of the nineteenth century and the Jewish enlightenment movement, whose roots run back to the eighteenth century in Berlin. For Feiner, the 1870s become an important point in a larger story of the secularization of modern Jewish identity. Bartal has been more cautious about employing a secularization theory but has also placed those addressed in this book on a continuum running from early-nineteenth-century Jewish Haskalah to late-nineteenth-century political movements. See Bartal's identification of Lieberman as a "radical enlightener," in *Letaken 'am* (Jerusalem: Karmel, 2013), 327–346. See most notably Shmuel Feiner, *Haskalah and History: The Emergence of Modern Jewish Historical Consciousness,* trans. Chaya Naor and Sondra Silverstone (Oxford: Littman Library of Jewish Civilization, 2002), 283–296; and Erich E. Haberer, *Jews*

and Revolution in Nineteenth-Century Russia (Cambridge: Cambridge University Press, 1995), 25. For a critique of this historiographical approach, see Ezra Mendelsohn's review of Erich E. Haberer's work, published in *Russian Review* 56, no. 1 (January 1997): 136–138. See also the position advanced by Bartal in his dissertation "Halo-yehudim veḥevratam besifrut 'ivrit veyidish bemizraḥ eiropa bein hashanim 1856–1914" (Ph.D. diss., Hebrew University, 1980). There Bartal follows the approach I have adopted in this work. He contrasts the early-nineteenth-century enlighteners with the materialists of the 1860s and 1870s, suggesting important political differences between the two groups (38). See also Eli Lederhendler's insights in *The Road to Modern Jewish Politics: Political Tradition and Political Reconstruction in the Jewish Community of Tsarist Russia* (New York: Oxford University Press, 1989), 147–149, in which the author differentiates the Jewish materialists of the 1870s from the enlighteners of 1840s. Lederhendler has also perceptively noted the difference between the forms of messianism advanced by those in 1870s and earlier models. See his "Interpreting the Messianic Rhetoric in the Russian Haskalah and Early Zionism," *Studies in Contemporary Jewry* 7 (1991): 20–23.

91. Pavel Axelrod, *Perezhitoe i peredumannoe* (1923; repr. Cambridge: Oriental Research Partners, 1975), 21. On Kovner's upbringing see Saul M. Ginzburg, *Meshumodim in tsarishn Rusland* (New York: Tsiko, 1946), 157.

92. See NYPL, ***P Joseph Sossnitz, Box 1.1, autobiography, p. 3.

93. Khasia Shur's father was a wealthy merchant. Her grandfather was the highly respected rabbi Jacob Barit of Vilna. See Khasia Shur, *Vospominaniia* (Kursk: 1928), 15–16. The Zuckermann family was one of the most distinguished rabbinic and scholarly families in eastern Europe; see Eliezer Zukermann, *Kitvei Eli'ezer Tsukerman,* ed. Tsvi Krol (Tel Aviv, 1940), 10–16. We should also include in this list the families of Grigory Gurevich and Judah Leib Levin. The latter was the son of merchants and the grandson of the Hasidic rebbe Moshe of Kobrin. On Levin, see Judah Leib Levin, *Yehuda Leib Levin: Zikhronot vehegyonot,* ed. Yehuda Slutsky (Jerusalem: Mosad Bialik, 1968), 36.

94. On Smolenskin's relationship to his family see Judah Leib Smolenskin, "Eleh toldot Perets," *Davar,* January 25, 1935. On Winchevsky see Kalman Marmor, "Moris Vintshevski: zayn lebn, virkn un shafn," in Morris Winchevsky, *Gezamlte verk,* 10 vols., ed. Kalman Marmor (New York: Frayhayt, 1927), 1:18–20.

95. On Zukermann's relationship to his parents see Zukermann, *Kitvei Eli'ezer Tsukerman,* 16–23. On Helfman's relationship to her parents see Henne Helfman, "A briv in der redaktsye," *Der alter Yisrolik,* October 5, 1875; and Lev Deutsch, "Gesya Helfman, di groyse shtile martirerin," *Di tsukunft* 21, no. 4 (1916): 322–325.

96. See the letter from Lilienblum to Gordon dated December 16, 1878, in Shlomo Breiman, ed., *Igrot M. L. Lilienblum le-Y. L. Gordon* (Jerusalem: Magnes, 1968), 157–158.

97. See Axelrod, *Perezhitoe i peredumannoe,* 17–32.

98. Shur, *Vospominaniia,* 40.

99. See Judah Leib Levin, *Yehuda Leib Levin: Zikhronot vehegyonot,* 46. On Lieberman's study of Kabbalah with his grandfather see Kalman Marmor, "Arn Libermans letste shrift," *Morgn frayhayt,* November 18, 1930. On Sossnitz, see his unedited autobiography, NYPL, ***P Joseph Sossnitz, box 1.1.

100. At age sixteen Ilya Orshanski had never even met a Gentile. See Yakov Moscow Mibaslow, "Toldot anshei shem: vehu ḥayyei heḥakham Eliyahu Orshanski," *Hakol,* January 26, 1879.

101. A. E. Kaufman, "Za mnogo let," *Evreiskaia starina* 5 (1913): 218.

102. See Deutsch, "Gesya Helfman, di groyse shtile martirerin," 322–325.

103. On the notes taken by the Berlin police of the Russian Jewish medical doctors, see the files in BINC, series 79, box 132.

104. On sexual experimentation within the Berlin commune, see Moshe Kamensky, "Nihilistim 'ivriyim bishnot hashiv'im," *Hashiloaḥ* 17 (1907): 260.

105. Using Talmudic innuendo, David Isaiah Silberbusch, who lived in Vienna in the 1880s and worked in the print shop of Peretz Smolenskin, suggested that Lieberman had been engaged in a sexual relationship with the Anglican missionary and apostate Isaac Salkinson. See D. I. Silberbusch, *Mipinkas zikhronotai* (Tel Aviv, 1936), 56. available at http://benyehuda.org/silberbusch/ishim_umeoraot.html#_ftn1 (accessed March 28, 2015).

106. See Krol, "Introduction," in Zuckermann, *Kitvei Eli'ezer Tsukerman,* 30.

107. See Eliezer Ben-Yehuda's description of his first encounter with "nihilistic literature" and "the material needs of life" in chapter 2 of "Haḥalom veshivro" (Jerusalem: Mosad Bialik, 1978), available at http://benyehuda.org/by/haidan_harishon.html (accessed April 3, 2017).

108. Mordechai Levin, *'Erkhei ḥevra vekhalkala ba'ide'ologya shel tekufat hahaskala,* 74 (quotation), 93–94.

109. On Russian Jews' enrollment in universities in the 1860s, see Nathans, *Beyond the Pale,* 214–256. The Vienna-trained philosopher and medical doctor Aaron Porjes, the Kiev-based physician Isaac Kaminer, and the Kiev lawyer Ilya Orshanski received university degrees.

110. See Shur, *Vospominaniia,* 60.

111. See Krol, "Introduction," in Zuckermann, *Kitvei Eli'ezer Tsukerman,* 29.

112. Weir, *Secularism and Religion in Nineteenth-Century Germany,* 118–129.

113. Lilienblum received twenty-five rubles a month as an editor of the Yiddish weekly *Kol mevaser.* See his letter to Y. L Gordon, December 16, 1870, in Breiman, ed., *Igrot M. L. Lilienblum le-Y. L. Gordon,* 107. Orshanski received thirty rubles a month as a lawyer in Odessa. See Mibaslow, "Toldot anshei shem." Judah Leib Levin received thirty-five rubles a month as a tutor and later became an accountant for the Brodsky family. See the letter from Eliezer Brodsky to Levin in Judah Leib Levin, *Yehuda Leib Levin: Zikhronot vehegyonot,* 51–52.

114. On the work conditions and salaries of Lithuanian handcrafters and factory workers, see Aaron Shemuel Lieberman, "Iz Vil'no," *Vpered!* September 1, 1875.

115. For an overview of the social impact of nineteenth-century Jewish newspapers see Israel Bartal, "'Mevaser umodi'a' le'ish yehudi': ha'itonut hayehudit ke'afik shel ḥidush," in his *Letaken 'am* (Jerusalem: Karmel, 2013), 315–325. For a study in English of the major Hebrew, Russian, and Yiddish newspapers in the 1860s and 1870s see Alexander Orbach, *New Voices of Russian Jews: A Study of the Russian Press of Odessa in the Era of the Great Reform, 1860–1871* (Leiden: Brill, 1980). On the Yiddish press in the

1860s and 1870s see most recently Alyssa Quint, "'Yiddish Literature for the Masses'? A Reconsideration of Who Read What in Jewish Eastern Europe," *AJS Review* 29, no. 1 (2005): 76–78. On the Hebrew press, see Lederhendler, *The Road to Modern Jewish Politics,* 119–133; and Oren Soffer, *Ein lefalpel! 'Iton "hatsefira" vehamodernizatsya shel hasiah hahevrati hapoliti* (Jerusalem: Mosad Bialik, 2007). On the Russian press, see Yehuda Slutsky, *Ha'itonut hayehudit-rusit bame'a hatesha' 'esreh* (Jerusalem: Mosad Bialik, 1970) 37–69, 102–120.

116. On the press as an arena of conflict see Lederhendler, *The Road to Modern Jewish Politics,* 130–133.

CHAPTER 1. TRADITION

1. For an overview of the Jews' economic situation in Polish lands see Israel Bartal *The Jews of Eastern Europe, 1772–1881,* trans. Chaya Naor (Philadelphia: University of Pennsylvania Press, 2006), 42–44. For more in-depth studies see Jacob Lestschinsky, "Di antviklung fun yidishn folk far di letste 100 yor," in *Shriftn far ekonomik un statistik* (1928): 1–64; Yisroel Yakhinson, *Sotsyal-ekonomisher shteyger bay yidn in rusland in XIX yor hundert* (Kharkov: Tsentraler farlag far di felker fun F.S.S.R., 1929); and Israel Sosis, *Di geshikhte fun di Yidishe gezelshaftlekhe shtremungen in Rusland in XIX yorhundert* (Minsk: Vaysrusisher melukhe-farlag, 1929).

2. Alexander I took steps to diversify the Jews' economic profile, assimilate them into the regional populations in which they resided, and encourage them to settle in the agricultural western and southwestern provinces. The first colonies were established in 1806 in Kherson on 80,000 acres of land. Soon some 1,690 families had begun making a livelihood by tilling Russian soil. In the face of miserable living conditions that drove away many of the settlers, the government recommitted its resources to supporting the new outposts. For an overview see Mordechai Levin, *'Erkhei hevra vekhalkala ba'ide'ologya shel tekufat hahaskala* (Jerusalem: Mosad Bialik, 1975), 187–256; and Mordechai Zalkin, "Can Jews Become Farmers? Rurality, Peasantry and Cultural Identity in the World of the Rural Jew in Nineteenth-Century Eastern Europe," *Rural History* 24, no. 2 (2013): 161–175.

3. See Yitskhok Fayn, "Di Londoner misyonern-gezelshaft far yidn: ir arbet in Poyln un Rusland bemeshekh fun 19tn y"h," *YIVO Bleter* 24 (1944): 27–46; Israel Bartal, "Misyonerim britim bimehozot habad," *Habad Hasidism: History, Thought, Image,* ed. Jonatan Meir and Gadi Sagiv (Jerusalem: Merkaz Zalman Shazar, 2016), 145–183; Agnieszka Jagodzinka, "English Missionaries Look at Polish Jews," in *Polin: Jews in the Kingdom of Poland, 1815–1918,* ed. Glenn Dynner, Antony Polonsky, Marcin Wodzinski (Oxford: Littman Library of Jewish Civilization, 2015), 89–116; John Klier, "State Policies and the Conversion of Jews in Imperial Russia," in *Of Religion and Empire: Missions, Conversion, and Tolerance in Tsarist Russia,* ed. Robert P. Geraci and Michael Khodarkovsky (Ithaca: Cornell University Press, 2011), 92–112; and Christopher Clark, "The Limits of the Confessional State: Conversions to Judaism in Prussia, 1814–1843," *Past and Present* 147 (1995): 159–79.

4. Charles Frederick Henningsen, *Eastern Europe and the Emperor Nicholas*, 3 vols. (London, 1846), 3:258.

5. On the economic positions of the rabbinic elite residing in Russian lands see Mordechai Levin, *'Erkhei ḥevra vekhalkala ba'ide'ologya shel tekufat hahaskala*, 23–32.

6. Ḥayyim of Volozhin, *Ru'aḥ ḥayyim* (Vilna, 1859), 6:4 (p. 76). Ḥayyim of Volozhin in other places (1:8, 16) asserted that that it is more virtuous to make a living through work than from study. However, he maintained that laborers should always honor clerics and see themselves as beneath them. He argues that men should work only so that they can devote the rest of their time to study (2:2, 26).

7. See Bernard D. Weinryb, "Latoldot hakalkaliyot vehaḥevratiyot etsel hayehudim bame'a hatesha' 'esreh," *Tarbiz* 7 (1936): 57–73; and Weinryb, "Toldot Ribal," *Tarbiz* 5, no. 2 (1934): 200n5. See also Mordechai Zalkin, "Economic and Occupational Aspects in the World of the East European Jewish Enlightenment in Russia in the First Half of the Nineteenth-Century," in *Enlightenment and Diaspora: The Armenian and Jewish Cases*, ed. Richard G. Hovannisian and David N. Myers (Atlanta: Scholars Press, 1999), 223–228.

8. See A. S. Katsenelenbogen, *Heḥarash vehamasger*, JNUL, A. S. Katsenelenbogen, MS. A236, p. 13. The work seems to have been written in 1821.

9. See Menashe Ilya, *Shekel hakodesh* (Kapust, 1823), 3a.

10. See Heinz-Dietrich Löwe, "Poles, Jews, and Tartars: Religion, Ethnicity and Social Structure in Tsarist Nationality Politics," *Jewish Social Studies* 6, no. 3 (2000): 81; and Frank Nesemann, "Aufgeklaerter Absolutismus and religioese Toleranz: Juden und Muslime unter Katharina II," *Leipziger Beitraege zur juedischen Geschichte und Kultur* 2 (2004): 75–99. More generally see Robert Crews, "Empire and the Confessional State: Islam and Religious Politics in Nineteenth-Century Russia," *American Historical Review* 108, no. 1 (2003): 50–83.

11. See Michael Stanislawski, *Tsar Nicholas I and the Jews: The Transformation of Jewish Society in Russia, 1825–1855* (Philadelphia: Jewish Publication Society, 1983), 15; and Yohanan Petrovsky-Shtern, *Jews in the Russian Army, 1827–1917* (Cambridge: Cambridge University Press, 2009), 64–66.

12. On the idea of Jews becoming "Russians of the Mosaic Faith" see Israel Zinberg, *The Haskalah Movement in Russia*, trans. Bernard Martin (New York: Hebrew Union College and Ktav Press, 1978), 75; and John Doyle Klier, *Imperial Russia's Jewish Question, 1855–1881* (Cambridge: Cambridge University Press, 1995), 84.

13. Mordecai Aaron Guenzburg, *Maggid emet* (Leipzig, 1843), 6.

14. Petrovsky-Shtern, *Jews in the Russian Army*, 89.

15. My theoretical equation of "traditional" economics and "traditional" religious worldviews follows Max Weber's economic-religious typology of "traditional authority." For Weber, traditionalists tended to reflect Catholics who remained entrenched in handcrafts and agricultural industries. Weber sharply contrasted the "fundamental characteristics of an individualistic capitalistic economy that [was] rationalized on the basis of rigorous calculation" with "the hand to mouth existence of the peasant and to the privileged traditionalism of the guild craftsman." Max Weber, *The Protestant Ethic*

and the Spirit of Capitalism, trans. Talcott Parsons (New York: Dover, 2003), 76. On Weber's category of traditional economics see Richard Swedberg, *Max Weber and the Idea of Economic Sociology* (Princeton: Princeton University Press, 2000), 66–69; and Philip S. Gorski, "The Protestant Ethic and the Bureaucratic Revolution: Ascetic Protestantism and the Administrative Rationalization in Early Modern Europe," in *Max Weber's Economy and Society: A Critical Companion,* ed. Philip S. Gorski and David M. Trubek (Stanford: Stanford University Press, 2005), 266–296.

16. See Mordechai Zalkin, "Ve'eleh yimaletu —heharash vehamasger," in *Yazamut yehudit ba'et hahadasha,* ed. Ran Aaronsohn and Shaul Stampfer (Jerusalem: Hebrew University Press, Magnes Press, 2000), 80–81, 92.

17. See Israel Klausner, *Vilna: Yerushalayim delita,* vol. 1: *Dorot rishonim 1495–1881* (Tel Aviv: Ghetto Fighters' House, 1988), 320. Klausner's calculations are probably based on archival documents, "Tekhunat toshavei Vilna," JNUL, Saul M. Ginzburg, ARC. 4*1281A, no. 311-331, and an anonymous pamphlet, "Matsav 'ir Vilna," ibid., no. 251-280. Both these documents list roughly thirty to forty professions, but stress that this economic diversity is misleading: rampant poverty engulfed the city.

18. "Tekhunat toshavei Vilna," JNUL, Saul M. Ginzburg, ARC. 4*1281A, no. 311-331.

19. See "Matsav 'ir Vilna," JNUL, Saul M. Ginzburg, ARC. 4* 1281A, no. 251-280, written for Moses Montefiore on the occasion of his visit to Vilna. Mordechai Zalkin informed me that the Vilna enlightener Abraham Dov Baer Levinsohn probably wrote the pamphlet.

20. Ibid., pp. 2–4.

21. Ibid., pp. 5–7.

22. Abraham Simha Katsenelenbogen, "Yalkut reshumot" (1845), St. Petersburg–Institute of Oriental Studies of the Russian Academy, B 525, JNUL, Yalkut Reshumot, F 69276, nos. 147, 148. This source contains numerous documents written by Katsenelenbogen, some of which span the 1840s and early 1850s. On Katsenelenbogen's claim that he was the chief accountant of Vilna see document no. 183. On Katsenelenbogen more generally see Zalkin, "Ve'eleh yimaletu—heharash vehamasger," 93–95.

23. In 1834 Russian officials described Katsenelenbogen as an "honest" and upright individual. See the Imperial Reports regarding his (and Solomon Salkin's) request to publish *Minhat bikkurim,* CAHJP, Tsvi Hirsch Katzenlenbogen, HM2/9776.7.

24. The report, titled "Ob ustroistve evreiskogo naroda v rossii," was published in two parts in Simon Dubnow, "Istoricheskie soobshcheniia," *Voskhod* 4 (1901): 25–40 (quotation on p. 29), and 5 (1902): 3–21.

25. See W. Bruce Lincoln, "Count P. D. Kiselev: A Reformer in Imperial Russia," *Australian Journal of Politics and History* 16 (1970): 177–188.

26. Dubnow, "Istoricheskie soobshcheniia," *Voskhod* 4 (1901): 30.

27. Benjamin Nathans, *Beyond the Pale: The Jewish Encounter with Late Imperial Russia* (Berkeley: University of California Press, 2002), 34.

28. See the detailed archival data on the taxes and school management in Peysekh Marek, *Ocherki po istorii prosvyeshcheniia evreev v Rossii* (Moscow, 1909), 71–83. Even at the end of the nineteenth century, Jews in agricultural settlements established by the Russian government refused to send their children to the state-sponsored schools. See Jew-

ish Colonial Association, *Recueil de materiaux sur la situation économique des Israelites de Russie,* 2 vols. (Paris, 1906), 1:105. A great deal of literature has been written about the *kheyder* system. See Nathaniel Deutsch, *The Dark Continent: Life and Death in the Russian Pale of Settlement* (Cambridge: Harvard University Press, 2011), 143–164. On the seminary graduates see Azriel Shochat, *Mosad harabbanut mita'am berusya* (Haifa: University of Haifa Press, 1976), 30–37.

29. See Stanislawski, *Tsar Nicholas I and the Jews* (Philadelphia: Jewish Publication Society, 1983), 66–69.

30. *Dopolnenie k "Sborniku postanovleniy" po ministerstvu narodnago prosvyeshcheniia 1803–1864,* 696. The report was originally issued on March 17, 1841.

31. Ibid., 700.

32. David Friedländer, *Avot* (Vienna, 1791), 14a. On Friedländer's economic theories see Derek Penslar, *Shylock's Children: Economics and Jewish Identity in Modern Europe* (Berkeley: University of California Press, 2001), 75.

33. Penslar, *Shylock's Children,* 75.

34. See Simon Dubnow, *History of the Jews in Russia and Poland, from the Earliest Times Until the Present Day,* trans. Israel Friedlaender, 3 vols. (Philadelphia: Jewish Publication Society, 1918), 1:242.

35. On the traditional character of Russian-Jewish enlightenment see Israel Sosis, *Di geshikhte fun di Yidishe gezelshaftlekhe shtremungen in Rusland in XIX yorhundert,* 46; and Stanislawski, *Tsar Nicholas I and the Jews,* 111.

36. See Stanislawski, *Tsar Nicholas I and the Jews,* 97–122. On Uvarov's general education policy and the Jews see Cynthia H. Wittaker, *The Origins of Modern Russian Education: An Intellectual Biography of Count Sergei Uvarov, 1786–1855* (Dekalb: Northern Illinois University Press, 1984), 200–204.

37. On Levinsohn's life see David Baer Nathansohn, *Sefer hazikhronot: divrei yemei hayyei . . . Yitshak Ber Levinzohn* (Warsaw, 1899), 5–6. For a complete English bibliography of Levinsohn's works see Louis S. Greenberg, *Isaac Baer Levinsohn: A Critical Investigation of the Works of Rabbi Isaac Baer Levinsohn (Ribal)* (New York: Bloch, 1930, 16.

38. See Immanuel Etkes, "Introduction," in *Yitshak Baer Levinsohn,* ed. Immanuel Etkes (Jerusalem: Merkaz Zalman Shazar, 1977), 3–19. On Levinsohn and his relationship to the Russian government see Stanislawski, *Tsar Nicholas I and the Jews,* 52–59; and Eli Lederhendler, *The Road to Modern Jewish Politics: Political Tradition and Political Reconstruction in the Jewish Community of Tsarist Russia* (New York: Oxford University Press, 1989), 102–106.

39. In 1817, Alexander I authorized the Englishman Lewis Way and his missionary group, the London Society for the Promotion of Christianity Among the Jews (LSPCJ), to missionize throughout the empire. See Fayn, "Di Londoner misyonern-gezelshaft far yidn."

40. On McCaul and the society's missionary activities in Warsaw see Michael R. Darby, *The Emergence of the Hebrew Christian Movement in Nineteenth-Century Britain* (Leiden: Brill, 2010), 121–125.

41. From 1821 to 1854 the LSPCJ, of which McCaul was a member, managed to persuade but 361 Jews (out of roughly 250,000 Jews living in Congress Poland) of the validity of

Christ's message, averaging 11 converts per year. See Fayn, "Di Londoner misyonern-gezelshaft far yidn."

42. There were nearly a dozen full-length Jewish responses to McCaul's work. Each response addressed different issues, according to when and where it was written. Fuenn's and Levinsohn's works were the two first and were produced during debates over Jewish rights in the Russian Empire in the 1840s. The Zhitomir enlightener Eliezer Zweifel also penned a response to McCaul, *Sanegor* (Protector). Zweifel's book was written in the 1870s but published in 1885. Zweifel used McCaul's tract to respond to the contemporary debates over the Talmud involving the anti-Semitic August Rohling and his Russian counterpart, Hippolytus Lutostansky. See Zweifel, *Sanegor* (Warsaw, 1885) 12, 63–65.

43. See the letter written by Levinsohn to David Luria in Nathansohn, *Sefer hazikhronot,* 103. Levinsohn's earlier work had been well received in Catholic circles. In a number of instances, Levinsohn informs his readers, "I shared my ideas with Christian scholars and theologians, who agreed with me." Isaac Baer Levinsohn, *Zerubavel* (Warsaw, 1886), 103–104. On Luther and the Jewish tradition see 100. Levinsohn found Christian scholarship at the library housed in the local Catholic Lyceum in Kremenets. On Levinsohn's use of the library's books see Isaac Baer Levinsohn "Introduction," to his *Efes damim: sefer hitnatslut neged 'alilat dam* (Bloodless: An Apologetic Against the Blood Libel; Vilna, 1837); and his biographer David Baer Nathansohn's discussion of the library in *Sefer hazikhronot,* 39.

44. With the financial support of the English Jewish philanthropist Moses Montefiore, Levinsohn's previously published play *Efes damim*—an allusion to Polish and Russian blood libels (Kovno, 1827; Zaslav 1830)—had been translated into numerous languages. As noted by Eli Lederhendler (*The Road to Modern Jewish Politics,* 102), Levinsohn wrote his tracts with the idea that they would be translated into Polish and Russian. On the reception history of Levinsohn's work and nineteenth-century blood libels see also the introduction of Louis Loewe's English translation, *Éfés dammîm: A Series of Conversations at Jerusalem Between a Patriarch of the Greek Church and a Chief Rabbi of the Jews, Concerning the Malicious Charge Against the Jews of Using Christian Blood.* (London, 1841). The task of translating *Zerubavel* was given to the young Kiev University student Rueven Kalisher and the enlightener Leon Mandelstamm. See Samuel Leib Zitron, *Shtadlonim: interesante Yidishe tipn fun noentn over* (Warsaw: Akhisefer, 1926), 262–266, and Nathansohn, *Sefer hazikhronot,* 100–101, which claim that Montefiore initiated contact with Levinsohn and encouraged him to write the response to McCaul. In general Nathansohn's account, based on letters Levinsohn penned to his friend Aron Reich, seems to have provided the basis for Zitron's narrative. Where Zitron offers new data, he seems to be historically inaccurate. See also Isaac Baer Levinsohn, *Bikurei Ribal* (Warsaw, 1891), 136–138. It is unclear why the translation failed to materialize.

45. See Fuenn's reflection on Levinsohn's work Mordechai Levin, *'Erkhei ḥevra vekhalkala ba'ide'ologya shel tekufat hahaskala,* 93.

46. When Montefiore visited Vilna in 1846 he interacted with Fuenn. See Saul M. Ginzburg, *Historishe verk,* 3 vols. (New York: Shoyl Ginzburg 70-yohriger yubiley komitet, 1937), 2:101.

47. Levinsohn, *Zerubavel,* 111–112.
48. JNUL, Samuel Joseph Fuenn Archive ARC. 4* 1527, *Darkhei Hashem* (hereafter *DH*), sect. I, p. 6.
49. It is important to note that Fuenn and Levinsohn were in contact with each other. In Fuenn's JNUL archive ARC. 4* 1527 03, folder 96, is a letter dated September 1839 in which Levinsohn asks Fuenn to make a number of changes to his manuscript *Beit yehuda.* Fuenn also explicitly cites Levinsohn's work in *Darkhei Hashem.* See ARC. 4* 1527, *DH,* sect. I, chap. 4, p. 60. Levinsohn composed a letter of support to Fuenn for the publication of *Pirhei tsafon* (1841).
50. "Bericht eines gelehrten russischen Israeliten aus Lithuauen, über den Bildungszustand der Israeliten in seinem Faterlande," parts 1–5, *Israelitische Annalen,* 5 (1840): 35–37; 6 (1840): 45–46; 7 (1840): 65–66; 9 (1840): 81–82; 10 (1840): 88–89.
51. "Bericht eines gelehrten russischen Israeliten aus Lithuauen," *Israeliten Annalen* 5, 46n2. On Levinsohn's relationship to Krochmal and other members of the Jewish enlightenment see Greenberg, *Isaac Baer Levinsohn,* 20n2, and Yisra'el Fieskin, "Toldot Yitshak Baer Levinson zts"l mikremenets," *Hamaggid,* November 25, 1863, 365.
52. Jay Harris, *Nachman Krochmal: Guiding the Perplexed of the Modern Age* (New York: New York University Press, 1991), 206–208; Kathryn Tanner, "Postmodern Challenges to 'Tradition,'" *Louvain Studies* 28 (2003), 175–193.
53. Isaac Baer Levinsohn, *Beit yehuda* (Vilna, 1858), I:151–152 (quotation), II:43.
54. On other Jewish enlighteners who adopted a similar view of the Oral Law see Moshe Pelli, "The Attitude of the First Maskilim in Germany Towards the Talmud," *Leo Beck Institute Year Book* 27 (1982): 243–269; Nancy Sinkoff, *Out of the Shtetl: Making Jews Modern in the Polish Borderlands* (Providence: Brown Judaic Studies, 2004), 241–270; and Talya Fishman, *Shaking the Pillars of Exile: "Voice of a Fool," an Early Modern Jewish Critique of Rabbinic Culture* (Stanford: Stanford University Press, 1997), 30–60.
55. In their use of "tradition" Fuenn and Levinsohn followed the theological pattern adopted by Jews living in other non-Protestant European lands. Most notably, Simone Luzzatto, writing in seventeenth-century Italy, also invoked the Catholic idea of tradition to argue that Jews shared more with Catholics than with Protestants. On Luzzatto's use of the Catholic template see David Ruderman, *Jewish Thought and Scientific Discovery in Early Modern Europe* (New Haven: Yale University Press, 1995), 156–158; and Giuseppe Veltri, *Renaissance Philosophy in Jewish Garb: Foundations and Challenges of Judaism on the Eve of Modernity* (Leiden: Brill, 2009), 187–192.
56. For a full presentation of Fuenn and Levinsohn's respective theologies see Eliyahu Stern, "Catholic Judaism: The Political Theology of the Nineteenth-Century Russian Jewish Enlightenment," *Harvard Theological Review* 109, no. 4 (Winter 2016): 483–511.
57. While living in Kremenets, Ukraine, Levinsohn was in contact with numerous Christian clergy, among them the Orthodox priest Antoni Rafalski, who would later become the Metropolitan of Saint Petersburg. Levinsohn's biographer David Baer Nathansohn claimed that in 1831 Levinsohn gave a copy of *Beit yehuda* to Rafalski to present to the scholar and archaeologist of Orthodox church history, Evgeny Bolkhovitinov, the Metropolitan of Kiev. In the first pages of *Beit yehuda* there appears a letter of endorsement, addressed to readers in Russian and Hebrew but written in Latin and signed

by the director of the Lyceum in Kremenets, Andrezja Lewicki. Lewicki notes that "a Polish translation of your [Levinsohn's] work on Judaism has been delivered at the Lyceum." On Levinsohn's ties to Rafalski see his letter to the censor Jacob Tugenhold in Bernard D. Weinryb, "Toldot Ribal," *Tarbiz* 5, no. 2 (1934): 203. Levinsohn's *Yemin tsidki* was explicitly written as a response to the theological questions posed to him by the rector of the Kiev Academy. See the introduction to *Yemin tsidki* (Warsaw, 1881), in which Levinsohn claims that he wrote his work as a response to the director of the Greek Orthodox seminary.

58. Levinsohn, in *Te'uda beyisra'el* (Vilna, 1828), 110, cites approvingly the French Jesuit Claude-Adrien Nonnotte's *Les Erreurs de Voltaire* (1762), in which Bossuet and the Catholic notion of tradition are defended against Voltaire's criticisms. See also Levinsohn, *Yemin tsidki*, 60–61. On Levinsohn's use of other French Catholic thinkers to support his arguments see pages 69–71 and his *Zerubavel*, 95.

59. See JNUL, Samuel Joseph Fuenn, ARC. 4* 1527, *DH*, sect. II, chap. 4, pp. 79–84.

60. See Jacques Bénigne Bossuet, *Einleitung in die Geschichte der Welt und der Religion,* trans. into German by D. Johann Andreas Cramer, 2 vols. (Leipzig: Verlegts Bernhard Christoph Breitkopf, 1757–1786), 1:205 and 1:176.

61. Levinsohn cites Cramer's edition of Bossuet's work in *Zerubavel*, 95. Fuenn cites Cramer's edition of Bossuet's work throughout his manuscript, particularly in *DH*, sect. II, chap. 4, pp. 79–84.

62. See Levinsohn, *Beit yehuda*, II:90.

63. Levinsohn, *Zerubavel*, 144–145.

64. Ibid., 28.

65. Israel Bartal correctly notes that by the 1840s Jewish enlighteners no longer referred to radical French revolutionary thinkers. Bartal, "Hamodel hamishni—tsorfat kimekor hashpa'a betahalikhei hamodernizatsya shel yehudei mizraḥ eiropa (1772–1863)," in *Hamahpekha hatsorfatit verishumah,* ed. Yermiel Cohen (Jerusalem: Merkaz Zalman Shazar, 1991), 281. Shmuel Feiner's excellent discussion of Guenzburg's criticisms of Levinsohn's "chain of tradition" is in his *Haskalah and History: The Emergence of Modern Jewish Historical Consciousness,* trans. Chaya Naor and Sondra Silverstone (Oxford: Littman Library of Jewish Civilization, 2002), 163–192.

66. Isaac Baer Levinsohn, *Aḥiya hashiloni haḥozeh* (Leipzig, 1864), 108–109. Here Levinsohn may have been influenced by allusions in Jewish polemical literature that identified Jewish reformers as Protestants. As Yosef Kaplan has argued, in the early eighteenth century Jews living among Catholic populations began describing Jewish heretics in the oblique language of "Karaites." Kaplan claims that *Karaite* was a code word among Catholic Hebraists for "Protestant." Levinsohn, however, explicitly makes the connection between reform versions of Judaism and Protestantism in the context of an attempt to appeal to Catholic and Orthodox Christians. Yosef Kaplan, "'Karaites' in Early Eighteenth-Century Amsterdam," in *Sceptics, Millenarians and Jews,* ed. D. Katz and J. Israel (Leiden: Brill, 1990), 196–236.

67. Levinsohn, *Yemin tsidki*, 72.

68. JNUL, Samuel Joseph Fuenn, ARC. 4* 1527, *DH*, sect. II, chap. 1, p. 2.

69. Ibid., sect. II, chap. 1, p. 1. For an analysis of Fuenn's radical theology see Eliyahu Stern, "Paul in the Jerusalem of Lithuania: Samuel Joseph Fuenn's Paths of God," in *Talmudic Transgressions: Essays in Honor of Daniel Boyarin,* ed. Moulie Vidas, Ishay Rosen-Zvi, Aharon Shemesh, and Charlotte Fonrobert (Leiden: Brill, 2017).

70. Georgy Florovsky, *Puti russkogo bogosloviia* (Paris: YMCA Press, 1981), 263. On the relationship between the Catholic church and Nicholas I's ministers, including Uvarov, see Eduard Winter, *Russland und das Papsttum,* 2 vols. (Berlin: Akadmie-Verlag, 1961), 2:240–247.

71. Florovsky, *Puti russkogo bogosloviia,* 135.

72. Paul Bushkovitch, "Orthodoxy and Old Rus' in the Thought of S. P. Shevyrev," *Forschungen zur Osteuropäischen Geschichte* 46 (1992): 204 (quotation), 212n18. On anti-Catholic sentiments in Russia see Theodore R. Weeks, "Religion and Russification, Russian Language in the Catholic Churches of the Northwest Provinces after 1863," *Kritika* 2, no. 1 (2001): 87–110; Weeks, "Russification and the Lithuanians, 1863–1905," *Slavic Review* 60, no. 1 (2001): 96–1114; and Löwe, "Poles, Jews, and Tartars," 68–69.

73. See Carolina Armenteros, "Preparing the Russian Revolution: Maistre and Uvarov on the History of Knowledge," in *Joseph de Maistre and His European Readers: From Friedrich von Gentz to Isaiah Berlin,* ed. Carolina Armenteros and Richard A. Lebrun (Leiden: Brill, 2011), 213–249. See also Florovsky, *Puti russkogo bogosloviia,* 135; Serhiy Bilenky, *Romantic Nationalism in Eastern Europe: Russian, Polish and Ukrainian Political Imaginations* (Stanford: Stanford University Press), 187–194.

74. See Cynthia H. Wittaker, "The Ideology of Sergei Uvarov: An Interpretive Essay," *Russian Review* 37, no. 2 (1978): 159–160.

75. S. S. Uvarov, *O prepodovanii istorii otnositel'no k narodnomu vospitaniiu* (Saint Petersburg, 1813).

76. Ibid., 15.

77. Ibid., 27n6.

78. Samuel Joseph Fuenn, *Nidhei yisra'el* (Vilna, 1850), 1.

79. Samuel Joseph Fuenn, "Amar rabbi El'azar 'atidim kol ba'alei umaniyyot sheya'amdu 'al hakarka'," *Hakarmel,* August 1, 1861.

80. On Levinsohn and Fuenn's precursors see Jonathan Karp, *The Politics of Jewish Commerce: Economic Thought and Emancipation in Europe, 1638–1848* (Cambridge: Cambridge University Press, 2008), 201–234; and Sinkoff, *Out of the Shtetl,* 135–141.

81. Levinsohn, *Zerubavel,* 70–73.

82. Jonathan Karp, "Can Economic History Date the Inception of Jewish Modernity?" in *The Economy in Jewish History: New Perspectives on the Interrelationship Between Ethnicity and Economic Life,* ed. Gideon Reuveni and Sarah Wobick-Segev (New York: Berghahn, 2011), 33.

83. Levinsohn, *Te'uda beyisra'el,* 182–183.

84. Mordechai Levin, *'Erkhei hevra vekhalkala ba'ide'ologya shel tekufat hahaskala,* notes that "though Levinsohn drew on the ideas espoused by German thinkers . . . he did not convey them to the Jewish public" (234). Levin suggests that Levinsohn wanted to provide a religious veneer for his ideas.

85. Carl August Buchholz, *Actenstükke die Verbesserung des bürgerlichen Zustandes der Israeliten* (Stuttgart, 1815), 77.

86. On the creation of a "Jewish tradition of agricultural work" see Mordechai Levin, *'Erkhei ḥevra vekhalkala ba'ide'ologya shel tekufat hahaskala*, 225–231.

87. Levinsohn, *Te'uda beyisra'el*, 173.

88. Fuenn, "Amar rabbi El'azar 'atidim kol ba'alei umaniyyot sheya'amdu 'al hakarka'."

89. Levinsohn, *Te'uda beyisra'el*, 178.

90. Fuenn, "Amar rabbi El'azar 'atidim kol ba'alei umaniyyot sheya'amdu 'al hakarka'."

91. Ibid.

92. Levinsohn, *Beit yehuda*, II:154.

93. Samuel Joseph Fuenn, "Iudaizm v otnoshenii k zhizni," *Prilozhenie k "Gakarmel'*," August 10, 1860.

94. Levinsohn, *Zerubavel*, 35.

95. In the first history written about the Jewish enlightenment on Russian lands, Menashe Morgulis noted that "the whole problem" between the Russian government and the Jewish population "involved a misunderstanding of the canons of interpretation regarding the Talmud." Menashe Morgulis, "K istorii obrazovaniia russkikh evreev," in *Evreiskaia biblioteka: istoriko-literaturnyi sbornik,* ed. Adolph E. Landau (Saint Petersburg, 1871), 163–164.

96. Meir Berlin (Bar-Ilan), *Fun Volozhin biz Yerusholayim* (New York, 1933), 1:69.

97. The poster appeared in the early 1840s and was an attack on Fuenn's publication *Pirḥei tsafon*. See JNUL, Saul M. Ginzburg, ARC. 4* 1281A, nos. 391–400.

98. See the first footnote to the second edition of Levinsohn, *Te'uda beyisra'el* (Warsaw, 1855); and Abraham Dov Baer Levinsohn's citation of the story in his introduction to the third printing (Warsaw: 1878), iii, iv. The story is also recorded by Benzion Hoffman, "Mit fuftsik yor tsurik," *Forverts,* May 25, 1947, 3.

99. See Israel Salanter's sermon in *'Ets pri* (New York, 1953), 12a–13b.

CHAPTER 2. SOCIAL MATERIALISM

1. Isaak Rülf, *Meine Reise nach Kowno um die Übersiedlung nothleidender Glaubensgenossen aus den Grenzbezirken nach dem Innern Russlands zu ordnen, sowie die in der dortigen Synagoge gehaltene Predigt* (Memel, 1869), 3–4.

2. See Samuel Joseph Fuenn, "Tikvat 'aniyim," *Hakarmel,* November 21, 1869; Mordechai Zalkin, "Al taḥdelu bo beineinu," *Kesher* 35 (Winter 2007): 63–69; Jacob Shatzky, "Kultur geshikhte fun der haskole bay yidn in Lite," in *Lite,* ed. Mendel Sudarsky, Uriah Katzenelenbogen, and J. Kissin, 2 vols. (New York: Jewish Lithuanian Culture Society, 1951), 1:735–741; Israel Klausner, *Vilna: Yerushalayim delita,* vol. 1: *Dorot rishonim 1495–1881* (Tel Aviv: Ghetto Fighters' House, 1988), 330–347.

3. When Saul Borovoi tried to write about people who called themselves "nihilists" in the 1860s, he was forced to admit that he could only muster the names of "two or three people, not more" who publicly identified themselves as such. "Before 1865," Borovoi writes, "there were no more than 150 students in Russian universities, and the number of nihilists certainly could not have totaled more than that." Saul Borovoi, "A farge-

sener nihilist (Yehude Leyb Lerner)," *Filologishe shriftn* 3 (1929): 474. For an overview of the Jews who identified themselves as nihilists (as opposed to those who identified themselves specifically as *Jewish* nihilists) in the 1860s see Elias Tcherikower, "Yidn-revolutsyonern in Rusland in di 60er un 70er yorn," in Tcherikower, ed., *Historishe shriftn*, 3 vols. (Vilna: YIVO, 1939), 3:79, 90–91; and Benjamin Nathans, *Beyond the Pale: The Jewish Encounter with Late Imperial Russia* (Berkeley: University of California Press, 2002), 60–61, 207.

4. See Moses Leib Lilienblum, "'Olam hatohu," *Hashahar*, 1873.

5. Moses Leib Lilienblum, "Tikkun medini vetikkun sifruti," *Hashahar*, 1871. See also Moshe Leib Lilienblum, *Ketavim otobiyografiyim*, ed. Shlomo Breiman, 3 vols. (Jerusalem: Mosad Bialik, 1970), 3:110 and n. 46.

6. Moses Lilienblum, letter to Mordecai ben-Hillel Hacohen, dated "the first day of Hannukah," 1894, JNUL, Mordecai ben Hillel Ha-Cohen, ARC 4* 1068 01, 272. The letter appeared in the newspaper *Davar* on February 15, 1935. Lilienblum is responding to Hacohen's biographical sketch in honor of Lilienblum's fiftieth birthday. See Mordecai ben-Hillel Hacohen, "Moshe Leib Lilienblum" (1894), in Hacohen, *Me'erev 'ad 'erev*, 2 vols. (Vilna, 1923), 1:245–263. On Lilienblum's later views in comparison to his positions in the 1870s, see Morris Winchevsky, "Lilienblum veyahaso lasotsyaliyut," *Lu'ah ahi'ezer* 2 (1921): 292–300; Samuel Leib Zitron, "Lilienblum vehasotsyaliyut hamarksit," *Hatsefira*, June 12, 1919; Zitron, "Moshe Leib Lilienblum," in Zitron, *Dray literarishe doyres*, 3 vols. (Vilna: Sh. Shreberk, 1921), 2:99–103; and Michal Berkowitz, "Lilienblum vesofrei ha'emet," *Hatsefira*, July 24, 1919. In YIVO, Kalman Marmor Collection, RG 205, folder 338, there is a series of letters sent by Berkowitz to Winchevsky addressing Lilienblum's political positions in the 1870s. In a letter dated February 2, 1922, Berkowitz admitted that Lilienblum was not interested in the question of socialism: "I will tell you a secret. Lilienblum did not understand socialism." In private correspondence, Zionist historians and activists objected to those who challenged Lilienblum's own account of events in the 1870s. "Throughout Lilienblum's life," Alter Druyanow uncritically maintained, "neither his lips nor his pen's tip ever issued a false word." Druyanow, letter to Winchevsky, December 8, 1921, YIVO, Kalman Marmor Collection, RG 205, folder 319.

7. Zitron, "Lilienblum vehasotsyaliyut hamarksit."

8. In his essay on the question of women's rights, for example, he deleted his original indictment of "liberalism" and his citation of Pisarev's essay on the subject. Similarly, he omitted his call for Jews to follow in Pisarev and Chernyshevsky's footsteps and see economics as the basis for the organization of society. Compare the last paragraph in Lilienblum's article "Tikkun medini vetikkun sifruti," *Hashahar*, 1871, to the version in Lilienblum, *Kol kitvei Moshe Leib Lilienblum*, 4 vols. (Krakow; Odessa, 1910–1913), 1:132–138.

9. Nathans, *Beyond the Pale*, 48, 62–69. For an overview of the laws issued by the Russian government against the Jewish population see J. B. Weber and W. Kempster, *A Report of the Commissioners of Immigration upon the Causes Which Incite Immigration to the United States* (Washington, D.C., 1892), 149–167.

10. On the Great Reforms see W. Bruce Lincoln, *Alexander's Great Reforms: Autocracy, Bureaucracy and the Politics of Change in Imperial Russia* (DeKalb: Northern Illinois

University Press, 1990). On Russian government policies regarding Jews following the emancipation of the serfs see Hans Rogger, *Jewish Policies and Right Wing Politics in Imperial Russia* (Berkeley: University of California, 1986), 113–153.

11. See the 1881 Russian census in Hans Rogger, *Jewish Policies and Right Wing Politics in Imperial Russia* (Berkeley: University of California Press, 1986), 145–146. On the 1897 census see Samuel Ettinger, "Demutah hayishuvit vehakalkalit shel yahadut rusya besof hame'a hatesha' 'esreh," in *Bein polin lerusya,* ed. Israel Bartal and Jonathan Frankel, 2 vols. (Jerusalem: Merkaz Zalman Shazar, Hebrew University, 1994), 2:258–261.

12. On the economic standing of Jewish handcrafters in Lithuania in the mid-nineteenth century, see the materials collected by S. Rombach, "Di yidishe balmelokhes in Rusland in der ershter helft fun 19tn yorhundert," *Tsaytshrift* 1 (1926):29–30; and Mark Wischnitzer, "Yidishe melokhe un balmelokhe-tzekhn in Lite," in *Lite,* ed. Sudarsky and Katzenelenbogen, 1:982–986. On the premodern history of Jewish handcrafters in Lithuania see Rivke Notik, "Tsu der geshikhte fun hantverk bay litvishe yidn," *YIVO Bleter* 1 (1936): 107–118.

13. Arcadius Kahan, "Impact of Industrialization on Jews in Tsarist Russia," in Kahan, *Essays in Jewish Social and Economic History,* ed. Roger Weiss (Chicago: University of Chicago Press, 1986), 2–4. On Jewish industrialization see Ezra Mendelsohn, *Class Struggle in the Pale: The Formative Years of the Jewish Workers' Movement in Tsarist Russia* (Cambridge: Cambridge University Press, 1970), 19–21.

14. See Israel Sosis, *Di geshikhte fun di Yidishe gezelshaftlekhe shtremungen in Rusland in XIX Yorhundert* (Minsk: Vaysrusisher melukhe-farlag, 1929), 122, 124–147. The lifting of residential restrictions for specified Jewish groups did not affect the majority of Jews, who remained in the Pale. Most stayed for fear that their rights might be rescinded. See Mendelsohn, *Class Struggle in the Pale,* 14. On the 1860s as an economic turning point for Jews see most recently Yohanan Petrovsky-Shtern, *The Golden Age Shtetl: A New History of Jewish Life in East Europe* (Princeton: Princeton University Press, 2014), 341–346.

15. Salo W. Baron, *The Russian Jew Under Tsars and Soviets* (New York: Schocken, 1987), 82. A number of Jews responded to the changes by petitioning the government for greater economic rights. On the response of Russian Jewish liberals to the emancipation of the serfs see John Doyle Klier, *Imperial Russia's Jewish Question, 1855–1881* (Cambridge: Cambridge University Press, 1995), 300–310. On the lack of influence of the Russian Jewish liberals in the 1860s see the somewhat overstated argument made by Israel Sosis in *Di geshikhte fun di Yidishe gezelshaftlekhe shtremungen in Rusland in XIX Yorhundert,* 99.

16. On Orshanski's education see Yakov Moscow Mibaslow, "Toldot anshei shem: vehu ḥayyei heḥakham Eliyahu Orshanski," *Hakol,* January 26, 1879; and more generally Menashe Morgulis, *Il'ia Grigorevich Orshanskiy i ego literaturnaia deiatel'nost'* (Saint Petersburg, 1904).

17. Isaiah Trunk, "Historians of Russian Jewry," in *Russian Jewry (1860–1917),* ed. Jacob Frumkin, Gregor Aronson, and Alexis Goldenweiser (New York: Yoseloff, 1966), 456 (453–477).

18. Ilya Orshanski, "Ocherki ekonomicheskogo polozheniia evreev v rossii," *Den'*, August 15, 1869.

19. Ibid.

20. Orshanski cites Shelgunov, as well as Pisarev's radical journal *Russkoe slovo*, ibid., October 18, 1869.

21. Ibid., November 29, 1869.

22. See the strong patriotic ideals expressed by Ilya Orshanski, *Evrei v Rossii* (Saint Petersburg, 1877), 2.

23. Like German Jewish scholars, Orshanski was a staunch supporter of acculturation on the basis that Jews were a religious group and not a national entity or an economic corporation. Still, in his approach to analyzing Jews he assumed that they could be understood as a distinct socioeconomic entity. Avraham Greenbaum alludes to this distinction in Orshanski's work in the context of historiographical debates over his legacy in *Perakim bahistoryografya shel yahadut rusya* (Jerusalem: Merkaz Dinur, 2006), 30.

24. On the employment of Orshanski's narrative by Jewish materialists see Judah Leib Levin, "She'eilat hayehudim," *Hakol*, January 5, 1879; and Mordecai ben-Hillel Hacohen, "Okhlei leḥem ha'atsavim," originally published in 1879 and reprinted in Hacohen, *Me'erev 'ad 'erev*, 1:44–49.

25. Moses Leib Lilienblum "Maka she'ein lah refua" (1872), in Lilienblum, *Kol kitvei Moshe Leib Lilienblum*, 2:20–21.

26. See Fuenn, "Tikvat 'aniyim." See also Mendelsohn, *Class Struggle in the Pale*, 8.

27. See the calculations in Rülf, *Meine Reise nach Kowno*, 14.

28. See Mordecai ben-Hillel Hacohen, "Dor holekh vedor ba," *Hashaḥar*, 1878, 10.

29. Kovner's exposé was part of a series of articles commissioned by the liberal Jewish Society for the Promotion of Culture Among the Jews of Russia. See Brian Horowitz, *Jewish Philanthropy and Enlightenment in Late-Tsarist Russia* (Seattle: University of Washington Press, 2009), 47.

30. The story first appeared in Kovner's autobiographical sketch, "Iz zapisek evreia," *Istoricheskiy vestnik* 91 (March–April): 977–1009, and is cited in Saul M. Ginzburg, *Meshumodim in tsarishn Rusland* (New York: Tsiko, 1946), 157–161.

31. In April 1875, Kovner, who was working as a bank clerk in Saint Petersburg, forged an employer's signature on a check and ran off to Moscow and then Kiev with 168,000 rubles. In September, Kovner was arrested, put on trial in Saint Petersburg, and sentenced to four years in prison. See Harriet Murav, *Identity Theft: The Jew in Imperial Russia and the Case of Avraam Uri Kovner* (Stanford : Stanford University Press, 2003), 109–114.

32. Abraham Uri Kovner, *Ḥeker davar* (Warsaw, 1865), 9. For an overview of responses to Kovner see Max Weinreich, *Fun beyde zaytn ployt: dos shturemdike lebn fun Uri Kovnern, dem nihilist* (Buenos Aires: Tsentral-farband fun Poylishe Yidn in Argentine, 1955), 103–110, 128. See also Abraham Baer Gottlober, *Iggeret tsa'ar ba'alei ḥayyim* (Zhitomir, 1868), 21–26, a response to Kovner's essay "Ru'aḥ ḥayyim," *Hakarmel*, December 11, 1866. For other critiques of Kovner's work see Shalom Jacob Abramowich, "Devarim aḥadim 'al divrei hameḥaber *ḥeker davar* me'et Avraham Uri Kovner," *Hamelits*,

August 8, 1866. Although Abramowich harshly criticized Kovner in the 1860s he would later adopt a realist position in his own writings. See also the pamphlet produced by Tsvi Daniel Habavli (TsD"H), *Shoresh davar* (Vilna, 1866), 10; and Yashe Bronshteyn, "Avrom Uri Kovner (1842–1909)," *Tsaytshrift* (1931): 227. For defenses of Kovner see his brother Yitsḥak Isaac Kovner, *Sefer hametsaref,* ed. Shmuel Feiner (Jerusalem: Mosad Bialik, 1998); and Yosef Yehuda Lerner, *Derush 'al hameitim* (Odessa, 1868). For an analysis of Kovner's work see Ginzburg, *Meshumodim in tsarishn Rusland,* 157–161.

33. See Shalom Jacob Abramowich, *Di Takse* (Zhitomir, 1869).

34. Eliezer Zweifel, *Shalom 'al yisra'el,* 3 vols. (Jerusalem: Mosad Bialik, 1972), 1:154. "In large [Hasidic] towns," an anonymous writer claimed, "there were multiple houses of prayer. Half of the people followed one master [tsaddik] and another half followed a different master. The inhabitants of the town had stopped supporting and had given up on [shared] communal organizations" ("Shim'u va'anaḥnu nedaber," *Hamelits,* July 23, 1863.

35. Sarah Foner, "Memories of My Childhood Days; or, A Look at the City of Dvinsk," *A Woman's Voice: Sarah Foner, Hebrew Author of the Haskalah,* ed. and trans. Morris Rosenthal (Wilbraham, Mass.: Dailey International, 2001), 19. On the fights among warring religious groups in Vilkomir see the recollections of Ya'akov Lifshutz in *Zikhron ya'akov* (Bnei Brak, 1968), 2:49–53.

36. Abraham Uri Kovner, "Yeshibotnaia bursa," *Den',* October 25, 1869.

37. Ibid., June 20, 1869. Compare these numbers to those in Shaul Stampfer, *Lithuanian Yeshivas of the Nineteenth Century: Creating a Tradition of Learning,* trans. Lindsey Taylor-Guthartz (Oxford: Littman Library of Jewish Civilization, 2012), 123–127; Stampfer notes that there were probably no more than two hundred students enrolled in Volozhin at any one time.

38. Mordechai Zalkin, "'Ir shel torah," in *Yeshivot uvattei midrash,* ed. Immanuel Etkes (Jerusalem: Merkaz Zalman Shazar, 2006), 131–160.

39. Kovner, "Yeshibotnaia bursa," October 25, 1869.

40. Kovner, *Ḥeker davar,* 109.

41. Ibid., 82.

42. Ibid., 9.

43. Kovner, "Yeshibotnaia bursa," October 25, 1869.

44. Ibid., June 11, 1869.

45. Ibid.

46. Compare Kovner's account with N. G. Pomialovsky, *Ocherki Bursy* (1862), translated into English by Alfred Kuhn under the title *Seminary Sketches* (Ithaca: Cornell University Press, 1973).

47. For an in-depth study of the games and pranks played in Jewish schools see the rich analysis of Yekhiel Shtern, "Kheyder un besmedresh," *YIVO Bleter* 31 (1948): 60–81. While many of those who attended smaller yeshivot did sleep in the women's sections of local synagogues, there were no "dormitories" in either the Volozhin or the Mir yeshivot (the two largest and most respected institutions of Jewish higher education in the Pale), so most of the students rented rooms in private homes. Only at the Vilna rabbinical seminary were there dormitories. On the history of the dormitory in Jewish institutions in eastern Europe see Shaul Stampfer, "Dormitory and Yeshiva in

Eastern Europe," in his *Families, Rabbis and Education: Traditional Jewish Society in Nineteenth-Century Eastern Europe* (Oxford: Littman Library of Jewish Civilization, 2010), 218–223. For an excellent analysis of the Russian archival documents on the students' behavior and living conditions see Verna Dohrn, "The Rabbinical Schools as Institutions of Socialization in Tsarist Russia, 1847–1873," *POLIN* 14 (2001): 83–104; and Efim Melamed, "The Zhitomir Rabbinical School: New Materials and Perspectives," *POLIN* 14 (2001): 105–115.

48. See Kovner, "Yeshibotnaia bursa," July 11, 1869.

49. Ibid.

50. Ibid., August 1, 1869. Kovner's tabulation is independently confirmed by the research of the historian Shaul Stampfer in *Lithuanian Yeshivas of the Nineteenth Century*, 110–111.

51. On the subsidies given to students at the government schools and universities see Bronshteyn, "Avrom Uri Kovner," 219; and Menashe Morgulis and David Rafaelovitch, "Kheshbn fun dem gelt," *Kol mevaser*, February 11, 1865.

52. Kovner, "Yeshibotnaia bursa," August 1, 1869. Despite the Volozhin yeshiva's flaws, "including its basis in the ancient abnormal economic condition of the Jews," Kovner expressed some tenderness and respect for the institution. He noted in the article that its students were distinguished in their erudition and were honest men. "If only this power had been given a different direction," he lamented, "it would have brought great fruits and Russian Jews would not occupy such a low standing compared to Jews in other states."

53. On the deficiencies of Jewish record keeping in the nineteenth century see Eugene Avrutin, *Jews and the Imperial State: Identification Politics in Tsarist Russia* (Ithaca: Cornell University Press, 2010), 79. The scholars Samuel Ettinger and Azriel Natan Frenk fail to provide data on religious functionaries in their respective calculations of Jewish professions in Russian and Polish lands. Ettinger's calculations do not even list as a category those who specifically engaged in religious professions. See Ettinger, "Demutah hayishuvit vehakalkalit shel yahadut rusya besof hame'a hatesha' 'esreh," 257–280, According to Azriel Natan Frenk, only 1.5 percent of Jews in Congress Poland in 1843 were *Klay koydesh* (beadles or rabbis associated with schools and study houses) and *melamdim* (teachers). Frenk's data are unreliable because he placed 24 percent of the population under the all-encompassing rubric *Tog loyn arbeter* (day laborers), which might well have included people paid to study or to engage in religious activities. See A. N. Frenk, "Di tsol yidn un zeyere basheftikungen in di shtet un derfer fun kenigraykh Poyln in 1843tn yor," *Bleter far Yidishe demografye, statistik un ekonomik* 3 (1923): 190–191. It is important to note that Jacob Lestschinsky, the editor of the journal, questioned Frenk's statistics (192).

54. Y. Magalski, "Kol 'aleh nirdaf," *Hakol*, September 14, 1879.

55. See Peretz Smolenskin's calculation in "Avoteinu ḥat'u ve'einam," in his *Perets ben Moshe Smolenskin: Ma'amarim*, 4 vols. (Jerusalem: Hapo'alim, 1926), 3:143.

56. See Fuenn, "Tikvat 'aniyim."

57. These percentages are based on combining the following professional categories of Jews out of a total of 5,063,106 persons: "Clergymen non-Christian" (26,214 total persons),

"Persons Serving About Churches" (61,697), "Living on Income from Capital or Supported by Family [*kest*]" (334,837) and "Supported by Charity of Charitable Institutions" (171,905). These categories account for 12 percent of the population. While a large percentage of those in the last two categories were not necessarily engaged in "religious occupations," my tabulation of 7–9 percent also factors in the number of weavers, slaughterers, undertakers, or merchants who might also have been drawing salaries as religious functionaries (for making prayer shawls, slaughtering kosher meat, or preparing bodies for funerals). For a full tabulation of the 1897 census of Russian Jews in English see Isaac Max Rubinow, "Economic Conditions of Jews in Russia," *United States Department of Commerce and Labor Bulletin of the Bureau of Labor* 25 (1907): 498–499. To be sure, this is an estimate and further research is required to identify the exact number of religious functionaries.

58. Glenn Dynner, *Yankel's Tavern: Jews, Liquor, and Life in the Kingdom of Poland* (New York: Oxford University, Press 2014), 137. It is important to note that many of those included under Frenk's label "day laborers" might be included under Dynner's category "religious functionaries." Dynner's figure of 6.5 percent (drawn from the Guttmacher Archive) seems low for the number of religious functionaries in the Pale of Settlement (as opposed to Congress Poland). Most religious functionaries and yeshiva students in Lithuanian lands were probably less predisposed to going to a Polish rabbi for blessings, even a non-Hasidic rabbi like Eliyahu Guttmacher. Furthermore, the Guttmacher Archive has no information about how many people who considered themselves "merchants" might have also been receiving money for religious functions. For example, those listed by Dynner as "weavers" were often engaged in weaving religious garments such as prayer shawls. Moreover, it is unclear if students at yeshivot and local study houses (both of which had certainly increased since 1843) were included, or how many unemployed individuals might have been living off of charities distributed by their families (*kest*) or religious institutions.

59. On the relationship between Kovner and Lilienblum see M. L. Lilienblum, letter to Y. L. Gordon, May 13, 1871, in Shlomo Breiman, ed., *Igrot M. L. Lilienblum le-Y. L. Gordon* (Jerusalem: Magnes, 1968), 121; Zitron, "Moshe Leib Lilienblum," 2:107; and Max Weinreich, "Di M. L. Lilienblum oysshtelung in YIVO," *YIVO Bleter* 23 (1944): 410–413. On Kovner's correspondence with Lilienblum see Ginzburg, *Meshumodim in tsarishn Rusland,* 162; and Bronshteyn, "Avrom Uri Kovner," 241–243.

60. For an analysis of Lilienblum's writings in the 1860s in English, see Michael Stanislawski, *For Whom Do I Toil: Judah Leib Gordon and The Crisis of Russian Jewry* (New York: Oxford University Press, 1988), 91–99.

61. On the *Voice of the Herald* see Alexander Orbach, *New Voices of Russian Jews: A Study of the Russian Press of Odessa in the era of the Great Reform, 1860–1871* (Leiden: Brill, 1980), 62–71. For an overview of the editorial agenda of its founding editor, Alexander Zederbaum, see Sosis, *Di geshikhte fun di Yidishe gezelshaftlekhe shtremungen in Rusland in XIX Yorhundert,* 95–99.

62. See Alexander Zederbaum, "Fanatizmus, nihilizmus," *Kol mevaser,* May 6, 1870. On the popularization of Jewish harmony in the 1860s see Bronshteyn, "Avrom Uri Kovner," 223. On Zederbaum's "pure faith Judaism" see as well his article "Ha'otiyot

le'aḥor," *Hamelits,* January 15, 1863. See also the editor's column in *Kol mevaser,* January 7, 1871.

63. The editor of the newspaper Alexander Zederbaum had published Lilienblum's earlier critiques of the rabbinic establishment for deeming slaughtered meat unkosher (based on restrictions that, according to Lilienblum, had no Talmudic basis) and ruling that even in a time of famine, any consumption of grains and even beans on Passover was forbidden. (The stricture against eating beans and other legumes on Passover is entirely without basis in Talmudic law, whereas even the prohibition of eating wheat and barley and their derivatives on Passover—a scriptural prohibition—is unquestionably suspended in any situation where there is a danger to life.) The rabbis, Lilienblum raged, were prepared to have people starve rather than allow them to eat matzah made out of grain. On the response of the rabbinic establishment to the famine and Lilienblum's attacks see Lifshutz, *Zikhron ya'akov,* 2:72–73.

64. See Shlomo Breiman's comments to the version recorded in Lilienblum's *Ḥattot ne'urim* in Lilienblum, *Ketavim otobiyografiyim,* 2:72, note 91.

65. Lilienblum, *Kol kitvei Moshe Leib Lilienblum,* 2:357. On Lilienblum and Chernyshevsky, see Sosis, *Di geshikhte fun di Yidishe gezelshaftlekhe shtremungen in Rusland in XIX Yorhundert,* 122; Elias Tcherikower, "Yidn-revolutsyonern in Rusland in di 60er un 70er yorn," 3:123–124; and Joseph Klausner, *Historya shel hasifrut ha'ivrit haḥadasha,* 6 vols. (Jerusalem: Hebrew University, 1952), 4:239–254.

66. Moses Leib Lilienblum, "Yaldei yom," CZA, Alter Druyanow Collection, A9/59/1–3 [p. 55].

67. On the publication and banning of Chernyshevsky's works see Irina Paperno, *Chernyshevsky and the Age of Realism: A Study in the Semiotics of Behavior* (Stanford: Stanford University Press, 1988), 28.

68. Samuel Leib Zitron, "Di ershter yidishe sotsyalistin in der hebrayisher literatur," in Zitron, *Dray literarishe doyres,* 2:121.

69. The heroine of the novel, Vera Pavlovna, was friends with a Jewish tradeswoman, Rachel, whom Chernyshevsky described as "absolutely honest, as are almost all small Jewish tradespeople, when dealing with decent people" Chernyshevsky, *What Is to Be Done?* trans. Michael B. Katz (Ithaca: Cornell University Press, 1989), 272.

70. Dmitry Pisarev, "Thinking Proletariat," in *Dmitry Pisarev: Selected Philosophical, Social and Political Essays,* trans. R. Dixon (Moscow: Foreign Languages Publishing House, 1958), 649.

71. William F. Woehrlin, *Chernyshevskii: The Man and the Journalist* (Cambridge: Harvard University Press, 1971), 141.

72. For an English overview of Lilienblum and Feyge Novakhovitch's relationship see Alan Mintz, *Banished from Their Father's Table: Loss of Faith and Hebrew Autobiography* (Bloomington: Indiana University Press, 1989), 43–47; and Michael Stanislawski, *Autobiographical Jews: Essays in Jewish Self-Fashioning* (Seattle: University of Washington Press, 2004), 60–66. Stanislawski suggests that Novakhovitch was related to the socialist leader Morris Winchevsky (Novakhovitch), but the source he cites indicates simply that Lilienblum felt a kinship with Winchevsky because he had the same last name as Feyge. See Morris Winchevsky, "Lilienblum veyaḥaso lasotsyaliyut,"

Lu'ah ahi'ezer 2 (1921): 292–295. Because of this, many mistakenly thought that Feyge was Winchevsky's sister. In a letter to Winchevsky dated September 26, 1921, the Zionist historian Alter Druyanow explained, "I had thought, and I had also heard from others, that Ms. Novakhovitch was a relative of yours (there was someone who also said she was your sister). This rumor was caused, as it would seem, by the fact that you both shared the same last name. However after reading your article in *Lu'ah ahi'ezer,* I now see that she was not your sister and might not have even been a relative." YIVO, Kalman Marmor Collection, RG 205, folder 319.

73. Lilienblum would later attempt to justify philosophically why it was impossible for him to remain with Fayge, and why he had ended the affair. See his "Maka she'ein lah refua" (1872), in Lilienblum, *Kol kitvei Moshe Leib Lilienblum,* 2:20–21.

74. On the first Jewish readers of Chernyshevsky see Morris Winchevsky, *Gezamlte verk,* ed. Kalman Marmor, 10 vols. (New York: Frayhayt 1927), 9:85.

75. On Chernyshevsky's impact on public Jewish reading culture see Jeffrey Veidlinger, *Jewish Public Culture in the Late Russian Empire* (Bloomington: Indiana University Press, 2009), 75–77. On Chernyshevsky's impact on Jewish historians and ethnographers in the 1880s and 1890s see Steven Cassedy, *To the Other Shore: The Russian Jewish Intellectuals Who Came to America* (Princeton: Princeton University Press, 1997), 15–37; Robert Seltzer, *Simon Dubnow's New Judaism: Diaspora Nationalism and the World History of the Jews* (Leiden: Brill, 2014), 36–37; Gabriela Safran, *Wandering Soul: The Dybbuk's Creator S. An-sky* (Cambridge: Harvard University Press, 2010), 17; Safran, *Rewriting the Jew: Assimilation Narratives in the Russian Empire* (Stanford: Stanford University Press, 2001), 20–25; Michael Katz's introduction to S. A. An-sky, *Pioneers: A Tale of Russian-Jewish Life in the 1880s,* trans. Michael R. Katz (Bloomington: Indiana University Press, 2014), vii, 75; and more generally Nathaniel Deutsch, *The Dark Continent: Life and Death in the Russian Pale of Settlement* (Cambridge: Harvard University Press, 2011).

76. On the Odessa pogrom of 1871 see Steven J. Zipperstein, *The Jews of Odessa: A Cultural History, 1794–1881* (Stanford: Stanford University Press, 1986), 114.

77. Ibid., 121.

78. M. L. Lilienblum, letter to Y. L Gordon, April 6, 1871, in Breiman, ed., *Igrot M. L. Lilienblum le-Y. L. Gordon,* 117.

79. Zipperstein, *The Jews of Odessa,* 14.

80. Moses Leib Lilienblum, "Yidishe lebnsfragn," *Kol mevaser,* March 11, 1871.

81. Ibid.

82. Ibid.

83. Ibid.

84. Ibid., March 24, 1871.

85. Ibid.

86. Ibid. As perceptively noted by Israel Bartal, Lilienblum was not adopting Levinsohn's logic that Jews ought to become peasants to appease the Russian government. Rather, he was stressing the need for them to engage in a full range of professions. See Israel Bartal, "Lilienblum, Mosheh Leib," in *YIVO Encyclopedia of Jews in Eastern Europe,* at http://www.yivoencyclopedia.org/article.aspx/Lilienblum_Mosheh_Leib (accessed March 2, 2016).

87. Lilienblum, "Yidishe lebnsfragn," March 24, 1871.

88. Lilienblum would later define a *batlan* as either a Jewish person engaged in unlawful economic activities or one who sat all day and did nothing but study. See Lilienblum, "Leḥem lare'evim," *Hamelits,* November 4, 1879.

89. Lilienblum, "Yidishe lebnsfragn," April 29, 1871.

90. Ibid.

91. Moses Aaron Shatzkes, *Der yudisher far-peysekh* (1881; Warsaw, 1896), 85–86.

92. Lilienblum was the first of many who equated women's problems with those of the Jews. See also Morris Winchevsky, "'Al ha'avanim," 3 parts, *Hakol,* March 26, April 20, and May 4, 1879; and Judah Leib Levin, "She'elot hazman," *Yehuda Leib Levin: Zikhronot vehegyonot,* ed. Yehuda Slutsky (Jerusalem: Mosad Bialik 1968), 17, 142.

93. On matchmakers in nineteenth-century Jewish literature see Naomi Seidman, *The Marriage Plot; or, How Jews Fell in Love with Love, and with Literature* (Stanford: Stanford University Press, 2016), 71–77. I would like to thank Prof. Seidman for her critical insights and assistance in helping me develop the core arguments in this section.

94. See Lilienblum, "Yidishe lebnsfragn," May 6, 1871.

95. Ibid. On the woman question in Lilienblum's writing see also Moses Leib Lilienblum, "Odessa," *Kol mevaser,* July 16, 1871.

96. Shaul Stampfer, "Gender Differentiation and the Education of Jewish Women," in his *Families, Rabbis and Education,* 184. See also the assessment in Rubinow, "Economic Conditions of Jews in Russia," that "the old-fashioned Jew of the Pale is readier to send his daughter than his son to a secular, Christian school" (581). For a more in-depth analysis of Jewish women's education see Iris Parush, *Reading Jewish Women: Marginality and Modernization in Nineteenth-Century Eastern European Jewish Society,* trans. Saadya Sternberg (Waltham, Mass.: Brandeis University Press, 2004), 59–62.

97. Observer in 1880 cited by Eliyana Adler, *In Her Hands: The Education of Jewish Girls in Tsarist Russia* (Detroit: Wayne State University Press, 2011), 119–120.

98. Ibid., 93, 124–131.

99. Lilienblum, "Yidishe lebnsfragn," May 6, 1871. A real-life story about a marriage that is strikingly similar to the one recounted in Lilienblum occurred in Mogilev in 1874. Far from being comical, however, it ended in tragedy when the woman committed suicide. The unpublished story, "Because of the Sin of the Parents" (Ba'avon avot), was written by the Yiddish writer Yankev Dinezon. See Zitron, "Yankev Dinezon," in Zitron, *Dray literarishe doyres,* 1:68.

100. See Lilienblum, "Ḥattot ne'urim," in his *Ketavim otobiyografiyim,* 2:89–93. Lilienblum's own behavior toward his wife suggests that he was better at preaching than practicing his progressive ideas about women.

101. Dmitry Pisarev, "Mysli Firkhova o vospitanii zhenshchin," in his *D. I. Pisarev. Sochineniia,* 5 vols. (Saint Petersburg, 1866), 5:198.

102. More generally, see Wendy Brown, "Tolerance and/or Equality? The 'Jewish Question' and the 'Woman Question,'" *differences: A Journal of Feminist Cultural Studies* 15, no. 2 (2004): 1–31.

103. On the discourse of tolerance among Jewish enlighteners see Moshe David Mitzkun, "Ma'amar hasavlanut vehahaskala davar be'ito," *Hamelits* May 23, 1861.

104. See Shlomo Lilienblum, letter to Reuven Brainin, March 1925, JPLM, Reuven Brainin Collection, no. 654.

105. See Jacob Shatzky, "Referatn un retsenzyes." *YIVO Bleter* 23 (1944): 133–134.

106. See Eliezer Zweifel, *Minim ve'ugav* (Vilna, 1858), 46; Zweifel, *Shalom 'al yisra'el*, 1:65, 2:56–59; Samuel Joseph Fuenn, *Kirya ne'emana* (Vilna, 1860), 142; and Fuenn, "Yisra'el ba'amim," *Hakarmel,* March 17, 1868, 42. On Zweifel see Shmuel Feiner, "Hamifneh beha'arakhat haḥasidut—Eli'ezer Zweifel vehahaskala hametuna berusya," in *Hada'at vehaḥayyim,* ed. Immanuel Etkes (Jerusalem: Merkaz Zalman Shazar, 1993), 355–360; and most recently Jonatan Meir, *Shivḥei Rodkinson: Mikha'el Levi Frumkin-Rodkinson vehaḥasidut* (Tel Aviv, 2012), 149–151, 178n89. On critiques of Zweifel by his contemporaries see Ḥayyim Melamed's review of Zweifel's *Shalom 'al yisra'el* in "Felyeton," *Kol mevaser,* October 7, 1868, 293; Shalom Jacob Abramowich, *Mishpat shalom* (Vilna, 1860), 37; and Abraham Baer Gottlober, *Toldot hakabbala vehaḥasidut* (Zhitomir, 1870).

107. See Eli Lederhendler, *The Road to Modern Jewish Politics: Political Tradition and Political Reconstruction in the Jewish Community of Russia* (New York: Oxford University Press, 1989), 73–75; and ChaeRan Freeze, *Jewish Marriage and Divorce in Imperial Russia* (Hanover, N.H.: Brandeis University Press and University Press of New England, 2002), 91. For a general overview of the way the Russian Empire sought to enforce "religious orthodoxy" among its various minority groups see Robert Crews, "Empire and the Confessional State: Islam and Religious Politics in Nineteenth-Century Russia," *American Historical Review* 108, no. 1 (2003): 52.

108. The new publisher of the newspaper, Moses Beilinson, dismissed Lilienblum. See Lilienblum, *Ketavim otobiyografiyim,* 2:86; and M. L. Lilienblum, letter to Y. L. Gordon, September 17, 1871, in Breiman, ed., *Igrot M. L. Lilienblum le-Y. L. Gordon,* 128.

109. Deeply depressed, or perhaps trying to style himself as a Jewish Rakhmetov, Lilienblum told Judah Leib Gordon that he was resigned to becoming a farmer. See M. L. Lilienblum, letter to Y. L. Gordon, April 6, 1871, in Breiman, ed., *Igrot M. L. Lilienblum le-Y. L. Gordon,* 118.

110. M. L. Lilienblum, letter to Judah Leib Gordon, October 16, 1878, ibid., 158.

111. Joseph Stern, *The Matter and the Form of Maimonides' Guide* (Cambridge: Harvard University Press, 2013), 97.

112. Ibid., 99.

113. Ibid., 158.

114. See Zipperstein, *The Jews of Odessa,* 146.

115. M. L. Lilienblum, letter to Y. L. Gordon, May 13, 1871, in Breiman, ed., *Igrot M. L. Lilienblum le-Y. L. Gordon,* 121.

116. Lilienblum, *Ketavim otobiyografiyim,* 2:96. Lilienblum used the term *krisis* in other contexts to describe the state of Jews in this period as well.

117. M. L. Lilienblum, "Tsara'at noshenet" (1873), in Lilienblum, *Kol kitvei Moshe Leib Lilienblum,* 2:37–38.

118. Ibid.

119. Dmitry Pisarev, "Realisty," in *Polnoe sobranie sochineniy i pisem v dvenadtsati tomakh,* ed. E. F. Kuznetsov et al., 12 vols. (Moscow: Nauka, 2003), 6:228.

120. Moses Leib Lilienblum, "'Olam hatohu," *Hashaḥar*, 1873, reprinted in edited form in Lilienblum, *Kol kitvei Moshe Leib Lilienblum*, 2:108–109. On the use of the word *life* as a code for materialism see James P. Scanlan, "Nicholas Chernyshevsky and Philosophical Materialism in Russia," *Journal of the History of Philosophy* 8, no. 1 (1970): 73–74.

CHAPTER 3. SCIENTIFIC MATERIALISM

1. See, e.g., Joseph Klausner, *Historya shel hasifrut ha'ivrit haḥadasha*, 6 vols. (Jerusalem: Hebrew University, 1952), 4:129. On the popularization and dissemination of scientific knowledge among eastern European Jews in the nineteenth century see Jacob Shavit and Jehuda Reinharz, *Ha'el hamadda'i* (Tel Aviv: Hakibbutz Hame'uḥad, 2011).

2. See Andreas W. Daum, *Wissenschaftspopularisierung im 19 Jahrhundert: Bürgerliche Kultur naturwissenchaftliche Bildung und die deutsche Öffentlichkeit 1848–1914* (Munich: Oldenbourg Verlag, 1998), 237–273.

3. On the role of natural sciences in the 1860s in Russia see Alexander Vucinich, *Darwin in Russian Thought* (Berkeley: University of California Press, 1988), 8. On the rise of the scientist as a new kind of public Jewish intellectual in late-nineteenth-century eastern Europe see Shavit and Reinharz, *Ha'el hamadda'i*, 12–13.

4. Very little has been published on Rabinowitz's or Sossnitz's life. For an overview of them in the context of other Hebrew scientific writers see Nehemiah Dov Hoffman, "Hashkafa 'al hitpatḥut sifruteinu hamadda'it haḥadasha," *'Ivri anokhi*, February 4, 1887. On Rabinowitz, see Yisra'el Ḥayyim Zagorodski, "Tsvi Hirsh Rabinovits," *Ha'asif* 3 (1887): 440–447. On Sossnitz see the eulogy delivered by his friend Reuven Brainin, "Yosef Leib Sossnitz," in *Kol kitvei Re'uven Brainin*, 3 vols. (New York, 1936), vol. 2, available at http://www.benyehuda.org/brainin/zosnits.html (accessed October 30, 2015); and Sossnitz's autobiography published in Benzion Eisenstadt's *Ḥakhmei yisra'el be'amerika* (New York, 1903), 43–45. Sossnitz's own recollections of his youth can be found in NYPL, ***P Joseph Sossnitz, Autobiography, box 1. For a full bibliography of Sossnitz's works see *Mazkeret ḥag hayovel shel Yosef Leib Sossnitz* (New York, 1908).

5. On nineteenth-century secular political projects see most recently Todd H. Weir, *Secularism and Religion in Nineteenth-Century Germany: The Rise of the Fourth Confession* (Cambridge: Cambridge University Press, 2015), 1–3.

6. Ludwig Büchner, *Force and Matter*, trans. and ed. J. Frederick Collingwood (London, 1864), 43. This phrase did not appear in the original edition of Büchner's *Kraft und Stoff: Empirisch-naturphilosophische Studien* (Frankfurt, 1855), but it was added in the second edition published in Frankfurt in 1856 (39–40).

7. Büchner, *Force and Matter*, 30–32.

8. Ibid., 221.

9. Ibid., 215–217. See Maurice Mandelbaum, *History, Man and Reason: A Study in Nineteenth-Century Thought* (Baltimore: Johns Hopkins University Press, 1971), 22.

10. See Ḥayyim Selig Slonimski, *Metsi'ut hanefesh* (Warsaw: 1858), 34.

11. Brainin, "Yosef Leib Sossnitz."

12. Ibid.

13. See Eisenstadt, *Ḥakhmei yisra'el be'amerika,* 43–45.

14. Sossnitz mentions that in his youth some thought he had supernatural powers. See his autobiographical documents in NYPL, ***P Joseph Sossnitz, Autobiography, box 1. The portrayal of Sossnitz as a miracle worker who had supernatural powers can also be found in Berl Kagan, *Yidishe shtet, shtetlekh un dorfishe yishuvim in Lite biz 1918* (New York: B. Kagan, 1991), 51, which cites the recollections of people who grew up in Birz. It was reported that women would come to him for his blessing and advice. More information on Sossnitz's early mystical tendencies can be found in M. D. Lippman, *Letoldot hayehudim belita-zamut* (Kieden, 1934), 80.

15. On Sossnitz's hope that Rabinowitz would promote his book among wealthy Jewish families in Saint Petersburg see his letter and response to Rabinowitz, "Metiv lir'ot," in JNUL, Joseph Sossnitz, B 710, Ms. Heb. 38°5774.

16. On Rabinowitz's cosmopolitanism and support for a rapprochement between Russians and Jews see Tsvi Hirsch Rabinowitz, "Sblizhenie evreev s obshchim naseleniem," *Razsvet,* October 17, 1879.

17. See Klausner, *Historya shel hasifrut ha'ivrit haḥadasha,* 4:133

18. See the recollections of Yehuda Leib Gamzu, "Dinanburg," *Hatsefira,* January 29, 1889.

19. On Rabinowitz's relationship to Ivan Delianov, see Kagan, *Yidishe shtet,* 259.

20. See the description of Sossnitz by the American journalist Hutchins Hapgood in *The Spirit of the Ghetto: Studies of the Jewish Quarter in New York* (New York: Funk and Wagnalls, 1902), 54.

21. Zagorodski, "Tsvi Hirsh Rabinovits," 444.

22. Tsvi Hirsch Rabinowitz, letter to Joseph Leib Sossnitz, in Sossnitz, *Akhen yesh Hashem* (Vilna, 1875), iv–v.

23. Daum, *Wissenschaftspopularisierung im 19 Jahrhundert,* 203–210.

24. Weir, *Secularism and Religion in Nineteenth-Century Germany,* 84.

25. Ibid., 119.

26. See Tsvi Hirsch Rabinowitz, *Otsar haḥokhma vehamadda': yesodei ḥokhmat hateva', sefer even hasho'evet* (Vilna, 1876), 90.

27. On the need for science to develop and embrace new theories see Rabinowitz's critique of Aaron Bernstein, ibid., 34–36.

28. See Elias Tcherikower, "Yidn-revolutsyonern in Rusland in di 60er un 70er yorn," in Tcherikower, ed., *Historishe shriftn,* 3 vols. (Vilna: YIVO, 1939), 3:64–65.

29. Eliyana Adler, *In Her Hands: The Education of Jewish Girls in Tsarist Russia* (Detroit: Wayne State University Press, 2011), 102.

30. On the increasing numbers of Jews in the Kiev University see statistical data compiled by M. F. Vladimirsky-Budanov, *Istoriia Imperatorskago Universiteta Sviatogo Vladimira* (Kiev, 1884), 1:263 and 479. On the support given by Jewish philanthropists to Jewish students in Kiev see the data compiled by Menashe Morgulis and David Rafaelovitch in "Kheshbn fun dem gelt," *Kol mevaser,* February 11, 1865, 99–101. On the student subsidies see Tcherikower, "Yidn-revolutsyonern in Rusland," 3:111. For an overview of the life of Russian Jews in medical schools see Lisa Rae Epstein, "Caring for the Soul's

House: The Jews of Russia and Health Care, 1860–1914" (Ph.D. diss., Yale University, 1995).

31. See Israel Bartal, *Kozak ubedvi* (Tel Aviv: Am Oved, 2007), 91.

32. Sossnitz, "Metiv lir'ot," JNUL, Joseph Sossnitz, B 710, Ms. Heb. 38°5774. Sossnitz's disapproval of Rabinowitz's "letter of endorsement" can also be found in his personal notes. In Sossnitz's copy of the book (in the possession of Sossnitz's great-grandson Fred Shaw) a line is drawn through Rabinowitz's letter, suggesting that it should be eliminated from the second edition he was proposing to publish.

33. Rabinowitz, *Otsar haḥokhma vehamadda': yesodei ḥokhmat hateva', sefer even hasho'evet*, title page.

34. See Mordechai Zalkin, "Scientific Thinking and Cultural Transformation in Nineteenth-Century East European Jewish Society," *Aleph* 5, no. 1 (2005): 268; Hoffman, "Hashkafa 'al hitpatḥut sifruteinu hamadda'it haḥadasha."

35. Tsvi Hirsch Rabinowitz, *Otsar haḥokhma vehamadda': sefer harkava vehafrada* (Vilna, 1876), 120; see also Rabinowitz, *Otsar haḥokhma vehamadda': yesodei ḥokhmat hateva', sefer even hasho'evet*, 60. Rabinowitz's study originally appeared as three volumes; these were then published as two separate books, which I consulted, and also as single volumes. On Bernstein's notion of ether see Frederick Gregory, "The Mysteries and Wonders of Natural Science: Aaron Bernstein's *Naturwissenschaftliche Volksbücher* and the Adolescent Einstein," in *Einstein: The Formative Years, 1879–1909,* ed. Don Howard and John Stachel (Berlin: Birkhäuser, 2000), 33.

36. Rabinowitz, *Otsar haḥokhma vehamadda': yesodei ḥokhmat hateva', sefer even hasho'evet,* 90. On Rabinowitz's theory of ether in relation to atomism see *Otsar haḥokhma vehamadda': sefer harkava vehafrada,* 102, 116.

37. Rabinowitz, *Otsar haḥokhma vehamadda': sefer harkava vehafrada,* 106–108.

38. Rabinowitz's theories echoed certain ideas expressed by the eleventh-century Andalusian Jewish philosopher Solomon ibn Gabirol (author of *Fons Vitae*), who believed that matter—albeit some pure, spiritual grade of matter—made up the "ontological core of reality." Like Rabinowitz, Ibn Gabirol considered this matter not to be a substance but something like ether, a kind of potential that made existence possible, something that unified and equalized all aspects of nature. Sarah Pessin, *Ibn Gabirol's Theology of Desire: Matter and Method in Jewish Medieval Neoplatonism* (Cambridge: Cambridge University Press, 2013), 37.

39. Rabinowitz, *Otsar haḥokhma vehamadda': yesodei ḥokhmat hateva', sefer even hasho'evet,* 93.

40. Sossnitz, "Metiv lir'ot," JNUL, Joseph Sossnitz, B 710, Ms. Heb. 38°5774, comment no. 42.

41. Rabinowitz, *Otsar haḥokhma vehamadda': yesodei ḥokhmat hateva', sefer even hasho'evet,* 114.

42. Ibid., 36. See also Jeremy Brown's perceptive reading of Rabinowitz's work in his *New Heavens and a New Earth: The Jewish Reception of Copernican Thought* (Oxford: Oxford University Press, 2013), 237.

43. Tsvi Hirsch Rabinowitz, "Ha'ivrim beyiḥusam laḥakirot beḥokhmat hateva'," *Hamelits,* January 24, 1871.

44. Ibid., May 2, 1871.

45. Rabinowitz, *Otsar hahokhma vehamadda': yesodei hokhmat hateva', sefer even hasho'evet,* 215.

46. Sossnitz, "Metiv lir'ot," JNUL, Joseph Sossnitz, B 710, Ms. Heb. 38°5774, comment no. 32.

47. On Slonimski and the telegraph see Nicolas Slonimsky, "My Grandfather Invented the Telegraph," *Commentary,* January 1, 1977, available athttps://www.commentarymaga zine.com/articles/my-grandfather-invented-the-telegraph/. On Slonimski and Humboldt see most recently Ela Bauer, "Ka'asher hamaskil hayehudi pagash et hamad'an hagermani," in *Sefer tavniyot nofim tarbutiyim,* ed. Arnon Soffer, Jacob O. Maos, and Ronit Cohen-Soffer (Haifa: Katedrat Haiken, Haifa University, 2011), 47–63.

48. Hayyim Selig Slonimski, "Atomei hagufim ve'ether ha'olam," *Hatsefira,* May 31, 1876.

49. Sossnitz, *Akhen yesh Hashem,* 51, note.

50. Sossnitz himself entertained the possibility of eternal matter. His archives contain a document in which he interprets the first verse of the book of Genesis as follows: "Something was created that did not exist, and perhaps there already existed matter from which he created." NYPL, ***P Joseph Sossnitz, "He'arot uvei'urim lekhitvei hakodesh," box 2.

51. On S. A. Rachinsky's translation of Darwin into Russian (*O proiskhozhdenii vidov,* 1864), see Vucinich, *Darwin in Russian Thought,* 8–50.

52. Much has been written about Darwin's reception in Jewish literature. Darwin's theory of evolution by natural selection was first addressed in Hebrew in Moses Bazilevsky's *Words of Understanding; or, Belief and Scientific Knowledge (Divrei bina: o emuna vehokhmat hateva',* 1870). In 1874 the newspaper *Hashahar* ran an article on Darwin's theory under the title "This Is the Book of Man," by the Franco-German scholar Naphtali Levy, which was anthologized a year later. See most notably, Michael Shai Cherry, "Creation, Evolution and Jewish Thought" (Ph.D. diss., Brandeis University, 2001); Jacob Shavit and Jehuda Reinharz, *Darvin vekhama mibnei mino* (Tel Aviv: Hakibbutz Hame'uhad, 2009); and the articles in Geoffrey Cantor and Marc Swetlitz, eds., *Jewish Tradition and the Challenge of Darwinism* (Chicago: University of Chicago Press, 2006).

53. Sossnitz, *Akhen yesh Hashem,* 47. See Julius Dub, *Kurze Darstellung der Lehre Darwin's über die Entstehung der Arten der Organismen* (Stuttgart, 1870), 281–282. See also M. Schleiden, *Über den Materialismus der neueren deutschen Materialismus, sein Wesen und seine Geschichte* (Leipzig, 1863), 45–46.

54. See Cherry, "Creation, Evolution and Jewish Thought," 137.

55. Sossnitz, *Akhen yesh Hashem,* 54–55. On Naturphilosophie see Timothy Lenoir, *The Strategy of Life: Teleology and Mechanics in Nineteenth-Century German Biology* (Dordrecht, Netherlands: Reidel, 1982), 69.

56. As astutely noted by Yitzchak Melamed, *acosmism* was originally invoked by the Jewish philosopher Solomon Maimon to describe Spinoza's pantheism, and later by Hegel to orientalize the ideas espoused by F. W. J. Schelling. Yitzhak Y. Melamed, "Salomon Maimon and the Rise of Spinozism in German Idealism," *Journal of the History of Philosophy* 42 (2004): 79–80; and "Acosmism or Weak Individuals? Hegel, Spinoza, and the Reality of the Finite," *Journal of the History of Philosophy* 48, no. 1 (2010): 77–92.

57. See Eisenstadt, *Ḥakhmei yisra'el be'amerika,* 43–45. Sossnitz wrote one of the first scholarly articles on Schneerson. See Joseph Leib Sossnitz, "Temunat haga'on heḥasid rav Menaḥem Mendel," in *Knesset Yisra'el,* ed. Saul P. Rabinowitz, 3 vols. (Warsaw, 1888), 3:213–218.

58. See Mordecai Kaplan, "The Influences That Have Shaped My Life," *Reconstructionist* 8, no. 10 (June 26, 1942): 30.

59. See Elliot R. Wolfson, *Open Secret: Postmessianic Messianism and the Mystical Revision of Menahem Mendel Schneerson* (New York: Columbia University Press, 2009), 63. For a different approach to understanding the nature of paradox in Ḥabad see Rachel Elior, "ḤaBaD: The Contemplative Ascent to God," in *Jewish Spirituality,* vol. 2: *From the Sixteenth-Century Revival to the Present,* ed. Arthur Green (New York: Crossroad, 1987), 60–61. See also Yoram Yacobson, "Bimvokhei ha'en vehayesh," *Kiryat sefer* 68 (1998): 229–243.

60. On Ḥabad and materiality see most recently S. Zalman Rothschild, "The Role of Materiality in Early Hasidism: Divine Immanence, Religious Service with the Corporeal, and Law in the Theology of the Maggid of Mezritch and Shneur Zalman of Lyady" (Ph.D. diss., New York University, 2016), 148–149.

61. See Sossnitz, *Akhen yesh Hashem,* 54.

62. According to Elliot Wolfson, "The leap . . . may be envisaged as the effort to think transcendence as the advance from place to no-place and immanence as the recoil from no-place to place. . . . [It] subverts the logic of cause and effect that is characteristic of the 'routine order,' marked by the term 'walking.' The causal agency of the leap defies the principle of causality, insofar as it signifies the occurrence of the event of being beyond being and nonbeing." Wolfson, "Achronic Time, Messianic Expectation, and the Secret of the Leap in Ḥabad," in *Ḥabad Hasidism: History, Theology and Image,* ed. Jonatan Meir and Gadi Sagiv (Jerusalem: Merkaz Zalman Shazar, 2016).

63. Fabius Mieses, "Korot hafilosofya haḥadasha," *Hatsefira,* June 18, 1878.

64. Gregory, *Scientific Materialism in Nineteenth-Century Germany,* 7 (quotation), 178–181.

65. See Sossnitz, *Akhen yesh Hashem,* 54.

66. Ibid., 53–61.

67. Emil du Bois-Reymond, "The Limits of our Knowledge of Nature," trans. J. Fitzgerald, *Popular Science Monthly* 5 (1874): 20. See also Vucinich, *Darwin in Russian Thought,* 160; and Joakim Philipson "The Purpose of Evolution: The Struggle for Existence in the Russian-Jewish Press, 1860–1900" (Ph.D. diss., Stockholm University, 2008), 54–55.

68. See Eisenstadt, *Ḥakhmei yisra'el be'amerika,* 43–45.

69. Slonimski's distributor in Warsaw Abraham Tsukerman, offered Sossnitz 400 rubles per year for the position. NYPL, ***P Joseph Sossnitz, 1.aaaa, box 5.

70. On Slonimski and Bernstein's relationship see Julius Bernstein, *Erinnerungen an das elterliche Haus* (Berlin: H. S. Hermann, 1913), 33. On Jewish scientists in German lands see Ulrich Charpa and Ute Deichmann, eds., *Jews and Sciences in German Contexts: Case Studies from the 19th and 20th Centuries* (Tübingen: Mohr Siebeck, 2007); and Shulamit Volkov, "Jewish Scientists in Imperial Germany (Parts I and II)," *Aleph* 1 (2001): 256–265.

71. Eisenstadt, *Ḥakhmei yisra'el be'amerika,* 44.

72. The Joseph Sossnitz archive at the New York Public Library contains a number of letters from prominent Jewish philanthropists offering Sossnitz various degrees of financial support. The Rothschild family provided him with 40 franks; see NYPL, ***P Joseph Sossnitz, 1.yyy, box 5. Acting on behalf of the Society for the Promotion of Enlightenment Among the Jews, Judah Leib Gordon also purchased books from Sossnitz and gave him financial support; ibid., 1.ccc, box 5. In personal correspondence Joseph Sossnitz's great-grandson Fred Shaw (October 15, 2015) informed me that Sossnitz worked on barges in order to earn extra money.

73. See Schweder, letter to Sossnitz, January 1877, regarding library privileges, NYPL, ***P Joseph Sossnitz, box 5, uncatalogued materials. In Sossnitz's handwritten notes (appearing in documents given to me by Fred Shaw) Sossnitz states that when he was twenty-four he met Schweder and "he allowed me to have access to all the books at the Riga Polytechnic Institute. And I was diligent in studying various knowledges and sciences."

74. See the Vilna enlightener Mordekhai Plungian, letter to Joseph Sossnitz, dated Tammuz 1881, NYPL, ***P Joseph Sossnitz 1.nnnnn, box 5.

75. Eisenstadt, *ḥakhmei yisra'el be'amerika,* 43.

76. See Yitsḥak Isaac Etkin, "Mikhtav," *Hame'asef,* January 1879.

77. The Joseph Sossnitz' archive at NYPL was catalogued on at least two occasions. In what seems to be an early bibliography and listing of manuscripts a bibliographer notes a document that offers a rebuttal to Etkin. However, I was unable to locate it in the archive. See NYPL, ***P Joseph Sossnitz, "Manuscripts in the New York Public Library," no. 3, box 1.

78. Ḥayyim Selig Slonimski, letter to Tsvi Hirsch Rabinowitz, copied by Joseph Sossnitz, NYPL, ***P Joseph Sossnitz, 1.5r, box 5. At no point in his apology did Slonimski retract any of his claims that Rabinowitz had adopted a materialist position. Rather, Slonimski apologized for not being more receptive toward Rabinowitz's theories.

79. "I have heard here a number of expressions against your book by Hasidim." Ibid.

80. Yitsḥak Isaac Etkin, *Torat haḥayyim veḥezyonoteihem* (Saint Petersburg, 1881). Etkin married Haeckel's biological materialism with the *princip "der arbietsteilung"* as described by Adam Smith in *The Wealth of Nations* (1776). According to Etkin an ideal polity would be self-sufficient and operate in a mechanistic matter in which all parts of society were productive and served the state. "The labor of all of the different organs were all intimately tied together and assist one another, and the goal of all of them is to establish and to strengthen the organism in its entirety" (*Torat haḥayyim veḥezyonoteihem,* 14–16).

81. Yitsḥak Isaac Etkin, "'Inyenei ḥokhma umadda'," *Hakol,* March 9, 1879.

82. Ḥayyim Selig Slonimski, foreword to Etkin, *Torat haḥayyim veḥezyonoteihem,* 14.

83. It seems that Sossnitz attempted to redraft parts of *Akhen yesh Hashem* and republish the work in 1893. See NYPL, ***P Joseph Sossnitz, "Akhen yesh Hashem," box 4.

84. Sossnitz, *Akhen yesh Hashem,* 54.

85. Sossnitz's great-grandson Fred Shaw possesses a copy of Sossnitz's emendations to *Akhen yesh Hashem.* This change is on page 54.

86. Michael Shai Cherry first noticed the discrepancy between the printed and emended versions of Sossnitz's work but incorrectly dismissed the idea that Sossnitz had changed his mind. Cherry assumed that Sossnitz omitted the miracles and the idea of God's leaping because "it seemed superfluous to [Sossnitz's] argument." Cherry, "Creation, Evolution and Jewish Thought," 140, n. 203. In a lecture delivered on April 7, 1900, titled "Tekhunat hayisre'eli" (The Israelite Character) Sossnitz explicitly reaffirmed his belief that nature did not leap and that differences between various races and ethnicities were historically produced. See the large notebook he kept of his various lectures, articles, and sermons in NYPL, ***P Joseph Sossnitz, box 4.

87. Sossnitz's new theory of God and the natural world is illuminated in Shaul Magid's description of Sossnitz's student Mordecai Kaplan's theology: "God is a not a cause that passes into the world (via revelation, for example). God is a cause that was, is, and will remain in and of the world." Shaul Magid, "The Spinozistic Spirit in Mordecai Kaplan's Revaluation of Judaism," *Modern Judaism,* 20, no. 2 (May 2000): 168.

88. See the draft of *Hama'or* in NYPL, ***P Joseph Sossnitz, "Hama'or," box 4, p. 34 and compare it with the published version of *Hama'or* (Warsaw, 1889).

89. NYPL, ***P Joseph Sossnitz, "Hama'or," box 4, pp. 34–35.

90. The discrepancy between Sossnitz's early and later positions was also recognized by some of his critics; see Judah Leib Luntz, *Ge'ula viyshu'a* (Petrikov, 1908), 97.

91. Joseph Leib Sossnitz, "Hadat vehahaskala," *Hatsefira,* October 21, 1879.

92. Ibid.

93. Ibid., October 14, 1879.

94. On Spinoza's influence on Sossnitz's students see the introduction to Simon Brainin, *Sefer orah lahayyim* (Vilna, 1884). Before the 1870s Spinoza was for the most part either depicted by Jewish thinkers as an idealist or a heretic. On the reception of Spinoza as a Jewish idealist, see Daniel B. Schwartz, *The First Modern Jew: Spinoza and the History of an Image* (Princeton: Princeton University Press, 2012), 31, 46–52. On the contradictory image of Spinoza's Jewishness among Enlightenment interpreters of Judaism see Adam Sutcliffe, *Judaism and Enlightenment,* 146–147.

95. See the partial notes of a speech delivered by Joseph Leib Sossnitz: "Derush lezikhron Ribal," delivered on "Shevat 24 (?) 1890," JNUL, Joseph Sossnitz, B 710, Ms. Heb. 38°5774.

96. See Mel Scult, *Judaism Faces the Twentieth Century: A Biography of Mordecai Kaplan* (Detroit: Wayne State University Press, 1993), 55; and Magid, "The Spinozistic Spirit in Mordecai Kaplan's Revaluation of Judaism," 165.

97. Sossnitz, "Hadat vehahaskala, October 14, 1879.

98. Ibid., October 21, 1879.

99. Tsvi Hirsch Rabinowitz, "Vvedenie," in Eliezer Berman, *Osnovy Moiseeva zakona: Rukovodstvo k zakonoucheniiu dlia evreiskogo iunoshestva* (Saint Petersburg, 1874). See Sossnitz, "Metiv lir'ot," JNUL, Joseph Sossnitz, B 710, Ms. Heb. 38°5774, comment no. 32.

100. See Adler, *In Her Hands*, 88.

101. Tsvi Hirsch Rabinowitz [G. Rabinovitch], "Vvedenie," in Berman, *Osnovy Moiseeva zakona* (Saint Petersburg, 1881), 10.

102. Rabinowitz [Rabinovitch], "Vvedenie," *Osnovy Moiseeva zakona* (1881), 10.

103. Ibid., 11.

104. Ibid. Rabinowitz's use of *vechnaia-zagrobnaia* and *nastoiashchaia-zemnaia* was a Russian translation of *Jeneseits* (what existed beyond the grave) and *Dieseits* (worldly knowledge). Rabinowitz shrewdly emphasized the latter over the former and made it a point to attack those who engaged in metaphysical interpretations of the Bible. See Weir, *Secularism and Religion in Nineteenth-Century Germany,* 79–81.

105. See Tsvi Hirsch Rabinowitz, *Otsar haḥokhma vehamadda': yesodei ḥokhmat hateva', sefer even hasho'evet*, 93.

106. Rabinowitz [Rabinovitch], "Vvedenie," *Osnovy Moiseeva zakona* (1881), 11.

107. See the biographical comments recorded in Ben-Ya'akov [pseud.], "Zikkaron leḥakham," *'Ivri anokhi,* March 1, 1889.

108. Sossnitz, "Hadat vehahaskala," October 21, 1879. Fred Shaw gave Michael Shai Cherry on May 15, 2000, a document that places Joseph Sossnitz in the late 1870s in a circle of Russian revolutionaries, some of whom would become involved in the assassination of Tsar Alexander II.

109. Sossnitz, *Akhen yesh Hashem*, 50.

110. See Carl Vogt, *Lectures on Man: His Place in Creation and the History of the Earth*, ed. James Hunt (London, 1864), 162–163.

111. Ibid., 448.

112. See Sossnitz, *Akhen yesh Hashem*, 55. On the publication and rejection of Vogt in Russian lands see Vucinich, *Darwin in Russian Thought*, 24.

113. Sossnitz, *Akhen yesh Hashem*, 63.

114. Joseph Sossnitz, "'Imrat elo'ah tserufa," 1890. Parts of the manuscript are in NYPL, ***P Joseph Sossnitz, boxes 2 and 4.

115. See Sossnitz's lecture "Tekhunat hayisre'eli," NYPL, ***P Joseph Sossnitz, box 4.

116. Sossnitz, "Hadat vehahaskala," October 28, 1879.

117. Lisa Moses Leff, "Self-Definition and Self-Defense: Jewish Racial Identity in Nineteenth-Century France," *Jewish History* 19 (2005): 19.

118. "Derekh mamona," *Halevanon*, December 26, 1879. The author of this article was given as "Shlomo Kohen ish Galitsya," which appears to be an alias. Perhaps it was written by Yehuda Halevi Lifshutz, who years later published a book under the same title attacking Sossnitz.

119. NYPL, ***P Joseph Sossnitz, 1.4a, box 5.

120. Sossnitz, "'Atsat emuna," unpublished response to *Halevanon*, NYPL, ***P Joseph Sossnitz, 1.5y, box 1.

121. See Lippman, *Letoldot hayehudim belita-zamut*, 80.

122. See Yehuda Halevi Lifshutz, *Derekh emuna* (Warsaw, 1895), 135.

123. Ibid., 136. Perceptively, Lifshutz recognized how the new Jewish scientific materialists (those whom he referred to as "atomists") were appropriating Kabbalistic theories.

124. Ibid. See also Sossnitz, *Hama'or,* 40. For multiple responses to Lifshutz see the un-catalogued documents in NYPL, ***P Joseph Sossnitz, boxes 1, 4, and 5.

125. See Zagorodski, "Tsvi Hirsh Rabinovits," 445. On Rabinowitz's ties to the mercantile elite and the publication of *Russkie Evrei* see A. E. Kaufman, "Za mnogo let," *Evreis-kaia starina* 5 (1913): 215–220.

126. Kaufman, "Za mnogo let," 218.

127. Chaim Weizmann, "Yedi'otav harishonot bekhimya misofer 'ivri," *Haboker* November 17, 1952.

128. On Rabinowitz and his role in promoting Russian Jewish liberal ideals see Benjamin Nathans, *Beyond the Pale: The Jewish Encounter with Late Imperial Russia* (Berkeley: University of California Press, 2002), 188.

129. Marina Mogliner, "Toward a History of Russian Jewish 'Medical Materialism': Russian Jewish Physicians and the Politics of Jewish Biological Normalization," *Jewish Social Studies* 19, no. 1 (Fall 2012): 96.

130. See the introduction to Brainin, *Sefer oraḥ laḥayyim,* as well as Brainin's own reflections presented at the Sossnitz Jubilee on November 30, 1907, recorded in Brainin, "Zosnits yubileum a zeltener erfolg," *Der morgn zhurnal,* December 1, 1907.

131. Kaplan, "The Influences That Have Shaped My Life," 30. It is not surprising that Jeffrey S. Gurock and Jacob J. Schacter, in their *A Modern Heretic and a Traditional Community: Mordecai M. Kaplan Orthodoxy and American Judaism* (New York: Columbia University Press, 1997), were unable to determine whether Sossnitz's theories strengthened Kaplan's beliefs or conversely "moved him along the road out of Orthodoxy," (175, n. 41). As I suggest in this chapter, this paradox lies at the heart of Sossnitz's worldview. Kaplan's indebtedness to Sossnitz further deepens Steven J. Zipperstein's incisive suggestion (citing Eli Lederhendler) in *Imagining Russian Jewry: Memory, History, Identity* (Seattle: University of Washington Press, 1999), 109–110, on the importance of looking at Kaplan's work within an eastern European Jewish context. Sossnitz's archive in NYPL provides important information regarding dates and the nature of the relationship between him and Kaplan. The archive contains two letters from Kaplan (and one from Kaplan's father). These letters attest to Kaplan's studying with Sossnitz in 1901 while he was attending rabbinical school at the Jewish Theological Seminary. NYPL, ***P Joseph Sossnitz, "Father's Correspondence," 1.zz.a, box 5. More information about Sossnitz and Kaplan's studies can be found in a letter Kaplan wrote to Sossnitz's great-grandson Fred Shaw on May 17, 1974 (copy in my possession) in which Kaplan describes his encounter with Sossnitz: "By the age of 15 I was a student at the Jewish Theological Seminary of New York and a freshman at the New York City College [*sic*]. By then I had arrived at what is known as 'the storm and stress period' of my life. Being dissatisfied with the courses in Jewish philosophy at Seminary [taught by Rabbi Bernard Drachman], my father z"l arranged with Mr. Sossnitz to read with me Maimonides, *The Guide for the Perplexed* (Hebrew text)." On Kaplan's studies with Sossnitz see also Mel Scult, *Communings of the Spirit: The Journals of Mordecai M. Kaplan, 1913–1934* (Detroit: Wayne State University Press, 2001), 46–47, 175. I hope to write about this subject in greater depth.

132. NYPL, ***P Joseph Sossnitz, 1.zz.a, box 5.

CHAPTER 4. PRACTICAL MATERIALISM

1. For an overview of the percentages of Jews in Russian educational and professional institutions see Yuri Slezkine, *The Jewish Century* (Princeton: Princeton University Press, 2004), 123–127.

2. The scholarship on the rise of Russian radicalism and the economic situation in Russia is too vast to cite here. In particular, see Franco Venturi, *Roots of Revolution: A History of the Populist and Socialist Movements in Nineteenth Century Russia,* trans. Francis Haskell (New York: Knopf, 1964); Mark Raeff, *Origins of the Russian Intelligentsia: The Eighteenth-Century Nobility* (New York: Harcourt, Brace and World, 1966); Daniel R. Brower, *Training Nihilists: Education and Radicalism in Tsarist Russia* (Ithaca: Cornell University Press, 1975); Gianni Stateri, *Death of a Utopia: The Development and Decline of Student Movements in Europe* (Oxford: Oxford University Press, 1975); and Robert J. Brym, *The Jewish Intelligentsia and the Russian Revolution: A Sociological Study of Intellectual Radicalism and Ideological Divergence* (London: Macmillan, 1978).

3. Slezkine, *The Jewish Century,* 98.

4. Ibid., 153.

5. Ibid., 137. On the early Russian Jewish revolutionaries see Erich Haberer, *Jews and Revolution in Nineteenth-Century Russia* (Cambridge: Cambridge University Press, 1995), 27–119. On the estrangement of Jewish socialists from the Jewish masses in the 1870s see Jonathan Frankel, *Politics and Prophecy: Socialism, Nationalism, and the Russian Jews, 1862–1917* (Cambridge: Cambridge University Press, 1981), 101–107; and Abraham Ascher, "Pavel Axelrod: A Conflict Between Jewish Loyalty and Revolutionary Dedication," *Russian Review* 24, no. 3 (July 1965): 249–265. On the Peoples' Will Party and its activities in the 1880s see Norman Naimark, *Terrorists and Social Democrats: The Russian Revolutionary Movement Under Alexander III* (Cambridge: Harvard University Press, 1983), 41–68.

6. Benjamin Jochelsohn, "Dalekoe proshloe, Iz vospominaniy starogo narodovol'tsa," *Byloe* 13 (1918): 56–57; Boris Frumkin, "Iz istorii revoliutsionnogo dvizheniia sredi evreev v 1870-kh godakh," *Evreiskaia starina* 2 (1911): 221.

7. See the data collected in Brym, *The Jewish Intelligentsia and the Russian Revolution,* 53–58. While Brym doubts that messianism exerted much influence on rates of radicalism, he still points to specific educational profiles (the university and the rabbinic institutions) as being the breeding ground for radicalism.

8. Slezkine, *The Jewish Century,* 155.

9. See Erich Goldhagen, "The Ethnic Consciousness of Early Russian Jewish Socialists," *Judaism,* 23, no. 4 (1974): 479–496. For other responses to Slezkine's work see the forum in *Ab Imperio* 1 (2005), particularly Marina Mogilner, "On Cabbages, Kings, and Jews," review of Yuri Slezkine, *The Jewish Century,* 138–150, and Natan Meir, "*The Jewish Century:* What Does Being a Jew Matter?" 171–174.

10. See Rebecca Trachtenberg Alpert, "The Quest for Economic Justice: Kaplan's Response to the Challenge of Communism, 1929–1940," in *The American Judaism of Mordecai M. Kaplan,* ed. Emanuel S. Goldsmith, Mel Scult, and Robert M. Seltzer (New York: New York University Press, 1990), 385–401.

11. Kook's positive position toward certain aspects of historical materialism can be seen in the letter he wrote to Shmuel Alexandrov on December 14, 1906: Abraham Isaac Kook, *Igrot harav Avraham Yitshak Hakohen Kook*, 3 vols. (Jerusalem: Mosad Harav Kook, 1961), 1:50.

12. On Jews ignoring of Marx's "On the Jewish Question" in the 1870s see Julius Carlebach, *Karl Marx and the Radical Critique of Judaism* (London: Routledge, 1978), 187–188. On its reception among acculturated Jews residing in German lands see Shlomo Na'aman, *Marxismus und Zionismus* (Gerlingen: Bleicher-Verlag, 1997), 68, 77–97; and Jack Jacobs, *On Socialists and "The Jewish Question" After Marx* (New York: New York University Press, 1992), 44–71.

13. The first allusion to Marx's "On the Jewish Question" to appear in a Jewish eastern European publication can be found in Isaac Joel Linetzky and Abraham Goldfaden's lead editorial in their short-lived Yiddish newspaper *The Old Jew* (*Der alter Yisrolik*), published in July 1875. In the context of a discussion on "the Jewish Question" the editors mention the position espoused by "der communist M." It is difficult to decipher which aspects in Marx's work the editors are referring to. The only copy of the newspaper I was able to find is damaged where Marx's name appears.

14. See Gareth Stedman Jones, *Karl Marx: Greatness and Illusion* (Cambridge: Harvard University Press, 2016), 155; and Carlebach, *Karl Marx and the Radical Critique of Judaism*, 187–188.

15. On the reception of Marx's "On the Jewish Question" among acculturated Jews in German lands, see Shlomo Na'aman, *Marxismus und Zionismus* (Gerlingen: Bleicher-Verlag, 1997), 68, 77–97; on Marx's lack of knowledge about Russian Jews see pages 73–74.

16. On Judah Leib Levin's translation of *Capital* into Hebrew see his autobiography, *Zikkaron basefer*, in Levin, *Yehuda Leib Levin: Zikhronot vehegyonot*, ed. Yehuda Slutsky (Jerusalem: Mosad Bialik, 1968), 53.

17. Boris Sapir, "Liberman et le Socialism Russe," *International Review of Social History* 3 (1938): 35–37.

18. See the recollections of Abraham Liessin in his *Zikhronot vahavayot* (Tel Aviv: Am Oved, 1943), 128.

19. For a partial listing of these works see Kalman Marmor's handwritten bibliography of Lieberman and his circle located in YIVO, Kalman Marmor Collection, RG 205, box 35. On Lieberman's influence on the Jewish labor movement see Abraham Menes, "Di Yidishe arbeter-bavegung in Rusland fun onheyb 70er bizn sof 90er yorn," in *Historishe shriftn*, ed. Elias Tcherikower, 3 vols. (Vilna: YIVO, 1939), 3:25–30.

20. The historian Jonathan Frankel has convincingly refuted earlier scholarship that described the materialists of the 1870 as being the sole inspiration behind the rise of Zionism and Bundism. However, often forgotten was Frankel's own caveat to his claims about the positions advanced in 1897, which were in many ways "essentially similar to, and even influenced by, the so-called Hebrew socialism developed by Aron Liberman in the 1870's." See Frankel, "The Roots of Jewish Socialism (1881–1892)," in *Essential Papers on Jews and the Left*, ed. Ezra Mendelsohn (New York: New York University Press, 1997), 61.

21. Zundelevich claimed that the Vilna circle read "*Istoricheskie pis'ma* [*Historical Letters*, 1869) of 'Mirtov'; certain articles by Nikolay Chernyshevsky in addition to his novel *What Is to Be Done;* [Nikolai Vasil'evich] Sokolov on the Schismatics, *Otshchepentsy* [*The Schismatics*, 1866]; the first volume of [Peter Lavrov's] journal *Vpered!*; and works by Erckmann-Chatrian[Émile Erckmann and Alexander Chatrian]." Frumkin, "Iz istorii revoliutsionnogo dvizheniia sredi evreev v 1870-kh godakh," 226–227. The book by the French authors Erckmann and Chatrian was probably *Historie d'un Paysan*, distributed by the Chaikovsky circle. On the books distributed by the Chaikovsky circle see Peter Kropotkin, *Memoirs of a Revolutionary* (New York: Black Rose Books, 1989), 287–306. On the role of Jews in the Chaikovsky circle see Haberer, *Jews and Revolution in Nineteenth-Century Russia*, 22–51.

22. On Zundelevich see Lev Deutsch, "Aron Zundelevitsh," *Di tsukunft* 19, no. 8 (August 1914): 831–840; and A. Litvak [Khayim Yankl Helfand], "Aron Zundelevitsh," *Royter pinkes: tsu der geshikhte fun der Yidisher arbeter-bavegung un* sotsyalistishe *shtremungen bay Yidn*, 2 vols. (Warsaw: Kultur lige, 1924), 2:80–106.

23. See Moshe Kamensky, "Nihilistim 'ivriyim bishnot hashiv'im," *Hashiloaḥ* 17 (1907): 258. On those who studied with Axelrod in Mogilev see Grigory Gurevich, "Zikhroynes," in *Historishe shriftn*, ed. Tcherikower, 3:225–226, 246n15. On the role played by the Luria and Gurevich libraries in the educational development of Mogilev's revolutionaries see Samuel Leib Zitron, "Yankev Dinezon," in his *Dray literarishe doyres*, 3 vols. (Vilna: Sh. Shreberk, 1921), 1:58–65. Axelrod tutored Dr. Isaac Kaminer's daughters Nadezhda, Sofia, and Augustina. Without Dr. Kaminer's blessing he married Nadezhda and moved to Kiev, where his disciples from Mogilev soon joined him. See Zitron, "Yankev Dinezon," 1:61. See also Abraham Ascher, *Pavel Axelrod and the Development of Menshevism* (Cambridge: Harvard University Press, 1972), 20–22.

24. Gurevich, "Zikhroynes, 3:226.

25. Pavel Axelrod, "Padenie evreiskogo kagala v Shklove," *Mogilevskie gubernskie vedomosti*, July 29, 1870. Seen in typed form in BINC, Aksel'rod, Pavel Borisovich, 47: 3. See also Pavel Axelrod, "Neskol'ko slov ob Evreev g. Mogileva," *Mogilevskie gubernskie vedomsti*, May 6, 1870.

26. Khasia Shur, *Vospominaniia* (Kursk, 1928), 35–36.

27. Ibid., 43.

28. See YIVO, Rabbinical School and Teachers' Seminary Archive, RG 24, folder 181. The folder includes correspondence between the Vilensk police, the seminary, and the Russian Ministry of Education. It seems the seminary was searched on June 29 and 30, 1875, and "a forbidden book" was found that was being read by students. See the letter written by the director of the police to the administration of the seminary dated July 17, 1875 (page 11, folder 181). The Rabbinical School Archives do not name the "book" but the Russian government files identify it as Nikolai Vasil'evich Sokolov's *Schismatics*. On material in the Russian government archives of the first Vilna group see Pinkhes Kon, "Oysforsh-materyaln vegn ershtn yidishn revolutsyonern krayzl in Vilne," *YIVO Bleter* 5 (1933): 171–176; and Max Weinreich, "Naye faktn vegn ershtn revolutsyonern kruzhok in Vilne," *Forverts*, May 27, 1928, 12.

29. On the liquidation of the Vilna group, see the letter sent on April 9, 1875, from the Director of the Vilna Education District to the Director of the Rabbinical School,

YIVO, Rabbinical School and Teachers' Seminary Archive, RG 24, folder 170. Material in folder 181 in the archive confirms the account of events described by Aaron Shemuel Lieberman in "Iz Vil'no," *Vpered!* September 1, 1875, 505–506. See also Elias Tcherikower, "Der onheyb fun der Yidisher sotsyalistisher bavegung," in Tcherikower, ed., *Historishe shriftn*, 1:474; and Aaron Shemuel Lieberman, *Arn Libermans briv*, ed. Kalman Marmor (New York: YIVO, 1951), 11. For an overview of the police roundups and trails of revolutionaries in 1873–1877 see Hugh Seaton Watson, *The Russian Empire, 1801–1917* (Oxford: Oxford University Press, 1988), 421–426.

30. See BINC, series 79, box 132, Geheime Präsidial-Registratur Lit. S. Nr. 1234, vol. I, 35, vol. II, 145.

31. On the establishment of the Jewish Section see BINC, series 79, box 132, Geheime Präsidial-Registratur Lit: S. Nr. 1234, vol. II, 147, 214–215. Gurevich noted that A. (Axelrod?) defined the relationship of the group to the "Jewish idea."

32. On the Jewish group in Berlin see Bernard D. Weinryb, *Bereshit hasotsyalism hayehudi* (Jerusalem Reuven Mas, 1940), 14; and Moshe Kamensky, "Hanihilistim," *Hatsefira*, April 16, 1913.

33. JNUL, Abraham Schwadron, 01 18, 26.

34. Elias Zuckermann, *Kitvei Eli'ezer Tsukerman*, ed. Tsvi Krol (Tel Aviv, 1940), 30.

35. Shur, *Vospominaniia*, 62.

36. Kamensky, "Nihilistim 'ivriyim bishnot hashiv'im," 260.

37. See Moshe Kamensky's claim in *Hatsefira*, April 14, 1913, that Eliezer Leventhal committed suicide because Augustina Kaminer rejected him.

38. See the Berlin police deposition of Nochum Broidi of Vilna in BINC, series 79, box 132, Geheime Präsidial-Registratur Lit. S. Nr. 1234, vol. I, 37.

39. Berlin police memo to London officials, July 20, 1878, in BINC, series 79, box 132, Geheime Präsidial-Registratur, Lit. S. Nr. 1234, vol. I, 187.

40. Students investigated included Moses Aronsohn, Carl Beilin, Nochum Broidi, Samuel Eliasberg, Joel Efron, the Gurevich brothers, Judah Leib Kantor, Abraham Meier Karatschunski, Josef Lion, Aaron Masie, the Romm brothers, and Herman Sack. Ibid. See also the memo titled "Die Ausweisung russischer Studenten wegen Verdachts des Nihilismus," February 7, 1879, in BINC, series 79, box 132, Lit. S. Nr. 1234, vol. II, 183; and the letter titled "An der Kaiserlich-Deutsche General Konsulat in Warschau. Secret!" ibid., 147–149.

41. Gurevich, "Zikhroynes," 3:238.

42. Later Lieberman may have had an affair with the Anglican priest Isaac Salkinson. But some speculate that it was actually a different romantic attachment that led him to commit suicide in 1881 in Syracuse, New York. See David Isaiah Silberbusch, *Mipinkas zikhronotai* (Tel Aviv, 1936), 56 available at http://benyehuda.org/silberbusch/ishim_umeoraot.html#_ftn1 (accessed on March 28, 2015).

43. See Boris Sapir, "Jewish Socialists Around *Vpered!*" *International Review of Social History* 10, no. 3 (1965): 370.

44. On Lieberman's attempt to translate *The Communist Manifesto* see the letters between Rosalya Idelsohn and Valerian Smirnov in Sapir, "Liberman et le Socialism Russe," 35–37.

45. See the letter from Lieberman to Eliezer Zuckermann dated February 17, 1876, in Lieberman, *Arn Libermans briv*, 53.

46. See letter from Levin to an unidentified individual, June 1910, PL, Judah Leib Levin, IV A104 71. His comments about words he attempted to translate in Marx appear on the second page.

47. Letter from Levin to Ephraim Deinard, October 15, 1878, JTS, Ephraim Deinard Papers, ARC 29, box 5.

48. Letter from Levin to an unidentified individual, June 1910, PL, Judah Leib Levin, IV A104 71.

49. Ibid. Levin in his autobiography mentions in passing that he translated Marx, but does not include any additional information. See Judah Leib Levin, *Zikkaron basefer*, in Levin, *Yehuda Leib Levin: Zikhronot vehegyonot*, 53n1.

50. Pavel Axelrod, *Perezhitoe i peredumannoe* (1923; repr. Cambridge: Oriental Research Partners, 1975), 88. Compare Axelrod's original statements regarding probably seeing *Capital* for the first time in Kaminer's home and the Yiddish translation of Axelrod's memoir by Jacob Krepliak, "Memuarn," *Di tsukunft* (June 1922): 362.

51. Over the course of the 1880s and 1890s there appeared numerous partial translations of Marx's works in Yiddish and Hebrew. But the first full Yiddish translation of *Capital* was not published until 1917–1918: Karl Marx, *Das Kapital: Kritik der politcischen Oekonomie*, trans. Jacob Merison as *Dos kapital* (New York: Krapotkin literatur gezelshaft, 1917–1918). Merison's translation was based on the edition published by Karl Kautsky in 1914. In 1947, Zevi Wislavsky published the first Hebrew translation of the first book of *Capital* under the title *Hakapital* in 1947.

52. Letter from Levin to an unidentified individual, June 1910, PL, Judah Leib Levin, IV A104 71. Levin's story is corroborated by Moshe Kamensky, who was in Kiev from the summer of 1874 to the summer of 1875. In his memoirs he writes that he read John Stuart Mill, Ferdinand Lassalle, and Marx during that period. See Kamensky, "Nihilistim 'ivriyim bishnot hashiv'im," 259.

53. Aaron Shemuel Lieberman "Hitpathut hayyei hahevra bishnot habeinayim," *Ha'emet* 2, 1877, in Tsvi Krol, *Ha'emet* (Tel Aviv, 1938), 25–31.

54. Ibid.

55. Marx, *Das Kapital, Capital,* trans. Samuel Moore and Edward Aveling as *Capital: A Critique of Political Economy* (Chicago: Charles H. Kerr, 1909), 8:27:2.

56. See Aaron Shemuel Lieberman, "Letoldot ha'utopya," in *Kitvei A. S. Liberman,* ed. Michal Berkowitz (Tel Aviv, 1928), 9–10n3.

57. Marx, *Capital,* 8.27.15.

58. Lieberman, "Letoldot ha'utopya," 2n1.

59. *Pinkas agudat hasotsyalistim ha'ivriyim belondon* (Jerusalem: Hebrew University, Merkaz Dinur, 1968), 42.

60. Aaron Shemuel Lieberman, "Ma'aseh Satan," *Ha-Emet,* 3, 1877, 52n1.

61. See Isaiah Tishby, *Torat hara' vehakelippa bekabbalat ha-Ari* (Jerusalem: Schocken, 1960), 48–49.

62. Ibid., 45.

63. For an in-depth analysis of the Lieberman's theory of Luzzatto's kabbalah and its relationship to a Marxist theory of historical development see Eliyahu Stern, "Marx and the Kabbalah: Aaron Shemuel Lieberman's Materialist Conception of Jewish History," *Journal of the History of Ideas* (forthcoming). On Luzzatto's political orientation see Jonathan Garb, "The Circle of Moshe Hayyim Luzzatto in Its Eighteenth-Century Context," *Eighteenth Century Studies* 44, no. 2 (2011): 189–202.

64. See Aaron Shemuel Lieberman, "Hitpathut hayyei hahevra bishnot habeinayim," 27–28n2.

65. Lieberman, "Ma'aseh Satan," 54–55.

66. Letter from Aaron Shemuel Lieberman to his brother Abraham Isaac Lieberman, August 1875, in Lieberman, *Arn Libermans briv,* 41.

67. Aaron Shemuel Lieberman, "Gevul kohot ha'adam," *Hamabit,* May 15, 1879.

68. Compare the positions advanced by Andrzej Walicki in "Marx, Engels and the Polish Question" in his *Philosophy and Romantic Nationalism: The Case of Poland* (Oxford: Oxford University Press, 1982), 358, and Roman Szporluk "Review of *Really Existing Nationalisms: A Post-Communist View from Marx and Engels,* by Erica Brenner," *American Journal of Sociology* 102, no. 4 (May 1997): 1236–1238.

69. Roman Szporluk, *Communism and Nationalism: Karl Marx Versus Friedrich List* (New York: Oxford University Press, 1988), 54.

70. See John Doyle Klier, *Imperial Russia's Jewish Question, 1855–1881* (Cambridge: Cambridge University Press, 1995), 102–122; and Benjamin Nathans, *Beyond the Pale: The Jewish Encounter with Late Imperial Russia* (Berkeley: University of California Press, 2002), 72–79.

71. See, for example, the description given by the newspaper editor Alexander Zederbaum in "Safa lene'emanim," *Hamelits,* November 8, 1860.

72. On the use of *plemia* by Russian liberals to describe Jews in the 1860s see Klier, *Imperial Russia's Jewish Question,* 118; and Darius Staliūnas, *Making Russians: Meaning and Practice of Russification in Lithuania and Belarus After 1863* (New York: Rodopi, 2007), 118. See also Lisa Moses Leff, "Self-Definition and Self-Defense: Jewish Racial Identity in Nineteenth-Century France," *Jewish History* 19 (2005): 12–22; and Till van Rahden, "Germans of the Jewish *Stamm:* Visions of Community Between Nationalism and Particularism, 1850–1933," in *German History from the Margins,* ed. Neil Gregor, Nils Roemer, and Mark Roseman (Bloomington: Indiana University Press, 2006), 27–48.

73. Sapir, "Jewish Socialists Around *Vpered!*" 367.

74. "Shelumei bahurei yisra'el" was reprinted in the Hebrew Labor newspaper *Davar* on April 30, 1936.

75. See Lieberman, "Ma'aseh Satan," 53. On the influence of Lavrov's *Historical Letters* on yeshiva students see Lev Deutsch, "Der ershter yeshive-bokher in der rusisher revolutsye," *Di tsukunft* 20, no. 8 (1915): 713–717.

76. Lieberman, "Ma'aseh Satan," 53.

77. Aaron Shemuel Lieberman, "Hayehudim bahagira," *Ha'emet* 2, 1877; reprinted in Krol, ed., *Ha'emet,* 22.

78. *Pinkas agudat hasotyalistim ha'ivriyim belondon,* 41. On Lieberman's propaganda

program see most recently Israel Bartal, *Letaken 'am* (Jerusalem: Karmel, 2013), 322–333.

79. Lieberman, "Iz Vil'no," 504.

80. On strikes in the 1870s see Menes, "Di Idishe arbeter-bavegung in Rusland fun onheyb 70er bizn sof 90er yorn," 3:10–17. On the conditions of the factories see Aaron Shemuel Lieberman, "Iz Belostoka," December 15, 1875. More generally on the working conditions of Jewish artisans and factory workers in the second half of the nineteenth century see Ezra Mendelsohn, *Class Struggle in the Pale: The Formative Years of the Jewish Workers' Movement in Tsarist Russia* (Cambridge: Cambridge University Press, 1970), 12–25.

81. Lieberman, "Iz Belostoka," *Vpered!* February 15, 1876, translated into Hebrew in *A. S. Lieberman: Ketavot uma'amarim be-'Vpered' (1875–1876)*, ed. Moshe Mishkinsky (Tel Aviv: Tel Aviv University, 1977), 138.

82. Lieberman's criticism of the haskalah can be found throughout his writings. See specifically "Letoldot ha'utopya," 12n4.

83. Eliezer Zuckermann, "Tikva tova," in Zuckermann, *Kitvei Eli'ezer Tsukerman*, 64–65.

84. Lieberman, letter to Smirnov, April 16, 1877, in Lieberman, *Arn Libermans briv*, 143.

85. Lieberman, "Hayehudim bahagira," 23.

86. Ibid., 22.

87. Reflections of Aaron Zundelevich, PL, Kalman Marmor, IV-104, 88, folder 13 (p. 24). On Lieberman's relationship to Zundelevich see also Morris Winchevsky, "Mit a dor tsurik," *Di tsukunft* 3, no. 11 (December 1894): 1–6; and Tcherikower, "Der onheyb fun der Yidisher sotsyalistisher bavegung," 1:507. Lieberman may have been thinking about similar models adopted by Mogilev revolutionaries, who dressed in traditional Jewish garb while teaching at local Jewish schools. See Zitron, "Yankev Dinezon," 1:61–64.

88. Samuel Leib Zitron, "Baym redaktor fun hashakhar," in his *Dray literarishe doyres*, 3:130–131. On the lack of impact and ineffectual nature of Lieberman's pamphlet see Tcherikower, "Der onheyb fun der Yidisher sotsyalistisher bavegung"; and Yosef Klausner, *Historya shel hasifrut ha'ivrit hahadasha*, 6 vols. (Jerusalem: Hebrew University, 1950), 6:256–257.

89. On Lieberman's animosity toward Landau (whom he referred to as the Vilna Maggid), see Sapir, "Liberman et le Socialism Russe," 59–61.

90. On Landau see Phinehas Pesis, *'Ir dubno verabbaneha* (Krakow, 1902), 34–35; and the lengthy entry in Hillel Noah Maggid-Steinschneider, *'Ir Vilna* (Vilna, 1900), 92–97.

91. Landau's business dealings are listed in the will of his Novogrudok business partner Abraham Shklefer (Yakov Abraham ben Yehuda Leib), "Tsava'a: hana'asa 'a.y. R. Ya'akov Avraham b.m. Yehuda Leyb hanikra R. Avraham Shklefer mi-Novohardak," in uncatalogued archival materials at the Beinecke Library, Yale University.

92. Landau's indictment seems to have followed a tense meeting between the head of Russia's Third Division, Alexander Potapov, and Vilna's rabbinic establishment. Potapov greeted him with "In addition to all other good qualities which you Jews possess, about the only thing you need is to become nihilists, too!" Cited in Jacob S. Raisin's *The Haskalah Movement in Russia* (Philadelphia: Jewish Publication Society of America, 1913), 259.

93. The quotation is from a Yiddish transcription of Landau's sermon, in PL, Kalman Marmor IV-104, 23, p. 1. The title page of the handwritten document in the archive also lists an article published in the Vilna newspaper *Hakarmel* on September 20, 1876. The article, written in Hebrew, bears some resemblance to the Yiddish transcription but seems to be a highly edited version of the original.

94. Ibid., p. 3.

95. Ibid., p. 4.

96. Ibid., p. 3. In his comments Landau mentions students who were caught "reading books." He was referring to the incident mentioned above concerning students who were found reading Nikolai Vasil'evich Sokolov's *Schismatics*.

97. Ibid., p. 4.

98. Isaac Elijah Landau, "Derush," *Hakarmel,* September 20, 1876.

99. Yehoshua Mordecai Lifshitz, letter to Aaron Shemuel Liberman, September 12, 1977. A photocopy of the original letter can be found in YIVO, Nokhem Shtif Archive, RG 57, folder 3075. On Lifshitz's argument for Yiddish as the primary Jewish language see his article "Di 4 klasn," *Kol mevaser,* June 18, 1863. A sharp criticism of Lifshitz is expressed in Michal Berkowitz, "Tsurik mit fuftsik yor: Arn Liberman un zayn 'ha'emes,'" in *Haynt (yubiley-numer)* (Warsaw, 1928). On why Lieberman wrote in Hebrew see Frumkin's note about Zundelevich's recollection on the subject in PL, Kalman Marmon, IV-104, 88, folder 13 (listed as page 24). Frumkin's note is based on recollections he gathered in the early twentieth century from Jewish revolutionaries. A Russian transcription of these recollections can be found in the Pinchas Lavon Institute (PL IV-104, 88, folder 1). Frumkin sent Zundelevich, Moses Aronsohn, Lazar Goldenberg, and others a series of questions about their activities in the 1870s. Among the subjects addressed in Frumkin's correspondences was the debate over what language was to be used for the dissemination of propaganda: Hebrew, Yiddish, or Russian. In his recollection of Lieberman's position, Dr. Aronsohn claimed that it seemed to him that Lieberman thought that "if his venture succeeded he would publish in Yiddish, but he had neither money nor an audience, nor collaborators nor other necessary conditions." See PL, Kalman Marmon, IV-104, 88, folder 13 (listed as p. 13). Frumkin's recollections were also cited by other scholars. See Tcherikower, "Der onhoyb fun der Yidisher sotsyalistisher bavenung," 1:470n1.

100. Levin's article was published in two installments: Judah Leib Levin, "Tsi badarf men shraybn hebreish?" *Der alter Yisrolik,* December 9 and 16, 1875. On *Der alter Yisrolik* and the Yiddish press in the 1870s see David E. Fishman, *The Rise of Modern Yiddish Culture* (Pittsburgh: University of Pittsburgh Press, 2005), 23.

101. Levin, "Tsi badarf men shraybn hebreish?" December 9. Levin's autobiographical comments can be found in Levin, *Zikkaron basefer,* 78.

102. Levin, "Tsi badarf men shraybn hebreish?" December 9.

103. Levin, letter to Moshe Kamensky, in Michal Berkowitz, "Mima'arekhet ha'emet," *Davar,* July 2, 1927; Levin, letter to Lieberman, ibid., December 4, 1927.

104. A decade earlier the Communist Moses Hess (1812–1875) wrote about the "nationalist" features of the Hasidic Jews residing in eastern Europe as making them ready for revolutionary activity. In 1862 Hess penned his major work on Jewish politics, *Rome*

and Jerusalem, in which he noted, "In those countries, which form a dividing line between the Occident and the Orient, namely, Russia, Poland, Prussia, Austria, and Turkey, there live millions of our brethren [*Stammesgenossen*] who earnestly believe in the restoration of the Jewish kingdom and pray for it fervently in their daily services. These Jews have preserved, by their belief in Jewish nationality [*jüdische Nationalität*], the very kernel of Judaism in a more faithful manner than have our Occidental Jews." Hess, *Rom und Jerusalem: die letzte Nationalitätenfrage* (1862), trans. Meyer Waxman as *Rome and Jerusalem* (New York: Bloch, 1918), 76. While Winchevsky and Zuckermann concurred with Hess in certain respects, they fundamentally differed with his assumption that Jewish nationality was based on fixed categories of race or Stamm. Hess believed in the eternality of the Jewish nation, whereas the Russian Jewish revolutionaries thought nationality was a historically relative identity.

105. Morris Winchevsky, "Erinerungen," in Winchevsky, *Gezamlte verk,* ed. Kalman Marmor, 10 vols. (New York: Frayhayt, 1927), 9:119.

106. See Gurevich, "Zikhroynes," 229.

107. Peter Lavrov, "Nasha programma," *Vpered!* August 1, 1873, 3.

108. Peter Lavrov, "Znanie i revoliutsiia," *Vpered!* August 1, 1873, 220.

109. Ibid., 228.

110. Gurevich, "Zikhroynes," 3:227. For an excellent overview of Bakunin's and Lavrov's standing among Jews in the 1870s see Moshe Mishkinsky, *'Iyunim basotsyalism hayehudi* (Kiryat Sdeh Bokér: Mechon Ben-Gurion, 2004), 223–235.

111. See Lev Deutsch, *Yidn in der Rusisher revolutsye,* translated from Russian into Yiddish by E. Korman (Berlin: Idisher literarisher farlag, 1923), 55. On Bakunin's influence among Jewish revolutionaries in the 1870s see Lev Deutsch, "Mikhail Bakunins Vide," *Di tsukunft* 29, no. 2 (February 1924): 115. Saul Yanovsky was first to translate of Bakunin's work into Yiddish, under the title *Got un der shtat* (Leeds: Lidzer anarkhistishe grupe, 1901).

112. Deutsch, *Yidn in der Rusisher revolutsye,* 55.

113. Axelrod, *Perezhitoe i peredumannoe,* 113.

114. Deutsch, "Mikhail Bakunins Veiduy," 115; see also Pavel Axelrod, *Perezhitoe i peredumannoe,* 113. As a general rule Tcherikower disagreed with Deutsch's recollections on the number of Jews involved in Bakunin's circle. Tcherikower, "Yidn-revolutsyonern in Rusland," in Tcherikower, ed., *Historishe shriftn,* 3:125–127.

115. See Tcherikower, "Yidn-revolutsyonern in Rusland," 3:97.

116. Lieberman, *Arn Libermans briv,* 80.

117. Ibid.

118. Ibid.

119. Ibid.

120. Peter Lavrov, *Istoricheskie pis'ma* (Saint Petersburg, 1870), trans. and ed. James P. Scanlan as *Peter Lavrov, Historical Letters* (Berkeley: University of California Press, 1967), 214, 217. It might be speculated that based on Lieberman's claim that Marx and Lassalle should be understood as part of Judaism's prophetic revolutionary system, Lavrov added them to his list in the 1891 edition of the *Historical Letters*. On Lav-

rov's views on religion see Lavrov, "Sotsializm i istoricheskoe khristianstvo," *Vpered!* December 15, 1875, and "Khristianskiy ide'al pered sudom sotsializma," *Vpered!* November 1, 1876. While Lavrov adamantly rejected using religion for socialist causes, he himself wrote numerous articles on the subject of religion and its relationship to socialist principles and propaganda throughout his life. See Peter Lavrov, *P. L. Lavrov. O religii,* ed. A. F. Okulovg et al. (Moscow, 1989).

121. Lavrov, *Peter Lavrov, Historical Letters,* 213 (letter 11).

122. Lavrov, "Nasha programma," 10.

123. Naum Bukhbinder, "Iz istorii revoliutsionnoi propagandy sredi evreev v Rossii v 70-kh gg," in *Istoriko-revoliutsionnyi sbornik,* ed. V. I. Nevsky (Moscow, 1924–1926), 47.

124. Ibid., 48.

125. Ibid., 47.

126. Ibid., 47–48.

127. See Mishkinsky, *'Iyunim basotsyalism hayehudi,* 227–228; on Ukrainian socialists' contacts with Lieberman and Levin, see Grigory Gurevich's reflections in PL, Kalman Marmor, IV-104, 88, folder 13.

128. Shur, *Vospominaniia,* 66.

129. See Franz Kursky, "Di Zhenever 'grupe sotsyalistn-yidn' un ir oyfruf (1880)," in Tcherikower, ed., *Historishe shriftn,* 3:557–562, and Tcherikower's notes, ibid., 563–567; and Jacobs, *On Socialists and "The Jewish Question" After Marx,* 48–51. On Dragamanov see Ivan L. Rudnysky, "Mykhailo Drahomanov and the Problem of Ukrainian-Jewish Relations," *Canadian Slavonic Papers* 11, no. 2 (Summer 1969): 182–198. For a Hebrew translation of the 1880 proposal see Shmuel Eisenstadt, *Perakim betoldot tenu'at hapo'alim hayehudit,* 2 vols. (Tel Aviv: Merhavya, 1970), 1:167–171.

130. Rodin [pseud.], "Ot gruppy sotsialistov-evreev," in *Sobranie politicheskikh sochineniy Dragomanova,* ed. B. A. Kistiakovsky (Paris, 1906), 2:, 320.

131. Ibid. On the authorship of the document see Krol, "Introduction," in Zuckermann, *Kitvei Eli'ezer Tsukerman,* 36n73.

132. Rodin [pseud.], "Ot gruppy sotsialistov-evreev,", 2:325.

133. Ibid., 2:326.

134. See Frankel, *Politics and Prophecy,* 101–104.

135. Salo W. Baron, *Modern Nationalism and Religion* (New York: Meridian, 1960), 22 (quotation), 225–226.

CHAPTER 5. THE MATERIALIZATION OF SPIRIT

1. Benedict Anderson, *Imagined Communities: Reflections on the Origin and Spread of Nationalism* (New York: Verso, 2006), 84. On the concept of Jewish ethnicity as the basis for nationalism see Gideon Shimoni, *The Zionist Ideology* (Hanover, N.H.: Brandeis University Press, 1995), 46–51. Shimoni applies to the case of Jewish nationalism Anthony D. Smith's concept of ethnie in Smith's *Theories of Nationalism* (London: Holmes and Meier, 1983), 192–210.

2. Samuel Leib Zitron, "Di ershter yidishe sotsyalistin in der hebrayisher literatur," in Zitron, *Dray literarishe doyres,* 3 vols. (Vilna: Sh. Sherberk, 1921), 2:110.

3. See Reuven Brainin, *Perets ben Moshe Smolenskin* (Warsaw, 1896), 87.

4. Salomon Simchowitz, "Vortwert," in his *Der Positivismus in Mosaismus: erläutert und entwickelt auf Grund der alten und mittelalterlichen philosophischen Literatur der Hebräer* (Vienna, 1880). On Simchowitz's work and the responses it generated see Joakim Philipson, "The Purpose of Evolution: The Struggle for Existence in the Russian-Jewish Press, 1860–1900" (Ph.D. diss., Stockholm University, 2008), 53–271. On the authorship of *Der Positivismus in Mosaismus* see Ch. D. Lippe, *Bibliographisches Lexicon der gesmmten Jüdischen Literatur der Gegenwart und Adress-Anzeiger* (Vienna, 1881), 456; and Majer Balaban, "Ya'akov Naftali Herts Simḥovits," *Hatsefira,* June 10, 1927.

5. Philipson, "The Purpose of Evolution," 257.

6. See Simchowitz, *Der Positivismus in Mosaismus,* 154.

7. Ibid., 131.

8. According to historian Israel Zinberg, "Kovner's writings had a large influence on the reading youth." Zinberg, "A. Kovner," *Perezhitoe* 2 (1910): 142. On Lilienblum's influence see Morris Winchevsky, "Lilienblum veyaḥaso lasotsyaliyut," *Lu'aḥ aḥi'ezer* 2 (1921): 293.

9. Compare the positions advanced by Shalom Jacob Abramowich in "Devarim aḥadim 'al divrei hameḥaber *ḥeker davar* me'et Avraham Uri Kovner," *Hamelits,* August 8, 1866, to those advanced in his "Ma na'aseh?" *Hamelits,* July 17, 1878.

10. M. L. Lilienblum, letter to Y. L. Gordon, December 16, 1878, in Shlomo Breiman, ed., *Igrot M. L. Lilienblum le-Y. L. Gordon* (Jerusalem: Magnes, 1968), 157–158.

11. Moses Leib Lilienblum, "'Olam hatohu," *Hashaḥar,* 1873.

12. Moses Leib Lilienblum, "Umstvennye potrebnosti russkikh evreev v sviazi s ikh material'nymi nuzhdami," *Razsvet* 9 (1879). Lilienblum's theory of a debt owed by Jews still differed from Lieberman's appropriation of Lavrov's theories. Whereas the later endorsed Jews spreading explicitly Marxist and Russian revolutionary propaganda, Lilienblum favored the spreading of Jewish national ideals.

13. See Esther Shechter's recollections about reading *Kol mevaser* in her memoir *Di geshikhte fun mayn lebn* (Winnipeg: Dos yidishe vort, 1951), 6.

14. See Henne Helfman, "A briv in der redaktsye," *Der alter Yisrolik,* October 5, 1875. Helfman's comments seem to have been provoked by Isaac Joel Linetzky's serial article in *Der alter Yisrolik,* titled "Der litvisher bokher," which reminded her of his anti-Hasidic satires for *Kol mevaser* published under the title "Dos poylishe yingl." On Linetzky and *Kol mevaser* see Jonatan Meir, *Shivḥei Rodkinson: Mikha'el Levi Frumkin-Rodkinson vehaḥasidut* (Tel Aviv: Hakibbutz Hame'uḥad, 2012), 129n38. Henne Helfman's Jewish background and publications have still not been adequately accounted for or explained. On her Jewish and intellectual background see the conflicting pictures presented by Lev Deutsch, "Gesya Helfman, di groyse shtile martirerin," *Di tsukunft,* 21, no. 4 (April 1916): 322–325; and Samuel Leib Zitron, "Hese Helfman," in Zitron *Dray literarishe doyres,* 2:78–80. See most recently the English translation of her 1881 trial transcript in ChaeRan Y. Freeze and Jay M. Harris, eds., *Everyday Jewish Life in Imperial Russia: Selected Documents, 1772–1914* (Waltham, Mass.: Brandeis University Press, 2013), no. 171.

15. Helfman, "A briv in der redaktsye."

16. Pauline Wengeroff, *Memoirs of a Grandmother: Scenes of the Cultural History of the Jews of Russia in the Nineteenth Century*, trans. Shulamit S. Magnus, 2 vols. (Stanford: Stanford University Press, 2015), 2:144.

17. See Elias Tcherikower, "Arbeter tsaytung," in Tcherikower, ed., *Historishe shriftn*, 3 vols. (Vilna: YIVO, 1939), 3:606.

18. See Mordecai ben-Hillel Hacohen, *'Olami*, 3 vols. (Jerusalem: Hapo'alim, 1927), 1:30, 39.

19. On the increased readership of *The Dawn* in 1873–1874 see Joseph Klausner, *Historya shel hasifrut ha'ivrit haḥadasha*, 6 vols. (Jerusalem: Hebrew University, 1953–1960), 5:76.

20. See Reuven Brainin, *Perets ben Moshe Smolenskin*, 62–64.

21. Judah Leib Kantor, "Ma'aminim anaḥnu," *Hashaḥar*, 1874.

22. Mordecai ben-Hillel Hacohen, "Dor holekh vedor ba," *Hashaḥar*, 1878. Hacohen's materialism is often ignored as a result of his somewhat misleading description of his own intellectual journey. In his autobiography he claimed, "After I started writing in the newspapers . . . people in Mogilev began revealing to me the whereabouts of 'open' libraries where I could obtain a copy of Chernyshevsky's *What Is to Be Done?* Now I was even given access to works written about nihilism that were illegally published. In one of these libraries run by Eliezer Luria I also found a volume of *The Dawn*. . . . The influence it exerted over me was decisive. Most notably, it stopped me from moving beyond the immediate interests of our nation, of Judaism, and all matters pertaining to work in a 'universal' sense—nihilism and its appendages—ceased to interest me." Hacohen, *'Olami*, 1:48–49.

23. Judah Leib Levin, *'Eved 'Avadim*, in his *Yehuda Leib Levin, ketavim nivḥarim*, ed. Menaḥem Mendel Feitelsohn, 2 vols. (Warsaw: 1911), 1:69. On Smolenskin's publishing of Naphtali Levy's work on Darwin, "Zeh sefer toldot ha'adam," in 1874 see Jacob Shavit and Jehuda Reinharz, *Darvin vekama mibnei mino* (Tel Aviv: Hakibbutz Hame'uḥad, 2009), 82–83.

24. Judah Leib Levin, "Kishron hama'aseh," in his *Yehuda Leib Levin, ketavim nivḥarim*, 2:7–62.

25. Judah Leib Levin, letter to unknown addressee, no date, PL, Judah Leib Levin papers, IV A104 71.

26. See Peretz Smolenskin's letter to Aaron Shemuel Lieberman in Michal Berkowitz, "Smolenskin vehasotsyaliyim ha'ivriyim," in *Lezekher Smolenskin*, ed. Aaron Verdei (Vienna, 1925), 22.

27. Abraham Tsukerman, letter to Ephraim Deinard, JTS, Ephraim Deinard Papers, ARC 29, box 5, letter 212.

28. Ibid. See also Mordecai ben-Hillel Hacohen, *'Olami*, 1:30, 48.

29. Abraham Tsukerman, letter to Ephraim Deinard, JTS, Ephraim Deinard Papers, ARC 29, box 5, letter 212. Deinard also considered Levin to be a friend. See Ephraim Deinard, letter to Ḥayyim Selig Slonimski, dated Iyar 28, 1876, ibid., box 5.

30. Abraham Tsukerman, letter to Ephraim Deinard, dated Elul 7, 1873, ibid., box 5, letter 242.

31. Peretz Smolenskin, letter to Judah Leib Levin, undated, JNUL, Abraham Schwadron, 01 15, 148.

32. Judah Leib Levin, letter to Mordecai ben-Hillel Hacohen, April 16, 1886, GN, Asher Braudes Archive, folder 29.

33. Ibid. It should be noted that Levin maintained that Smolenskin had the same positive feelings toward the articles published in Lieberman's newspaper.

34. Peretz Smolenskin, "Hakesef vehakavod," in *Bikoret tihyeh,* ed. Smolenskin (Odessa, 1867), 17–22.

35. See Joseph Klausner, *Historya shel hasifrut ha'ivrit hahadasha,* 5:92–97.

36. See Peretz Smolenskin, letter to Ephraim Deinard, undated (1873?), JTS, Ephraim Deinard Papers, box 5, letter 93. Smolenskin also noted that in Vienna the paper was cheaper. "Quartos (four leaves or eight book pages) purchased for five hundred copies of *The Dawn* cost 18 rubles and on superior paper 20 rubles. One thousand copies of the newspaper printed on standard paper cost 22 rubles and with superior paper only 28 rubles." Furthermore, he maintained, "no extra time was lost due to the censor."

37. See Gurevich, letter to Lieberman, recorded by Berlin Police in PR Lit S. Nr. 1234 vol. 1, 174

38. Aaron Shemuel Lieberman, "Ma'aseh Satan," *Ha'emet* 3, 1877.

39. See Grigory Gurevich, "Zikhroynes," in *Historishe shriftn,* ed. Elias Tcherikower, 3 vols. (Vilna: YIVO, 1939), 3:233.

40. David Isaiah Silberbusch, *Mipinkas zikhronotai* (Tel Aviv, 1936), available at http://benyehuda.org/silberbusch/ishim_umeoraot.html#_ftn1 (accessed on March 28, 2015).

41. See Smolenskin's letter to Lieberman in Berkowitz, "Smolenskin vehasotsyaliyim ha'ivriyim," 22.

42. Peretz Smolenskin, letter to Judah Leib Levin, undated, JNUL, Abraham Schwadron, 01 15, 148. Smolenskin also was concerned about Levin's crude language, reprimanding him, "Among readers are many women and even some men who are not accustomed to your disgusting language [*nibbul peh*]."

43. Joseph Klausner, *Historya shel hasifrut ha'ivrit hahadasha,* 5:107. See also Mordecai ben-Hillel Hacohen, "Perets ben Moshe Smolenskin," in his *Me'erev 'ad 'arev,* 2 vols. (Vilna, 1923), 1:222.

44. Ya'akov Lifshutz, letter to Ephraim Deinard, dated Tevet 14, 1881, JTS, Ephraim Deinard Papers, ARC 29, box 2.

45. Ya'akov Lifshutz, letter to Ephraim Deinard, with remarks by Yehuda Lifshutz, dated Tammuz 15, 1878, ibid.

46. Shlomo Kohen [pseud.], "Derekh emuna," *Halevanon,* December 19, 1879.

47. Quoted in Eliezer Raphael Malachi, "Morris Winchevsky," in Malachi, *Masot ureshimot* (New York, 1937), 160.

48. See the letter from Levin to Lieberman dated June 22, 1877, in Michal Berkowitz, "Smolenskin vehasotsyaliyim ha'ivriyim," 23.

49. Judah Leib Levin, letter to Mordecai ben-Hillel Hacohen, April 16, 1886, GN, Asher Braudes Archive, folder 29.

50. Netanneh Tokef (Isaac Kaminer), letter to Eliezer Zuckermann undated, JNUL, Abraham Schwadron, 01 19, 218.

51. At one point Lieberman even told Levin to stop sending articles to Smolenskin. See the letter from Lieberman to Levin in Berkowitz, "Smolenskin vehasotsyaliyim ha'ivriyim," 23.

52. See Peretz Smolenskin's notes to Mordecai ben-Hillel Hacohen, "Dor holekh vedor ba," *Hashaḥar*, 1878.

53. On Smolenskin's views of socialism see Berkowitz, "Smolenskin vehasotsyaliyim ha'ivriyim," 21–26; and Reuven Brainin, *Perets ben Moshe Smolenskin*, 87–89.

54. See Joseph Klausner, *Historya shel hasifrut ha'ivrit haḥadasha*, 5:117.

55. "Habikoret shel Perets Smolenskin," in Tsvi Krol, ed., *Ha'emet* (Tel Aviv, 1938), 116.

56. Aaron Shemuel Lieberman, "She'eilat hayehudim," *Ha'emet* 1 (1877), in Krol, ed., *Ha'emet*, 3.

57. See Judah Leib Levin, "She'eilat hayehudim," *Hakol*, January 5, 1879.

58. Judah Leib Levin, letter to Mordecai ben-Hillel Hacohen, April 16, 1886, GN, Asher Braudes Archive, folder 29.

59. Peretz Smolenskin, "She'eilat hayehudim—she'eilat haḥayyim: ma'amar rishon," in his *Perets ben Moshe Smolenskin: Ma'amarim*, 4 vols. (Jerusalem: Hapo'alim, 1926), 3:5.

60. Ibid.

61. Aaron Shemuel Lieberman, "Gevul koḥot ha'adam," *Hamabit*, May 15, 1879.

62. Mordecai ben-Hillel Hacohen, "Perets ben Moshe Smolenskin," 1:225.

63. Peretz Smolenskin, "She'eilat hayehudim—she'eilat haḥayyim," 3:26. On Hobsbawm's notion of tradition see Eric J. Hobsbawm and Terence O. Ranger, *The Invention of Tradition* (Cambridge: Cambridge University Press, 1992), 5.

64. Peretz Smolenskin, "'Et la'asot," in Smolenskin, *Perets Ben Moshe Smolenskin: Ma'amarim*, 1:192.

65. Peretz Smolenskin, "'Et lata'at," in Smolenskin, *Perets ben Moshe Smolenskin: Ma'amarim*, 2:22.

66. Ibid., 2:191.

67. Ibid., 2:185.

68. See Isaac E. Barzilay, "Smolenskin's Polemic Against Mendelssohn in Historical Perspective," *Proceedings of the American Academy for Jewish Research* 53 (1986): 11–48.

69. Peretz Smolenskin, "'Et la'asot," 1:192.

70. On Smolenskin's personal religiosity in Odessa and the rumors surrounding the cat story see Joseph Klausner, *Historya shel hasifrut ha'ivrit haḥadasha*, 5:32.

71. See Peretz Smolenskin, "'Et lata'at," 2:30.

72. See Peretz Smolenskin, "She'eilat hayehudim—she'eilat haḥayyim: ma'amar rishon," 3:25. Smolenskin's criticism of both movements centered on the emphasis they placed on the question of Judaism's relationship to the law and their denial of a Jewish national character. "In the days of old, Torah was revered over prayer," Smolenskin asserted, "but now the Baal Shem Tov and his circle, as well as Mendelssohn, have risen against Torah." Smolenskin believed that the emphasis placed by Israel Baal Shem Tov and Moses Mendelssohn—leaders of the Hasidic and Reform movements, respectively—on "the importance of law . . . gave rise to hatred and fragmentation among our people." Peretz Smolenskin, "'Et la'asot," 1:193.

73. See Peretz Smolenskin, "'Et la'asot," 1:193.

74. On Lenora and Peretz's relationship see Judah Leib Smolenskin, "Eleh toldot Perets," *Davar,* January 25, 1935.

75. See Smolenskin's claim that he wanted his paper to be read by women in Peretz Smolenskin, letter to Judah Leib Levin, undated, JNUL, Abraham Schwadron, 01 15, 148.

76. Quoted in Ben David, "Yom zikkaron le-Smolenskin," *Hamelits,* February 27, 1890.

77. See Peretz Smolenskin, "'Et lata'at," 2:193–195.

78. See Smolenskin's response to Lieberman regarding yeshiva students and revolution in Zitron, "Peretz Smolenskin," in Zitron, *Dray literarishe doyres,* 3:135–138.

79. See Judah Leib Smolenskin, "Eleh toldot Perets."

80. This information came from letters exchanged between the Russian doctor Vladimir Havkin and the Zionist leader Mordecai ben-Hillel Hacohen from 1896 to 1897. Havkin's knowledge of Smolenskin and Axelrod came from one of Smolenskin's teachers in Shklov, the enlightener, M. D. Malkin. See Havkin, letter to Mordecai ben-Hillel Hacohen, undated, in JNUL, Mordecai ben Hillel Ha-Cohen, ARC. 4* 1068 01, 182. Havkin's claims are supported by the fact that both men were in Shklov in in 1858.

81. Pavel Axelrod, *Perezhitoe i peredumannoe* (1923; reprint Cambridge: Oriental Research Partners, 1975), 28–29.

82. On Smolenskin's national historiography see David N. Myers, *Re-Inventing the Jewish Past: European Jewish Intellectuals and the Zionist Return to History* (New York: Oxford University Press, 1995), 29–32.

83. Tsvi Hacohen Shershevsky, "Pesher davar," *Hatsefira,* October 10, 1877. On the use of the Hebrew term "ru'ah le'umi" see Zavia Nardi, "Mishnato hale'umit shel Perets Smolenskin umikumah beyahadut rusya" (M.A. thesis, Hebrew University, 1976), 77–79. On the idea of a "national character" comprising the religious spirit, beliefs, and historical experiences of one people (*eines Volksstamms*), see Heinrich Graetz, *Geschichte der Juden,* 11 vols. (Magdeburg, 1860), 5:8. On the idea of a Jewish national character in German Jewish literature of the period see Michael Silber, "Alliance of the Hebrews, 1863–1875: The Diaspora Roots of an Ultra-Orthodox Proto-Zionist Utopia in Palestine," *Journal of Israeli History: Politics, Society, Culture* 27, no. 2 (2008) : 119–147; and in Russian literature, Israel Sosis, "Natsional'nyi vopros v literature kontsa 60kh i nachala 70kh godov," *Evreiskaia starina* 7, no. 2 (1915) : 324–337.

84. Brian Porter, *When Nationalism Began to Hate: Imagining Modern Politics in Nineteenth-Century Poland* (Oxford: Oxford University Press, 2000), 19–21. On Smolenskin as an idealist see Nardi, "Mishnato hale'umit shel Perets Smolenskin umikumah beyahadut rusya," 44–47.

85. While Smolenskin never claimed to have been influenced by Wolf's or Zunz's positions, he greatly admired the latter and repeatedly praised his work. Smolenskin met Zunz in the 1870s when he visited Prussia. See Peretz Smolenskin, "'Et lata'at," 2:234n1. Smolenskin's theory of Geist also drew on the work of other Jewish western European scholars, most notably his friend and supporter Adolf Jellinek. See Smolenskin's "Even yisra'el" (1869), in his *Perets ben Moshe Smolenskin,* in which he reviewed Jellinek's *Der Jüdische Stamm.* It should be noted that Smolenskin undoubtedly was in-

fluenced by the way the term *ru'ah* appeared in the writings of the Galician enlightener Nachman Krochmal. Zunz had edited Krochmal's writings and was himself greatly indebted to the Galician maskil's notion of Jewish Geist as a proto-national identity. For Krochmal, like Smolenskin, the Jewish people had a collective identity that could not be reduced to a religious phenomenon. However, Smolenskin vehemently rejected Krochmal's claims that Jewish Geist was located in the development of Jewish law. Smolenskin read Krochmal's work *Moreh nevukhei hazeman* in the late 1850s when he studied in the yeshiva in Shklov. See Vladimir Havkin, letter to Mordecai ben-Hillel Hacohen, undated, in JNUL, Mordecai ben Hillel Ha-Cohen, ARC. 4* 1068 01, 182. On Smolenskin's use of the term *Geist* see Joseph Klausner, *Historya shel hasifrut ha'ivrit hahadasha,* 5:93–94.

86. See Amos Bitzan, "Leopold Zunz and the Meanings of Wissenschaft," *Journal of the History of Ideas* 78, no. 2 (2017): 233–254.

87. Peretz Smolenskin, "'Et lata'at," 2:23.

88. Peretz Smolenskin, "'Am 'olam," in his *Perets ben Moshe Smolenskin,* 1:145. On Smolenskin's theory of messianism see Eli Lederhendler, "Interpreting the Messianic Rhetoric in the Russian Haskalah and Early Zionism," *Studies in Contemporary Jewry* 7 (1991): 20–23.

89. Peretz Smolenskin, "'Et lata'at," 2:199.

90. See Eliezer Ben-Yehuda, *Hahalom veshivro* (Jerusalem: Mosad Bialik, 1978), available at http://benyehuda.org/by/haidan_harishon.html.

91. Ibid., chap. 2.

92. Eliezer Ben-Yehuda, "Mikhtav le-Ben-Yehuda," *Hashahar,* 1880.

93. On Adelman, see Eliezer Raphael Malachi, letter to Kalman Marmor, October 5, 1932, YIVO, Kalman Marmor Collection, RG 205, folder 340. On Mordecai Adelman's influence on Ben-Yehuda see the excellent article by George Mandel, "Who Was Ben-Yehuda with in Boulevard Montmartre," *Oxford Centre Papers* 2 (1984): 1–15. Ben-Yehuda refers to Adelman as Zundelmann in his memoir.

94. Ibid., 7.

95. Eliezer Ben-Yehuda, *Hahalom veshivro* (Jerusalem: Mosad Bialik) 1978, available at http://benyehuda.org/by/haidan_harishon.html. On the influence of the Balkan revolution on Smolenskin's thinking see Joseph Klausner, *Historya shel hasifrut ha'ivrit hahadasha,* 5:70–71.

96. On the publication history of Judah Leib Gordon's *Die judische Frage in der orientalischen Frage* (Vienna, 1877), see Gedaliah Elkoshi, ed., *Tseror igrot shel Perets Smolenskin el Yehuda Leib Gordon* (Jerusalem: Kiryat Sefer, 1959), 3–7. Later, Gordon retracted this position and expressed reservations regarding the establishment of "an earthly Jewish State . . . governed by rabbinical authorities." See his letter to M. M. Doltzki, December 1, 1882, in *Igrot Yehuda Leib Gordon: 1830–1892,* ed., Isaac Jacob Weisberg, 2 vols. (Warsaw, 1894), 2:10.

97. Peretz Smolenskin, "'Et la'asot," 1:186.

98. Ibid., 1:187.

99. Ben-Yehuda, "Mikhtav le-Ben-Yehuda."

100. To be sure, Ahad Ha'am rejected being classified as Smolenskin's disciple. On the historical relationship of Ahad Ha'am to Smolenskin see David Patterson, "Ahad Ha-Am and Smolenskin" in *The Crossroads: Essays on Ahad Ha-am,* ed. Jacques Kornberg (Albany: State University of New York Press, 1983), 36–45; and Joseph Klausner, *Historya shel hasifrut ha'ivrit hahadasha,* 5:94–96.

101. Peretz Smolenskin, "Teshuva," *Hashahar,* 1880.

102. Ibid.

103. Ibid.

104. Moses Leib Lilienblum, "'Al yisra'el ve'al artso," *Hashahar,* 1881.

105. Ibid.

106. Ibid. See also Peretz Smolenskin, "Lehashiv davar," *Hashahar,* 1881, reprinted in his *Perets ben Moshe Smolenskin,* 4:244. In his original article Lilienblum declared, "I am not of the opinion that Jews are a spiritual nation. This is idealism and I am no idealist." In the reprinted version in his *Kol kitvei Moshe Leib Lilienblum,* 4 vols. (Krakow; Odessa, 1910–1913), Lilienblum omitted his original disavowal of "idealism" and removed the word *idealist* from the article. Instead, he substituted the less philosophically loaded term *dreamer.* The fundamental philosophical debate was downplayed as tactical nationalist differences. On Lilienblum's self-editing of his biographical works see Michael Stanislawski, *Autobiographical Jews: Essays in Jewish Self-Fashioning* (Seattle: University of Washington Press, 2004), 60–63.

107. Moses Lilienblum, letter to Mordecai ben-Hillel Hacohen, dated "the first day of Hanukkah," 1894, JNUL, Mordecai ben Hillel Ha-Cohen, ARC 4* 1068 01, 272.

108. Smolenskin, "Lehashiv davar." Smolenskin's frank assessment of Lilienblum's animus toward him can be found in a letter from Peretz Smolenskin to Judah Leib Levin located in JNUL, Abraham Schwadron, 01 15, 148. These and other personal matters were edited from the published version of the article in *Hamaggid,* May 7, 1885.

109. On sacralization among Zionist thinkers more generally see David Sorkin, "Between Messianism and Survival: Secularization and Sacralization in Modern Judaism," *Journal of Modern Jewish Studies* 3, no. 1 (2004): 73–86.

110. Lederhendler, "Interpreting the Messianic Rhetoric in the Russian Haskalah and Early Zionism," 30, 24, 15.

111. On the relationship of Smolenskin to Hess see Joseph Klausner, *Historya shel hasifrut ha'ivrit hahadasha,* 5:72–74.

112. Peretz Smolenskin, *Nekam berit* (Vienna, 1883), translated into English in Steven Adams, *Peretz Smolenskin's "Nekam Berit" as a Response to the Russian Pogroms of 1881: A Translation and Literary-Critical Analysis of the Novel* (Hebrew Union College: 1982).

113. On the historical background of *Nekam berit* see Joseph Klausner, *Historya shel hasifrut ha'ivrit hahadasha,* 5:144–146, 255–262.

114. Smolenskin, *Nekam berit,* trans. Adams, 73.

115. Ibid., 84–85.

116. Quoted in Walter Laqueur, *A History of Zionism* (New York: Schocken, 1972), 234.

CONCLUSION

1. Judah Leib Gordon, "Hakitsa 'ammi," *Hakarmel,* April 18, 1866.

2. James Loeffler, *Rooted Cosmopolitans: Human Rights and Jewish Politics in the Twentieth Century* (New Haven: Yale University Press, forthcoming).

3. Philip Nord, *The Republican Moment: Struggles for Democracy in Nineteenth-Century France* (Cambridge: Harvard University Press, 1995), 80.

4. Abigail Green, "Liberal, Jewish and/or Secular: Thinking About International Jewish Activism," paper delivered at the Oxford Advanced Seminar in Jewish Studies on "Jews, Liberalism, Anti-Semitism: the Dialectics of Inclusion, 1780–1950," October 11, 2015, Oxford, U.K. On the European roots to American Jewish liberalism see Ben Halpern, "The Roots of American Jewish Liberalism," *American Jewish Historical Quarterly* 66, no. 2 (1976): 190–214.

5. Leon Pinsker, *Auto-Emancipation,* trans. D. S. Blondheim (New York: Maccabaean, 1906), 3.

6. It should be noted that Pinsker's materialism represented a noticeable break with his earlier assertion that nations were constituted by "spirit" and not by "external forms." Dmitry Shumsky has astutely noted the transformation of Pinsker's theory of nationality in his "Leon Pinsker and *Autoemancipation!* A Reevaluation," *Jewish Social Studies* 18, no. 1 (Fall 2011): 45–47.

7. See the lead editorial "Eine Alte Frage," *Allgemeine Zeitung des Judenthums,* October 17, 1882.

8. Saul Phinehas Rabbinowitz, letter to Judah Leib Levin, [1881], CZA, Alter Druyanow Collection, A987, 175–179.

9. Judah Leib Levin, *Yehuda Leib Levin: Zikhronot vehegyonot,* ed. Yehuda Slutsky (Jerusalem: Mosad Bialik, 1968), 69.

10. See Benny Kraut, "Towards the Establishment of the National Conference of Christians and Jews: The Tenuous Road to Religious Goodwill in the 1920s," *American Jewish History* 77 (1988): 388–412.

11. On the secular and religious elements encompassed in *Yiddishkeit* see most recently Annie Polland, "'May a Freethinker Help a Pious Man?': The Shared World of the 'Religious' and the 'Secular' Among Eastern European Jewish Immigrants to America," *American Jewish History* 93, no. 4 (December 2007): 378.

12. See Asher Ginsberg, "Truth from Eretz Yisrael," trans. Alan Dowty, *Israel Studies* 5, no. 2 (2000): 160. On Russian Jewish immigration to Palestine and the United States as an economic movement see Gur Alroey, *Hamahpekha hashketa: hahagira hayehudit meha'imperya harusit 1924–1875* (Jerusalem: Zalman Shazar, 2008).

13. Avraham Shlonsky, "Jezreel," *Bagalgal* (Tel Aviv, 1927), 23.

14. See Rebecca Trachtenberg Alpert, "The Quest for Economic Justice: Kaplan's Response to the Challenge of Communism, 1929–1940," in *The American Judaism of Mordecai M. Kaplan,* ed. Emanuel S. Goldsmith, Mel Scult, and Robert M. Seltzer (New York: New York University Press, 1990), 385–401.

15. Mordecai M. Kaplan, *Judaism in Transition* (New York: Behrman's Jewish Book House, 1941), 255–266.

16. See Kaplan's critique of Asher Ginsberg, ibid., 124.

17. On Kaplan's detractors labeling him a "materialist" see Bernard Drachman, "An Examination of Prof. Mordecai Kaplan's Views on Judaism," *The Jewish Forum* 4, no. 2 (1921): 729. Ken Koltun-Fromm, in *Material Culture and Jewish Thought in America* (Bloomington: Indiana University Press, 2010), 13–53, has also insightfully noted a materialist orientation in Kaplan's writing.

18. James Loeffler, "Nationalism Without a Nation? On the Invisibility of American Jewish Politics," *Jewish Quarterly Review* 105, no. 3 (Summer 2015): 371. See also Loeffler, *Rooted Cosmopolitans,* chap. 1.

19. Pew Research Center, "A Portrait of Jewish Americans," October 2013, chapter 4, available at http://www.pewforum.org/2013/10/01/chapter-4-religious-beliefs -and-practices/ (accessed May 12, 2017).

20. Leon Wieseltier "Jewish Bodies Jewish Minds," *Jewish Quarterly Review* 95, no. 3 (Summer 2005): 435–442. For a critique of Wieseltier's position see Barbara Kirshenblatt-Gimblett and Jeffrey Shandler, "Introduction," *Material Religion: The Journal of Objects Art and Belief* 3, no. 3 (2007): 308–312.

21. Michael Meyer, *The Origins of the Modern Jew: Jewish Identity and European Culture, 1749–1824* (Detroit: Wayne State University Press, 1967), 168.

22. For a critique of the Protestant narrative of modern Judaism see Eliyahu Stern, "Catholic Judaism: The Political Theology of the Nineteenth-Century Russian Jewish Enlightenment," *Harvard Theological Review* 109, no. 4 (Winter 2016): 508–511.

Abramowich, Shalom Jacob. "Devarim aḥadim 'al divrei hameḥaber *ḥeker davar
me'et Avraham Uri Kovner." Hamelits,* August 8, 1866.
———. "Ma na'aseh?" *Hamelits,* July 17, 1878.
———. *Mishpat shalom.* Vilna, 1860.
———. *Di Takse.* Zhitomir, 1869.
Adler, Eliyana. *In Her Hands: The Education of Jewish Girls in Tsarist Russia.* Detroit:
Wayne State University Press, 2011.
Alpert, Rebecca Trachtenberg. "The Quest for Economic Justice: Kaplan's Response
to the Challenge of Communism, 1929–1940." In *The American Judaism of Mor-
decai M. Kaplan,* ed. Emanuel S. Goldsmith, Mel Scult, and Robert M. Seltzer,
385–401. New York: New York University Press, 1990.
Alroey, Gur. *Hamahpekha hashketa: hahagira hayehudit meha'imperya harusit
1924–1875.* Jerusalem: Zalman Shazar, 2008.
Anderson, Benedict. *Imagined Communities: Reflections on the Origin and Spread of
Nationalism.* New York: Verso, 2006.
An-sky, S. A. *Pioneers: A Tale of Russian-Jewish Life in the 1880s.* Trans. Michael R.
Katz. Bloomington: Indiana University Press, 2014.
Armenteros, Carolina. "Preparing the Russian Revolution: Maistre and Uvarov on
the History of Knowledge." In *Joseph de Maistre and His European Readers: From
Friedrich von Gentz to Isaiah Berlin,* ed. Carolina Armenteros and Richard A.
Lebrun, 213–249. Leiden: Brill, 2011.

Arnal, William, and Russell T. McCutcheon. *The Sacred Is the Profane: The Political Nature of Religion.* New York: Oxford University Press, 2013.

Ascher, Abraham. "Pavel Axelrod: A Conflict Between Jewish Loyalty and Revolutionary Dedication." *Russian Review* 24, no. 3 (July 1965): 249–265.

———. *Pavel Axelrod and the Development of Menshevism.* Cambridge: Harvard University Press, 1972.

Assad, Talal. *Genealogies of Religion: Disciplines and Reasons of Power in Christianity and Islam.* Baltimore: Johns Hopkins University Press, 1993.

Avineri, Shlomo. *The Social and Political Thought of Karl Marx.* Cambridge: Cambridge University Press, 1968.

Avrutin, Eugene. *Jews and the Imperial State: Identification Politics in Tsarist Russia.* Ithaca: Cornell University Press, 2010.

———. "The Politics of Jewish Legibility: Documentation Practices and Reform During the Reign of Nicholas I." *Jewish Social Studies* 11, no. 2 (2005): 136–169.

———. "Visibility and Invisibility in Modern Jewish History: A Comment on *The Jewish Century.*" *Ab Imperio* 1 (2005): 151–156.

Axelrod, Pavel. *Perezhitoe i peredumannoe.* 1923. Repr. Cambridge: Oriental Research Partners, 1975. Translated into Yiddish by Jacob Krepliak and serialized in "Memuarn." *Di tsukunft* (1922–1923).

Bacon, Gershon. "Prolonged Erosion, Organization and Reinforcement: Reflections on Orthodox Jewry in Congress Poland (up to 1914)." In *Major Changes Within the Jewish People in Wake of the Holocaust,* ed. Yisra'el Gutman, 71–91. Jerusalem: Yad Vashem, 1996.

Baer, Yitzchak (Fritz). *Yisra'el ba'amim.* Jerusalem: Mosad Bialik, 1955.

Balaban, Majer. "Ya'akov Naftali Herts Simḥovits." *Hatsefira,* June 10, 1927.

Baron, Salo W. *Modern Nationalism and Religion.* New York: Meridian, 1960.

———. *The Russian Jew Under Tsars and Soviets.* New York: Schocken, 1987.

Bartal, Israel. "Halo-yehudim veḥevratam besifrut 'ivrit veyidish bemizraḥ eiropa bein hashanim 1856–1914." Ph.D. Diss. Hebrew University, 1980.

———. "Hamodel hamishni—tsorfat kimekor hashpa'a betahalikhei hamodernizatsya shel yehudei mizraḥ eiropa (1772–1863)." In *Hamahpekha hatsorfatit verishumah,* ed. Yermiel Cohen, 271–285. Jerusalem: Merkaz Zalman Shazar, 1991.

———. *The Jews of Eastern Europe, 1772–1881.* Trans. Chaya Naor. Philadelphia: University of Pennsylvania Press, 2006.

———. *Kozak ubedvi.* Tel Aviv: Am Oved, 2007.

———. *Letaken 'am.* Jerusalem: Karmel, 2013.

———. "Lilienblum, Mosheh Leib." *YIVO Encyclopedia of Jews in Eastern Europe.* http://www.yivoencyclopedia.org/article.aspx/Lilienblum_Mosheh_Leib.

———. "Misyonerim britim bimeḥozot ḥabad." In *Habad Hasidism: History, Thought, Image,* ed. Jonatan Meir and Gadi Sagiv, 145–183. Jerusalem: Merkaz Zalman Shazar, 2016.

————. "Mordecai Aaron Günzberg: A Lithuanian Maskil Faces Modernity." In *From East and West: Jews in a Changing Europe, 1750–1870*, ed. Frances Malino and David Sorkin, 126–147. Oxford: Blackwell, 1991.

————. "The Secularization of Jewish Spirituality: Hasidism Reinvented." The American Association of Polish-Jewish Studies. http://www.aapjstudies.org/ index.php?id=42 (accessed January 14, 2016).

Barzilay, Isaac E. "Smolenskin's Polemic Against Mendelssohn in Historical Perspective." *Proceedings of the American Academy for Jewish Research* 53 (1986): 11–48.

Batnitzky, Leora. *How Judaism Became a Religion: An Introduction to Modern Jewish Thought.* Princeton: Princeton University Press, 2011.

Bauer, Ela. *Between Poles and Jews: The Development of Nahum Sokolow's Political Thought.* Jerusalem: Hebrew University Magnes Press, 2005.

————. "Ka'asher hamaskil hayehudi pagash et hamad'an hagermani." In *Sefer tavniyot nofim tarbutiyim*, ed. Arnon Soffer, Jacob O. Maos, and Ronit Cohen-Soffer, 47–63. Haifa: Katedrat Ḥaiken, Haifa University, 2011.

Bazilevsky, Moses. *Divrei bina: o emuna veḥokhmat hateva'.* Zhitomir, 1870.

Beiser, Fredrick C. *The Genesis of Neo-Kantianism, 1796–1880.* Oxford: Oxford University Press, 2014.

Benedict, Philip. *Christ's Churches Purely Reformed: A Social History of Calvinism.* New Haven: Yale University Press, 2002.

Ben-Ya'akov [pseud.]. "Zikkaron leḥakham." *'Ivri anokhi*, March 1, 1889.

Ben-Yehuda, Eliezer. *Haḥalom veshivro.* Jerusalem: Mosad Bialik, 1978. Available at http://benyehuda.org/by/haidan_harishon.html.

————. "Mikhtav le-Ben-Yehuda." *Hashaḥar*, 1880.

Berditsevski, Mikhah Yosef. "Lezekher Moshe Leib Lilienblum." *Davar*, February 15, 1935.

"Bericht eines gelehrten russischen Israeliten aus Lithuauen, über den Bildungszustand der Israeliten in seinem Faterlande." Pts. 1–5. *Israelitische Annalen* 5 (1840): 35–37; 6 (1840): 45–46; 7 (1840): 65–66; 9 (1840): 81–82; 10 (1840): 88–89.

Berkowitz, Michal. "Lilienblum vesofrei ha'emet." *Hatsefira*, July 24, 1919.

————. "Mikitvei Perets Smolenskin." *Hatsefira*, October 2, 1919.

————. "Mima'arekhet ha'emet." *Davar*, July 2, December 4, 1927.

————. "Smolenskin vehasotsyaliyim ha'ivriyim." In *Lezekher Smolenskin,* ed. Aaron Verdei, 21–26. Vienna, 1925.

Berlin (Bar-Ilan), Meir. *Fun Volozhin biz Yerusholayim.* 2 vols. New York, 1933.

Bernstein, Julius. *Erinnerungen an das elterliche Haus.* Berlin: H. S. Hermann, 1913.

Biale, David. "Jewish Consumer Culture in Historical and Contemporary Perspective." In *Longing, Belonging and the Making of Jewish Consumer Culture,* ed. Gideon Reuveni and Nils H. Roemer, 23–38. Leiden: Brill, 2010.

Bilenky, Serhiy. *Romantic Nationalism in Eastern Europe: Russian, Polish and Ukrainian Political Imaginations.* Stanford: Stanford University Press, 2012.

Birnbaum, Pierre. "A Jacobin Regenerator: Abbé Grégoire." In *Jewish Destinies: Citizenship, State and Community in Modern France,* ed. Pierre Birnbaum, 11–30. New York: Hill and Wang, 2000.

Birnbaum, Pierre, and Ira Katznelson, eds. *Paths of Emancipation: Jews, States and Citizenship.* Princeton: Princeton University Press, 1995.

Bitzan, Amos. "Leopold Zunz and the Meanings of Wissenschaft." *Journal of the History of Ideas* 78, no. 2 (2017): 233–254.

Blejwas, Stanislaus A. "Polish Positivism and the Jews." *Jewish Social Studies* 46, no. 1 (1984): 21–36.

Borovoi, Saul. "A fargesener nihilist (Yehude Leyb Lerner)." *Filologishe shriftn* 3 (1929): 473–484.

Bossuet, Jacques-Bénigne. *Einleitung in die Geschichte der Welt und der Religion.* Translated from French into German by D. Johann Andreas Cramer. 2 vols. Leipzig, 1757–1786.

Boyarin, Daniel. *Carnal Israel: Reading Sex in Talmudic Judaism.* Berkeley: University of California Press, 1993.

Boyarin, Jonathan, and Daniel Boyarin eds. *Jews and Other Differences: The New Jewish Cultural Studies.* Minneapolis: University of Minnesota Press, 1997.

Brainin, Reuven. *Perets ben Moshe Smolenskin.* Warsaw, 1896.

———. "Yosef Leib Sossnitz." In *Kol kitvei Re'uven Brainin.* 3 vols. New York, 1936. Available at http://www.benyehuda.org/brainin/zosnits.html.

Brainin, Simon. *Sefer oraḥ laḥayyim.* Vilna, 1884.

———. "Zosnits yubileum a zeltener erfolg." *Der morgn zhurnal,* December 1, 1907.

Breiman, Shlomo, ed. *Igrot M. L. Lilienblum le-Y. L. Gordon.* Jerusalem: Magnes, 1968.

Brenner, Michael, Vicki Caron, and Uri R. Kaufmann, eds. *Jewish Emancipation Reconsidered: The French and German Models.* Tübingen: Mohr Siebeck, 2003.

Brill, Alan. *Judaism and World Religions: Encountering Christianity, Islam and Eastern Traditions.* New York: Palgrave Macmillan, 2012.

Brill, Yosef. "Toldot Oyev." In *Otsar hasifrut,* ed. Shaltiel Isaac Graber Bi'arslovei, 645–649. Krakow, 1892.

Bronshteyn, Yashe. "Avrom Uri Kovner (1842–1909)." *Tsaytshrift* (1931): 211–243.

Brower, Daniel R. *Training Nihilists: Education and Radicalism in Tsarist Russia.* Ithaca: Cornell University Press, 1975.

Brown, Jeremy. *New Heavens and a New Earth: The Jewish Reception of Copernican Thought.* Oxford: Oxford University Press, 2013.

Brown, Wendy. "Rights and Identity in Late Modernity." In *Identities, Politics, and Rights,* ed. Austin Sarat and Thomas R. Kearns, 85–131. Ann Arbor: University of Michigan Press, 1995.

———. "Tolerance and/or Equality? The 'Jewish Question' and the 'Woman Question.'" *differences: A Journal of Feminist Cultural Studies* 15, no. 2 (2004): 1–31.

Brubaker, Rogers. "Religion and Nationalism: Four Approaches." *Nations and Nationalism* 18, no. 1 (2012): 2–20.

Brym, Robert J, *The Jewish Intelligentsia and the Russian Revolution: A Sociological Study of Intellectual Radicalism and Ideological Divergence.* London: Macmillan, 1978.

Buchholz, Carl August. *Actenstükke die Verbesserung des bürgerlichen Zustandes der Israeliten.* Stuttgart, 1815.

Büchner, Ludwig. *Kraft und Stoff: Empirisch-naturphilosophische Studien.* Frankfurt, 1855. 2nd ed. Frankfurt, 1856. Trans. and ed. J. Frederick Collingwood as *Force and Matter* (London, 1864).

Bukhbinder, Naum. "Iz istorii revoliutsionnoi propagandy sredi evreev v Rossii v 70-kh godakh." In *Istoriko-revoliutsionnyi sbornik,* ed. V. I. Nevsky, 37–66. Moscow, 1924–1926.

Bushkovitch, Paul. "Orthodoxy and Old Rus' in the Thought of S. P. Shevyrev." *Forschungen zur Osteuropäischen Geschichte* 46 (1992): 203–220.

Bynum, Carolyn Walker. *Christian Materiality: An Essay on Religion in Late Medieval Europe.* New York: Zone, 2011.

Cahen, Isidore. "Chronique israélite de la Quinzain," *Archives israélites de France* 29 (1868): 387–393.

———. "Sur une polémique récente a propos du Darwinisme," *Archives israélites de France* 36 (1875): 175–178.

Caldwell, Peter C. *Love, Death and Revolution in Central Europe.* New York: Palgrave Macmillan, 2009.

Cantor, Geoffrey, and Marc Swetlitz, eds. *Jewish Tradition and the Challenge of Darwinism.* Chicago: University of Chicago Press, 2006.

Carlebach, Julius. *Karl Marx and the Radical Critique of Judaism.* London: Routledge, 1978.

Cassedy, Steven. *To the Other Shore: The Russian Jewish Intellectuals Who Came to America.* Princeton: Princeton University Press, 1997.

Chakrabarty, Dipesh. *Provincializing Europe: Postcolonial Thought and Historical Difference.* Princeton: Princeton University Press, 2000.

Charpa, Ulrich. "Aaron Bernstein's *Nachster Grosser Reformator:* Einstein, Reform Judaism and the Fries School." In Charpa and Deichmann, eds., *Jews and Sciences in German Contexts,* 155–180.

Charpa, Ulrich, and Ute Deichmann, eds. *Jews and Sciences in German Contexts: Case Studies from the Nineteenth and Twentieth Centuries.* Tübingen: Mohr Siebeck, 2007.

Chatterjee, Margaret. *Studies in Modern Jewish and Hindu Thought.* New York: St. Martin's, 1997.

Chernyshevsky, Nikolai. *What Is to Be Done?* Trans. Michael B. Katz. Ithaca: Cornell University Press, 1989.

Cherry, Michael Shai. "Creation, Evolution and Jewish Thought." Ph.D. Diss. Brandeis University, 2001.

Clark, Christopher. "The 'Christian State' and the 'Jewish Citizen' in Nineteenth-Century Prussia." In *Protestants, Catholics and Jews in Germany, 1800–1914,* ed. Helmut Walser Smith, 67–93. London: Bloomsbury, 2001.

———. "The Limits of the Confessional State: Conversions to Judaism in Prussia, 1814–1843." *Past and Present* 147 (1995): 159–179.

Crews, Robert. "Empire and the Confessional State: Islam and Religious Politics in Nineteenth-Century Russia." *American Historical Review* 108, no. 1 (2003): 50–83.

Dalmia, Vasudha. *Nationalization of Hindu Traditions: Bharatendu Harischandra and Nineteenth-Century Banaras.* Delhi: Oxford University Press, 1997.

Dalmia, Vasudha, and Heinrich von Stietencron, eds. *Representing Hinduism: The Construction of Religious Traditions and National Identity.* London: Sage, 1995.

Darby, Michael R. *The Emergence of the Hebrew Christian Movement in Nineteenth-Century Britain.* Leiden: Brill, 2010.

Daum, Andreas W. *Wissenschaftspopularisierung im 19 Jahrhundert: Bürgerliche Kultur naturwissenschaftliche Bildung und die deutsche Öffentlichkeit 1848–1914.* Munich: Oldenbourg Verlag, 1998.

David, Ben. "Yom zikkaron le-Smolenskin." *Hamelits,* February 27, 1890.

Deutsch, Lev. "Aron Zundelevitsh." *Di tsukunft* 19, no. 8 (August 1914): 831–840.

———. "Der ershter yeshive-bokher in der rusisher revolutsye." *Di tsukunft* 20, no. 8 (1915): 713–717.

———. "Gesya Helfman, di groyse shtile martirerin." *Di tsukunft* 21, no. 4 (April 1916): 322–325.

———. "Mikhail Bakunins vide." *Di tsukunft* 29, no. 2 (February 1924): 114–117.

———. *Yidn in der Rusisher revolutsye.* Translated from Russian into Yiddish by E. Korman. Berlin: Yidisher literarisher farlag, 1923.

Deutsch, Nathaniel. *The Dark Continent: Life and Death in the Russian Pale of Settlement.* Cambridge: Harvard University Press, 2011.

Dikker, Pesah. "Isaac Baer Levinsohnin." *Prilozhenie k "Gakarmel',"* August 24, 1862.

Dohrn, Verna. "The Rabbinical Schools as Institutions of Socialization in Tsarist Russia, 1847–1873." *POLIN* 14 (2001): 83–104.

Dopolnenie k "Sborniku postanovleniy" po ministerstvu narodnago prosvyeshcheniia 1803–1864. Saint Petersburg, 1867.

Drachman, Bernard. "An Examination of Prof. Mordecai Kaplan's Views on Judaism." *Jewish Forum* 4, no. 2 (1921): 724–731.

Dub, Julius. *Kurze Darstellung der Lehre Darwin's über die Entstehung der Arten der Organismen.* Stuttgart, 1870.

Dubnow, Simon. *History of the Jews in Russia and Poland, from the Earliest Times Until the Present Day.* Trans. Israel Friedlaender. 3 vols. Philadelphia: Jewish Publication Society, 1918.

———. "Istoricheskie soobshcheniia." *Voskhod* 4 (1901): 25–40, and 5 (1902): 3–21.

Du Bois-Reymond, Emil. "The Limits of our Knowledge of Nature." Trans. J. Fitzgerald. *Popular Science Monthly* 5 (1874): 17–32.

Dynner, Glenn. *Yankel's Tavern: Jews, Liquor, and Life in the Kingdom of Poland.* New York: Oxford University Press, 2014.

Efron, John. *Defenders of the Race: Jewish Doctors and Race Science in Fin-de-Siècle Europe.* New Haven: Yale University Press, 1994.

"Eine Alte Frage." *Allgemeine Zeitung des Judenthums,* October 17, 1882.

Eisenstadt, Benzion. *Ḥakhmei yisra'el be'amerika.* New York, 1903.

Eisenstadt, Shmuel. *Perakim betoldot tenu'at hapo'alim hayehudit.* 2 vols. Tel Aviv: Merhavya, 1970.

Elior, Rachel. "HaBaD: The Contemplative Ascent to God." In Green, ed., *Jewish Spirituality,* 2:157–205.

Elkoshi, Gedaliah, ed. *Tseror igrot shel Perets Smolenskin el Yehuda Leib Gordon.* Jerusalem: Kiryat Sefer, 1959.

Elshakry, Marwa. *Reading Darwin in Arabic, 1860–1950.* Chicago: University of Chicago Press, 2013.

Enloe, Cynthia. "Religion and Ethnicity." In *Ethnic Diversity and Conflict in Eastern Europe,* ed. P. Sugar, 350–360. Santa Barbara, Calif.: ABC-Clio, 1980.

Epstein, Lisa Rae. "Caring for the Soul's House: The Jews of Russia and Health Care, 1860–1914." Ph.D. Diss. Yale University, 1995.

Etkes, Immanuel, ed. *Yitsḥak Baer Levinson.* Jerusalem: Merkaz Zalman Shazar, 1977.

Etkin, Yitsḥak Isaac. "'Inyenei ḥokhma umadda'." *Hakol,* March 9, 1879.

———. "Mikhtav." *Hame'asef,* January 1879.

———. *Torat haḥayyim veḥezyonoteihem.* Saint Petersburg, 1881.

Ettinger, Samuel. "Demutah hayishuvit vehakalkalit shel yahadut rusya besof hame'a hatesha' 'esreh." In *Bein polin lerusya,* ed. Israel Bartal and Jonathan Frankel, 2 vols., 2:257–280. Jerusalem: Merkaz Zalman Shazar, Hebrew University, 1994.

Fayn, Yitskhok. "Di Londoner misyonern-gezelshaft far yidn: ir arbet in Poyln un Rusland bemeshekh fun 19tn y"h." *YIVO Bleter* 24 (1944): 27–46.

Feigenbaum, Benjamin. "Materyalizmus in yidishkayt oder religyon un lebn—ver firt vemen?" *Di tsukunft* 5, no. 6 (June 1896): 15–20; 5, no. 7 (July 1896): 15–23; 5, no. 8 (August 1896): 17–24; 5, no. 9 (September 1896): 30–35; 5, no. 10 (October 1896): 12–20.

Feiner, Shmuel. "Hamifneh beha'arakhat haḥasidut—Eli'ezer Zweifel vehahaskala hametuna berusya." In *Hada'at vehaḥayyim,* ed. Immanuel Etkes, 355–360. Jerusalem: Merkaz Zalman Shazar, 1993.

———. *Haskalah and History: The Emergence of Modern Jewish Historical Consciousness.* Trans. Chaya Naor and Sondra Silverstone. Oxford: Littman Library of Jewish Civilization, 2002.

Fenton, Steve. *Ethnicity.* Malden, Mass.: Blackwell, 2003.

Fieskin, Yisra'el. "Toldot Yitsḥak Baer Levinson zts"l mikremenets." *Hamaggid,* November 25, 1863.

Fishman, David E. *The Rise of Modern Yiddish Culture.* Pittsburgh: University of Pittsburgh Press, 2005.

Fishman, Talya. *Shaking the Pillars of Exile: "Voice of a Fool," an Early Modern Jewish Critique of Rabbinic Culture.* Stanford: Stanford University Press, 1997.

Florovsky, Georgy. *Puti russkogo bogosloviia.* Paris: YMCA Press, 1981.

Foner, Sarah. *A Woman's Voice: Sarah Foner, Hebrew Author of the Haskalah.* Ed. and trans. Morris Rosenthal. Wilbraham, Mass.: Dailey International, 2001.

Fraade, Steven. "Ascetical Aspects of Ancient Judaism." In Green, ed., *Jewish Spirituality,* 1:253–277.

Frankel, Jonathan. *Prophecy and Politics: Socialism, Nationalism and the Russian Jews, 1862–1917.* Cambridge: Cambridge University Press, 1981.

———. "The Roots of Jewish Socialism (1881–1892)." In *Essential Papers on Jews and the Left,* ed. Ezra Mendelsohn, 58–77. New York: New York University Press, 1997.

———. *Vladimir Akimov on the Dilemmas of Russian Marxism, 1895–1903.* Cambridge: Cambridge University Press, 1969.

Frede, Victoria S. *Doubt, Atheism and the Russian Intelligentsia.* Madison: University of Wisconsin Press, 2011.

———. "Materialism and the Radical Intelligentsia: 1860s." In *A History of Russian Philosophy, 1830–1930: Faith, Reason and the Defense of Human Dignity,* ed. G. M. Hamburg and Randall A. Poole, 69–89. Cambridge: Cambridge University Press, 2013.

Freeze, ChaeRan. *Jewish Marriage and Divorce in Imperial Russia.* Hanover, N.H.: Brandeis University Press and the University Press of New England, 2002.

Freeze, ChaeRan, and Jay M. Harris, eds. *Everyday Jewish Life in Imperial Russia: Selected Documents, 1772–1914.* Waltham, Mass.: Brandeis University Press, 2013.

Frenk, A. N. "Di tsol yidn un zeyere basheftikungen in di shtet un derfer fun Kenigraykh Poyln in 1843tn yor." *Bleter far Yidishe demografye, statistik un ekonomic* 3 (1923): 190–191.

Friedländer, David. *Avot.* Vienna, 1791.

Frumkin, Boris. "Iz istorii revoliutsionnogo dvizheniia sredi evreev v 1870-kh godakh." *Evreiskaia starina* 2 (1911): 221–248, 513–540.

Fuenn, Samuel Joseph. "Amar rabbi El'azar 'atidim kol ba'alei umaniyyot sheya'amdu 'al hakarka'." *Hakarmel,* August 1, 1861.

———. "Iudaizm v otnoshenii k zhizni." *Prilozhenie k "Gakarmel',"* August 10, 1860.

———. *Kirya ne'emana.* Vilna, 1860.

———. *Nidḥei yisra'el.* Vilna, 1850.

———. *Pirḥei tsafon.* Vilna, 1841.

———. "Tikvat 'aniyim." *Hakarmel,* November 21, 1869.

———. "Yisra'el ba'amim." *Hakarmel,* March 17, 1868.

Gamzu, Yehuda Leib. "Dinanburg." *Hatsefira,* January 29, 1889.

Garb, Jonathan. "The Circle of Moshe Hayyim Luzzatto in Its Eighteenth-Century Context." *Eighteenth Century Studies* 44, no. 2 (2011): 189–202.

Gilman, Sander L. "Karl Marx and the Secret Language of Jews." *Modern Judaism* 4, no. 3 (1984): 275–294.

Ginzburg, Saul M. *Historishe verk.* 3 vols. New York: Shoyl Ginzburg 70-yohriger yubiley komitet, 1937.

———. *Meshumodim in tsarishn Rusland.* New York: Tsiko, 1946.

Goldhagen, Erich. "The Ethnic Consciousness of Early Russian Jewish Socialists." *Judaism* 23, no. 4 (1974): 479–496.

Gordon, Judah Leib. "Hakitsa 'ammi." *Hakarmel,* April 18, 1866.

———. *Igrot Yehuda Leib Gordon: 1830–1892.* Ed. Isaac Jacob Weisberg. 2 vols. Warsaw, 1894.

———. *Die judische Frage in der orientalischen Frage.* Vienna, 1877.

Gorski, Philip S. "The Protestant Ethic and the Bureaucratic Revolution: Ascetic Protestantism and the Administrative Rationalization in Early Modern Europe." In *Max Weber's Economy and Society: A Critical Companion,* ed. Philip S. Gorski and David M. Trubek, 266–296. Stanford: Stanford University Press, 2005.

Gottlober, Abraham Baer. *Iggeret tsa'ar ba'alei ḥayyim.* Zhitomir, 1868.

———. *Toldot hakabbala vehaḥasidut.* Zhitomir, 1870.

Graetz, Heinrich. *Geschichte der Juden.* 11 vols. Magdeburg, 1860.

Green, Arthur, ed. *Jewish Spirituality.* 2 vols. New York: Crossroad, 1986–1987.

Greenbaum, Avraham. *Perakim bahistoryografya shel yahadut rusya.* Jerusalem: Merkaz Dinur, 2006.

Greenberg, Louis S. *Isaac Baer Levinsohn: A Critical Investigation of the Works of Rabbi Isaac Baer Levinsohn (Ribal).* New York: Bloch, 1930.

Gregory, Frederick. "The Mysteries and Wonders of Natural Science: Aaron Bernstein's *Naturwissenschaftliche Volksbücher* and the Adolescent Einstein." In *Einstein: The Formative Years, 1879–1909,* ed. Don Howard and John Stachel, 23–41. Berlin: Birkhäuser, 2000.

———. *Scientific Materialism in Nineteenth-Century Germany.* Dordrecht: D. Reidel, 1977.

———. "Scientific Versus Dialectical Materialism: A Clash of Ideologies in Nineteenth-Century German Radicalism." *History of Science Society* 68, no. 2 (June 1977): 206–223.

Grözinger, Karl Erich. *Jüdisches Denken. Theologie-Philosophie-Mystik.* Vol. 4: *Zionismus und Schoah.* Frankfort: Campus Verlag, 2015.

Guenzburg, Mordecai Aaron. *Maggid emet.* Leipzig, 1843.

Gurevich, Grigory. "Zikhroynes." In Tcherikower, ed., *Historishe shriftn*, 3:224–255.

Gurock, Jeffrey S., and Jacob J. Schacter. *A Modern Heretic and a Traditional Community: Mordecai M. Kaplan, Orthodoxy, and American Judaism.* New York: Columbia University Press, 1997.

Habavli, Tsvi Daniel [TsD″H]. *Shoresh davar.* Vilna, 1866.

Haberer, Erich E. *Jews and Revolution in Nineteenth-Century Russia.* Cambridge: Cambridge University Press, 1995.

Hacohen, Mordecai ben-Hillel. "Dor holekh vedor ba." *Hashahar,* 1878.

———. *Me'erev 'ad 'erev.* 2 vols. Vilna, 1923.

———. *'Olami.* 3 vols. Jerusalem: Hapo'alim, 1927.

Halpern, Ben, and Jehuda Reinharz. "Nationalism and Jewish Socialism: The Early Years." *Modern Judaism* 8, no. 3 (1988): 217–248.

Hanioğlu, M. Şükrü. "Blueprints for a Future Society: Late Ottoman Materialists on Science, Religion and Art." In *Late Ottoman Society: The Intellectual Legacy,* ed. Elisabeth Özdalga, 28–116. New York: Routledge Curzon, 2005.

———. *The Young Turks in Opposition.* Oxford: Oxford University Press, 1995.

Hapgood, Hutchins. *The Spirit of the Ghetto: Studies of the Jewish Quarter in New York.* New York: Funk and Wagnalls, 1902.

Harris, Jay. *Nachman Krochmal: Guiding the Perplexed of the Modern Age.* New York: New York University Press, 1991.

Hart, Mitchell B. *The Healthy Jew: Symbioses of Judaism and Modern Medicine.* New York: Cambridge University Press, 2007.

Hayes, Carlton. *A Generation of Materialism, 1871–1900.* New York: Harper and Row, 1941.

Hayyim of Volozhin. *Ru'ah hayyim.* Vilna, 1859.

Heinze, Andrew R. *Adapting to Abundance: Jewish Immigrants, Mass Consumption and the Search for American Identity.* New York: Columbia University Press, 1992.

Helfman, Henne. "A briv in der redaktsye." *Der alter Yisrolik,* October 5, 1875.

Helmholtz, Hermann. *Über die Wechselwirkung der Naturkräft.* Köningsberg, 1854.

Henningsen, Charles Frederick. *Eastern Europe and the Emperor Nicholas.* 3 vols. London, 1846.

Heschel, Susannah. *Abraham Geiger and the Jewish Jesus.* Chicago: University of Chicago Press, 1998.

Hess, Jonathan M. *Germans, Jews and the Claims of Modernity.* New Haven: Yale University Press, 2002.

Hess, Moses. *Dynamische Stofflehre.* Paris, 1877.

———. *Rom und Jerusalem: die letzte Nationalitätenfrage.* Leipzig, 1862. Trans. Meyer Waxman as *Rome and Jerusalem* (New York: Bloch, 1918).

———. "Die Soziale Revolution." *Volksstaat,* February 1870. Reprinted in William Liebknecht, *Der Hochverrats-prozess wider Liebknecht, Bebel, Hepner vor dem Schwurgericht zu Leipzig vom 11. bis 26. März 1872,* 742–758. Berlin, 1894.

Hirsch, Samson Raphael. *Judaism Eternal.* Trans. Isidor Grunfeld. 2 vols. London: Soncino, 1959.

Hobsbawm, Eric J., and Terence O. Ranger. *The Invention of Tradition.* Cambridge: Cambridge University Press, 1992.

Hoffman, Benzion. "Mit fuftsik yor tsurik." *Forverts,* May 25, 1947.

Hoffman, Nehemiah Dov. "Hashkafa 'al hitpathut sifruteinu hamadda'it hahadasha." *'Ivri anokhi,* February 4, 1887.

Horowitz, Brian. *Jewish Philanthropy and Enlightenment in Late-Tsarist Russia.* Seattle: University of Washington Press, 2009.

Hvithamar, Annika, and Margit Warburg. "Introducing Civil Religion, Nationalism and Globalisation." In *Holy Nations and Global Identities: Civil Religion, Nationalism and Global Identities,* ed. Annika Hvithamar, Margit Warburg, and Brian Arly Jacobson, 1–10. Leiden: Brill, 2009.

Ilya, Menashe. *Shekel hakodesh.* Kapust, 1823.

Israel, Jonathan I. *European Jewry in the Age of Mercantilism.* Oxford: Oxford University Press, 1985.

Jacobs, Jack. *On Socialists and "The Jewish Question" After Marx.* New York: New York University Press, 1992.

Jagodzinka, Agnieszka. "English Missionaries Look at Polish Jews." In *Jews in the Kingdom of Poland, 1815–1918,* edited by Glenn Dynner, Antony Polonsky, and Marcin Wodzinski, 89–116. Oxford: Littman Library of Jewish Civilization, 2015.

Jellinek, Adolph. *Der Jüdische Stamm.* Vienna, 1869.

Jenkins, Richard. *Rethinking Ethnicity: Arguments and Explorations.* London: Sage, 1997.

Jewish Colonial Association. *Recueil de materiaux sur la situation économique des Israélites de Russie.* 2 vols. Paris, 1906.

Jochelsohn, Benjamin. "Dalekoe proshloe, Iz vospominaniy starogo narodovol'tsa." *Byloe* 13 (1918): 53–75.

Jones, Kenneth W. *Arya Dharm: Hindu Consciousness in Nineteenth-Century Punjab.* Berkeley: University of California Press, 1976.

Jordan, Zbigniew A. *The Evolution of Dialectical Materialism: A Philosophical and Sociological Analysis.* New York: St. Martin's, 1967.

Joselit, Jenna Weissman. *The Wonders of America: Reinventing Jewish Culture, 1880–1950.* New York: Henry Holt, 1994.

"Joseph Sossnitz, Philosopher, Dead." *New York Times,* March 3, 1910.

Joskowicz, Ari. *The Modernity of Others: Jewish Anti-Catholicism in Germany and France.* Stanford: Stanford University Press, 2014.

Kagan, Berl. *Yidishe shtet, shtetlekh un dorfishe yishuvim in Lite biz 1918.* New York: Kagan, 1991.

Kahan, Arcadius. *Essays in Jewish Social and Economic History.* Ed. Roger Weiss. Chicago: University of Chicago Press, 1986.

———. "The First Wave of Jewish Immigration from Eastern Europe to the United States." In Kahan, *Essays in Jewish Social and Economic History*, 118–148.

———. "Impact of Industrialization on Jews in Tsarist Russia." In Kahan, *Essays in Jewish Social and Economic History*, 1–69.

Kalisher, Reuven. *Ma'amar 'al hakoḥot hapo'alim babri'a.* Warsaw, 1862.

Kamensky, Moshe. "Hanihilistim," *Hatsefira*, April 16, 1913.

———. "Nihilistim 'ivriyim bishnot hashiv'im." *Hashiloaḥ* 17 (1907): 257–263.

Kaminer, Isaac. "'Al derekh avodat ha'adama," *Hakol*, May 7, 1879.

———. *Shirei Yitsḥak ben Avraham doktor Kaminer.* Ed. Asher Ginsberg. Odessa, 1905.

Kantor, Judah Leib. "Ma'aminim anaḥnu." *Hashaḥar*, 1874.

Kaplan, Mordecai M. "The Influences That Have Shaped My Life." *Reconstructionist* 8, no. 10 (June 26, 1942): 27–36.

———. *Judaism in Transition.* New York: Behrman's Jewish Book House, 1941.

Kaplan, Yosef. "'Karaites' in Early Eighteenth-Century Amsterdam." In *Sceptics, Millenarians and Jews,* ed. D. Katz and J. Israel, 196–236. Leiden: Brill, 1990.

Karp, Jonathan. "Can Economic History Date the Inception of Jewish Modernity?" In *The Economy in Jewish History: New Perspectives on the Interrelationship Between Ethnicity and Economic Life,* ed. Gideon Reuveni and Sarah Wobick-Segev, 23–42. New York: Berghahn, 2011.

———. *The Politics of Jewish Commerce: Economic Thought and Emancipation in Europe, 1638–1848.* Cambridge: Cambridge University Press, 2008.

Katz, Jacob. *Out of the Ghetto: The Social Background of Jewish Emancipation, 1770–1870.* Cambridge: Schocken, 1973.

———. *Tradition and Crisis: Jewish Society at the End of the Middle Ages.* Trans. Bernard Dov Cooperman. Rev. ed. Syracuse, N.Y.: Syracuse University Press, 2000.

Kaufman, A. E. "Za mnogo let." *Evreiskaia starina* 5 (1913): 201–220.

Kautsky, Karl. "Forvert." In Karl Marx and Friedrich Engels, *Dos manifest fun di komunistishe partey.* Geneva: algemeynem idishn arbeter bund in Rusland un Poyln, 1899.

Keane, Webb. "Materialism, Missionaries and Modern Subjects on Colonial Indonesia." In *Conversion to Modernities: The Globalization of Christianity,* ed. Peter van der Veer, 137–170. New York: Routledge, 1996.

———. "Sincerity, 'Modernity' and the Protestants." *Cultural Anthropology* 17, no. 1 (2002): 67–74.

Kirshenblatt-Gimblett, Barbara. "The Corporeal Turn." *Jewish Quarterly Review* 95, no. 3 (Summer 2005): 447–461.

———. "Objects of Ethnography." In *Exhibiting Cultures: The Poetics and Politics of Museum Display,* ed. Ivan Karp and Steven D. Lavine, 386–443. Washington, D.C.: Smithsonian, 1991.

Kirshenblatt-Gimblett, Barbara, and Jeffrey Shandler. "Introduction." *Material Religion: The Journal of Objects, Art, and Belief* 3, no. 3 (2007): 308–312.

Klausner, Israel. *Vilna: Yerushalayim delita.* Vol. 1: *Dorot rishonim 1495–1881.* Tel Aviv: Ghetto Fighters' House, 1988.

Klausner, Joseph. "Hamaterialismus hahistori vehatnu'a hale'umit." In Klausner, *Kitvei prof. Yosef Klausner: yahadut ve'enoshiyut,* 2 vols., 1:81–106. Tel Aviv: Massada, 1955.

———. *Historya shel hasifrut ha'ivrit hahadasha.* 6 vols. Jerusalem: Hebrew University, 1953–1960.

———. *Kitvei prof. Yosef Klausner: otobiyografya.* 2 vols. Tel Aviv: Massada, 1955.

Klier, John Doyle. *Imperial Russia's Jewish Question, 1855–1881.* Cambridge: Cambridge University Press, 1995.

———. "State Policies and the Conversion of Jews in Imperial Russia." In *Of Religion and Empire: Missions, Conversion, and Tolerance in Tsarist Russia,* ed. Robert P. Geraci and Michael Khodarkovsky, 92–112. Ithaca: Cornell University Press, 2011.

Knörzer, Heidi. "Ludwig Philippson et Isidore Cahen: Deux journalists, deux pays, un discours politique commun." *Archives juives* 43 (2010): 122–131.

Kobrin, Rebecca, ed. *Chosen Capital: The Jewish Encounter with American Capitalism.* New Brunswick, N.J.: Rutgers University Press, 2012.

Kohen, Shlomo [pseud.] "Derekh mamona." *Halevanon,* December 26, 1879.

———. "Derekh emuna." *Halevanon,* December 19, 1879.

Koltun-Fromm, Ken. *Material Culture and Jewish Thought in America.* Bloomington: Indiana University Press, 2010.

Kon, Pinkhes. "Oysforsh-materyaln vegn ershtn yidishn revolutsyonern krayzl in Vilne." *YIVO Bleter* 5 (1933): 171–176.

Kook, Abraham Isaac. *Igrot harav Avraham Yitshak Hakohen Kook.* 3 vols. Jerusalem: Mosad Harav Kook, 1961.

Kopf, David. *The Brahmo Samaj and the Shaping of the Modern Indian Mind.* Princeton: Princeton University Press, 1979.

Kosicki, Piotr H. "Masters in Their Own Home or Defenders of the Human Person? Wojciech Korfanty, Anti-Semitism, and Polish Christian Democracy's Illiberal Rights Talk." *Modern Intellectual History.* Published online January 23, 2015. DOI: http://dx.doi.org/10.1017/S1479244314000857.

Kovner, Abraham Uri. "Yeshibotnaia bursa." *Den',* June 11, June 20, July 11, August 1, October 25, 1869.

———. *Heker davar.* Warsaw, 1865.

———. "Ru'ah hayyim." *Hakarmel,* December 11, 1866.

Kovner, Yitshak Isaac. *Sefer hametsaref.* Ed. Shmuel Feiner. Jerusalem: Mosad Bialik, 1998.

Kraut, Benny. "Towards the Establishment of the National Conference of Christians and Jews: The Tenuous Road to Religious Goodwill in the 1920s." *American Jewish History* 77 (1988): 388–412.

Krol, Tsvi, ed. *Ha'emet.* Tel Aviv, 1938.

Kropotkin, Peter. *Memoirs of a Revolutionary.* New York: Black Rose Books, 1989.

Kursky, Franz. "Di Zhenever 'grupe sotsyalistn-yidn' un ir oyfruf (1880)." In Tcherikower, ed., *Historishe shriftn,* 3:557–562.

Landau, Isaac Elijah. "Derush," *Hakarmel,* September 20, 1876.

Landauer, Gustav. "Sind das Ketzergedanken." In *Gustav Landauer, Der Werdende Mensch: Aufsätze über Leben und Schrifttum,* ed. Martin Buber, 170–174. Potsdam: Kiepenheuer, 1921.

Lange, Friedrich Albert. *Die Arbeiterfrage: Ihre Bedeutung für Gegenwart und Zukunft.* Duisburg, 1865.

———. *Geschichte des Materialismus und Kritik seiner Bedeutung in der Gegenwart.* 2 vols. Leipzig, 1873–1875. Translated from German into Russian by Nikolia Starkhov as *Istoriia Materializma.* Saint Petersburg, 1881–1883. Translated into Hebrew by Shraga Feivel Frankel as *Toldot hamaterialismus uvikoret 'erko bizmaneinu.* Warsaw, 1922. Translated into English by Ernst Chester Thomas as Frederick Albert Lange, *The History of Materialism and Criticism of Its Present Importance,* 3 vols. Boston: Houghton, Mifflin, 1881.

Langerman, Tzvi. "Yosef Shlomo Delmedigo's Engagement with Atomism." In *Jewish Culture in Early Modern Europe: Essays in Honor of David B. Ruderman,* ed. Richard I. Cohen, Natalie Dohrmann, Adam Shear, and Elchanan Reiner, 124–133. Cincinnati: Hebrew Union College, University of Pittsburgh Press, 2014.

Laqueur, Walter. *A History of Zionism.* New York: Schocken, 1972.

Lavrov, Peter. *Istoricheskie pis'ma.* St. Petersburg, 1870. Trans. and ed. James P. Scanlan as *Peter Lavrov, Historical Letters* (Berkeley: University of California Press, 1967).

———. "Khristianskiy ide'al pered sudom sotsializma." *Vpered!* November 1, 1876.

———. "Nasha programma." *Vpered!* August 1, 1873.

———. *P. L. Lavrov. O religii.* Ed. A. F. Okulovg et al. Moscow, 1989.

———. "Sotsializm i istorecheskoe khristianstvo." *Vpered!* December 15, 1875.

———. "Znanie i revoliutsiia." *Vpered!* August 1, 1873.

Lederhendler, Eli. "Interpreting the Messianic Rhetoric in the Russian Haskalah and Early Zionism." *Studies in Contemporary Jewry* 7 (1991): 14–33.

———. *Jewish Immigrants and American Capitalism, 1880–1920: From Caste to Class.* New York: Cambridge University Press, 2009.

———. *The Road to Modern Jewish Politics: Political Tradition and Political Reconstruction in the Jewish Community of Tsarist Russia.* New York: Oxford University Press, 1989.

Leff, Lisa Moses. *Sacred Bonds of Solidarity: The Rise of Jewish Internationalism in Nineteenth-Century France.* Stanford: Stanford University Press, 2006.

———. "Self-Definition and Self-Defense: Jewish Racial Identity in Nineteenth-Century France." *Jewish History* 19 (2005): 7–28.

Lehmann, Hartmut. "Über die Varianten einer komplementären Relation. Die Säkularisierung der Religion und die Sakralisierung der Nation im 20. Jahrhundert." In *Religion im Nationalstaat zwischen den Weltkriegen,* ed. Christian Maner and Martin Schulze Wessel, 13–27. Stuttgart: Fritz Steiner Verlag, 2002.

Lenoir, Timothy. *The Strategy of Life: Teleology and Mechanics in Nineteenth-Century German Biology.* Dordrecht, Netherlands: Reidel, 1982.

Lerner, Yosef Yehuda. *Derush 'al hameitim.* Odessa, 1868.

Lestschinsky, Jacob. "Di antviklung fun yidishn folk far di letste 100 yor." *Shriftn far ekonomik un statistik* 1 (1928): 1–64.

Levin, Judah Leib. "She'eilat hayehudim." *Hakol,* January 5, 1879.

———. "Tsi badarf men shraybn hebreish?" *Der alter Yisrolik,* December 9 and 16, 1875.

———. *Yehuda Leib Levin: Zikhronot vehegyonot.* Ed. Yehuda Slutsky. Jerusalem: Mosad Bialik, 1968.

———. *Yehuda Leib Levin, ketavim nivharim.* Ed. Menaḥem Mendel Feitelsohn. 2 vols. Warsaw, 1911.

Levin, Mordechai. *'Erkhei ḥevra vekhalkala ba'ide'ologya shel tekufat hahaskala.* Jerusalem: Mosad Bialik, 1975.

Levinsohn, Isaac Baer. *Aḥiya hashiloni haḥozeh.* Leipzig, 1864.

———. *Beit yehuda.* Vilna, 1858.

———. *Bikurei Ribal.* Warsaw, 1891.

———. *Efes damim: sefer hitnatslut neged 'alilat dam.* Vilna, 1837. Translated from Hebrew into English by Louis Loewe as *Éfés dammîm: A Series of Conversations at Jerusalem Between a Patriarch of the Greek Church and a Chief Rabbi of the Jews, Concerning the Malicious Charge Against the Jews of Using Christian Blood.* London, 1841.

———. *Te'uda beyisra'el.* Vilna, 1828.

———. *Yemin tsidki.* Warsaw, 1881.

———. *Zerubavel.* Warsaw, 1886.

Lieberman, Aaron Shemuel. *Arn Libermans briv.* Ed. Kalman Marmor. New York: YIVO, 1951.

———. *A. S. Lieberman: Ketavot uma'amarim be-'Vpered' (1875–1876).* Ed. Moshe Mishkinsky. Tel Aviv: Tel Aviv University, 1977.

———. "Gevul koḥot ha'adam." *Hamabit,* May 15, 1879.

———. "Hayehudim bahagira." In Krol, ed., *Ha'emet,* 21–25. Originally published in *Ha'emet* 2, 1877.

———. "Hitpatḥut ḥayyei haḥevra bishnot habeinayim." In Krol, ed., *Ha'emet,* 25–31. Originally published in *Ha'emet* 2, 1877.

———. "Iz Belostoka." *Vpered!* February 15, 1875.

———. "Iz Belostoka." *Vpered!* December 15, 1875.

———. "Iz Vil'no." *Vpered!* September 1, 1875.

———. "Letoldot ha'utopya." In *Kitvei A. S. Liberman,* ed. Michal Berkowitz, 1–62. Tel Aviv, 1928.

———. "Ma'aseh Satan." *Ha'emet* 3, 1877, 51–56.

———. "She'eilat hayehudim." *Ha'emet* 1, 1877. In Krol, ed., *Ha'emet,* 1–5.

———. "Shelumei baḥurei yisra'el." *Davar,* April 30, 1936.

Liedtke, Rainer, and Stephan Wendehorst, eds. *The Emancipation of Catholics, Jews and Protestants: Minorities and the Nation-State in Nineteenth-Century Europe.* Manchester: Manchester University Press, 1999.

Liessin, Abraham. "Epizodn." In Tcherikower, ed., *Historishe shriftn,* 3:173–224.

———. *Zikhronot vaḥavayot.* Tel Aviv: Am Oved, 1943.

Lifshitz, Yehoshua Mordecai. "Di 4 klasn." *Kol mevaser,* June 18, 1863.

Lifshutz, Ya'akov. *Zikhron ya'akov.* 3 vols. Bnei Brak, 1968.

Lifshutz, Yehuda Halevi. *Derekh emuna.* Warsaw, 1895.

Lilienblum, Moses Leib. "'Al yisra'el ve'al artso." *Hashaḥar,* 1881.

———. *Ketavim otobiyografiyim.* Ed. Shlomo Breiman. 3 vols. Jerusalem: Mosad Bialik, 1970.

———. *Kol kitvei Moshe Leib Lilienblum.* 4 vols. Krakow; Odessa, 1910–1913.

———. "Leḥem lare'evim." *Hamelits,* November 4, 1879.

———. "Maka she'ein lah refua." *Hamelits,* October, 17, 1872.

———. "Mikhtav lamotsi la'or." *Hashaḥar,* 1874.

———. "Odessa." *Kol mevaser,* July 16, 1871.

———. "'Olam hatohu." *Hashaḥar,* 1873.

———. "Tikkun medini vetikkun sifruti." *Hashaḥar,* 1871.

———. "Umstvennye potrebnosti russkikh evreev v sviazi s ikh material'nymi nuzhdami." *Razsvet* 9 (1879).

———. "Yidishe lebnsfragn." *Kol mevaser,* March 11, 18, and 24, April 22 and 29, May 6, June 3 and 10, July 1 and 23, 1871.

Lincoln, W. Bruce. *Alexander's Great Reforms: Autocracy, Bureaucracy and the Politics of Change in Imperial Russia.* DeKalb: Northern Illinois University Press, 1990.

———. "Count P. D. Kiselev: A Reformer in Imperial Russia." *Australian Journal of Politics and History* 16 (1970): 177–188.

Lippe, Ch. D. *Bibliographisches Lexicon der gesmmten jüdischen Literatur der Gegenwart und Adress-Anzeiger.* Vienna, 1881.

Lippman, M. D. *Letoldot hayehudim belita-zamut.* Kieden, 1934.

Litvak, A. [Khayim Yankl Helfand]. "Aron Zundelevitsh." In *Royter pinkes: tsu der geshikhte fun der Yidisher arbeter-bavegung un* sotsyalistishe *shtremungen bay Yidn.* 2 vols. 2:80–106. Warsaw: Kultur lige, 1924.

Litvak, Olag. *Haskalah: The Romantic Movement in Judaism.* New Brunswick, N.J.: Rutgers University Press, 2012.

Loeffler, James. "Nationalism Without a Nation? On the Invisibility of American Jewish Politics." *Jewish Quarterly Review* 105, no. 3 (Summer 2015): 367–398.

Löwe, Heinz-Dietrich. "Poles, Jews, and Tartars: Religion, Ethnicity and Social Structure in Tsarist Nationality Politics." *Jewish Social Studies* 6 (2000): 52–96.

Löwy, Michael. *Redemption and Utopia: Jewish Libertarian Thought in Central Europe: A Study in Elective Affinity.* Trans. Hope Heaney. Stanford: Stanford University Press, 1992.

Luntz, Judah Leib. *Ge'ula viyshu'a.* Petrikov, 1908.

Magalski, Y. "Kol 'aleh nirdaf." *Hakol,* September 14, 1879.

Maggid-Steinschneider, Hillel Noah. *'Ir Vilna.* Vilna, 1900.

Magid, Shaul. "The Spinozistic Spirit in Mordecai Kaplan's Revaluation of Judaism." *Modern Judaism* 20, no. 2 (May 2000): 159–180.

Malachi, Eliezer Raphael. "Morris Winchevsky." In Malachi, *Masot ureshimot,* 157–182. New York: 1937.

Mandel, George. "Who Was Ben-Yehuda with in Boulevard Montmartre?" *Oxford Centre Papers* 2 (1984): 1–15.

Mandelbaum, Maurice. *History, Man and Reason: A Study in Nineteenth-Century Thought.* Baltimore: Johns Hopkins University Press, 1971.

Marek, Peysekh. *Ocherki po istorii prosvyeshcheniia evreev v Rossii.* Moscow, 1909.

Marmor, Kalman. "Arn Libermans letste shrift." *Morgn frayhayt,* November 18, 1930.

Marx, Karl. *Das Kapital: Kritik der politcischen Oekonomie.* Hamburg: 1867. Translated into Yiddish by Jacob Merison as *Dos kapital.* New York: Krapotkin literatur gezelshaft, 1917–1918. Translated into Hebrew by Zevi Wislavsky as *Hakapital.* Jerusalem: Po'alim, 1947. Translated into English by Samuel Moore and Edward Aveling as *Capital: A Critique of Political Economy.* Chicago: Charles H. Kerr, 1909.

———. *Manifest der Kommunistischen Partei.* London: Office der Bildungs-Gesellschaft für Arbeiter" von J. E. Burghard, [1848]. Later revised and translated into English as Karl Marx and Frederick Engels, *The Manifesto of the Communist Party.* Authorized English translation. Ed. and annot. Frederick Engels. London: William Reeves, 1888. Now Karl Marx and Friedrich Engels, *The Communist Manifesto.* Harmondsworth, U.K.: Penguin, 1985. Translated into Yiddish as *Dos manifest fun di komunistishe partey.* Geneva: algemeynem idishn arbeter bund in Rusland un Poyln, 1899.

———. "On the Jewish Question." In *The Marx- Engels Reader.* 2nd ed. Ed. and trans. Robert Tucker, 26–53. New York: Norton, 1978.

"Materialismus in der Naturwissenschaft, Der." *Jeschurun* 2, no. 5 (1856): 271–279.

Megill, Allan, and Jaeyoon Park. "Misrepresenting Marx: A Lesson in Historical Method." Unpublished manuscript, July 2016. In author's possession.

Meir, Jonatan. *Shivḥei Rodkinson: Mikha'el Levi Frumkin-Rodkinson vehaḥasidut.* Tel Aviv: Hakibbutz Hame'uḥad, 2012.

Meir, Natan. "*The Jewish Century:* "What Does Being a Jew Matter?" *Ab Imperio* 1 (2005): 171–174.

Melamed, Efim. "The Zhitomir Rabbinical School: New Materials and Perspectives." *POLIN* 14 (2001): 105–115.

Melamed, Ḥayyim. "Felyeton." Review of *Shalom 'al yisra'el,* by Eliezer Zweifel. *Kol mevaser,* October 7, 1868.

Melamed, Yitzhak Y. "Acosmism or Weak Individuals? Hegel, Spinoza, and the Reality of the Finite." *Journal of the History of Philosophy* 48, no. 1 (2010): 77–92.

———. "Salomon Maimon and the Rise of Spinozism in German Idealism." *Journal of the History of Philosophy* 42 (2004): 67–96.

Mendelsohn, Ezra. *Class Struggle in the Pale: The Formative Years of the Jewish Workers' Movement in Tsarist Russia.* Cambridge: Cambridge University Press, 1970.

———. Review of *Jews and Revolution in Nineteenth-Century Russia,* by Erich E. Haberer. *Russian Review* 56, no. 1 (January 1997): 136–138.

Menes, Abraham. "Di Yidishe arbeter-bavegung in Rusland fun onheyb 70er bizn sof 90er yorn." In Tcherikower, ed., *Historishe shriftn,* 3:1–59.

Meyer, Brigit. "Aesthetics of Persuasion: Global Christianity and Pentecostalism's Sensational Forms." *South Atlantic Quarterly* 9 (2010): 744–750.

Meyer, Brigit, and Dick Houtman, eds. *Things: Religion and the Question of Materiality,* New York: Fordham University Press, 2012.

Meyer, Michael. *The Origins of the Modern Jew: Jewish Identity and European Culture, 1749–1824.* Detroit: Wayne State University Press, 1967.

Mibaslow, Yakov Moscow. "Toldot anshei shem: vehu ḥayyei heḥakham Eliyahu Orshanski." *Hakol,* January 26, 1879.

Michael, Reuwen. "Graetz and Hess." *Leo Baeck Institute Yearbook* 9 (1964): 91–121.

Mieses, Fabius. "Korot hafilosofya haḥadasha." *Hatsefira,* June 18, 1878.

"Mikhtav me-Yehalel le-Yalag." *He'avar* 1 (1918): 193–197.

Miller, Daniel, ed. *Materiality.* Durham, N.C.: Duke University Press, 2005.

Mintz, Alan. *Banished from Their Father's Table: Loss of Faith and Hebrew Autobiography.* Bloomington: Indiana University Press, 1989.

Mishkinsky, Moshe. *'Iyunim basotsyalism hayehudi.* Kiryat Sdeh Bokér: Mechon Ben-Gurion, 2004.

Mitzkun, Moshe David. "Ma'amar hasavlanut vehahaskala davar be'ito." *Hamelits,* May 23, 1861.

Mogilner, Marina. "On Cabbages, Kings, and Jews." Review of *The Jewish Century,*
by Yuri Slezkine. *Ab Imperio* 1 (2005): 138–150.

———. "Toward a History of Russian Jewish 'Medical Materialism': Russian Jewish Physicians and the Politics of Jewish Biological Normalization." *Jewish Social
Studies* 19, no. 1 (Fall 2012): 70–106.

Morgulis, Menashe. *Il'ia Grigorevich Orshanskiy i ego literaturnaia deiatel'nost'.* Saint
Petersburg, 1904.

———. "K istorii obrazovaniia russkikh evreev." In *Evreiskaia biblioteka: istoriko-
literaturnyi sbornik,* ed. Adolph E. Landau, 135–191. Saint Petersburg, 1871.

Morgulis, Menashe, and David Rafaelovitch. "Kheshbn fun dem gelt." *Kol mevaser,*
February 11, 1865.

Mosse, George L. *The Nationalization of the Masses: Political Symbolism and Mass
Movements in Germany from the Napoleonic Wars Through the Third Reich.* Ithaca:
Cornell University Press, 1975.

Muller, Jerry Z. *Capitalism and the Jews.* Princeton: Princeton University Press, 2010.

Murav, Harriet. *Identity Theft: The Jew in Imperial Russia and the Case of Avraam Uri
Kovner.* Stanford: Stanford University Press, 2003.

Myers, David N. "Between Diaspora and Zion: History, Memory, and the Jerusalem Scholars." In *The Jewish Past Revisited: Reflections on Modern Jewish Historians,* ed. David N. Myers and David B. Ruderman, 88–103. New Haven: Yale
University Press, 1998.

———. *Re-inventing the Jewish Past: European Jewish Intellectuals and the Zionist
Return to History.* New York: Oxford University Press, 1995.

Na'aman, Shlomo. *Marxismus und Zionismus.* Gerlingen: Bleicher-Verlag, 1997.

Naimark, Norman. *Terrorists and Social Democrats: The Russian Revolutionary Movement Under Alexander III.* Cambridge: Harvard University Press, 1983.

Nardi, Zavia. "Mishnato hale'umit shel Perets Smolenskin umikumah beyahadut
rusya." M.A. Thesis. Hebrew University, 1976.

Nathans, Benjamin. *Beyond the Pale: The Jewish Encounter with Late Imperial Russia.*
Berkeley: University of California Press, 2002.

Nathansohn, David Baer. *Sefer hazikhronot: divrei yemei ḥayyei . . . Yitsḥak Ber
Levinzohn.* Warsaw, 1899.

Nesemann, Frank. "Aufgeklaerter Absolutismus und religioese Toleranz: Juden und
Muslime unter Katharina II." *Leipziger Beitraege zur juedischen Geschichte und
Kultur* 2 (2004): 75–99.

Neumann-Schliski, Jens. *Konfession oder Stamm? Konzepte jüdischer Identität bei
Redakteuren jüdischer Zeitschriften 1840 bis 1881 im internationalen Vergleich.*
Bremen: Lumiere, 2011.

Nirenberg, David. *Anti-Judaism: The Western Tradition.* New York: Norton, 2013.

———. "Judaism as a Political Concept: Toward a Critique of Political Theology."
Representations 128, no. 1 (Fall 2014): 1–29.

Nord, Philip. *The Republican Moment: Struggles for Democracy in Nineteenth-Century France.* Cambridge: Harvard University Press, 1995.

Notik, Rivke. "Tsu der geshikhte fun hantverk bay litvishe yidn." *YIVO Bleter* 1 (1936): 107–118.

Orbach, Alexander. *New Voices of Russian Jews: A Study of the Russian Press of Odessa in the Era of the Great Reform, 1860–1871.* Leiden: Brill, 1980.

Orshanski, Ilya. *Evrei v rossii.* Saint Petersburg, 1877.

———. "Ocherki ekonomicheskogo polozheniia evreev v rossii." *Den',* August 15, October 18, and November 29, 1869.

Ozment, Steven. *Reformation Europe: A Guide to Research.* Saint Louis: Center for Reformation Study, 1982.

Paperno, Irina. *Chernyshevsky and the Age of Realism: A Study in the Semiotics of Behavior.* Stanford: Stanford University Press,1988.

Parush, Iris. *Reading Jewish Women: Marginality and Modernization in Nineteenth-Century Eastern European Jewish Society.* trans. Saadya Sternberg. Waltham, Mass.: Brandeis University Press, 2004.

Patterson, David. "Ahad Ha-Am and Smolenskin." In *The Crossroads: Essays on Ahad Ha-am,* ed. Jacques Kornberg, 36–45. Albany: State University of New York Press, 1983.

Peled, Yoav. "From Theology to Sociology: Bruno Bauer and Karl Marx on the Question of Jewish Emancipation." *History of Political Thought* 13, no. 3 (1992): 464–485.

Pelli, Moshe. "The Attitude of the First Maskilim in Germany Towards the Talmud." *Leo Beck Institute Year Book* 27 (1982): 243–269.

Pels, Peter. "The Modern Fear of Matter: Reflections on the Protestantism of Victorian Science." In Meyer and Houtman, eds., *Things: Religion and the Question of Materiality,* 264–283.

Penslar, Derek. *Shylock's Children: Economics and Jewish Identity in Modern Europe.* Berkeley: University of California Press, 2001.

Peretz, Isaac Leib. *Di verk fun Yitskhok Leybush Perets.* Ed. David Pinski. 10 vols. New York, 1920.

Pesis, Phinehas. *'Ir dubno verabbaneha.* Krakow, 1902.

Pessin, Sarah. *Ibn Gabirol's Theology of Desire: Matter and Method in Jewish Medieval Neoplatonism.* Cambridge: Cambridge University Press, 2013.

———. "Matter, Form and the Corporeal World." In *The Cambridge History of Jewish Philosophy: From Antiquity Through the Seventeenth Century,* ed. Steven Nadler and Tamar Rudavsky, 269–302. Cambridge: Cambridge University Press, 2009.

Petrovsky-Shtern, Yohanan. *The Golden Age Shtetl: A New History of Jewish Life in East Europe.* Princeton: Princeton University Press, 2014.

————. *Jews in the Russian Army, 1827–1917: Drafted into Modernity.* Cambridge: Cambridge University Press, 2009.

Pew Research Center. "A Portrait of American Jews." October 1, 2013. http://www .pewforum.org/2013/10/01/jewish-american-beliefs-attitudes-culture-survey/.

Philipson, Joakim. "The Purpose of Evolution: The Struggle for Existence in the Russian-Jewish Press, 1860–1900." Ph.D. Diss. Stockholm University, 2008.

Pinkas agudat hasotsyalistim ha'ivriyim belondon. Jerusalem: Hebrew University, Merkaz Dinur, 1968.

Pinsker, Leo. *Auto-Emancipation.* Trans. D. S. Blondheim. New York: Maccabaean, 1906.

Pisarev, Dmitry. *D. I. Pisarev. Sochineniia.* 5 vols. Saint Petersburg, 1866.

————. "Realisty." In *Polnoe sobranie sochineniy i pisem v dvenadtsati tomakh,* ed. E. F. Kuznetsov et al., 12 vols., 6:222–353. Moscow: Nauka, 2003.

————. "Thinking Proletariat." In *Dmitry Pisarev: Selected Philosophical, Social and Political Essays,* trans. R. Dixon, 624–674. Moscow: Foreign Languages Publishing House, 1958.

Plekhanov, Georgi. *Beiträge zur Geschichte des Materialismus.* Stuttgart, 1896.

————. *Selected Philosophical Works.* Trans. Julius Katzer. 5 vols. Moscow, 1976.

Polland, Annie. "'May a Freethinker Help a Pious Man?': The Shared World of the 'Religious' and the 'Secular' Among Eastern European Jewish Immigrants to America." *American Jewish History* 93, no. 4 (December 2007): 375–407.

Pomialovsky, N. G. *Seminary Sketches.* Trans. Alfred Kuhn. Ithaca: Cornell University Press, 1973.

Porter, Brian. "The Social Nation and Its Futures: English Liberalism and Polish Nationalism in Late Nineteenth-Century Warsaw." *American Historical Review* 101, no. 5 (December 1996): 1470–1492.

————. *When Nationalism Began to Hate: Imagining Modern Politics in Nineteenth-Century Poland.* Oxford: Oxford University Press, 2000.

Porter-Szűcs, Brian. *Faith and Fatherland: Catholicism and Modernity.* Oxford: Oxford University Press, 2011.

Quint, Alyssa. "'Yiddish Literature for the Masses'? A Reconsideration of Who Read What in Jewish Eastern Europe." *AJS Review* 29, no. 1 (2005): 61–89.

Rabinovitch, Simon. *Jews and Diaspora Nationalism: Writings on Jewish Peoplehood in Europe.* Waltham, Mass.: Brandeis University Press, 2012.

Rabinowitz, Tsvi Hirsch. "Ha'ivrim beyiḥusam laḥakirot beḥokhmat hateva'." *Hamelits,* January 24, May 2, 1871.

————. "Haskama." In Sossnitz, *Akhen yesh Hashem,* iv–v.

————. *Otsar haḥokhma vehamadda': sefer harkava vehafrada.* Vilna, 1876.

————. *Otsar haḥokhma vehamadda': yesodei ḥokhmat hateva', sefer even hasho'evet.* Vilna, 1876.

———. "Sblizhenie evreev s obshchim naseleniem." *Razsvet,* October 17, 1879.

———. "Vvedenie." In Eliezer Berman, *Osnovy Moiseeva zakona.* Saint Petersburg, 1874.

———."Vvedenie." In Eliezer Berman, *Osnovy Moiseeva zakona: Rukovodstvo k zakonoucheniiu dlia evreiskogo iunoshestva.* Saint Petersburg, 1881.

Raeff, Mark. *Origins of the Russian Intelligentsia: The Eighteenth-Century Nobility.* New York: Harcourt, Brace and World, 1966.

Rahden, Till van. "Germans of the Jewish *Stamm:* Visions of Community Between Nationalism and Particularism, 1850–1933." In *German History from the Margins,* ed. Neil Gregor, Nils Roemer, and Mark Roseman, 27–48. Bloomington: Indiana University Press, 2006.

Raisin, Jacob S. *The Haskalah Movement in Russia.* Philadelphia: Jewish Publication Society of America, 1913.

Rall, Yisra'el. "Hametaharim." *Hamaggid,* February 27, 1861.

Ravid, Benjamin. *Economics and Toleration in Seventeenth-Century Venice: The Background and Context of the 'Discorso' of Simone Luzzatto.* Jerusalem: American Academy of Jewish Research, 1978.

Rivkind, Isaac. *Yidishe gelt in lebnshteyger kultur-geshikhte un folklor: leksikologishe shtudye.* New York: American Academy for Jewish Research, 1959.

Rochelson, Meri-Jane. *A Jew in the Public Arena: The Career of Israel Zangwill.* Detroit: Wayne State University Press, 2008.

———. "'A Religion of Pots and Pans': Jewish Materialism and Spiritual Materiality in Israel Zangwill's *Children of the Ghetto.*" In *Victorian Vulgarity: Taste in Verbal and Visual Culture,* ed. Susan David Bernstein and Elsie B. Michie, 119–135. Burlington, Vt.: Ashgate, 2009.

Rodin [pseud.]. "Ot gruppy sotsialistov-evreev." In *Sobranie politicheskikh sochineniy Dragomanova,* ed. B. A. Kistiakovsky, 2 vols., 2:320–325. Paris, 1906.

Rogger, Hans. *Jewish Policies and Right Wing Politics in Imperial Russia.* Berkeley: University of California Press, 1986.

Rombach, Sh. "Di yidishe balmelokhes in Rusland in der ershter helft fun 19tn yorhundert." *Tsaytshrift* 1 (1926): 25–30.

Rothschild, S. Zalman. "The Role of Materiality in Early Hasidism: Divine Immanence, Religious Service with the Corporeal, and Law in the Theology of the Maggid of Mezritch and Shneur Zalman of Lyady." Ph.D. Diss. New York University, 2016.

Rubinow, Isaac Max. "Economic Conditions of the Jews in Russia." *United States Department of Commerce and Labor, Bulletin of the Bureau of Labor* 25 (1907): 487–583.

Ruderman, David. *Jewish Thought and Scientific Discovery in Early Modern Europe.* New Haven: Yale University Press, 1995.

Rudnysky, Ivan L. "Mykhailo Drahomanov and the Problem of Ukrainian-Jewish Relations." *Canadian Slavonic Papers* 11, no. 2 (Summer 1969): 182–198.

Rülf, Isaak. *Meine Reise nach Kowno um die Übersiedlung nothleidender Glaubensgenossen aus den Grenzbezirken nach dem Innern Russlands zu ordnen, sowie die in der dortigen Synagoge gehaltene Predigt.* Memel, 1869.

Safran, Gabriela. *Rewriting the Jew: Assimilation Narratives in the Russian Empire.* Stanford: Stanford University Press, 2001.

———. *Wandering Soul: The Dybbuk's Creator S. An-sky.* Cambridge: Harvard University Press, 2010.

Salanter, Israel. *'Ets pri.* New York, 1953.

Sapir, Boris. "Jewish Socialists Around *Vpered!*" *International Review of Social History* 10, no. 3 (1965): 365–384.

———. "Liberman et le Socialism Russe." *International Review of Social History* 3 (1938): 25–88.

Sarvarkar, V. D. *Hindutva.* Bombay: Veer Savarkar Prakashan, 1969.

———. *The Story of My Transportation for Life.* Trans. Majhi Janmathep. Bombay, 1984.

Scanlan, James. "Nicholas Chernyshevsky and Philosophical Materialism in Russia." *Journal of the History of Philosophy* 8, no. 1 (1970): 65–86.

Schleiden, M. *Über den Materialismus der neueren deutschen Materialismus, sein Wesen und seine Geschichte.* Leipzig, 1863.

Schutte, Anne Jacobson; Susan C. Karant-Nunn, and Heinz Schilling, eds. *Reformationsforschung in Europa und Nordamerika: Eine historiographische Bilanz anlässlich des 100. Bandes des Archivs für Reformationsgeschichte.* Gütersloh: Gütersloher Verlagshaus, 2009.

Schwartz, Daniel B. *The First Modern Jew: Spinoza and the History of an Image.* Princeton: Princeton University Press, 2012.

Scult, Mel. *Communings of the Spirit: The Journals of Mordecai M. Kaplan, 1913–1934.* Detroit: Wayne State University Press, 2001.

———. *Judaism Faces the Twentieth Century: A Biography of Mordecai Kaplan.* Detroit: Wayne State University Press, 1993.

Seidman, Naomi. *The Marriage Plot; or, How Jews Fell in Love with Love, and with Literature.* Stanford: Stanford University Press, 2016.

———. "Secularization and Sexuality: Theorizing the Erotic Transformation of Ashkenaz." Association for Jewish Studies. Available at http://www.ajsnet.org/seidman.pdf.

Seltzer, Robert. *Simon Dubnow's New Judaism: Diaspora Nationalism and the World History of the Jews.* Leiden: Brill, 2014.

"Shim'u va'anaḥnu nedaber." *Hamelits,* July 23, 1863.

Sharshevsky, Benjamin. *Shisha sidrei madda'.* Odessa, 1911.

Shatzkes, Moses Aaron. *Der yudisher far-peysekh.* 1881. Warsaw, 1896.

Shatzky, Jacob. "Kultur-geshikhte fun der haskole bay yidn in Lite." In Sudarsky, Katzenelenbogen, and Kissin, eds., *Lite,* 1:735–741.

———. "Referatn un retsenzyes." *YIVO Bleter* 23 (1944): 125–139.

Shavit, Jacob, and Jehuda Reinharz. *Darvin vekhama mibnei mino.* Tel Aviv: Hakibbutz Hame'uḥad, 2009.

———. *Ha'el hamadda'i.* Tel Aviv: Hakibbutz Hame'uḥad, 2011.

Shechter, Esther. *Di geshikhte fun mayn lebn.* Winnipeg: Dos Yidishe vort, 1951.

Sheinbaum, Eliezer Y. *Hatsiyonut vehamateryaliyut.* Vilna: 1906.

Shershevsky, Tsvi Hacohen. "Pesher davar." *Hatsefira,* October 10, 1877.

Shimoni, Gideon. *The Zionist Ideology.* Hanover, N.H.: Brandeis University Press, 1995.

Shlomo Hakohen Ish Galician [pseud.]. "Derekh emuna." *Halevanon,* December 26, 1879.

Shlonsky, Avraham. "Jezreel." *Bagalgal.* Tel Aviv, 1927, 23.

Shochat, Azriel. *Mosad harabbanut mita'am berusya.* Haifa: University of Haifa Press, 1976.

Shtern, Yekhiel. "Kheyder un besmedresh." *YIVO Bleter* 31 (1948): 60–81.

Shumsky, Dmitry. "Leon Pinsker and *Autoemancipation!* A Reevaluation." *Jewish Social Studies* 18, no. 1 (Fall 2011): 33–62.

Shur, Khasia. *Vospominaniia.* Kursk, 1928.

Silber, Michael. "Alliance of the Hebrews, 1863–1875: The Diaspora Roots of an Ultra-Orthodox Proto-Zionist Utopia in Palestine." *Journal of Israeli History: Politics, Society, Culture* 27, no. 2 (2008): 119–147.

Silberbusch, David Isaiah. *Mipinkas zikhronotai.* Tel Aviv, 1936.

Simchowitz, Salomon. *Der Positivismus in Mosaismus: erläutert und entwickelt auf Grund der alten und mittelalterlichen philosophischen Literatur der Hebräer.* Vienna, 1880.

Sinkoff, Nancy. *Out of the Shtetl: Making Jews Modern in the Polish Borderlands.* Providence, R.I.: Brown Judaic Studies, 2004.

Slezkine, Yuri. *The Jewish Century.* Princeton: Princeton University Press, 2004.

Slonimski, Ḥayyim Selig. "Atomei hagufim ve'ether ha'olam." *Hatsefira,* May 31, 1876.

———. *Metsi'ut hanefesh.* Warsaw, 1858.

Slonimsky, Nicolas. "My Grandfather Invented the Telegraph." *Commentary,* January 1, 1977, available at https://www.commentarymagazine.com/articles/my-grandfather-invented-the-telegraph/.

Slutsky, Yehuda. *Ha'itonut hayehudit-rusit bame'a hatesha' 'esreh.* Jerusalem: Mosad Bialik, 1970.

Smith, Anthony D. *Theories of Nationalism.* London: Holmes and Meier, 1983.

Smith, Jonathan Z. *Relating Religion: Essays in the Study of Religion.* Chicago: University of Chicago Press, 2004.

Smolenskin, Judah Leib. "Eleh toldot Perets." *Davar,* January 25, 1935.

Smolenskin, Peretz. "Hakesef vehakavod." In *Bikoret tihyeh,* ed. Smolenskin, 17–22. Odessa, 1867.

———. *Hato'eh bedarkhei hahayyim.* 4 vols. Vienna, 1878.

———. *Nekam berit.* Vienna, 1883. Translated by Steven Adams as *Peretz Smolenskin's "Nekam Berit" as a Response to the Russian Pogroms of 1881: A Translation and Literary-Critical Analysis of the Novel* (Cincinnati: Hebrew Union College Press, 1982).

———. *Perets ben Moshe Smolenskin: Ma'amarim.* 4 vols. Jerusalem: Hapo'alim, 1926.

———. "Teshuva." *Hashahar,* 1880.

Soffer, Oren. *Ein lefalpel! 'Iton "hatsefira" vehamodernizatsya shel hasiah hahevrati hapoliti.* Jerusalem: Mosad Bialik, 2007.

Sokolov, Nikolai Vasil'evich. *Otshchepentsy.* Zurich, 1866.

Sommerville, C. John. *Secularization of Early Modern England: From Religious Culture to Religious Faith.* Oxford: Oxford University Press, 1992.

Sorkin, David. "Between Messianism and Survival: Secularization and Sacralization in Modern Judaism." *Journal of Modern Jewish Studies* 3, no. 1 (2004): 73–86.

Sosis, Israel. *Di geshikhte fun di Yidishe gezelshaftlekhe shtremungen in Rusland in XIX yorhundert.* Minsk: Vaysrusisher melukhe-farlag, 1929.

———. "Natsional'nyi vopros v literature kontsa 60kh i nachala 70kh godov." *Evreiskaia starina* 7, no. 2 (1915): 324–337.

Sossnitz, Joseph Leib. *Akhen yesh Hashem.* Vilna, 1875.

———. "Hadat vehahaskala." *Hatsefira,* October 14, 21, and 28, 1879.

———. *Hama'or.* Warsaw, 1889.

———. "Temunat haga'on hehasid rav Menahem Mendel." In *Knesset Yisra'el,* ed. Saul P. Rabinowitz, 3 vols., 3:213–218. Warsaw, 1888.

Spiller, Philip. *Die Urkraft des Weltalls.* Berlin, 1876.

Staliūnas, Darius. *Making Russians: Meaning and Practice of Russification in Lithuania and Belarus After 1863.* New York: Rodopi, 2007.

Stampfer, Shaul. *Families, Rabbis and Education: Traditional Jewish Society in Nineteenth-Century Eastern Europe.* Oxford: Littman Library of Jewish Civilization, 2010.

———. *Lithuanian Yeshivas of the Nineteenth Century: Creating a Tradition of Learning.* Trans. Lindsey Taylor-Guthartz. Oxford: Littman Library of Jewish Civilization, 2012.

Stanislawski, Michael. *Autobiographical Jews: Essays in Jewish Self-Fashioning.* Seattle: University of Washington Press, 2004.

————. *For Whom Do I Toil? Judah Leib Gordon and The Crisis of Russian Jewry.* New York: Oxford University Press, 1988.

————. "Russian Jewry, the Russian State, and the Dynamics of Jewish Emancipation." In Birnbaum and Katznelson, eds., *Paths of Emancipation,* 262–284.

————. *Tsar Nicholas I and the Jews: The Transformation of Jewish Society in Russia, 1825–1855.* Philadelphia: Jewish Publication Society, 1983.

Stateri, Gianni. *Death of a Utopia: The Development and Decline of Student Movements in Europe.* Oxford: Oxford University Press, 1975.

Stedman Jones, Gareth. *Karl Marx: Greatness and Illusion.* Cambridge: Harvard University Press, 2016,

Steinberg, Yehoshua. "Kevod sefat kodesh." *Hamaggid,* January 11, 1860.

Stern, Eliyahu. "Catholic Judaism: The Political Theology of the Nineteenth-Century Russian Jewish Enlightenment." *Harvard Theological Review* 109, no. 4 (Winter 2016): 483–511.

————. "Marx and the Kabbalah: The First Translations of Marx into Hebrew." *Journal of the History of Ideas* Forthcoming.

————. "Paul in the Jerusalem of Lithuania: Samuel Joseph Fuenn's Paths of God." In *Talmudic Transgressions: Essays in Honor of Daniel Boyarin,* ed. Moulie Vidas, Ishay Rosen-Zvi, Aharon Shemesh, and Charlotte Fonrobert, 407–417. Leiden: Brill, 2017.

Stern, Joseph, *The Matter and the Form of Maimonides' Guide.* Cambridge: Harvard University Press, 2013.

Strakhov, Nikolia. *Istoriia materializma.* Saint Petersburg, 1881–1883.

Sudarsky, Mendel, Uriah Katzenelenbogen, and J. Kissin, eds. *Lite.* 2 vols. New York: Jewish Lithuanian Culture Society, 1951.

Sutcliffe, Adam. *Judaism and Enlightenment.* Cambridge: Cambridge University Press, 2003.

————. "Ludwig Börne, Jewish Messianism, and the Politics of Money," Leo Baeck Year Book 57 (2012): 213–237.

Swedberg, Richard. *Max Weber and the Idea of Economic Sociology.* Princeton: Princeton University Press, 2000.

Szporluk, Roman. *Communism and Nationalism: Karl Marx Versus Friedrich List.* New York: Oxford University Press, 1988.

————. Review of *Really Existing Nationalisms: A Post-Communist View from Marx and Engels,* by Erica Brenner. *American Journal of Sociology* 102, no. 4 (May, 1997): 1236–1238.

Tanner, Kathryn. "Postmodern Challenges to 'Tradition.'" *Louvain Studies* 28 (2003): 175–193.

Tartakoff, Paula. *Between Christian and Jew: Conversion and Inquisition in the Crown of Aragon, 1250–1391.* Philadelphia: University of Pennsylvania Press, 2012.

Tcherikower, Elias, ed. *Historishe shriftn.* 3 vols. Vilna: YIVO, 1939.

Tishby, Isaiah. *Torat hara' vehakelippa bekabbalat ha-Ari.* Jerusalem: Schocken, 1960.

Tiwari, Brij Gopal. *Secularism and Materialism in Modern India.* Jabalpur: Motilal Banarsidass, 1964.

Trunk, Isaiah. "Historians of Russian Jewry." In *Russian Jewry (1860–1917),* ed. Jacob Frumkin, Gregor Aronson, and Alexis Goldenweiser, 453–477. New York: Yoseloff, 1966.

Tsunzer, Elyokem. *A Jewish Bard: Being the Biography of Eliakum Zunser.* Trans. Simon Hirsdansky. New York, 1905.

Urbach, Ephraim E. *The Sages: Their Concepts and Beliefs.* Jerusalem: Magnes, 1975.

Uvarov, S. S. *O prepodovanii istorii otnositel'no k narodnomu vospitaniiu.* Saint Petersburg, 1813.

Veer, Peter van der. "Hindus: A Superior Race." *Nations and Nationalism* 5, no. 3 (1999): 419–430.

———. *Religious Nationalism: Hindus and Muslims in India.* Berkeley: University of California Press, 1994.

Veer, Peter van der, and Hartmut Lehmann, eds. *Nation and Religion: Perspectives on Europe and Asia.* Princeton: Princeton University Press, 1999.

Veidlinger, Jeffrey. *Jewish Public Culture in the Late Russian Empire.* Bloomington: Indiana University Press, 2009.

Veltri, Giuseppe. *Renaissance Philosophy in Jewish Garb: Foundations and Challenges of Judaism on the Eve of Modernity.* Leiden: Brill, 2009.

Venturi, Franco. *Roots of Revolution: A History of the Populist and Socialist Movements in Nineteenth Century Russia.* Trans. Francis Haskell. New York: Knopf, 1964.

Vogt, Carl. *Lectures on Man: His Place in Creation and the History of the Earth.* Ed. James Hunt. London, 1864.

Volkov, Shulamit. "Jewish Scientists in Imperial Germany (Parts I and II)." *Aleph* 1 (2001): 215–281.

Vucinich, Alexander. *Darwin in Russian Thought.* Berkeley: University of California Press, 1988.

———. *Science in Russian Culture, 1861–1917.* Stanford: Stanford University Press, 1970.

Walicki, Andrzej. *A History of Russian Thought from the Enlightenment to Marxism.* Stanford: Stanford University Press, 1979.

———. *Philosophy and Romantic Nationalism: The Case of Poland.* Oxford: Oxford University Press, 1982.

Wallet, Bart. "Napoleon's Legacy—National Government and Jewish Community in Western Europe." *Simon Dubnow Institute Yearbook* 6 (2007): 291–309.

Watson, Hugh Seaton. *The Russian Empire, 1801–1917.* Oxford: Oxford University Press, 1988.

Weber, J. B., and W. Kempster. *A Report of the Commissioners of Immigration upon the Causes Which Incite Immigration to the United States.* Washington, D.C., 1892.

Weber, Max. *The Protestant Ethic and the Spirit of Capitalism.* Trans. Talcott Parsons. New York: Dover, 2003.

Weeks, Theodore R. "Religion and Russification, Russian Language in the Catholic Churches of the Northwest Provinces After 1863." *Kritika* 2, no. 1 (2001): 87–110.

———. "Russification and the Lithuanians, 1863–1905." *Slavic Review* 60, no. 1 (2001): 96–114.

Weikart, Richard. "The Impact of Social Darwinism on Anti-Semitic Ideology in Germany and Austria, 1860–1945." In Cantor and Swetlitz, eds., *Jewish Tradition and the Challenge of Darwinism,* 93–116.

Weinreich, Max. *Fun beyde zaytn ployt: dos shturemdike lebn fun Uri Kovnern, dem nihilist.* Buenos Aires: Tsentral-farband fun Poylishe Yidn in Argentine, 1955.

———. "Di M. L. Lilienblum oysshtelung in YIVO." *YIVO Bleter* 23 (1944): 407–415.

———. "Naye faktn vegn ershtn revolutsyonern kruzshok in Vilne." *Forverts,* May 27, 1928.

Weinryb, Bernard D. *Bereshit hasotsyalism hayehudi.* Jerusalem: Reuven Mas, 1940.

———. "Latoldot hakalkaliyot vehaḥevratiyot etsel hayehudim bame'a hatesha' 'esreh." *Tarbiz* 7 (1936): 57–73.

———. "Toldot Ribal." *Tarbiz* 5, no. 2 (1934): 199–207.

Weir, Todd H. *Secularism and Religion in Nineteenth-Century Germany: The Rise of the Fourth Confession.* Cambridge: Cambridge University Press, 2015.

Weizmann, Chaim. "Yedi'otav harishonot bekhimya misofer 'ivri." *Haboker,* November 17, 1952.

Wengeroff, Pauline. *Memoirs of a Grandmother: Scenes of the Cultural History oft he Jews of Russia in the Nineteenth Century.* Trans. Shulamit S. Magnus. 2 vols. Stanford: Stanford University Press, 2015.

Wessel, Martin Schulze, ed. *Nationalisierung der Religion und Sakralisierung der Nation im östlichen Europa.* Stuttgart: Franz Steiner Verlag, 2006.

Widover, C. G. Halevi. "Hayehudim uleshon eiropa." *Hamaggid,* March 9, May 11, 1859.

Wieseltier, Leon. "Jewish Bodies, Jewish Minds." *Jewish Quarterly Review* 95, no. 3 (Summer 2005): 435–442.

Winchevsky, Morris. "'Al ha'avanim." *Hakol,* March 26, April 20, and May 4, 1879.

———. *Gezamlte verk.* Ed. Kalman Marmor. 10 vols. New York: Frayhayt, 1927.

———. "Lilienblum veyaḥaso lasotsyaliyut." *Lu'aḥ aḥi'ezer* 2 (1921): 292–300.

———. "Mit a dor tsurik." *Di tsukunft* 3, no. 11 (December 1894): 1–6.

Winter, Eduard. *Russland und das Papsttum.* 2 vols. Berlin: Akadmie-Verlag, 1961.

Wischnitzer, Mark. "Yidishe melokha un bal melokha tzekhn in Lite." In Sudarsky, Katzenelenbogen, and Kissin, eds., *Lite,* 1:982–986.

Wise, Isaac. *The Cosmic God.* Cincinnati, 1876.

Wittaker, Cynthia H. "The Ideology of Sergei Uvarov: An Interpretive Essay." *Russian Review* 37, no. 2 (1978): 158–176.

———. *The Origins of Modern Russian Education: An Intellectual Biography of Count Sergei Uvarov, 1786–1855.* Dekalb: Northern Illinois University Press, 1984.

Woehrlin, William F. *Chernyshevskii: The Man and the Journalist.* Cambridge: Harvard University Press, 1971.

Wolfson, Elliot R. "Achronic Time, Messianic Expectation, and the Secret of the Leap in Ḥabad." In *Habad Hasidism: History, Theology and Image,* ed. Jonatan Meir and Gadi Sagiv. Jerusalem: Merkaz Zalman Shazar, 2016.

———. *Open Secret: Postmessianic Messianism and the Mystical Revision of Menahem Mendel Schneerson.* New York: Columbia University Press, 2009.

Yacobson, Yoram. "Bimvokhei ha'en vehayesh." *Kiryat sefer* 68 (1998): 229–243.

Yakhinson, Yisroel. *Sotsyal-ekonomisher shteyger bay yidn in rusland in XIX yor hundert.* Kharkov: Tsentraler farlag far di felker fun F.S.S.R., 1929.

Zagorodski, Yisra'el Ḥayyim. "Tsvi Hirsh Rabinovits." *Ha'asif* 3 (1887): 440–447.

Zalkin, Mordechai. "Al taḥdelu bo beineinu." *Kesher* 35 (Winter 2007): 63–69.

———. "Can Jews Become Farmers? Rurality, Peasantry and Cultural Identity in the World of the Rural Jew in Nineteenth-Century Eastern Europe." *Rural History* 24, no. 2 (2013): 161–175.

———. "Economic and Occupational Aspects in the World of the East European Jewish Enlightenment in Russia in the First Half of the Nineteenth Century." In *Enlightenment and Diaspora: The Armenian and Jewish Cases,* ed. Richard G. Hovannisian and David N. Myers, 223–228. Atlanta, Ga.: Scholars, 1999.

———. "'Ir shel torah." In *Yeshivot uvatei midrash,* ed. Immanuel Etkes, 131–160. Jerusalem: Merkaz Zalman Shazar, 2006.

———. "Scientific Thinking and Cultural Transformation in Nineteenth-Century East European Jewish Society." *Aleph* 5, no. 1 (2005): 249–271.

———. "Ve'eleh yimaletu—heḥarash vehamasger." In *Yazamut yehudit ba'et haḥadasha,* ed. Ran Aaronsohn and Shaul Stampfer, 67–95. Jerusalem: Hebrew University Press, Magnes, 2000.

Zederbaum, Alexander. "Besora motset." *Hamelits,* August 17, 1865.

———. "Fanatizmus, Nihilismus." *Kol mevaser,* May 6, 1870.

———. "Ha'otiyot le'aḥor." *Hamelits,* January 15, 1863.

———. "Safa lene'emanim." *Hamelits,* November 8, 1860.

Zelizer, Viviana A. *Pricing the Priceless Child: The Changing Social Value of Children.* New York: Basic, 1981.

Zimmerman, Joshua D. *Poles and Jews: The Politics of Nationality.* Madison: University of Wisconsin Press, 2004.

Zinberg, Israel. "A. Kovner." *Perezhitoe* 2 (1910): 130–159.

———. *The Haskalah Movement in Russia.* Trans. Bernard Martin. New York: Hebrew Union College and Ktav Press, 1978.

Zipperstein, Steven J. *Imagining Russian Jewry: Memory, History, Identity.* Seattle: University of Washington Press, 1999.

———. *The Jews of Odessa: A Cultural History, 1794–1881.* Stanford: Stanford University Press, 1986.

———. Review of *The Jewish Century,* by Yuri Slezkine. *American Historical Review* 112, no. 2 (2007): 463–465.

Zitron, Samuel Leib. *Dray literarishe doyres.* 3 vols. Vilna: Sh. Shreberk, 1921.

———. "Lilienblum." *Hatsefira,* June 19, 1919.

———. "Lilienblum vehasotsyaliyut hamarksit." *Hatsefira,* June 12, 1919.

———. *Shtadlonim: interesante Yidishe tipn fun noentn over.* Warsaw: Akhisefer, 1926.

Zlocisti, Theodor. *Moses Hess, Jüdische Schriften.* Berlin: von Lious Lamm, 1905.

Zuckermann, Eliezer. *Kitvei Eli'ezer Tsukerman.* Ed. Tsvi Krol. Tel Aviv, 1940.

Zweifel, Eliezer. *Minim ve'ugav.* Vilna, 1858.

———. *Sanegor.* Warsaw, 1885.

———. *Shalom 'al yisra'el.* 3 vols. Jerusalem: Mosad Bialik, 1972.

Index

Abramowich, Shalom Jacob, 27, 136, 152;
    Fathers and Sons, 152
absolutism, "enlightened," 34
acosmism, 96, 101, 105
Adelman, Moritz (Mordecai), 158, 171
African Americans, 161
agriculture, 33–36, 39, 43, 49, 51–54, 62,
    72, 171; agrarian economy, 51
Alexander I, Tsar, 34, 50, 135
Alexander II, Tsar, 59, 91, 124, 153
Alliance Israélite Universelle, 157
American Jewish Committee, 188
Amsterdam, 107
Anderson, Benedict, 7, 148, 163
anthropology, 7, 12, 17, 116
anti-Semitism: American Jewish combat-
    ing of, 189, 190; Christian theologi-
    cal, 182; conspiracy theories, 182; as
    disease, 184; economic, 39; German,
    8, 169; and Jewish mercantilism, 52;
    and Jewish wealth, 62; in legisla-
    tion, 162; liberal responses to, 183;
    motivating pogroms, 1; Pinsker

accused of fueling, 185; in sermons
    and theater, 3
Aquinas, Saint Thomas, 126
Arendt, Hannah, 9
aristocracy: "ghetto," 28; Jewish, 127, 132;
    Polish, 32, 50; Talmudic, 139
Aristotle, 81
Aronsohn, Moses, 123
art movement, Jewish, 113
asceticism, 74, 126, 129
atheism, 17, 18, 88, 96, 153, 185, 189
atomism, 13, 93
Axelrod, Nadezhda, 119
Axelrod, Pavel (Pinchas), 27, 28, 118–120,
    125, 140, 167, 168

Bakunin, Mikhail, 139, 140
Baron, Salo W., 60, 146
Bazilevsky, Moses, 88
Bebel, August, 19
beit midrash (study hall), 121, 135, 174
Belarus: 27; Grodno, 61, 156; Minsk, 22;
    Mogilev, 28, 60, 62, 118–121, 139,

Belarus (*continued*)
140, 153; Shklov, 167; within Pale of
Settlement, 33
Ben-Gurion, David, 22, 186
Ben Israel, Menashe, 53
Ben-Yehuda, Eliezer, 27, 170–177; in
Zionist dispute, 149
Ben Zvi, Yitzhak, 22, 186
Berlin: commune of Jewish materialists
in, 29; education of Jewish young,
35; Great Powers conference (1878),
183; Jewish "doctors," 36; Jewish
religious norms, 35; police, 120–122;
printing of materialist works in,
157; Russian Jewish materialists flee
to, 119, 120; Talmud study in, 40;
universities, 29
Berlin, Naftali Tsvi, 88
Bernstein, Aaron, 92, 101
Bernstein, Eduard, 121, 123
Bible: and agriculture, 51, 52; and
Darwin, 5; ethics of, 9; Jewish *Geist*,
163; Luther's translation of, 89; and
Marx, 23, 117, 145; materialist ideas
in, 6, 21; Messiah in, 15; on Oral
Law, 44; as propaganda, 24; respect
for kings in, 136; socialism in, 24;
trade laws in, 51; women in, 165
Borochov, Ber, 186
Borsky, Shayndle, 165
Bossuet, Jacques-Bénigne, 46–49
Brainin, Simon, 113
Brenner, Yosef Haim, 159
Brog, Georg, 153
Bucharest, 157
Buchholz, Carl August, 50
Büchner, Ludwig: criticism of, 13, 90, 91,
100, 102, 111; *Darwin's Theory of the
Origin and Development of the Living
World* (*Die Darwin'sche Theorie von
der Entstehung und Umwandlung
der Lebewelt*), 95; disciples, 90; on
eternality of matter, 151; *Force and
Matter* (*Kraft und Stoff*), 87; "Heat

and Life" (Wärme und Leben), 64;
heretical ideas, 89, 111; ideas touted
by dissidents, 90; *Physiological
Portraits* (*Physiologische Bilder*), 64;
on science, 13, 87–90, 95; superseded
by Marx, 115
Bulgaria, 170, 171
Bundists: hermeneutics, 22; historiography, 21, 186; on Jewish materialism, 21, 24; on Marx, 22, 116, 118,
130; and *What Is to Be Done?* 70;
Winchevsky as leader of, 28, 138

Cahen, Isidore, 9
Calvin, John, 127
Capital (*Das Kapital,* Marx), 22, 23, 115,
117, 118, 125, 126, 156
capitalism: and acts of "mercy," 134; as
foreign influence on Judaism, 127;
influence of materialism on, 4; and
Kabbalah, 128; Levin on, 154; Marx
on Judaism and, 15, 115; negative
impact on Jews, 161; relation to
feudalism, 126, 127; relation to Protestantism, 127; in western Europe
and United States, 130
Catholicism: church fathers, 47; confessional polities, 7; influence on human intellect, 127; marginalization
of, 18; nonmaterial understanding
of religion, 8; Polish and eastern
European, 16; Russian discrimination against, 10
Ceba, Ansaldo, 165
censorship, 43, 88, 157, 160, 173
Cevdet, Abdullah, 17
Chaikovsky Circle, 116, 118
charity, 10, 66, 174
Chernyshevsky, Nikolai: *The Contemporary* (*Sovremennik*), 152; influence on
Jewish intellectuals, 21; influence on
Lilienblum, 58, 79, 81–85; superseded by Marx, 115; *What Is to Be
Done?* (*Chto delat'?*), 29, 69, 121

Christian Democratic Party, 16
Christianity: Anglican Church, 43;
    differentiated from Judaism, 48,
    185; how transformed by materialist
    theories, 26; as influence on liberal
    Judaism, 127; Jewish converts to,
    8; material resources of, 7; McCaul
    on relationship of Judaism and, 43;
    medieval, 125; Orshanski's refusal
    to convert to, 60, 63; Orthodox, 35,
    36, 46–48, 54; proselytizing of Jews,
    34; slavery allowed by, 50; Sullam's
    refusal to convert to, 165; theology
    of spirit in, 7
Chto delat? (*What Is to Be Done?*,
    Chernyshevsky), 29, 69, 121
civil rights, 9, 183
Cohen, Hermann, 13, 14
Columbus Platform of 1937 (Reform
    Judaism), 189
Committee for Defining Measures for
    the Radical Transformation of the
    Jews of Russia, 39
communism, 58, 121, 130, 142, 182, 185;
    influence of materialism on, 4
Communist International, 130
Communist Manifesto (*Manifest der
    Kommunistischen Partei,* Marx), 22,
    23, 117, 124, 130
Communist Party, 116
Community (*Hromada,* newspaper),
    144
consciousness: du Bois-Reymond's
    theory of, 100; God's relation to,
    129; Marx's theories of, 16, 129;
    materialist, 26; social Zionism as
    new form of, 22; as transformer of
    material world, 177; as unbounded,
    102; as unknowable, 13, 14, 100
conservation of energy, 6
conservatism, 28, 90; Jewish religious,
    41, 74, 111, 134; of Russian censor-
    ship, 157; of P. Smolenskin's critics,
    158–159

conspiracy theories, 182, 184
consumption, 19, 57, 62, 70
conversion: from Judaism, 63, 158; to
    Judaism, 191
corporations, 8–10, 30, 32, 33, 35, 50, 191
cosmopolitanism, 5, 110, 113
Cossacks, 1, 179
Cramer, Johann Andreas, 47
Creation: foundational ether preceded,
    92; as God's plan to eliminate evil,
    128; Ḥabad views on, 98, 99; scien-
    tific materialists' theories on, 93–95;
    of the universe, 128; use of outside
    forces to explain, 103
Crémieux, Adolphe, 92

Daniel Deronda (George Eliot), 171
Darwin, Charles: on the Creator, 95;
    Dub on, 95; Feigenbaum on, 24;
    Hebrew translation of, 154; Hess on,
    15; and Judaism, 95; Kaplan's ad-
    vocacy of, 113; and Marx in eastern
    Europe, 27; monogenetic theory of
    human evolution, 108, 109; *On the
    Origin of Species,* 5, 95; Rabinowitz
    on, 93; Savarkar on, 17; Sossnitz on,
    95, 96, 104; survival of the fittest, 17;
    Vogt's criticism of, 109
dat ḥomrit (materialistic religion), 106
Dawn (*Hashaḥar,* journal), 147, 149, 153,
    156, 158–160, 171
Day (*Den',* Jewish weekly), 60, 62, 63, 65
Delianov, Ivan, 89
democratic movement, Hasidism as, 139
Democritus, 13, 93
demography, 8, 18, 172
Den' (*Day,* Jewish weekly), 60, 62, 63, 65
depression and suicide among young
    materialists, 29, 121
Deutsch, Lev, 116, 140, 145
Deutsch-Französische Jahrbücher (*Ger-
    man-French Annual,* journal), 117
diaspora, 4, 169, 174
dillug (leap), 98–102, 104, 105

discrimination: basis for Jews' involvement in finance, 50; of gender in revolutionary movement, 121; in Jewish professions, 161; against Jews, economic conditions as cause of, 160; as justification for Jewish state, 178; materialism as concession to, 6; in rabbinic Judaism, 51; by Russian Empire, 10; as source of Jews' economic woes, 62; against women, 79

divorce, 70

Dragomanov, Mykhailo, 144, 145

Dub, Julius, 95

du Bois-Reymond, Emil, 99, 100, 102, 103

education: *Bildung,* 72, 90; Bossuet's theories on religious, 49; elementary (see *kheyder*); of German Jews, 35; government-backed, 87, 89; Jewish women's, 77–78, 165; Kovner on Jewish institutions, 62; of masses as precondition for revolution, 139; Russian, 48; Russian minister of, 89; Russian reform of Jewish, 40, 42; self-education, promoted by Chaikovsky Circle, 118; as solution to Jews' problems, 154, 161

Elijah ben Solomon (Gaon of Vilna), 166, 167

Eliot, George, 171

empirical knowledge, 83, 97, 105

empirical methods, 56, 57, 60, 93, 99, 151

emuna (faith), 48

Engels, Friedrich, 14, 15, 24, 60

England, 6, 145

"enlightened rationalism," 36

enlighteners. See *maskilim*

Enlightenment, 107; French, 47; Jewish, 26, 29, 43, 68, 116, 168. *See also* Haskalah

Epicurus, 93

Epstein, Anna, 118

equality: economic, 19, 69, 79, 145, 149, 161, 189; gender, 70, 121, 165, 167; Marx on, 146

Eretz Israel, 174–179, 186, 191. *See also* Palestine

etherism, 93, 94, 102

ethical literature. See *musar*

ethics, 9, 11, 108, 113, 164, 168, 174, 187

ethnic minorities, 3, 4

Etkin, Yitshak Isaac, 27, 102, 103; *Theory of Life and Its Forms (Torat haḥayyim veḥezyonoteihem),* 102

evil, 81, 108, 125, 126, 128, 129, 136

evolution: causal theory of, 99; Darwin's theory of, 109; divine spirit within the process of, 96; human, 108, 109; of knowledge, 91

Fathers and Sons (Ottsy i dety) (Turgenev), 68

Feigenbaum, Benjamin, 24–26

feminism, 80

feudalism, 36, 49–51, 125–127; imperial, 49; and Kabbalah, 128; and scholasticism, 125

Feuerbach, Ludwig, 69, 88

First Fruits (Minḥat bikkurim, newspaper), 38

Florovsky, Georgy, 48

Foner, Sara, 63

forced conscription, 35

Forward! (Vpered!, journal), 123, 132

foundational ether, 92–95

Fourier, Charles, 24, 69

Frankel, Jonathan, 26

Free Religious Movement, 90

free speech, 136

Friedländer, David, 40, 41

Fuenn, Samuel Joseph, 35, 36, 43–58, 68, 80, 81, 83, 88

Fundamentals of the Law of Moses (Osnovy Moiseeva zakona, Russian-sponsored government publication), 107

Galileo, 88
Gans, Eduard, 190
Gaon of Vilna. *See* Elijah ben Solomon
Garden Land (*Hakarmel,* newspaper), 136
Gazelle (*Hatsvi,* newspaper), 171
Geist, Jewish, 144, 149, 153, 163–169, 171, 173–179
genetics, 191
Geneva Congress, 145
German-French Annual (*Deutsch-Französische Jahrbücher,* journal), 117
German Social Democratic Party, 22, 29, 121
Germany, 6, 8–10, 113, 131, 142, 144, 152
Geschichte des Materialismus (*History of Materialism,* Lange), 12
Ginsberg, Asher. *See* Ha'am, Ahad
Gintsburg family, 112, 132
Gnosticism, 128
God: conceptions of, 7; enemy of, 111; existence/absence of, 86, 95, 105; fear of king equivalent to fear of, 136; impersonal, 105; as "Natural Selector," 96; in nature, 96; political criticism tantamount to denial of, 136; rulers as messengers of, 127, 135; secularization of, 86; as unifying principle, 107
Goethe, Johann Wolfgang von, 58
Gordon, Judah Leib, 71, 131, 171, 183
government: discrimination against Jews of, 50; investigation of revolutionaries by, 121; investment opportunities to Jews provided by, 50; pricing of commodities by, 154; western European, 8
Great Reforms (Alexander II), 59
Guenzburg, Mordecai Aaron, 76
guilds, 30, 33, 36, 53, 54, 59, 60
Gumplowicz, Ludwig, 181
Gurevich, Grigory, 27, 29, 120, 122, 139, 157, 158
gymnasiums, 28, 78, 91, 101, 114

Ha'am, Ahad, 173, 186
Ḥabad, 96–101, 125, 186; theology, 98
Hacohen, Mordecai ben-Hillel, 27, 153, 162
Hadassah (organization), 165
Haeckel, Ernst, 17, 102, 104, 111
Ha'emet (*The Truth,* newspaper), 144, 149, 157–162, 171
Ḥagiz, Moses, 105
Haifa, 22
Hakarmel (*The Garden Land,* newspaper), 136
Halbgebildete, 30, 90, 91
Halevanon (*The Lebanon,* newspaper), 111
ḥalukka (religious charity), 174
ḥalutsim (pioneers), 186
Hamburg, 35, 50
Hashaḥar (*The Dawn,* journal), 147, 149, 153, 156, 158–160, 171
Hasidim: competition with Mitnagdim, 63; as critics of scientific materialism, 102; divide between *maskilim* and, 68; interpretation of Talmud by, 41; opposition to Enlightenment, 54; as potential revolutionaries, 138, 140; rebbes, 33; Sossnitz as exemplar of, 89, 97, 101; as sympathetic to Jewish masses, 138
Hasidism: competition with Mitnagdism, 64; as democratic movement, 138; economic/social influence, 74; leaders mocked by P. Smolenskin, 147; materialism and *avodah bagashmiyut,* 100; materialist ideas in, 6; predisposed to socialism, 4; seeds of socialist revolution in, 138; theology, 96; worldview vs. materialism, 86
Haskalah, 26, 80. See also *maskilim*
Hato'eh bedarkhei haḥayyim (*The Wanderer in the Paths of Life,* P. Smolenskin), 160
Hatsefira (*The Morning,* newspaper), 98
Hatsvi (*The Gazelle,* newspaper), 171
Hayes, Carlton, 12

Hebrew Educational Alliance, 113

Hebrew language: as culture, 172; as end in itself, 176; Levin on, 137; modern, 149; as national language, 148, 170; newspapers, 30, 43, 98, 102, 141, 147, 153, 171; opposition to, 137; prohibitions of, 141; propaganda, 136; scientific materialists' knowledge of, 89; scientific works in, 150; as spoken language, 171, 173; translations to, 58, 64, 125, 126, 136, 154, 155, 158

Hebrew literature: J. Klausner's work on history of, 21; of Lilienblum, 68; of Sossnitz, 88

Hebrew University of Jerusalem, 21

Helfman, Henne (Hessia), 27, 28, 153

Herzl, Theodore, 172, 181; proposal for Jewish state in Uganda, 172

Hess, Moses, 15, 89, 178

Hinduism, 17, 18; civilization, 17, 18; national movements, 17; values, 18

Hindutva, 17

historiography: Marxist, 24; modern Jewish, 20–27, 179, 186; political, 26; Zionist, 22, 148, 184

History of Materialism (Geschichte des Materialismus, Lange), 12

Hobsbawm, Eric, 163

Hoffman, Nehemiah Dov, 113

Holocaust, 9, 189, 190; gas chambers, 182

holy men. See tsadikim

homosexuality, 29, 65, 158

Hovevei Tsiyon (Lovers of Zion; movement), 21

Hromada (Community, newspaper), 144

Humboldt, Alexander von, 94

idealism: anti-idealism as a form of, 177; of Ben-Yehuda and P. Smolenskin, 175–177; vs. economics, 186; fostered by the yeshiva, 167, 168; Jewish bias toward, 11; of Jewish national-

ism, 171; Judaism as religious, 151; Kovner's attack on Jewish, 64; vs. materialism, 13, 14, 96; philosophical, 3; renounced by Lilienblum, 176; of L. Smolenskin, 165; Torah as system of, 168, 169; Zionism and, 169–181; Zionist, 24, 186

Idelsohn, Rosalya, 118, 141

imperialism, 18; anti-imperialism, 59

India, 17

industrialization, 4, 59, 60, 72, 126

intelligentsia, 132, 145; Hebrew as language of, 137; Jewish, 26, 132, 136–138, 152; Lavrov's theories of, 132, 140; liberal Russian, 71; rabbinic, 63, 136; revolutionary, 135; Russian, 85; students as, 135, 139–140

intermarriage, 167, 189, 191

Islam, 10, 16–18, 20, 40, 44

Israel, State of, 112, 189, 191; president of, 22, 112; prime minister of, 22

Israelitische Annalen (Jewish Yearbook, newspaper), 45

Italy, 128, 145, 164, 178

Jerusalem, 174

Jesus of Nazareth, 182

Jewish law, 4, 86, 164, 167; Oral Law, 44–48, 53; Written Law, 44

"Jewish Protestants," 127

"Jewish Question," 15, 39, 79, 117, 161–163, 170, 181

Jewish Section of the Revolutionary International League, 120, 123

Jewish socialist union, 28; London, 123

Jewish Yearbook (Israelitische Annalen, newspaper), 45

Jochelsohn, Benjamin, 116

Judah Loew ben Bezalel (Maharal of Prague), 105

justice: injustice, 128, 134; for the oppressed, 161; for the poor, 171; social, 190

Kabbalah, 5, 28, 105, 106, 117, 123, 128, 145; importance of science in, 105, 106; nature of God in, 106; *sephirot*, 129; as speculative knowledge, 106; teaching of, as Jewish profession, 74

Kabbalists, 99, 106, 125, 142

Kahan, Arcadius, 60

Kamensky, Moses, 75, 158

Kaminer, Isaac, 5, 15, 27, 118, 159, 160

Kant, Immanuel, 13, 93

Kantor, Judah Leib, 27, 29, 153

Kapital (*Capital*, Marx), 22, 23, 115, 117, 118, 125, 126, 156

Kaplan, Mordecai, 97, 107, 113, 116, 186–190

Katsenelenbogen, Abraham Simha, on Jewish life in Vilna, 38

Kautsky, Karl, 22, 23

Kemal, Mustafa, 17

kheyder (elementary schools), 28, 40, 63

Kiev: cell members' escape to, 119; Jewish students' understanding of Marx, 125; Kiev University, 66, 91; pogrom in (1872), 11; tanneries, 61

Kiselev, Count Pavel Dimitrievitch, 39, 40, 42, 51

Klausner, Fannie, 23

Klausner, Joseph, 21–23

Kol mevaser (*Voice of the Herald*, newspaper), 68, 152

Kook, Abraham Isaac, 116

Kovner, Abraham Uri, 27–29, 57, 58, 62–68, 74, 81, 152, 159; *Analyzing the Issue* (*Heker davar*), 63

Kovno, 56, 62, 101, 112, 159

Kraft und Stoff (*Force and Matter*, Büchner), 87

Krochmal, Nachman, 45, 168

labor: as commodity, 15, 156; deemed non-Jewish, 77; as first principle, 5; in Hinduism, 18; Jewish lack of knowledge needed for, 37; Jewish materialism based on, 16; manual, 29, 83; by married women, 11; necessary for Redemption, 175; relations, 15, 67, 126, 141; strikes, 132; vs. study, 12, 34, 42, 55; unions, 190; yeshiva students unfit for, 65

Laborers of Zion. *See* Po'alei Tsiyon

Landau, Isaac Elijah, 135, 136

Landauer, Gustav, 6

Lange, Friedrich Albert, 12–14, 100

Laplace, Pierre-Simon, 93

Lassalle, Ferdinand, 22

Lavrov, Peter, 123, 124, 132, 139–143, 152, 170

Law of Nations, 187

leap. See *dillug*

Lebanon (*Halevanon*, newspaper), 111

Lenin, Vladimir, 70

Levin, Judah Leib, 137–140, 154–159; emphasis on Jewish bodies, 11; as Hebrew translator of Marx, 125; indictment of Lieberman, 137; as interpreter of Marx, 15; on "Jewish Question," 161; on Jewish underpinnings of materialism, 5; Jewish upbringing and education of, 125; methodology for studying Marx, 117; "propaganda strategy" of, 145; rejection of *Stamm*, 131; as student of Kabbalah, 28

Levinsohn, Isaac Baer, 35, 36, 41–58, 68, 71, 81, 83

Liakhotsky, Antin, 144

liberalism, 16, 61, 113, 180, 183

Lieberman, Aaron Shemuel, 117–121, 123–145, 147–149, 156–163; Adelman as assistant to, 171; behavior toward wife, 165; criticized for focusing on the material, 190; ideas as basis for cultural nationalism, 177; influence on Lilienblum, 152; as interpreter of Marx, 15; and Jewish *Geist*, 168; on Jewish underpinnings of material-

Lieberman, Aaron Shemuel (*continued*) ism, 5; Jews defined by history of oppression, 178; on labor as first principle, 5; rejection of *Stamm,* 131; as student of Kabbalah, 28; theory of "crisis of fork and knife," 186

Lifshitz, Yehoshua Mordecai, 136, 137

Lifshutz, Ya'akov Halevi, 112, 159

Lifshutz, Yehuda Halevi, 112

Lilienblum, Moses Leib, 57–59, 67–72, 74–84, 152–153, 175–177; behavior toward wife, 165; castigation of Kovner, 29; criticized, 190; and cultural nationalism, 177; denied entry to Russian universities, 114, 115; on economic gender roles, 165; Jewish "material perspective," 5, 6; Jews defined by history of oppression, 178; rejection of *Stamm,* 131; as social materialist, 13

Lithuania: Grand Duchy of, 27; Jewish materialists' origins in, 27; labor strikes in, 132; Lieberman's charter to, 143

Lovers of Zion. *See* Ḥovevei Tsiyon

Lubavitch (movement). *See* Ḥabad

Lubavitch (town), 96

luftmenschen, 71

Luria, Isaac, 128

Luria, Shlomo Zalman, 27

Luther, Martin, 89

Luzzatto, Moses Hayyim, *138 Gates of Wisdom,* 128

Maharal of Prague. *See* Judah Loew ben Bezalel

Maimonides, 81, 107, 112, 126, 190

manufacturing, 33, 50, 60, 62, 71, 72, 123, 126

Mao Zedong, 19

maritime activities, 52, 53

marriage, 11, 13, 29, 66, 74–79, 118, 121, 180

Marx, Karl, 22–25, 115–118, 124–126, 129–131, 140–145, 154–156; *Capital (Das Kapital),* 22, 23, 115, 117, 118, 125, 126, 156; capitalist mode of production, 126; *The Communist Manifesto (Manifest der Kommunistischen Partei),* 22, 23, 117, 124, 130; "The Jewish Question" (Zur Judenfrage), 15; vs. Lilienblum on "nature," 83; materialism as defined by, 14–16; never read by P. Smolenskin, 149; reception of in eastern Europe, 27; theory of the commodity form, 125, 155

Marxism, 115–142, 158; Feigenbaum on, 24; Jewish nationalism as side effect of, 146; Judaism reformulated in terms of, 146; and Kabbalah according to Jewish materialists, 5; Levin and, 154

Masie, Aaron Meir, 27, 29

maskilim: adoration of Gaon of Vilna, 167; approach of Lilienblum vs., 71, 72; and Bossuet's theories, 49; connection to Russian government, 37, 41; denunciation of P. Smolenskin, 159; divide between Hasidim and, 68; on early marriage, 76; emancipatory politics of, 81; employed by Nicholas I, 35; German, 40; on Jewish professions, 37; and materialism, 55; proposal to government, 41; rejected by Lieberman, 132, 134; rejected by P. Smolenskin, 174; on Russian religious reform, 36, 38, 53, 54; Russian vs. German, 41; on Talmud, 41, 45, 49; theory of tradition, 45; on tolerance, 79

materialism, 3; biological, 9, 69; Catholic, 18, 20; Christian, 6; dialectical, 14; economic, 9, 187; Hindu, 16–20; historical, 14, 21, 116, 154, 156, 187; historicization of, 12–20; Islamic, 16–20; Jewish, definition of, 12–14;

Judaism defined as opposing, 9;
Marxist, 141, 168; vs. materiality, 6;
philosophical, 9, 93, 97; practical, 14,
15, 114, 147–149, 160; quantitative,
57, 59, 61, 67, 81; scientific, 85–114,
151, 187; social, 58; substantive, 57,
67
Mazzini, Giuseppe, 178
McCaul, Alexander, 43, 44, 49
Meisel, Eliyahu Ḥayyim, 101
Mendele Moykher-Sforim. *See* Abramo-
wich, Shalom Jacob
Mendelssohn, Moses, 41, 167
Menshevik Party, 28, 118, 125, 140
mercantilism, Jewish, 52
Messiah, 48, 162, 164, 172; belief in es-
sential to Jewish *Geist*, 163
messianic age, 51, 110, 173, 174
messianism, 15, 110, 178
metaphysics, 16–18, 92–96, 175–179;
American Jews and, 189; Jewish vs.
Christian, 55; and Kabbalah, 106;
relationship to materialism, 26;
Zionism as end of Jewish, 185
Mickiewicz, Adam, 16, 178
Middle East, 16, 21, 144
Mieses, Fabius, 99
Mikveh Yisrael (agricultural school),
171
Mill, John Stuart, 79
Minḥat bikkurim (*First Fruits*, newspaper), 38
minority rights, 35, 113, 130 187; movement, 116, 182, 187–189
missionaries, 34, 43
Mitnagdim, 63, 64, 77, 89, 139; opposition to enlightenment, 54
Moleschott, Jacob, 88, 111
moneylending and borrowing, 3, 40, 50,
51. *See also* usury
monism, 12, 19, 90, 102
monotheism, 164, 168, 169; essential to
Jewish *Geist*, 163

Montefiore, Moses, 37, 43
Morning (*Hatsefira*, newspaper), 98
Moses, 2, 48, 106–109, 163; Mosaic
Faith, 10, 35, 36, 54, 127; political
authority of, 107
musar (ethical literature), 125
mysticism, 48, 96, 164. *See also* Kabbalah

Narodnaia Volia (Peoples' Will) Party,
28, 116
Natanson, Mark, 116
nationalism: cultural, 159, 163, 166,
177–179; European Romantic, 176;
Jewish, 21, 80, 113, 146–149, 168–173,
178, 181, 184–185; Turkish, 17
nation-states, 86, 127, 182, 184
natural selection, 95, 96, 154
"Natural Selector," God as, 96
nature, 13–15, 83–114, 128–130; human
beings as a part of, 162; immutable,
125; knowledge of God through, 152;
society as mirroring, 83; as the will
of Heaven, 125
Naturphilosophie, 96, 99, 105
nebular theory, 93
Nekam berit (*Revenge of the Covenant*,
Smolenskin), 179–181
New Testament, 48
Nicholas I, Tsar, 34–36, 41, 42, 52, 136;
ultimate goal for Jews of, 35
Nieman River, 32
nihilism, 81, 121, 123, 152, 153, 159, 185;
"half-nihilism," 67
Novakhovitch, Feyge, 69, 80

Odessa, 22, 71, 77
oral transmission, 48
organic matter, origins of, 99, 100
Orshanski, Ilya, 27, 31, 57, 58, 60–63, 67
Osnovy Moiseeva zakona (*Fundamentals of the Law of Moses*, Russian-
sponsored government publication),
107

Ottoman Empire, 16, 158, 170, 171, 183
Owen, Robert, 69

paganism, 189
Pale of Settlement: defined, 33; "epochal
    transformation" of, 60; Jews as per-
    cent of gymnasium population of,
    114; Jews' reception of Marx in, 118
Palestine, 169–181, 186; chief rabbi of,
    116; ideological ocean between
    America and, 186; Jewish immigra-
    tion to, 113, 185; Jews in slavery
    except in, 39; Kaplan and Jewish
    Zionist cause in, 113; Lieberman on
    Jewish homeland in, 141
pantheism, 96, 100, 101, 105, 107
Paperna, Abraham Jacob, 27
Paris, 29, 48, 170, 171; Great Powers
    conference (1856), 183
Pavlovna, Vera (character in *What Is to
    Be Done?*), 79, 121
Pavlyk, Mykhailo, 144
Peoples' Will (*Narodnaia Volia*) Party,
    28, 116
Perlman, Eliezer. *See* Ben-Yehuda,
    Eliezer
Petrovsky-Shtern, Yochanan, 36
Pew report on Jewish life (2013), 189
Pharisees, 8, 182
Philipson, Joakim, 151
physiology, 13, 64, 99, 103, 107
Pinsker, Leon, 184, 185, 187, 189, 190;
    Auto-Emancipation, 184
Pisarev, Dmitry, 21, 30, 58, 69, 79, 81–84,
    118, 177
Plekhanov, Georgi, 12, 14
Po'alei Tsiyon (Laborers of Zion; move-
    ment), 21
pogroms, 1, 2, 182; of 1871 (Odessa),
    71; of 1872 (Kiev), 11; of 1881 (Pale
    of Settlement), 4, 31, 71, 108, 113,
    170, 179, 185; in Romania, 157; in
    Smolenskin's *Revenge of the Covenant
    (Nekam berit)*, 180

Poland, 16, 32, 40, 111, 144, 168; rebellion
    of 1831 in, 136; uprising of 1833 in,
    168; uprising of 1863 in, 60
Poliakov family, 112, 132
Polish-Lithuanian Commonwealth, 16,
    32, 33
Porjes, Aaron, 27
positivism, 107–109; once under rubric
    of materialism, 12; overlap with ma-
    terialism, 5; Rabinowitz as staunch
    adherent of, 86, 112, 113; religious,
    108; of Simchowitz, 150, 151; state-
    based, 16
prayer, 69, 74; house of, 62, 66
proletariat, 126, 132, 140, 152
Protestantism, 7, 9, 40, 127, 190; ascetic
    qualities of, 127; and economic
    secularization, 7; and Kabbalah, 128;
    relation to capitalism, 127
Protestants, 7, 34–36, 43, 47, 127, 158,
    186, 190; confessional polities, 7;
    nonmaterial understanding of
    religion, 8
Proudhon, Pierre-Joseph, 149
Prussia: assimilation of Jews in, 57;
    dismantler of corporations, 33;
    epicenter of science-religion debate,
    87; feudalism and guilds abolished
    in, 33; Jewish reforms used as model
    in, 35, 41; role in third partition of
    Polish-Lithuanian Commonwealth,
    32

quietism, political, 127, 136

rabbis: coercive power by, 33; compared
    with church fathers, 47; costly sala-
    ries of, 63; encouraged to be more
    lenient, 68; Orthodox, 187; Reform,
    189; P. Smolenskin's quarrels with,
    147, 167, 174; visited by Sossnitz,
    101; state-appointed, 63
Rabinowitz, Tsvi Hirsch, 85–95, 102,
    107–113, 131; on human beings

reflected in nature, 13; ignorance of Russian, 28; as lifelong observant Jew, 28; as public defender of Russian Jews, 89; rift with Slonimski, 102

race: differences, 110, 113, 141, 142; theories, 15, 16, 86, 109

raznochintsy (members of mixed classes), 29

rebbe, 76, 78; of Ḥabad, 96

Redemption, 169, 173, 175, 177–179

residential restrictions, 60; on Jews, 54, 60

revelation, 58, 86, 100, 163, 183

Revenge of the Covenant (*Nekam berit*, Smolenskin), 179–181

Revolutionary International League, 121, 123, 144, 145, 157

Ricardo, David, 154, 155

Riga, 29, 101, 113

Russia: aiding Jews' return to Palestine, 170; Alexander II's reforms, 59; beginnings of Zionism in, 175; Catholic and Orthodox Christian populations of, 36; census (1897), 67; distinct character of yeshivot in, 64; economic and religious reform, 37–41; education institutions, 114; effects of Crimean War on, 59; feudalism in, 51; financial strains of 1860s, 56; first Jewish periodicals, 43; geographical expansion (1795), 32; Jewish "factories" in, 61; Jewish intelligentsia in, 26, 36; Jewish liberals in, 10, 110, 131, 182; Jewish occupations in nineteenth-century, 66; Jews as distinct entity in, 142, 144; Jews restricted from sciences in, 152; major religious groups, 36; Marx and oppressed groups of, 142; Nicholas I's Christian vision for, 36; religious minorities in, 40; supporting Balkan independence, 157, 158, 170, 171; world's largest Jewish population, 32

Russkie Evrei (*Russian Jews*, newspaper), 112

Sabbatai Zevi, 107; anti-Sabbateans, 105

Saint Petersburg: capitalist elite in, 89, 109; Chaikovsky Circle founded in, 118; exodus of guild merchants and wealthy Jews to, 56, 60; Jewish girls school in, 107; *Saint Petersburg Record* (*Sankt-Peterburgskie vedomosti*, newspaper), 71; universities, 29, 92; women's medical courses in, 91

Salkinson, Isaac, 158

Sankt-Peterburgskie vedomosti (*Saint Petersburg Record*, newspaper), 71

Sapir, Boris, 132

Savarkar, V. D., 17, 18

Schatz, Boris, 97, 113

Schelling, F. W. J., 98, 99, 101, 105; and *Naturphilosophie*, 105

Schiller, Friedrich, 58

Schneersohn, Menachem Mendel, 96

scholasticism, 125–128, 190; ascetic qualities of, 127; and feudalism, 125; and Kabbalah, 128

Schweder, Gothard, 101

Seed of Babylon (*Zerubavel*, Levinsohn), 43

sephirot. See Kabbalah

Serbia, 170

serfs, emancipation of, 33, 59, 60, 72

settler movement, 116

sexism. *See* equality: gender

sexuality, 29, 67, 69, 70, 81, 121, 158

Shakespeare, William, 158

Shakharistin, 159

Shelgunov, Nikolai, 60

Shlonsky, Avraham, 186

Shur, Khasia, 27, 28, 119, 121, 144

Siberia, 116

Simchowitz, Salomon Shachne, 27, 150, 151

Simon, Saint, 24

Sion (Russian-Jewish weekly), 184

slavery, 39, 50

Slonimski, Ḥayyim Selig, 27, 88, 94, 95, 101–104

Smirnov, Valerian, 124, 134, 140–142, 151

Smith, Adam, 154, 155

Smolenskin, Lenora, 165, 166, 172

Smolenskin, Peretz, 147–150, 156–181; publishes materialist literature, 153, 154; *Revenge of the Covenant* (*Nekam berit*), 179; *The Wanderer in the Paths of Life* (*Hato'eh bedarkhei haḥayyim*), 160; in Zionist dispute, 149

socialism, 19, 21–24, 26, 123, 143, 149; basis for Jews' predisposition to, 5; influence of materialism on, 4

socialitsischen Utopien, 121

Society for the Promotion of Culture Among the Jews of Russia, 89

Sorbonne. *See* University of Paris

Sossnitz, Joseph, 85–102, 104–114; as Darwinian, 5; family life, 28; on human beings reflected in nature, 13; *The Luminary* (*Hama'or*), 105; "materialische religion" of, 106, 109, 111, 113, 159; as student of Kabbalah, 28; as teacher of Kaplan, 187

Sovremennik (*The Contemporary*, Chernyshevsky), 152

Spektor, Yitsḥak Elḥanan, 101

Spencer, Herbert, 17, 172

Spiller, Philip, 92, 94; *The Primordial Force of the Universe* (*Die Urkraft des Weltalls*), 94

Spinoza, Baruch: as basis for worldview of Sossnitz, 107; "the Enlightened Spinozist," 107; Kaplan on, 107; Lilienblum's assessment of, 81; materialist ideas in writings of, 6; on Moses, 107; pantheism of, 107

Sprung (leap), 98, 99. See also *dillug*

Stalin, Joseph, 94

Stamm, 131, 144

study hall, 63–65, 77, 167, 174, See also *beit midrash*

Sullam, Sara Copia, 164, 165, 167

Syrkin, Nachman, 22

Talmud: agricultural metaphors of, 51; canonicity of, 45; commentarial methods not employed by quantitative materialists, 57; contempt of by Hasidim, 138; on economics, 53; on Gentiles, 51; on humanity's creating evil, 126; "jurisprudential malleability," 45; Lilienblum's positive relationship to, 81–82; and metaphysics, 94; productive labor vs. study of, 12, 34; rejection of, 55; respect for kings in, 136; respect of sciences in, 105; role in Russia's religious reform agenda, 37–49; seen as inimical to Jews' honesty, 43; students as intelligentsia, 135; "Talmudic prodigy" in marriage, 75–80

Tchernichovsky, Shaul, 23

Tel Aviv, 154

Temkin (Smolenskin), Lenora, 158. *See also* Smolenskin, Lenora

terrorism, groups, 116; tactics, 118

Trial of the Fifty, 153

Truth (*Ha'emet*, newspaper), 144, 149, 157–162, 171

tsadikim (holy men), 129

Turgenev, Ivan Sergeyevitch, 68, 152; *Fathers and Sons* (*Ottsy i dety*), 68

Ukraine, 27, 41, 144, 170; Berdichev, 3, 153; Kremenets, 41; Lieberman's 1876 charter addressed to, 143; within Pale of Settlement, 33; Volhynian, 32; Zhitomir, 118

universities, 64, 84, 91; entry for Jews to, 28, 29, 54, 59, 91, 114–116

University of Paris (Sorbonne), 171

University of Saint Vladimir, 91

Ural Mountains, 139

urbanization, 59, 60
usury, 51. *See also* moneylending and
borrowing
Uvarov, Count Sergey, 40–42, 48, 49, 51

Vienna: Congress of, 50; Great Powers
conference (1815), 183; lack of censorship in, 157; print shops in, 149, 153
Vilkomir, 67, 69
Vilna, 118–120; accusations of revolution
in (1875), 120; as birthplace of Jewish socialism, 22; chief accountant,
38; "death" and "starvation" in, 37;
Gaon of, 166, 167; plethora of study
houses in, 62, 64; socialist reading
cell in, 143;
Vivekananda, Swami, 18
Vogt, Karl, 13, 88, 109–111, 159
Voice of the Herald (*Kol mevaser,* newspaper), 68, 152
Voltaire, 47
Vpered! (*Forward!,* journal), 123, 132

Wanderer in the Paths of Life (*Hato'eh
bedarkhei hahayyim,* P. Smolenskin),
160
Warsaw, 43, 121
Warshavsky family, 132
Weber, Max, 36, 127
Weinryb, Bernard D., 121
Weizmann, Chaim, 112
Wengeroff, Pauline, 153
Winchevsky, Morris, 27, 28, 138–140
Wisdom, Understanding, and Knowledge (Ḥabad doctrine), 99
Wissenschaft des Judentums, 168
Wolf, Friedrich August, 168
women, 74–81, 165–167; economic role
of Jewish, 11; education of Jewish, 77–78; female revolutionaries,
121 foreign appearance of Jewish,
34; Jewish material well-being as
gendered issue, 11; labor, 12; medical
courses for, 91; private schools for

Jewish, 91; readers of Yiddish but
not Hebrew, 153; as Torah scholars,
165, 166

yeshiva students: charity distributed
to, 66; compared with Hasidim,
138–140; as defilers of Jewish state,
174; health issues of, 65; ignorance of
Hebrew language by, 77; as a "klass,"
66; overlooked in statistical studies,
66, 67; as potential revolutionaries,
131–135, 140; pranks of, 65; in satire
of Lilienblum, 74; unfit for labor, 65
yeshivot: as corrupters of youth, 65; and
dissipation of funds, 78; economic/
social influence of, 74; Gaon of
Vilna and, 167; Kovner's criticism of,
62–66; Mir, 64, 66; P. Smolenskin's
scorn of and praise of, 167; state-
sponsored, 43, 64, 118; Volozhin, 64,
88, 135
Yiddishkeit, 186; vs. Zionism, 186
Yiddish language: Levin on, 137; as living
Jewish language, 137; propaganda,
145; writers, 136
Young Turks, 16, 17

Zagorski, Ephraim Menkin, 88
Zangwill, Israel, 6
Zederbaum, Alexander, 80, 131
Zerubavel (*Seed of Babylon,* Levinsohn),
43
Zionism: break from rabbinic Judaism,
179; compared with Hindutva e, 18;
Cultural, 15, 22, 147, 148, 173, 187;
idealism and, 169–181; influence of
materialism on, 4; Jewish *Geist* and,
163; Jewish materialism as framework for understanding of, 182;
J. Klausner on, 21, 22; Lilienblum
as founder in eastern Europe, 58;
Marxist, 21, 145; polemics against,
136; political, 175; relation to Jewish
religion, 185; vs. *Yiddishkeit,* 186

Zohar, 105, 125

Zuckermann, Eliezer: disdain for accepted norms, 119; on greed of *maskilim,* 134; on Hasidim, 138; importance of overshadowed by P. Smolenskin, 147; on Jews as distinct national entity, 144, 145; as rebel, 121; on Yiddish as proper language of propaganda, 145

Zundelevich, Aaron, 116, 118, 120, 123, 135

Zunz, Leopold, 168

Zweifel, Eliezer, 80, 131